50% OFF Online Praxis Core Prep Course!

Dear Customer,

We consider it an honor and a privilege that you chose our Praxis Core Study Guide. As a way of showing our appreciation and to help us better serve you, we partnered with Mometrix Test Preparation to offer **50% off their online Praxis Core Online Course**. Many Praxis courses are needlessly expensive and don't deliver enough value. With their course, you get access to the best Praxis Core prep material, and **you only pay half price**.

Mometrix has structured their online course to perfectly complement your printed study guide. The Praxis Core Online Course contains **in-depth lessons** that cover all the most important topics, **250+ video reviews** that explain difficult concepts, over **1,450 practice questions** to ensure you feel prepared, and more than **550 digital flashcards**, so you can study while you're on the go.

Online Praxis Core Prep Course

Topics Covered:
- Reading
  - Key Ideas and Details
  - Craft, Structure, and Language Skills
  - Integration of Knowledge and Ideas
- Writing
  - Language Skills
  - Text Types, Purposes, and Production
  - Common Errors
- Mathematics
  - Number and Quantity
  - Algebra
  - Geometry

Course Features:
- Praxis Core Study Guide
  - Get content that complements our best-selling study guide.
- Full-Length Practice Tests
  - With over 700 practice questions, you can test yourself again and again.
- Mobile Friendly
  - If you need to study on the go, the course is easily accessible from your mobile device.
- Praxis Core Flashcards
  - Their course includes a flashcards mode with over 550 content cards for you to study.

To receive this discount, visit their website: mometrix.com/university/praxis-core/ and add the course to your cart. At the checkout page, enter the discount code: **TPBCORE50**

If you have any questions or concerns, please contact them at support@mometrix.com.

Sincerely,

 in partnership with **Mometrix** TEST PREPARATION

SCAN HERE

FREE Test Taking Tips Video/DVD Offer

To better serve you, we created videos covering test taking tips that we want to give you for FREE. **These videos cover world-class tips that will help you succeed on your test.**

We just ask that you send us feedback about this product. Please let us know what you thought about it—whether good, bad, or indifferent.

To get your **FREE videos**, you can use the QR code below or email freevideos@studyguideteam.com with "Free Videos" in the subject line and the following information in the body of the email:

     a. The title of your product

     b. Your product rating on a scale of 1-5, with 5 being the highest

     c. Your feedback about the product

If you have any questions or concerns, please don't hesitate to contact us at info@studyguideteam.com.

Thank you!

Praxis Core Study Guide 2025-2026
5 Practice Tests and Academic Skills for Educators Exam Prep (Math 5733, Writing 5723, Reading 5713) [8th Edition]

Lydia Morrison

Written and edited by TPB Publishing.

TPB Publishing is not associated with or endorsed by any official testing organization. TPB Publishing is a publisher of unofficial educational products. All test and organization names are trademarks of their respective owners. Content in this book is included for utilitarian purposes only and does not constitute an endorsement by TPB Publishing of any particular point of view.

Interested in buying more than 10 copies of our product? Contact us about bulk discounts:
bulkorders@studyguideteam.com

ISBN 13: 9781637753637

Table of Contents

Welcome

Dear Reader,

Welcome to your new Test Prep Books study guide! We are pleased that you chose us to help you prepare for your exam. There are many study options to choose from, and we appreciate you choosing us. Studying can be a daunting task, but we have designed a smart, effective study guide to help prepare you for what lies ahead.

Whether you're a parent helping your child learn and grow, a high school student working hard to get into your dream college, or a nursing student studying for a complex exam, we want to help give you the tools you need to succeed. We hope this study guide gives you the skills and the confidence to thrive, and we can't thank you enough for allowing us to be part of your journey.

In an effort to continue to improve our products, we welcome feedback from our customers. We look forward to hearing from you. Suggestions, success stories, and criticisms can all be communicated by emailing us at info@studyguideteam.com.

Sincerely,
Test Prep Books Team

FREE Videos/DVD OFFER

Doing well on your exam requires both knowing the test content and understanding how to use that knowledge to do well on the test. We offer completely FREE test taking tip videos. **These videos cover world-class tips that you can use to succeed on your test.**

To get your **FREE videos**, you can use the QR code below or email freevideos@studyguideteam.com with "Free Videos" in the subject line and the following information in the body of the email:

   a. The title of your product
   b. Your product rating on a scale of 1-5, with 5 being the highest
   c. Your feedback about the product

If you have any questions or concerns, please don't hesitate to contact us at info@studyguideteam.com.

SCAN HERE

Quick Overview

As you draw closer to taking your exam, effective preparation becomes more and more important. Thankfully, you have this study guide to help you get ready. Use this guide to help keep your studying on track and refer to it often.

This study guide contains several key sections that will help you be successful on your exam. The guide contains tips for what you should do the night before and the day of the test. Also included are test-taking tips. Knowing the right information is not always enough. Many well-prepared test takers struggle with exams. These tips will help equip you to accurately read, assess, and answer test questions.

A large part of the guide is devoted to showing you what content to expect on the exam and to helping you better understand that content. In this guide are practice test questions so that you can see how well you have grasped the content. Then, answer explanations are provided so that you can understand why you missed certain questions.

Don't try to cram the night before you take your exam. This is not a wise strategy for a few reasons. First, your retention of the information will be low. Your time would be better used by reviewing information you already know rather than trying to learn a lot of new information. Second, you will likely become stressed as you try to gain a large amount of knowledge in a short amount of time. Third, you will be depriving yourself of sleep. So be sure to go to bed at a reasonable time the night before. Being well-rested helps you focus and remain calm.

Be sure to eat a substantial breakfast the morning of the exam. If you are taking the exam in the afternoon, be sure to have a good lunch as well. Being hungry is distracting and can make it difficult to focus. You have hopefully spent lots of time preparing for the exam. Don't let an empty stomach get in the way of success!

When travelling to the testing center, leave earlier than needed. That way, you have a buffer in case you experience any delays. This will help you remain calm and will keep you from missing your appointment time at the testing center.

Be sure to pace yourself during the exam. Don't try to rush through the exam. There is no need to risk performing poorly on the exam just so you can leave the testing center early. Allow yourself to use all of the allotted time if needed.

Remain positive while taking the exam even if you feel like you are performing poorly. Thinking about the content you should have mastered will not help you perform better on the exam.

Once the exam is complete, take some time to relax. Even if you feel that you need to take the exam again, you will be well served by some down time before you begin studying again. It's often easier to convince yourself to study if you know that it will come with a reward!

2

Test-Taking Strategies

1. Predicting the Answer

When you feel confident in your preparation for a multiple-choice test, try predicting the answer before reading the answer choices. This is especially useful on questions that test objective factual knowledge. By predicting the answer before reading the available choices, you eliminate the possibility that you will be distracted or led astray by an incorrect answer choice. You will feel more confident in your selection if you read the question, predict the answer, and then find your prediction among the answer choices. After using this strategy, be sure to still read all of the answer choices carefully and completely. If you feel unprepared, you should not attempt to predict the answers. This would be a waste of time and an opportunity for your mind to wander in the wrong direction.

2. Reading the Whole Question

Too often, test takers scan a multiple-choice question, recognize a few familiar words, and immediately jump to the answer choices. Test authors are aware of this common impatience, and they will sometimes prey upon it. For instance, a test author might subtly turn the question into a negative, or he or she might redirect the focus of the question right at the end. The only way to avoid falling into these traps is to read the entirety of the question carefully before reading the answer choices.

3. Looking for Wrong Answers

Long and complicated multiple-choice questions can be intimidating. One way to simplify a difficult multiple-choice question is to eliminate all of the answer choices that are clearly wrong. In most sets of answers, there will be at least one selection that can be dismissed right away. If the test is administered on paper, the test taker could draw a line through it to indicate that it may be ignored; otherwise, the test taker will have to perform this operation mentally or on scratch paper. In either case, once the obviously incorrect answers have been eliminated, the remaining choices may be considered. Sometimes identifying the clearly wrong answers will give the test taker some information about the correct answer. For instance, if one of the remaining answer choices is a direct opposite of one of the eliminated answer choices, it may well be the correct answer. The opposite of obviously wrong is obviously right! Of course, this is not always the case. Some answers are obviously incorrect simply because they are irrelevant to the question being asked. Still, identifying and eliminating some incorrect answer choices is a good way to simplify a multiple-choice question.

4. Don't Overanalyze

Anxious test takers often overanalyze questions. When you are nervous, your brain will often run wild, causing you to make associations and discover clues that don't actually exist. If you feel that this may be a problem for you, do whatever you can to slow down during the test. Try taking a deep breath or counting to ten. As you read and consider the question, restrict yourself to the particular words used by the author. Avoid thought tangents about what the author *really* meant, or what he or she was *trying* to say. The only things that matter on a multiple-choice test are the words that are actually in the question. You must avoid reading too much into a multiple-choice question, or supposing that the writer meant something other than what he or she wrote.

5. No Need for Panic

It is wise to learn as many strategies as possible before taking a multiple-choice test, but it is likely that you will come across a few questions for which you simply don't know the answer. In this situation, avoid panicking. Because most multiple-choice tests include dozens of questions, the relative value of a single wrong answer is small. As much

3

as possible, you should compartmentalize each question on a multiple-choice test. In other words, you should not allow your feelings about one question to affect your success on the others. When you find a question that you either don't understand or don't know how to answer, just take a deep breath and do your best. Read the entire question slowly and carefully. Try rephrasing the question a couple of different ways. Then, read all of the answer choices carefully. After eliminating obviously wrong answers, make a selection and move on to the next question.

6. Confusing Answer Choices

When working on a difficult multiple-choice question, there may be a tendency to focus on the answer choices that are the easiest to understand. Many people, whether consciously or not, gravitate to the answer choices that require the least concentration, knowledge, and memory. This is a mistake. When you come across an answer choice that is confusing, you should give it extra attention. A question might be confusing because you do not know

the subject matter to which it refers. If this is the case, don't eliminate the answer before you have affirmatively settled on another. When you come across an answer choice of this type, set it aside as you look at the remaining choices. If you can confidently assert that one of the other choices is correct, you can leave the confusing answer aside. Otherwise, you will need to take a moment to try to better understand the confusing answer choice. Rephrasing is one way to tease out the sense of a confusing answer choice.

7. Your First Instinct

Many people struggle with multiple-choice tests because they overthink the questions. If you have studied sufficiently for the test, you should be prepared to trust your first instinct once you have carefully and completely read the question and all of the answer choices. There is a great deal of research suggesting that the mind can come to the correct conclusion very quickly once it has obtained all of the relevant information. At times, it may seem to you as if your intuition is working faster even than your reasoning mind. This may in fact be true. The knowledge you obtain while studying may be retrieved from your subconscious before you have a chance to work out the associations that support it. Verify your instinct by working out the reasons that it should be trusted.

8. Key Words

Many test takers struggle with multiple-choice questions because they have poor reading comprehension skills. Quickly reading and understanding a multiple-choice question requires a mixture of skill and experience. To help with this, try jotting down a few key words and phrases on a piece of scrap paper. Doing this concentrates the process of reading and forces the mind to weigh the relative importance of the question's parts. In selecting words and phrases to write down, the test taker thinks about the question more deeply and carefully. This is especially true for multiple-choice questions that are preceded by a long prompt.

9. Subtle Negatives

One of the oldest tricks in the multiple-choice test writer's book is to subtly reverse the meaning of a question with a word like *not* or *except*. If you are not paying attention to each word in the question, you can easily be led astray by this trick. For instance, a common question format is, "Which of the following is...?" Obviously, if the question instead is, "Which of the following is not...?," then the answer will be quite different. Even worse, the test makers are aware of the potential for this mistake and will include one answer choice that would be correct if the question were not negated or reversed. A test taker who misses the reversal will find what he or she believes to be a correct answer and will be so confident that he or she will fail to reread the question and discover the original error. The only way to avoid this is to practice a wide variety of multiple-choice questions and to pay close attention to each and every word.

10. Reading Every Answer Choice

It may seem obvious, but you should always read every one of the answer choices! Too many test takers fall into the habit of scanning the question and assuming that they understand the question because they recognize a few key words. From there, they pick the first answer choice that answers the question they believe they have read. Test takers who read all of the answer choices might discover that one of the latter answer choices is actually *more* correct. Moreover, reading all of the answer choices can remind you of facts related to the question that can help you arrive at the correct answer. Sometimes, a misstatement or incorrect detail in one of the latter answer choices will trigger your memory of the subject and will enable you to find the right answer. Failing to read all of the answer choices is like not reading all of the items on a restaurant menu: you might miss out on the perfect choice.

11. Spot the Hedges

One of the keys to success on multiple-choice tests is paying close attention to every word. This is never truer than with words like *almost*, *most*, *some*, and *sometimes*. These words are called "hedges" because they indicate that a statement is not totally true or not true in every place and time. An absolute statement will contain no hedges, but

in many subjects, the answers are not always straightforward or absolute. There are always exceptions to the rules in these subjects. For this reason, you should favor those multiple-choice questions that contain hedging language. The presence of qualifying words indicates that the author is taking special care with his or her words, which is certainly important when composing the right answer. After all, there are many ways to be wrong, but there is only one way to be right! For this reason, it is wise to avoid answers that are absolute when taking a multiple-choice test. An absolute answer is one that says things are either all one way or all another. They often include words like *every*, *always*, *best*, and *never*. If you are taking a multiple-choice test in a subject that doesn't lend itself to absolute answers, be on your guard if you see any of these words.

12. Long Answers

In many subject areas, the answers are not simple. As already mentioned, the right answer often requires hedges. Another common feature of the answers to a complex or subjective question are qualifying clauses, which are groups of words that subtly modify the meaning of the sentence. If the question or answer choice describes a rule to which there are exceptions or the subject matter is complicated, ambiguous, or confusing, the correct answer will require many words in order to be expressed clearly and accurately. In essence, you should not be deterred by answer choices that seem excessively long. Oftentimes, the author of the text will not be able to write the correct answer without offering some qualifications and

5

modifications. Your job is to read the answer choices thoroughly and completely and to select the one that most accurately and precisely answers the question.

13. Restating to Understand

Sometimes, a question on a multiple-choice test is difficult not because of what it asks but because of how it is written. If this is the case, restate the question or answer choice in different words. This process serves a couple of important purposes. First, it forces you to concentrate on the core of the question. In order to rephrase the question accurately, you have to understand it well. Rephrasing the question will concentrate your mind on the key words and ideas. Second, it will present the information to your mind in a fresh way. This process may trigger your memory and render some useful scrap of information picked up while studying.

14. True Statements

Sometimes an answer choice will be true in itself, but it does not answer the question. This is one of the main reasons why it is essential to read the question carefully and completely before proceeding to the answer choices. Too often, test takers skip ahead to the answer choices and look for true statements. Having found one of these, they are content to select it without reference to the question above. The savvy test taker will always read the entire question before turning to the answer choices. Then, having settled on a correct answer choice, he or she will refer to the original question and ensure that the selected answer is relevant. The mistake of choosing a correct-but-irrelevant answer choice is especially common on questions related to specific pieces of objective knowledge.

15. No Patterns

One of the more dangerous ideas that circulates about multiple-choice tests is that the correct answers tend to fall into patterns. These erroneous ideas range from a belief that B and C are the most common right answers, to the idea that an unprepared test-taker should answer "A-B-A-C-A-D-A-B-A." It cannot be emphasized enough that pattern-seeking of this type is exactly the WRONG way to approach a multiple-choice test. To begin with, it is highly unlikely that the test maker will plot the correct answers according to some predetermined pattern. The questions are scrambled and delivered in a random order. Furthermore, even if the test maker was following a pattern in the assignation of correct answers, there is no reason why the test taker would know which pattern he or she was using. Any attempt to discern a pattern in the answer choices is a waste of time and a distraction from the real work of taking the test. A test taker would be much better served by extra preparation before the test than by reliance on a pattern in the answers.

Bonus Content

We host multiple bonus items online, including all five practice tests in digital format. Scan the QR code or go to this link to access this content:

testprepbooks.com/bonus/praxiscore

The first time you access the page, you will need to register as a "new user" and verify your email address.

If you have any issues, please email support@testprepbooks.com.

Introduction to the Praxis Core Tests

Function of the Test

The **Praxis Core** tests are taken by college students or professionals who wish to apply to teacher preparation programs. There are three separate tests involved in the Praxis Core: the Reading Test, Writing Test, and Mathematics Test. These tests are designed to measure the skills of teaching candidates and assess their overall knowledge in certain subject areas.

Evaluation of test scores depends on the particular program candidates are interested in. Some universities use test scores to determine admission into teacher education programs, while some states look at test scores for their teacher licensing process.

The Praxis Core tests are computer-based tests that can be taken internationally. If taken outside the United States, they must be taken for either entrance or certification into a teacher education program or employment inside the United States.

Test Administration

To find test dates and centers, go to https://www.ets.org/praxis/register/centers_dates/. This has information about where and when tests are offered. The core tests all have a "continuous testing" window. Note that all three tests can be taken at the same time; this option is called **Combined Test**.

Retesting is an option if a test taker feels they did not perform well on the test; however, the retest must be taken at least twenty-eight days after the initial test was taken.

Those who have need of accommodation in the testing environment will need to apply to have their accommodation approved by ETS Disability Services. Note that this process may take up to six weeks to review. Additional documentation can take up to another six weeks, so be sure and begin the process well in advance of the testing date. Once approved, ETS will send instructions on how to register for the test. Don't register for the test until documentation has been approved and sent back to you.

Test Format

On the day of the test, a photo ID as well as the admission ticket should be brought with you to the testing center. Test takers should arrive at least half an hour before the test starts to ensure they are on time and have all the available resources. Scientific, graphic, and four-function calculators are allowed in the testing area for some Praxis tests. The ETS website will provide information to determine if the test being taken permits the use of a calculator. Food and drink are not permitted in the testing area.

There are three different tests that can be taken for the Praxis Core: Reading, Writing, and Math. The Combined Test offers all three of these tests at the same time. Here is the breakdown of each test:

Test	Questions	Time
Reading	56	85 minutes
Mathematics	56	85 minutes
Writing (2 sections)	40 + 2 essays	40 minutes + 60 minutes

Scoring

Score information on the score report will be available 10 to 16 business days after the test. Test takers can find online scores through an account set up with the Praxis website, and they have the option to send scores to up to four agencies when they first register for the test. Test scores are downloadable for ten years from the reporting date.

To determine what score is considered a passing one, test takers will have to check with the state, institution, or association that requires the test. On the ETS website, there is a link that provides information on every state that requires the Praxis Core. The information will lead to the agency's website where it can be determined what the passing score will be for a specific agency or institution.

Recent/Future Developments

The ETS updates the Praxis website annually to show how states or agencies have altered their requirements for passing the test. Check with the state or agency on the ETS website to get detailed information about passing scores and requirements. The test content and outlines were modified in 2020.

Study Prep Plan for the Praxis Core Tests

1 **Schedule -** Use one of our study schedules below or come up with one of your own.

2 **Relax -** Test anxiety can hurt even the best students. There are many ways to reduce stress. Find the one that works best for you.

3 **Execute -** Once you have a good plan in place, be sure to stick to it.

One Week Study Schedule		
Day 1	Reading	
Day 2	Writing	
Day 3	Mathematics	
Day 4	Data Interpretation and Representation...	
Day 5	Practice Test #1	
Day 6	Practice Test #2	
Day 7	Take Your Exam!	

Two Week Study Schedule			
Day 1	Reading	Day 8	Data Interpretation and Representation...
Day 2	Organization and Structure	Day 9	Algebra and Geometry
Day 3	Integration of Knowledge and Ideas	Day 10	Geometry
Day 4	Writing	Day 11	Practice Test #1
Day 5	Language and Research Skills for Writing	Day 12	Practice Test #2
Day 6	Mathematics	Day 13	Practice Test #3
Day 7	Solving Problems Involving Constant Rates	Day 14	Take Your Exam!

<table>
<tr><td rowspan="20" style="writing-mode: vertical-lr;">**One Month Study Schedule**</td></tr>
</table>

One Month Study Schedule					
Day 1	Reading	Day 11	Research Skills and Strategies	Day 21	Answer Explanations #1
Day 2	Supporting Ideas	Day 12	Mathematics	Day 22	Practice Test #2
Day 3	Organization and Structure	Day 13	Solving Problems Involving Ratios...	Day 23	Answer Explanations #2
Day 4	Meaning of Words	Day 14	Solving Problems Involving Constant...	Day 24	Practice Test #3
Day 5	Integration of Knowledge and Ideas	Day 15	Counterexamples	Day 25	Answer Explanations #3
Day 6	Analysis and Comparison of Texts	Day 16	Data Interpretation and Representation...	Day 26	Practice Test #4
Day 7	Writing	Day 17	Using Data from a Random Sample...	Day 27	Answer Explanations #4
Day 8	Text Production: Writing Informative...	Day 18	Algebra and Geometry	Day 28	Practice Test #5
Day 9	Language and Research Skills...	Day 19	Geometry	Day 29	Answer Explanations #5
Day 10	The Conventions of Standard English...	Day 20	Practice Test #1	Day 30	Take Your Exam!

Build your own prep plan by visiting:
testprepbooks.com/prep

11

As you study for your test, we'd like to take the opportunity to remind you that you are capable of great things! With the right tools and dedication, you truly can do anything you set your mind to. The fact that you are holding this book right now shows how committed you are. In case no one has told you lately, you've got this! Our intention behind including this coloring page is to give you the chance to take some time to engage your creative side when you need a little brain-break from studying. As a company, we want to encourage people like you to achieve their dreams by providing good quality study materials for the tests and certifications that improve careers and change lives. As individuals, many of us have taken such tests in our careers, and we know how challenging this process can be. While we can't come alongside you and cheer you on personally, we can offer you the space to recall your purpose, reconnect with your passion, and refresh your brain through an artistic practice. We wish you every success, and happy studying!

Math Reference Sheet

Symbol	Phrase
+	added to, increased by, sum of, more than
-	decreased by, difference between, less than, take away
×	multiplied by, 3 (4, 5 . . .) times as large, product of
÷	divided by, quotient of, half (third, etc.) of
=	is, the same as, results in, as much as
x, t, n, etc.	a variable which is an unknown value or quantity
<	is under, is below, smaller than, beneath
>	is above, is over, bigger than, exceeds
≤	no more than, at most, maximum; less than or equal to
≥	no less than, at least, minimum; greater than or equal to
√	square root of, exponent divided by 2

Geometry	Description
$P = 2l + 2w$	for perimeter of a rectangle
$P = 4 \times s$	for perimeter of a square
$P = a + b + c$	for perimeter of a triangle
$A = \frac{1}{2} \times b \times h = \frac{bh}{2}$	for area of a triangle
$A = b \times h$	for area of a parallelogram
$A = \frac{1}{2} \times h(b_1 + b_2)$	for area of a trapezoid
$A = \frac{1}{2} \times a \times P$	for area of a regular polygon
$C = 2 \times \pi \times r$	for circumference (perimeter) of a circle
$A = \pi \times r^2$	for area of a circle
$c^2 = a^2 + b^2; c = \sqrt{a^2 + b^2}$	for finding the hypotenuse of a right triangle
$SA = 2xy + 2yz + 2xz$	for finding surface area
$V = \frac{1}{3}xyh$	for finding volume of a rectangular pyramid
$V = \frac{4}{3}\pi r^3; \frac{1}{3}\pi r^2 h; \pi r^2 h$	for volume of a sphere; a cone; and a cylinder

Radical Expressions	Description
$\sqrt[n]{a} = a^{\frac{1}{n}}; \sqrt[n]{a^m} = (\sqrt[n]{a})^m = a^{\frac{m}{n}}$	a is the radicand, n is the index, m is the exponent
$\sqrt{x^2} = (x^2)^{\frac{1}{2}} = x$	to convert square root to exponent
$a^m \times a^n = a^{m+n}$	multiplying radicands with exponents
$(a^m)^n = a^{m \times n}$	multiplying exponents
$(a \times b)^m = a^m \times b^m$	parentheses with exponents

Property	Addition	Multiplication
Commutative	$a + b = b + a$	$a \times b = b \times a$
Associative	$(a + b) + c = a + (b + c)$	$(a \times b) \times c = a \times (b \times c)$
Identity	$a + 0 = a; 0 + a = a$	$a \times 1 = a; 1 \times a = a$
Inverse	$a + (-a) = 0$	$a \times \frac{1}{a} = 1; a \neq 0$
Distributive		$a(b + c) = ab + ac$

Data	Description
Mean	equal to the total of the values of a data set, divided by the number of elements in the data set
Median	middle value in an odd number of ordered values of a data set, or the mean of the two middle values in an even number of ordered values in a data set
Mode	the value that appears most often
Range	the difference between the highest and the lowest values in the set

Graphing	Description
(x, y)	ordered pair, plot points in a graph
$y = mx + b$	slope-intercept form; m represents the slope of the line and b represents the y-intercept
$f(x)$	read as f of x, which means it is a function of x
(x_2, y_2) and (x_2, y_2)	two ordered pairs used to determine the slope of a line
$m = \frac{y_2 - y_1}{x_2 - x_1}$	to find the slope of the line, m, for ordered pairs
$Ax + By = C$	standard form of an equation, also for solving a system of equations through the elimination method
$M = (\frac{x_1 + x_2}{2}, \frac{y_1 + y_2}{2})$	for finding the midpoint of an ordered pair
$y = ax^2 + bx + c$	quadratic function for a parabola
$y = a(x - h)^2 + k$	quadratic function for a parabola with vertex
$y = ab^x; y = a \times b^x$	function for exponential curve
$y = ax^2 + bx + c$	standard form of a quadratic function
$x = \frac{-b}{2a}$	for finding axis of symmetry in a parabola; given quadratic formula in standard form
$f = \sqrt{\frac{\Sigma(x - \bar{x})^2}{n - 1}}$	function for standard deviation of the sample; where $\bar{x}$ = sample mean and n = sample size

Proportions and Percentage	Description
$\frac{gallons}{cost} = \frac{gallons}{cost}; \frac{7\ gallons}{\$14.70} = \frac{x}{\$20}$	written as equal ratios with a variable representing the missing quantity
$\frac{y_1}{x_1} = \frac{y_2}{x_2}$	for direct proportions
$(y_1)(x_1) = (y_2)(x_2)$	for indirect proportions
$\frac{change}{original\ value} \times 100 = percent\ change$	for finding percentage change in value
$\frac{new\ quantity - old\ quantity}{old\ quantity} \times 100$	for calculating the increase or decrease in percentage

14

Reading

Key Ideas and Details

Main Idea and Primary Purpose

Topic Versus Main Idea

It is very important to know the difference between the topic and the main idea of the text. Even though these two are similar because they both present the central point of a text, they have distinctive differences. A **topic** is the subject of the text; This can usually be described in a concise one- to two-word phrase. On the other hand, the **main idea** is more detailed and provides the author's central point of the text. It can be expressed through a complete sentence and is often found in the beginning, the middle, or at the end of a paragraph. In most nonfiction books, the first sentence of the passage usually (but not always) states the main idea. Review the passage below to explore the topic versus the main idea.

> Cheetahs are one of the fastest mammals on the land, reaching up to 70 miles an hour over short distances. Even though cheetahs can run as fast as 70 miles an hour, they usually only have to run half that speed to catch up with their choice of prey. Cheetahs cannot maintain a fast pace over long periods of time because their bodies will overheat. After a chase, cheetahs need to rest for approximately 30 minutes prior to eating or returning to any other activity.

In the example above, the topic of the passage is "Cheetahs" simply because that is the subject of the text. The main idea of the text is "Cheetahs are one of the fastest mammals on the land but can only maintain a fast pace for shorter distances." While it covers the topic, it is more detailed and refers to the text in its entirety. The text continues to provide additional details called supporting details, which will be discussed in the next section.

Central Ideas in Informational Texts

Informational text is specifically designed to relate factual information, and although it is open to a reader's interpretation and application of the facts, the structure of the presentation is carefully designed to lead the reader to a particular conclusion or central idea. When reading informational text, it is important that readers are able to understand its organizational structure as the structure often directly relates to an author's intent to inform and/or persuade the reader.

The first step in identifying the text's structure is to determine the thesis or main idea. The thesis statement and organization of a work are closely intertwined. A **thesis statement** indicates the writer's purpose and may include the scope and direction of the text. It may be presented at the beginning of a text or at the end, and it may be explicit or implicit.

Once a reader has a grasp of the thesis or main idea of the text, he or she can better determine its organizational structure. Test takers are advised to read informational text passages more than once in order to comprehend the material fully. It is also helpful to examine any text features present in the text including the table of contents, index, glossary, headings, footnotes, and visuals. The analysis of these features and the information presented within them can offer additional clues about the central idea and structure of a text.

The following questions should be asked when considering structure:

- How does the author assemble the parts to make an effective whole argument?
- Is the passage linear in nature and if so, what is the timeline or thread of logic?

15

- What is the presented order of events, facts, or arguments? Are these effective in contributing to the author's thesis?

- How can the passage be divided into sections? How are they related to each other and to the main idea or thesis?

- What key terms are used to indicate the organization?

Next, test takers should skim the passage, noting the first line or two of each body paragraph—the **topic sentences**—and the conclusion. Key **transitional terms**, such as *on the other hand*, *also*, *because*, *however*, *therefore*, *most importantly*, and *first*, within the text can also signal organizational structure. Based on these clues, readers should then be able to identify what type of organizational structure is being used. The following organizational structures are most common:

- **Problem/solution**: organized by an analysis/overview of a problem, followed by potential solution(s)

- **Cause/effect**: organized by the effects resulting from a cause or the cause(s) of a particular effect

- **Spatial order**: organized by points that suggest location or direction—e.g., top to bottom, right to left, outside to inside

- **Chronological/sequence order**: organized by points presented to indicate a passage of time or through purposeful steps/stages

- **Comparison/contrast**: organized by points that indicate similarities and/or differences between two things or concepts

- **Order of importance**: organized by priority of points, often most significant to least significant or vice versa

Theme

The **theme** is the central message of a fictional work, whether that work is structured as prose, drama, or poetry. It is the heart of what an author is trying to say to readers through the writing, and theme is largely conveyed through literary elements and techniques.

In literature, a theme can often be determined by considering the overarching narrative conflict within the work. Though there are several types of conflicts and several potential themes within them, the following are the most common:

- Individual against the self—relevant to themes of self-awareness, internal struggles, pride, coming of age, facing reality, fate, free will, vanity, loss of innocence, loneliness, isolation, fulfillment, failure, and disillusionment

- Individual against nature—relevant to themes of knowledge vs. ignorance, nature as beauty, quest for discovery, self-preservation, chaos and order, circle of life, death, and destruction of beauty

- Individual against society—relevant to themes of power, beauty, good, evil, war, class struggle, totalitarianism, role of men/women, wealth, corruption, change vs. tradition, capitalism, destruction, heroism, injustice, and racism

- Individual against another individual—relevant to themes of hope, loss of love or hope, sacrifice, power, revenge, betrayal, and honor

For example, in Hawthorne's *The Scarlet Letter*, one possible narrative conflict could be the individual against the self, with a relevant theme of internal struggles. This theme is alluded to through characterization—Dimmesdale's moral struggle with his love for Hester and Hester's internal struggles with the truth and her daughter, Pearl. It's

16

also alluded to through plot—Dimmesdale's suicide and Hester helping the very townspeople who initially condemned her.

Sometimes, a text can convey a **message** or **universal lesson**—a truth or insight that the reader infers from the text, based on analysis of the literary and/or poetic elements. This message is often presented as a statement. For example, a potential message in Shakespeare's *Hamlet* could be "Revenge is what ultimately drives the human soul." This message can be immediately determined through plot and characterization in numerous ways, but it can also be determined through the setting of Norway, which is bordering on war.

Authors employ a variety of techniques to present a theme. They may compare or contrast characters, events, places, ideas, or historical or invented settings to speak thematically. They may use analogies, metaphors, similes, allusions, or other literary devices to convey the theme. An author's use of diction, syntax, and tone can also help convey the theme. Authors will often develop themes through the development of characters, use of the setting, repetition of ideas, use of symbols, and through contrasting value systems. Authors of both fiction and nonfiction genres will use a variety of these techniques to develop one or more themes.

Regardless of the literary genre, there are commonalities in how authors, playwrights, and poets develop themes or central ideas.

Authors often do research, the results of which contribute to theme. In prose fiction and drama, this research may include real historical information about the setting the author has chosen or include elements that make fictional characters, settings, and plots seem realistic to the reader. In nonfiction, research is critical since information contained within this literature must be accurate.

In fiction, authors present a narrative conflict that will contribute to the overall theme. This conflict may involve the storyline itself and some trouble within characters that needs resolution. In nonfiction, this conflict may be an explanation or commentary on factual people and events.

Authors will sometimes use character motivation to convey theme, such as in the example from *Hamlet* regarding revenge. In fiction, the characters an author creates will think, speak, and act in ways that effectively convey the theme to readers. In nonfiction, the characters are factual, as in a biography, but authors pay particular attention to presenting those motivations to make them clear to readers.

Authors also use literary devices as a means of conveying theme. For example, the use of moon symbolism in Mary Shelley's *Frankenstein* is significant as its phases can be compared to the phases that the Creature undergoes as he struggles with his identity.

The selected point of view can also contribute to a work's theme. The use of first-person point of view in a fiction or non-fiction work engages the reader's response differently than third person point of view. The central idea or theme from a first-person narrative may differ from a third-person limited text.

In literary nonfiction, authors usually identify the purpose of their writing, which differs from fiction, where the general purpose is to entertain. The purpose of nonfiction is usually to inform, persuade, or entertain the audience. The stated purpose of a non-fiction text will drive how the central message or theme, if applicable, is presented.

Authors identify an audience for their writing, which is critical in shaping the theme of the work. For example, the audience for J.K. Rowling's *Harry Potter* series would be different than the audience for a biography of George Washington. The audience an author chooses to address is closely tied to the purpose of the work. The choice of an audience also drives the choice of language and level of diction an author uses. Ultimately, the intended audience determines the level to which that subject matter is presented and the complexity of the theme.

Summaries of the Main Idea or Primary Purpose of a Reading Selection

Creating an outline that identifies the **main ideas** of a passage as well as the **supporting details** is a helpful tool in effectively summarizing a text. Most outlines will include a title that reveals the topic of the text and is usually a single phrase or word, such as "whales." If the passage is divided up into paragraphs, or the paragraphs into sections, each paragraph or section will have its own main idea. These "main ideas" are usually depicted in outlines as roman numerals. Next, writers use supporting details in order to support or prove the main ideas. The supporting details should be listed underneath each main idea in the outline.

For example:

> Title: Whales
> I. Killer whales
>   a. Highly social
>   b. Apex predator
> II. Humpback whales
>   a. Males produce "song"
>   b. Targeted for whaling industry
> III. Beluga whales
>   a. Complex sense of hearing
>   b. Slow swimmers

Making an outline is a useful method of summarization because it forces the reader to deconstruct the text as a whole and to identify only the most important parts of the text.

Ideas from a text can also be organized using graphic organizers. A **graphic organizer** is a way to simplify information and take key points from the text. A graphic organizer such as a timeline may have an event listed for a corresponding date on the timeline while an outline may have an event listed under a key point that occurs in the text. Each reader needs to create the type of graphic organizer that works the best for him or her in terms of being able to recall information from a story. Examples include a **spider-map**, which takes a main idea from the story and places it in a bubble with supporting points branching off the main idea. An **outline** is useful for diagramming the main and supporting points of the entire story, and a **Venn diagram** classifies information as separate or overlapping.

Writing a summary is similar to creating an outline. In both instances, the reader wants to relay the most important parts of the text without being too verbose. A **summary** of a text should begin with stating the main idea of that text. Then, the reader must decide which supporting details are absolutely essential to the main idea of the text and leave any irrelevant information out of the summary. A summary shouldn't be too brief—readers should include important details depicted in the text—but it also shouldn't be too long either. The appeal of a summary to an audience is that they are able to receive the message of the text without being distracted by the style or detours of the author.

Another effective reading comprehension strategy is paraphrasing. Paraphrasing is usually longer than a summary. **Paraphrasing** is taking the author's text and rewriting, or "translating," it into their own words. A tip for paraphrasing is to read a passage over three times. Once you read the passage and understand what the author is saying, cover the original passage and begin to write everything you remember from that passage into your own words. Usually, if you understand the content well enough, you will have translated the main idea of the author into your own words with your own writing style. An effective paraphrase will be as long as the original passage but will have a different writing structure.

18

Summaries of Informational Texts

Informational text is written material that has the primary function of imparting information about a topic. It is often written by someone with expertise in the topic and directed at an audience that has less knowledge of the topic. Informational texts are written in a different fashion from storytelling or narrative texts. Typically, this type of text has several organizational and structural differences from narrative text. In informational texts, there are features such as charts, graphs, photographs, headings and subheadings, glossaries, indexes, bibliographies, or other guidance features. With the aid of technology, embedded hyperlinks and video content are also sometimes included. Informational material may be written to compare and contrast, be explanatory, link cause and effect, provide opinion, persuade the reader, or serve a number of other purposes. Finally, informational texts typically use a different style of language than narrative texts, which instead, focus more on storytelling. Historically, informational texts were not introduced until students were ready to read to learn versus still learning to read. However, research is now suggesting that informational text can be developmentally appropriate for students at a much younger age.

One very effective strategy for increasing comprehension of informational text is reciprocal teaching. **Reciprocal teaching** is a method of small group teaching that relies on students assuming different roles to practice four reading strategies particularly helpful for readers of informational texts. Predicting, summarizing, questioning, and clarifying will lead students to understand and apply what they read. Skilled readers have acquired a set of techniques that make informational reading effective for them. They begin by previewing text selections and making educated guesses as to what the content will include. They then identify the purpose for reading the text and can explain why the content will be important to know. They are able to filter the reading selection to screen out the trivial points and focus on the most important facts. Using critical thinking skills, they monitor their own understanding of the information by asking themselves questions about what they have read. They use multiple methods to determine the meaning of unknown vocabulary. Finally, they can concisely and succinctly form an overall summary of what they have learned from the text.

Predicting

Predicting requires thinking ahead and, after reading, verifying whether predictions were correct. This method engages students with the text and gets them to pay attention to details that tell them whether their predictions might be coming true. The goal is to help students learn to base their predictions on clues from the text. They should not only state what they predict but also be able to comment on the specifics of the text that lead them to make those predictions.

Summarizing

Through **summarizing**, students learn to identify the main ideas and differentiate them from the less important information in the text. It helps them remember what they read and retell the central concepts in their own words. As students learn to break down larger chunks of information into more concise sentences, they use analytical thinking skills and hone their critical reading capabilities.

Questioning Techniques

Questioning has immeasurable value in the reading process. Answering questions about a text gives purpose for reading to students and focuses them on reading to learn information. Similarly, generating questions about a text for others to answer enables a student to analyze what is important to learn in the text and glean summarizing skills. Keeping Bloom's Taxonomy in mind, teachers can scaffold students toward increased critical thinking capabilities. **Bloom's Taxonomy** shows the hierarchy of learning progressing through the following stages:

- Remembering
- Understanding
- Applying
- Analyzing

- Evaluating
- Creating

Clarifying

Clarifying is the post-reading phase where students learn to clear up any misunderstandings and unanswered questions. Strategies for clarifying include defining any unknown words, rereading at a slower pace, reviewing previous segments of the text, referring to their summaries, and skimming future portions of the text.

Supporting Ideas

Supporting details help readers better develop and understand the main idea. Supporting details answer questions like *who, what, where, when, why,* and *how*. Different types of supporting details include examples, facts and statistics, anecdotes, and sensory details.

Persuasive and informative texts often use supporting details. In persuasive texts, authors attempt to make readers agree with their points of view, and supporting details are often used as "selling points." If authors make a statement, they need to support the statement with evidence in order to adequately persuade readers. Informative texts use supporting details such as examples and facts to inform readers. Review the previous "Cheetahs" passage to find examples of supporting details.

> Cheetahs are one of the fastest mammals on the land, reaching up to 70 miles an hour over short distances. Even though cheetahs can run as fast as 70 miles an hour, they usually only have to run half that speed to catch up with their choice of prey. Cheetahs cannot maintain a fast pace over long periods of time because their bodies will overheat. After a chase, cheetahs need to rest for approximately 30 minutes prior to eating or returning to any other activity.

In the example, supporting details include:

- Cheetahs reach up to 70 miles per hour over short distances.
- They usually only have to run half that speed to catch up with their prey.
- Cheetahs will overheat if they exert a high speed over longer distances.
- Cheetahs need to rest for 30 minutes after a chase.

Look at the diagram below (applying the cheetah example) to help determine the hierarchy of topic, main idea, and supporting details.

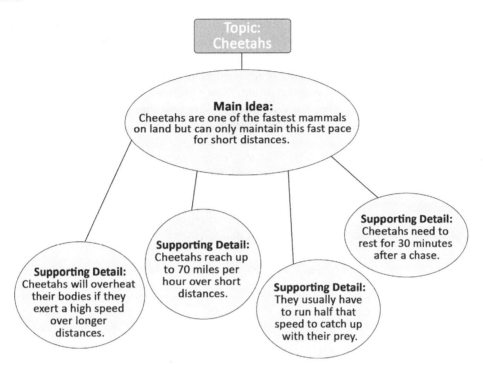

Determining How Ideas or Details Inform the Author's Argument

Once a reader has determined an author's thesis or main idea, he or she will need to understand how textual evidence supports interpretation of that thesis or main idea. Test takers will be asked direct questions regarding an author's main idea and may be asked to identify evidence that would support those ideas. This will require test takers to comprehend literal and figurative meanings within the text passage, be able to draw inferences from provided information, and be able to separate important evidence from minor supporting details. It's often helpful to skim test questions and answer options prior to critically reading informational text; however, test takers should avoid the temptation to solely look for the correct answers. Just trying to find the "right answer" may cause test takers to miss important supporting textual evidence. Making mental note of test questions is only helpful as a guide when reading.

After identifying an author's thesis or main idea, a test taker should look at the supporting details that the author provides to back up their assertions, identifying those additional pieces of information that help expand the thesis. From there, test takers should examine the additional information and related details for credibility, the author's use of outside sources, and be able to point to direct evidence that supports the author's claims. It's also imperative that test takers be able to identify what is strong support and what is merely additional information that is nice to know but not necessary. Being able to make this differentiation will help test takers effectively answer questions regarding an author's use of supporting evidence within informational text.

Inferences

Identifying Inferences and Implications that Can be Drawn From a Text

Engaged readers should constantly self-question while reviewing texts to help them form conclusions. Self-questioning is when readers review a paragraph, page, passage, or chapter and ask themselves, "Did I understand what I read?," "What was the main event in this section?," "Where is this taking place?," and so on. Authors can provide clues or pieces of evidence throughout a text or passage to guide readers toward a conclusion. This is why

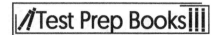
active and engaged readers should read the text or passage in its entirety before forming a definitive conclusion. If readers do not gather all the pieces of evidence needed, then they may jump to an illogical conclusion.

At times, authors **directly state** conclusions while others simply **imply** them. Of course, it is easier if authors outwardly provide conclusions to readers because it does not leave any information open to interpretation. On the other hand, implications are things that authors do not directly state but can be assumed based off of information they provided. If authors only imply what may have happened, readers can form a menagerie of ideas for conclusions. For example, look at the following statement: "Once we heard the sirens, we hunkered down in the storm shelter." In this statement, the author does not directly state that there was a tornado, but clues such as "sirens" and "storm shelter" provide insight to the reader to help form that conclusion.

Readers should be able to make inferences. Making an **inference** requires the reader to read between the lines and look for what is implied rather than what is explicitly stated. That is, using information that is known from the text, the reader is able to make a logical assumption about information that is not explicitly stated but is probably true. Read the following passage:

> "Hey, do you wanna meet my new puppy?" Jonathan asked.
>
> "Oh, I'm sorry but please don't—" Jacinta began to protest, but before she could finish, Jonathan had already opened the passenger side door of his car and a perfect white ball of fur came bouncing towards Jacinta.
>
> "Isn't he the cutest?" beamed Jonathan.
>
> "Yes—achoo!—he's pretty—aaaachooo!!—adora—aaa—aaaachoo!" Jacinta managed to say in between sneezes. "But if you don't mind, I—I—achoo!—need to go inside."

Which of the following can be inferred from Jacinta's reaction to the puppy?
a. She hates animals.
b. She is allergic to dogs.
c. She prefers cats to dogs.
d. She is angry at Jonathan.

An inference requires the reader to consider the information presented and then form their own idea about what is probably true. Based on the details in the passage, what is the best answer to the question? Important details to pay attention to include the tone of Jacinta's dialogue, which is overall polite and apologetic, as well as her reaction itself, which is a long string of sneezes. Choices *A* and *D* both express strong emotions ("hates" and "angry") that are not evident in Jacinta's speech or actions. Choice *C* mentions cats, but there is nothing in the passage to indicate Jacinta's feelings about cats. Choice *B*, "she is allergic to dogs," is the most logical choice. Based on the fact she began sneezing as soon as a fluffy dog approached her, it makes sense to guess that Jacinta might be allergic to dogs. So even though Jacinta never directly states, "Sorry, I'm allergic to dogs!," using the clues in the passage, it is still reasonable to guess that this is true.

Making inferences is crucial for readers of literature because literary texts often avoid presenting complete and direct information to readers about characters' thoughts or feelings, or they present this information in an unclear way, leaving it up to the reader to interpret clues given in the text. In order to make inferences while reading, readers should ask themselves:

- What details are being presented in the text?
- Is there any important information that seems to be missing?
- Based on the information that the author does include, what else is probably true?
- Is this inference reasonable based on what is already known?

Craft, Structure, and Language Skills

Attitude and Tone

An Author's Tone or Attitude Toward Material in a Text

An author's **tone** is the use of particular words, phrases, and writing style to convey an overall meaning. Tone expresses the author's attitude towards a particular topic. For example, a historical reading passage may begin like the following:

> The presidential election of 1960 ushered in a new era, a new Camelot, a new phase of forward thinking in U.S. politics that embraced brash action and unrest and responded with admirable leadership.

From this opening statement, a reader can draw some conclusions about the author's attitude towards President John F. Kennedy. Furthermore, the reader can make additional, educated guesses about the state of the Union during the 1960 presidential election. By close reading, the test taker can determine that the repeated use of the word *new* and words such as *admirable leadership* indicate the author's tone of admiration regarding President Kennedy's boldness. In addition, the author assesses that the era during President Kennedy's administration was problematic through the use of the words *brash action* and *unrest.* Therefore, if a test taker encountered a test question asking about the author's use of tone and their assessment of the Kennedy administration, the test taker should be able to identify an answer indicating admiration. Similarly, if asked about the state of the Union during the 1960s, a test taker should be able to correctly identify an answer indicating political unrest.

When identifying an author's tone, the following list of words may be helpful. This is not an inclusive list. Generally, parts of speech that indicate attitude will also indicate tone:

- Comical
- Angry
- Ambivalent
- Scary
- Lyrical
- Matter-of-fact
- Judgmental
- Sarcastic
- Malicious
- Objective
- Pessimistic
- Patronizing
- Gloomy
- Instructional
- Satirical
- Formal
- Casual

An author's **message** is the same as the overall meaning of a passage. It is the main idea, or the main concept the author wishes to convey. An author's message may be stated outright, or it may be implied. Regardless, the test taker will need to use careful reading skills to identify an author's message or purpose.

Often, the message of a particular passage can be determined by thinking about why the author wrote the information. Many historical passages are written to inform and to teach readers established, factual information. However, many historical works are also written to convey biased ideas to readers. Gleaning bias from an author's

23

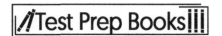
message in a historical passage can be difficult, especially if the reader is presented with a variety of established facts as well. Readers tend to accept historical writing as factual. This is not always the case. Any discerning reader who has tackled historical information on topics such as United States political party agendas can attest that two or more works on the same topic may have completely different messages supporting or refuting the value of the identical policies.

Therefore, it is important to critically assess an author's message separate from factual information. One author, for example, may point to the rise of unorthodox political candidates in an election year based on the failures of the political party in office while another may point to the rise of the same candidates in the same election year based on the current party's successes. The historical facts of what has occurred leading up to an election year are not in refute. Labeling those facts as a failure or a success is a bias within an author's overall message, as is excluding factual information in order to further a particular point. In a standardized testing situation, a reader must be able to critically assess what the author is trying to say separate from the historical facts that surround their message.

Using the example of Lincoln's Gettysburg Address, a test question may ask the following:

> What message is the speaker trying to convey through this address?

Then they will ask the test taker to select an answer that best expresses Lincoln's message to his audience. Based on the options given, a test taker should be able to select the answer expressing the idea that Lincoln's audience should recognize the efforts of those who died in the war as a sacrifice to preserving human equality and self-government.

An author may want to challenge a reader's intellect, inspire imagination, or spur emotion. An author may present information to appeal to a physical, aesthetic, or transformational sense.

Take the following text as an example:

> In 1963, Martin Luther King stated "I have a dream." The gathering at the Lincoln Memorial was the beginning of the Civil Rights movement and, with its reference to the Emancipation Proclamation, Dr. King's words electrified those who wanted freedom and equality while rising from hatred and slavery. It was the beginning of radical change.

The test taker may be asked about the effect this statement might have on King's audience. Through careful reading of the passage, the test taker should be able to choose an answer that best identifies an effect of grabbing the audience's attention. The historical facts are in place: King made the speech in 1963 at the Lincoln Memorial, kicked off the civil rights movement, and referenced the Emancipation Proclamation. The words *electrified* and *radical change* indicate the effect the author wants the reader to understand as a result of King's speech. In this historical passage, facts are facts. However, the author's message goes beyond the facts to indicate the effect the message had on the audience and, in addition, the effect the event should have on the reader.

How an Author's Word Choice Conveys Attitude and Shapes Meaning, Style, and Tone

Authors choose their words carefully in order to artfully depict meaning, style, and tone, which is most commonly inferred through the use of adjectives and verbs. The **tone** is the predominant emotion present in the text and represents the attitude or feelings that an author has towards a character or event.

To review, an **adjective** is a word used to describe something, and usually precedes the **noun**, a person, place, or object. A **verb** is a word describing an action. For example, the sentence "The scary woodpecker ate the spider" includes the adjective "scary," the noun "woodpecker," and the verb "ate." Reading this sentence may rouse some negative feelings, as the word "scary" carries a negative charge. The **charge** is the emotional connotation that can be derived from the adjectives and verbs and is either positive or negative. Recognizing the charge of a particular sentence or passage is an effective way to understand the meaning and tone the author is trying to convey.

Many authors have conflicting charges within the same text, but a definitive tone can be inferred by understanding the meaning of the charges relative to each other. It's important to recognize key **conjunctions**, or words that link sentences or clauses together. There are several types and subtypes of conjunctions. Three are most important for reading comprehension:

- **Cumulative conjunctions** add one statement to another.
  - Examples: *and, both, also, as well as, not only*
  - e.g. The juice is sweet *and* sour.
- **Adversative conjunctions** are used to contrast two clauses.
  - Examples: *but, while, still, yet, nevertheless*
  - e.g. She was tired, *but* she was happy.
- **Alternative conjunctions** express two alternatives.
  - Examples: *or, either, neither, nor, else, otherwise*
  - e.g. He must eat, *or* he will die.

Identifying the meaning and tone of a text can be accomplished with the following steps:

- Identify the adjectives and verbs.
- Recognize any important conjunctions.
- Label the adjectives and verbs as positive or negative.
- Understand what the charge means about the text.

To demonstrate these steps, examine the following passage from the classic children's poem, "The Sheep":

Lazy sheep, pray tell me why

In the pleasant fields you lie,

Eating grass, and daisies white,

From the morning till the night?

Everything can something do,

But what kind of use are you?

–Taylor, Jane and Ann. "The Sheep."

This selection is a good example of conflicting charges that work together to express an overall tone. Following the first two steps, identify the adjectives, verbs, and conjunctions within the passage. For this example, the adjectives are underlined, the verbs are in **bold**, and the conjunctions *italicized*:

<u>Lazy</u> sheep, pray **tell** me why

In the <u>pleasant</u> fields you **lie**,

Eating grass, and daisies <u>white,</u>

From the morning till the night?

Everything can something do,

But what kind of use are you?

For step three, read the passage and judge whether feelings of positivity or negativity arose. Then assign a charge to each of the words that were outlined. This can be done in a table format, or simply by writing a + or − next to the word.

The word <u>lazy</u> carries a negative connotation; it usually denotes somebody unwilling to work. To **tell** someone something has an exclusively neutral connotation, as it depends on what's being told, which has not yet been revealed at this point, so a charge can be assigned later. The word <u>pleasant</u> is an inherently positive word. To **lie** could be positive or negative depending on the context, but as the subject (the sheep) is lying in a pleasant field, then this is a positive experience. **Eating** is also generally positive.

After labeling the charges for each word, it might be inferred that the tone of this poem is happy and maybe even admiring or innocuously envious. However, notice the adversative conjunction, "but" and what follows. The author has listed all the pleasant things this sheep gets to do all day, but the tone changes when the author asks, "What kind of use are you?" Asking someone to prove their value is a rather hurtful thing to do, as it implies that the person asking the question doesn't believe the subject has any value, so this could be listed under negative charges. Referring back to the verb **tell**, after reading the whole passage, it can be deduced that the author is asking the sheep to tell what use the sheep is, so this has a negative charge.

+	−
• Pleasant • Lie in fields • From morning to night	• Lazy • Tell me • What kind of use are you

Upon examining the charges, it might seem like there's an even amount of positive and negative emotion in this selection, and that's where the conjunction "but" becomes crucial to identifying the tone. The conjunction "but" indicates there's a contrasting view to the pleasantness of the sheep's daily life, and this view is that the sheep is lazy and useless, which is also indicated by the first line, "lazy sheep, pray tell me why."

It might be helpful to look at questions pertaining to tone. For this selection, consider the following question:

The author of the poem regards the sheep with a feeling of what?
a. Respect
b. Disgust
c. Apprehension
d. Intrigue

Considering the author views the sheep as lazy with nothing to offer, Choice *A* appears to reflect the opposite of what the author is feeling.

Choice *B* seems to mirror the author's feelings towards the sheep, as laziness is considered a disreputable trait, and people (or personified animals, in this case) with unfavorable traits might be viewed with disgust.

Choice *C* doesn't make sense within context, as laziness isn't usually feared.

Choice *D* is tricky, as it may be tempting to argue that the author is intrigued with the sheep because they ask, "pray tell me why." This is another out-of-scope answer choice as it doesn't *quite* describe the feelings the author experiences and there's also a much better fit in Choice *B*.

Organization and Structure

Good writing is not merely a random collection of sentences. No matter how well written, sentences must relate and coordinate appropriately with one another. If not, the writing seems random, haphazard, and disorganized. Therefore, good writing must be organized, where each sentence fits a larger context and relates to the sentences around it.

Transition Words

The writer should act as a guide, showing the reader how all the sentences fit together. Consider this seat belt example:

> Seat belts save more lives than any other automobile safety feature. Many studies show that airbags save lives as well. Not all cars have airbags. Many older cars don't. Air bags aren't entirely reliable. Studies show that in 15% of accidents, airbags don't deploy as designed. Seat belt malfunctions are extremely rare.

There's nothing wrong with any of these sentences individually, but together they're disjointed and difficult to follow. The best way for the writer to communicate information is through the use of transition words. Here are examples of transition words and phrases that tie sentences together, enabling a more natural flow:

To show causality: *as a result, therefore*, and *consequently*
To compare and contrast: *however, but,* and *on the other hand*
To introduce examples: *for instance, namely,* and *including*
To show order of importance: *foremost, primarily, secondly,* and *lastly*

Note that this is not a complete list of transitions. There are many more that can be used; however, most fit into these or similar categories. The important point is that the words should clearly show the relationship between sentences, supporting information, and the main idea.

Here is an update to the previous example using transition words. These changes make it easier to read and bring clarity to the writer's points:

> Seat belts save more lives than any other automobile safety feature. Many studies show that airbags save lives as well; however, not all cars have airbags. For instance, some older cars don't. Furthermore, air bags aren't entirely reliable. For example, studies show that in 15% of accidents, airbags don't deploy as designed, but, on the other hand, seat belt malfunctions are extremely rare.

Also, test takers should be prepared to analyze whether the writer is using the best transition word or phrase for the situation. For example, the sentence: "As a result, seat belt malfunctions are extremely rare" doesn't make sense in the context above because the writer is trying to show the contrast between seat belts and airbags, not the causality.

Organizational Structure

Depending on what the author is attempting to accomplish, certain formats or text structures work better than others. For example, a sequence structure might work for narration but not for identifying similarities and differences between concepts. Similarly, a comparison-contrast structure is not useful for narration. It's the author's job to put the right information in the correct format.

Readers should be familiar with the five main literary structures:

1. **Sequence** structure (sometimes referred to as the order structure) is when the order of events proceed in a predictable order. In many cases, this means the text goes through the plot elements: exposition, rising action, climax, falling action, and resolution. Readers are introduced to characters, setting, and conflict in the exposition. In

27

the rising action, there's an increase in tension and suspense. The climax is the height of tension and the point of no return. Tension decreases during the falling action. In the resolution, any conflicts presented in the exposition are solved, and the story concludes. An informative text that is structured sequentially will often go in order from one step to the next.

2. In the **problem-solution** structure, authors identify a potential problem and suggest a solution. This form of writing is usually divided into two parts (the problem and the solution) and can be found in informational texts. For example, cell phone, cable, and satellite providers use this structure in manuals to help customers troubleshoot or identify problems with services or products.

3. When authors want to discuss similarities and differences between separate concepts, they arrange thoughts in a **comparison-contrast** paragraph structure. Venn diagrams are an effective graphic organizer for comparison-contrast structures because they feature two overlapping circles that can be used to organize similarities and differences. A comparison-contrast essay organizes one paragraph based on similarities and another based on differences. A comparison-contrast essay can also be arranged with the similarities and differences of individual traits addressed within individual paragraphs. Words such as *however*, *but*, and *nevertheless* help signal a contrast in ideas.

4. **Descriptive** writing structure is designed to appeal to your senses. Much like an artist who constructs a painting, good descriptive writing builds an image in the reader's mind by appealing to the five senses: sight, hearing, taste, touch, and smell. However, overly descriptive writing can become distracting; whereas sparse descriptions can make settings and characters seem flat. Good authors must strike a balance between the two and provide enough detail to enable the reader to really see and experience what is happening in the plot without distracting the reader with excessive details.

5. Passages that use the **cause-and-effect** structure are simply asking *why* by demonstrating some type of connection between ideas. Words such as *if, since, because, then, or consequently* indicate a cause-and-effect relationship. By switching the order of a complex sentence, the writer can rearrange the emphasis on different clauses. Saying, *If Sheryl is late, we'll miss the dance*, is different from saying *We'll miss the dance if Sheryl is late*. One emphasizes Sheryl's tardiness while the other emphasizes missing the dance. Paragraphs can also be arranged in a cause-and-effect format. Cause-and-effect writing discusses the impact of decisions that have been made or could be made. Researchers often apply this paragraph structure to the scientific method.

Regardless as to the specific text structure used, organized writing should have an introduction and conclusion. Examining the writer's strategies for introductions and conclusions puts the reader in the right mindset to interpret the rest of the text. Look for methods the writer might use for introductions such as:

> Stating the main point immediately, followed by outlining how the rest of the piece supports this claim.

> Establishing important, smaller pieces of the main idea first, and then grouping these points into a case for the main idea.

> Opening with a quotation, anecdote, question, seeming paradox, or other piece of interesting information, and then using it to lead to the main point.

Whatever method the writer chooses, the introduction should make their intention clear, establish their voice as a credible one, and encourage a person to continue reading.

Conclusions tend to follow a similar pattern. In them, the writer restates their main idea a final time, often after summarizing the smaller pieces of that idea. If the introduction uses a quote or anecdote to grab the reader's attention, the conclusion often makes reference to it again. Whatever way the writer chooses to arrange the

conclusion, the final restatement of the main idea should be clear and simple for the reader to interpret. Finally, conclusions shouldn't introduce any new information.

Identifying the Role that an Idea, Reference, or Piece of Information Plays in an Author's Argument

Readers should always identify the author's position or stance in a text. No matter how objective a piece may seem, assume the author has preconceived beliefs. Reduce the likelihood of accepting an invalid argument by looking for multiple articles on the topic, including those with varying opinions. If several opinions point in the same direction, and are backed by reputable peer-reviewed sources, it's more likely the author has a valid argument. Positions that run contrary to widely held beliefs and existing data should invite scrutiny. There are exceptions to the rule, so be a careful consumer of information.

Though themes, symbols, and motifs are buried deep within the text and can sometimes be difficult to infer, an author's purpose is usually obvious from the beginning. There are four purposes of writing: to inform, to persuade, to describe, and to entertain. Informative writings present facts in an accessible way and are also known as expository writing. Persuasive writing appeals to emotions and logic to inspire the reader to adopt a specific stance. Be wary of this type of writing, as it often lacks objectivity. Descriptive writing is designed to paint a picture in the reader's mind, while texts that entertain are often narratives designed to engage and delight the reader.

The various writing styles are usually blended, with one purpose dominating the rest. For example, a persuasive piece might begin with a humorous tale to make readers more receptive to the persuasive message, or a recipe in a cookbook designed to inform might be preceded by an entertaining anecdote that makes the recipe more appealing.

In an argument or persuasive text, an author will strive to sway readers to an opinion or conclusion. To be effective, an author must consider their intended audience. Although an author may write text for a general audience, he or she will use methods of appeal or persuasion to convince that audience. Aristotle asserted that there were three methods or modes by which a person could be persuaded. These are referred to as **rhetorical appeals**.

The three main types of rhetorical appeals are shown in the following graphic.

Ethos, also referred to as an **ethical appeal**, is an appeal to the audience's perception of the writer as credible (or not), based on their examination of their ethics and who the writer is, their experience or incorporation of relevant information, or their argument. For example, authors may present testimonials to bolster their arguments. The reader who critically examines the veracity of the testimonials and the credibility of those giving the testimony will be able to determine if the author's use of testimony is valid to their argument. In turn, this will help the reader determine if the author's thesis is valid. An author's careful and appropriate use of technical language can create an overall knowledgeable effect and, in turn, act as a convincing vehicle when it comes to credibility. Overuse of technical language, however, may create confusion in readers and obscure an author's overall intent.

Pathos, also referred to as **emotional appeal**, is an appeal to the audience's sense of identity, self-interest, or emotions. A critical reader will notice when the author is appealing to pathos through anecdotes and descriptions that elicit an emotion such as anger or pity. Readers should also beware of factual information that uses generalization to appeal to the emotions. While it's tempting to believe an author is the source of truth in their text, an author who presents factual information as universally true, consistent throughout time, and common to all groups is using **generalization**. Authors who exclusively use generalizations without specific facts and credible sourcing are attempting to sway readers solely through emotion.

Logos, also referred to as a **logical appeal**, is an appeal to the audience's ability to see and understand the logic in a claim offered by the writer. A critical reader has to be able to evaluate an author's arguments for validity of reasoning and for sufficiency when it comes to argument.

Rhetorical Strategies and Devices

A **rhetorical device** is the phrasing and presentation of an idea that reinforces and emphasizes a point in an argument. A rhetorical device is often quite memorable. One of the more famous uses of a rhetorical device is in John F. Kennedy's 1961 inaugural address: "Ask not what your country can do for you, ask what you can do for your country." The contrast of ideas presented in the phrasing is an example of the rhetorical device of antimetabole.

Some other common examples are provided below, but test takers should be aware that this is not a complete list.

Device	Definition	Example
Allusion	A reference to a famous person, event, or significant literary text as a form of significant comparison	"We are apt to shut our eyes against a painful truth, and listen to the song of that siren till she transforms us into beasts." Patrick Henry
Anaphora	The repetition of the same words at the beginning of successive words, phrases, or clauses, designed to emphasize an idea	"We shall not flag or fail. We shall go on to the end. We shall fight in France, we shall fight on the seas and oceans, we shall fight with growing confidence ... we shall fight in the fields and in the streets, we shall fight in the hills. We shall never surrender." Winston Churchill
Understatement	A statement meant to portray a situation as less important than it actually is to create an ironic effect	"The war in the Pacific has not necessarily developed in Japan's favor." Emperor Hirohito, surrendering Japan in World War II

30

Device	Definition	Example
Parallelism	A syntactical similarity in a structure or series of structures used for impact of an idea, making it memorable	"A penny saved is a penny earned." Ben Franklin
Rhetorical question	A question posed that is not answered by the writer though there is a desired response, most often designed to emphasize a point	"Can anyone look at our reduced standing in the world today and say, 'Let's have four more years of this?'" Ronald Reagan

Meaning of Words

Individual words are constructed from building blocks of meaning. An **affix** is an element that is added to a root or stem word that can change the word's meaning.

For example, the stem word *fix* is a verb meaning *to repair*. When the ending *–able* is added, it becomes the adjective *fixable*, meaning "capable of being repaired." Adding *un–* to the beginning changes the word to *unfixable*, meaning "incapable of being repaired." In this way, affixes attach to the word stem to create a new word and a new meaning. Knowledge of affixes can assist in deciphering the meaning of unfamiliar words.

Affixes are also related to inflection. **Inflection** is the modification of a base word to express a different grammatical or syntactical function. For example, countable nouns such as *car* and *airport* become plural with the addition of *–s* at the end: *cars* and *airports*.

Verb tense is also expressed through inflection. **Regular verbs**—those that follow a standard inflection pattern—can be changed to past tense using the affixes *–ed*, *–d*, or *–ied*, as in *cooked* and *studied*. Verbs can also be modified for continuous tenses by using *–ing*, as in *working* or *exploring*. Thus, affixes are used not only to express meaning but also to reflect a word's grammatical purpose.

31

A **prefix** is an affix attached to the beginning of a word. The meanings of English prefixes mainly come from Greek and Latin origins. The chart below contains a few of the most commonly used English prefixes.

Prefix	Meaning	Example
a-	not	amoral, asymptomatic
anti-	against	antidote, antifreeze
auto-	self	automobile, automatic
circum-	around	circumference, circumspect
co-, com-, con-	together	coworker, companion
contra-	against	contradict, contrary
de-	negation or reversal	deflate, deodorant
extra-	outside, beyond	extraterrestrial, extracurricular
in-, im-, il-, ir-	not	impossible, irregular
inter-	between	international, intervene
intra-	within	intramural, intranet
mis-	wrongly	mistake, misunderstand
mono-	one	monolith, monopoly
non-	not	nonpartisan, nonsense
pre-	before	preview, prediction
re-	again	review, renew
semi-	half	semicircle, semicolon
sub-	under	subway, submarine
super-	above	superhuman, superintendent
trans-	across, beyond, through	trans-Siberian, transform
un-	not	unwelcome, unfriendly

While the addition of a prefix alters the meaning of the base word, the addition of a **suffix** may also affect a word's part of speech. For example, adding a suffix can change the noun *material* into the verb *materialize* and back to a noun again in *materialization*.

Suffix	Part of Speech	Meaning	Example
-able, -ible	adjective	having the ability to	honorable, flexible
-acy, -cy	noun	state or quality	intimacy, dependency
-al, -ical	adjective	having the quality of	historical, tribal
-en	verb	to cause to become	strengthen, embolden
-er, -ier	adjective	comparative	happier, longer
-est, -iest	adjective	superlative	sunniest, hottest
-ess	noun	female	waitress, actress
-ful	adjective	full of, characterized by	beautiful, thankful

Suffix	Part of Speech	Meaning	Example
-fy, -ify	verb	to cause, to come to be	liquefy, intensify
-ism	noun	doctrine, belief, action	Communism, Buddhism
-ive, -ative, -itive	adjective	having the quality of	creative, innovative
-ize	verb	to convert into, to subject to	Americanize, dramatize
-less	adjective	without, missing	emotionless, hopeless
-ly	adverb	in the manner of	quickly, energetically
-ness	noun	quality or state	goodness, darkness
-ous, -ious, -eous	adjective	having the quality of	spontaneous, pious
-ship	noun	status or condition	partnership, ownership
-tion	noun	action or state	renovation, promotion
-y	adjective	characterized by	smoky, dreamy

Through knowledge of prefixes and suffixes, a student's vocabulary can be instantly expanded with an understanding of **etymology**—the origin of words. This, in turn, can be used to add sentence structure variety to academic writing.

Context Clues

Familiarity with common prefixes, suffixes, and root words assists tremendously in unraveling the meaning of an unfamiliar word and making an educated guess as to its meaning. However, some words do not contain many easily-identifiable clues that point to their meaning. In this case, rather than looking at the elements within the word, it is useful to consider elements around the word—i.e., its context. **Context** refers to the other words and information within the sentence or surrounding sentences that indicate the unknown word's probable meaning. The following sentences provide context for the potentially-unfamiliar word *quixotic*:

> Rebecca had never been one to settle into a predictable, ordinary life. Her quixotic personality led her to leave behind a job with a prestigious law firm in Manhattan and move halfway around the world to pursue her dream of becoming a sushi chef in Tokyo.

A reader unfamiliar with the word *quixotic* doesn't have many clues to use in terms of affixes or root meaning. The suffix *–ic* indicates that the word is an adjective, but that is it. In this case, then, a reader would need to look at surrounding information to obtain some clues about the word. Other adjectives in the passage include *predictable* and *ordinary*, things that Rebecca was definitely not, as indicated by "Rebecca had never been one to settle." Thus, a first clue might be that *quixotic* means the opposite of predictable.

The second sentence doesn't offer any other modifier of *personality* other than *quixotic*, but it does include a story that reveals further information about her personality. She had a stable, respectable job, but she decided to give it up to follow her dream. Combining these two ideas together, then—unpredictable and dream-seeking—gives the reader a general idea of what *quixotic* probably means. In fact, the root of the word is the character Don Quixote, a romantic dreamer who goes on an impulsive adventure.

While context clues are useful for making an approximate definition for newly-encountered words, these types of clues also come in handy when encountering common words that have multiple meanings. The word *reservation* is used differently in each the following sentences:

> A. That restaurant is booked solid for the next month; it's impossible to make a reservation unless you know somebody.

> B. The hospital plans to open a branch office inside the reservation to better serve Native American patients who cannot easily travel to the main hospital fifty miles away.

C. Janet Clark is a dependable, knowledgeable worker, and I recommend her for the position of team leader without reservation.

All three sentences use the word to express different meanings. In fact, most words in English have more than one meaning—sometimes meanings that are completely different from one another. Thus, context can provide clues as to which meaning is appropriate in a given situation. A quick search in the dictionary reveals several possible meanings for *reservation*:

- An exception or qualification
- A tract of public land set aside, such as for the use of American Indian tribes
- An arrangement for accommodations, such as in a hotel, on a plane, or at a restaurant

Sentence A mentions a restaurant, making the third definition the correct one in this case. In sentence B, some context clues include Native Americans, as well as the implication that a reservation is a place—"inside the reservation," both of which indicate that the second definition should be used here. Finally, sentence C uses *without reservation* to mean "completely" or "without exception," so the first definition can be applied here.

Using context clues in this way can be especially useful for words that have multiple, widely varying meanings. If a word has more than one definition and two of those definitions are the opposite of each other, it is known as an **auto-antonym**—a word that can also be its own antonym. In the case of auto-antonyms, context clues are crucial to determine which definition to employ in a given sentence. For example, the word *sanction* can either mean "to approve or allow" or "a penalty." Approving and penalizing have opposite meanings, so *sanction* is an example of an auto-antonym. The following sentences reflect the distinction in meaning:

A. In response to North Korea's latest nuclear weapons test, world leaders have called for harsher sanctions to punish the country for its actions.

B. The general has sanctioned a withdrawal of troops from the area.

A context clue can be found in sentence A, which mentions "to punish." A punishment is similar to a penalty, so sentence A is using the word *sanction* according to this definition.

Other examples of auto-antonyms include *oversight*—"to supervise something" or "a missed detail," *resign*—"to quit" or "to sign again, as a contract," and *screen*—"to show" or "to conceal." For these types of words, recognizing context clues is an important way to avoid misinterpreting the sentence's meaning.

A context clue is a hint that an author provides to the reader in order to help define difficult or unique words. When reading a passage, a test taker should take note of any unfamiliar words, and then examine the sentence around them to look for clues to the word meanings. Let's look at an example:

He faced a *conundrum* in making this decision. He felt as if he had come to a crossroads. This was truly a puzzle, and what he did next would determine the course of his future.

The word **conundrum** may be unfamiliar to the reader. By looking at context clues, the reader should be able to determine its meaning. In this passage, context clues include the idea of making a decision and of being unsure. Furthermore, the author restates the definition of conundrum in using the word *puzzle* as a synonym. Therefore, the reader should be able to determine that the definition of the word *conundrum* is a difficult puzzle.

Similarly, a reader can determine difficult vocabulary by identifying antonyms. Let's look at an example:

Her *gregarious* nature was completely opposite of her twin's, who was shy, retiring, and socially nervous.

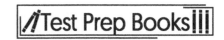

The word *gregarious* may be unfamiliar. However, by looking at the surrounding context clues, the reader can determine that *gregarious* does not mean shy. The twins' personalities are being contrasted. Therefore, *gregarious* must mean sociable, or something similar to it.

At times, an author will provide contextual clues through a cause and effect relationship. Look at the next sentence as an example:

> The athletes were excited with *elation* when they won the tournament; unfortunately, their off-court antics caused them to forfeit the win.

The word elated may be unfamiliar to the reader. However, the author defines the word by presenting a cause and effect relationship. The athletes were so elated at the win that their behavior went overboard, and they had to forfeit. In this instance, *elated* must mean something akin to overjoyed, happy, and overexcited.

Cause and effect is one technique authors use to demonstrate relationships. A **cause** is why something happens. The **effect** is what happens as a result. For example, a reader may encounter text such as *Because he was unable to sleep, he was often restless and irritable during the day.* The cause is insomnia due to lack of sleep. The effect is being restless and irritable. When reading for a cause and effect relationship, look for words such as "if," "then," "such," and "because." By using cause and effect, an author can describe direct relationships, and convey an overall theme, particularly when taking a stance on their topic.

An author can also provide contextual clues through comparison and contrast. Let's look at an example:

> Her torpid state caused her parents, and her physician, to worry about her seemingly sluggish well-being.

The word *torpid* is probably unfamiliar to the reader. However, the author has compared *torpid* to a state of being and, moreover, one that's worrisome. Therefore, the reader should be able to determine that *torpid* is not a positive, healthy state of being. In fact, through the use of comparison, it means sluggish. Similarly, an author may contrast an unfamiliar word with an idea. In the sentence *Her __torpid__ state was completely opposite of her usual, bubbly self,* the meaning of *torpid*, or sluggish, is contrasted with the words *bubbly self*.

A test taker should be able to critically assess and determine unfamiliar word meanings through the use of an author's context clues in order to fully comprehend difficult text passages.

Syntax

Syntax refers to the arrangement of words, phrases, and clauses to form a sentence. Knowledge of syntax can also give insight into a word's meaning. The section above considered several examples using the word *reservation* and applied context clues to determine the word's appropriate meaning in each sentence. Here is an example of how the placement of a word can impact its meaning and grammatical function:

> A. The development team has reserved the conference room for today.

> B. Her quiet and reserved nature is sometimes misinterpreted as unfriendliness when people first meet her.

In addition to using *reserved* to mean different things, each sentence also uses the word to serve a different grammatical function. In sentence A, *reserved* is part of the verb phrase *has reserved*, indicating the meaning "to set aside for a particular use." In sentence B, *reserved* acts as a modifier within the noun phrase "her quiet and reserved nature." Because the word is being used as an adjective to describe a personality characteristic, it calls up a different definition of the word—"restrained or lacking familiarity with others." As this example shows, the function of a word within the overall sentence structure can allude to its meaning. It is also useful to refer to the earlier chart about suffixes and parts of speech as another clue into what grammatical function a word is serving in a sentence.

Analyzing Nuances of Word Meaning and Figures of Speech

Language is not as simple as one word directly correlated to one meaning. Rather, one word can express a vast array of diverse meanings, and similar meanings can be expressed through different words. However, there are very few words that express exactly the same meaning. For this reason, it is important to be able to pick up on the nuances of word meaning.

Many words contain two levels of meaning: connotation and denotation as discussed previously in the informational texts and rhetoric section. A word's **denotation** is its most literal meaning—the definition that can readily be found in the dictionary. A word's **connotation** includes all of its emotional and cultural associations.

In literary writing, authors rely heavily on connotative meaning to create mood and characterization. The following are two descriptions of a rainstorm:

A. The rain slammed against the windowpane, and the wind howled through the fireplace. A pair of hulking oaks next to the house cast eerie shadows as their branches trembled in the wind.

B. The rain pattered against the windowpane, and the wind whistled through the fireplace. A pair of stately oaks next to the house cast curious shadows as their branches swayed in the wind.

Description A paints a creepy picture for readers with strongly emotional words like *slammed*, connoting force and violence. *Howled* connotes pain or wildness, and *eerie* and *trembled* connote fear. Overall, the connotative language in this description serves to inspire fear and anxiety.

However, as can be seen in description B, swapping out a few key words for those with different connotations completely changes the feeling of the passage. *Slammed* is replaced with the more cheerful *pattered*, and *hulking* has been swapped out for *stately*. Both words imply something large, but *hulking* is more intimidating whereas *stately* is more respectable. *Curious* and *swayed* seem more playful than the language used in the earlier description. Although both descriptions represent roughly the same situation, the nuances of the emotional language used throughout the passages create a very different sense for readers.

Selective choice of connotative language can also be extremely impactful in other forms of writing, such as editorials or persuasive texts. Through connotative language, writers reveal their biases and opinions while trying to inspire feelings and actions in readers:

- Parents won't stop complaining about standardized tests.
- Parents continue to raise concerns about standardized tests.

Readers should be able to identify the nuance in meaning between these two sentences. The first one carries a more negative feeling, implying that parents are being bothersome or whiny. Readers of the second sentence, though, might come away with the feeling that parents are concerned and involved in their children's education. Again, the aggregate of even subtle cues can combine to give a specific emotional impression to readers, so from an early age, students should be aware of how language can be used to influence readers' opinions.

Another form of non-literal expression can be found in *figures of speech*. As with connotative language, figures of speech tend to be shared within a cultural group and may be difficult to pick up on for learners outside of that group. In some cases, a figure of speech may be based on the literal denotation of the words it contains, but in other cases, a figure of speech is far removed from its literal meaning. A case in point is **irony**, where what is said is the exact opposite of what is meant:

The new tax plan is poorly planned, based on faulty economic data, and unable to address the financial struggles of middle-class families. Yet legislators remain committed to passing this brilliant proposal.

36

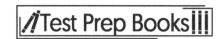

When the writer refers to the proposal as brilliant, the opposite is implied—the plan is "faulty" and "poorly planned." By using irony, the writer means that the proposal is anything but brilliant by using the word in a non-literal sense.

Another figure of speech is **hyperbole**—extreme exaggeration or overstatement. Statements like "I love you to the moon and back" or "Let's be friends for a million years" utilize hyperbole to convey a greater depth of emotion, without literally committing oneself to space travel or a life of immortality.

Figures of speech may sometimes use one word in place of another. **Synecdoche**, for example, uses a part of something to refer to its whole. The expression "Don't hurt a hair on her head!" implies protecting more than just an individual hair, but rather her entire body. "The art teacher is training a class of Picassos" uses Picasso, one individual notable artist, to stand in for the entire category of talented artists. Another figure of speech using word replacement is **metonymy**, where a word is replaced with something closely associated to it. For example, news reports may use the word Washington to refer to the American government or the crown to refer to the British monarch.

Figurative Language

Literary texts also employ rhetorical devices. Figurative language like simile and metaphor is a type of rhetorical device commonly found in literature. In addition to rhetorical devices that play on the *meanings* of words, there are also rhetorical devices that use the *sounds* of words. These devices are most often found in poetry but may also be found in other types of literature and in non-fiction writing like speech texts.

Alliteration and assonance are both varieties of sound repetition. Other types of sound repetition include: **anaphora**, repetition that occurs at the beginning of the sentences; **epiphora**, repetition occurring at the end of phrases; **antimetabole**, repetition of words in reverse order; and **antiphrasis**, a form of denial of an assertion in a text.

Alliteration refers to the repetition of the first sound of each word. Recall Robert Burns' opening line:

> My love is like a red, red rose

This line includes two instances of alliteration: "love" and "like" (repeated *L* sound), as well as "red" and "rose" (repeated *R* sound). Next, assonance refers to the repetition of vowel sounds, and can occur anywhere within a word (not just the opening sound). Here is the opening of a poem by John Keats:

> When I have fears that I may cease to be
> Before my pen has glean'd my teeming brain

Assonance can be found in the words "fears," "cease," "be," "glean'd," and "teeming," all of which stress the long *E* sound. Both alliteration and assonance create a harmony that unifies the writer's language.

Another sound device is **onomatopoeia**, or words whose spelling mimics the sound they describe. Words such as "crash," "bang," and "sizzle" are all examples of onomatopoeia. Use of onomatopoetic language adds auditory imagery to the text.

Readers are probably most familiar with the technique of pun. A **pun** is a play on words, taking advantage of two words that have the same or similar pronunciation. Puns can be found throughout Shakespeare's plays, for instance:

> Now is the winter of our discontent
> Made glorious summer by this son of York

These lines from *Richard III* contain a play on words. Richard III refers to his brother, the newly crowned King Edward IV, as the "son of York," referencing their family heritage from the house of York. However, while drawing a comparison between the political climate and the weather (times of political trouble were the "winter," but now the new king brings "glorious summer"), Richard's use of the word "son" also implies another word with the same pronunciation, "sun"—so Edward IV is also like the sun, bringing light, warmth, and hope to England. Puns are a clever way for writers to suggest two meanings at once.

Some examples of figurative language are included in the following table.

Term	Definition	Example
Simile	Compares two things using "like" or "as"	Her hair was like gold.
Metaphor	Compares two things as if they are the same	He was a giant teddy bear.
Idiom	Using words with predictable meanings to create a phrase with a different meaning	The world is your oyster.
Alliteration	Repeating the same beginning sound or letter in a phrase for emphasis	The busy baby babbled.
Personification	Attributing human characteristics to an object or an animal	The house glowered menacingly with a dark smile.
Foreshadowing	Giving an indication that something is going to happen later in the story	I wasn't aware at the time, but I would come to regret those words.
Symbolism	Using symbols to represent ideas and provide a different meaning	The ring represented the bond between us.
Onomatopoeia	Using words that imitate sound	The tire went off with a bang and a crunch.
Imagery	Appealing to the senses by using descriptive language	The sky was painted with red and pink and streaked with orange.
Hyperbole	Using exaggeration not meant to be taken literally	The girl weighed less than a feather.

Figurative language can be used to give additional insight into the theme or message of a text by moving beyond the usual and literal meaning of words and phrases. It can also be used to appeal to the senses of readers and create a more in-depth story.

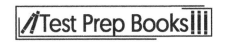

Relating Unfamiliar Words to Familiar Words

The Reading section will test a reader's ability to use context clues, and then relate unfamiliar words to more familiar ones. Using the word *torpid* as an example, the test may ask the test taker to relate the meaning of the word to a list of vocabulary options and choose the more familiar word as closest in meaning. In this case, the test may say something like the following:

Which of the following words means the same as the word *torpid* in the above passage?

Then they will provide the test taker with a list of familiar options such as happy, disgruntled, sluggish, and animated. By using context clues, the reader has already determined the meaning of *torpid* as slow or sluggish, so the reader should be able to correctly identify the word *sluggish* as the correct answer.

One effective way to relate unfamiliar word meanings to more familiar ones is to substitute the provided word in each answer option for the unfamiliar word in question. Although this will not always lead to a correct answer every time, this strategy will help the test taker narrow answer options. Be careful when utilizing this strategy. Pay close attention to the meaning of sentences and answer choices because it's easy to mistake answer choices as correct when they are easily substituted, especially when they are the same part of speech. Does the sentence mean the same thing with the substituted word option in place or does it change entirely? Does the substituted word make sense? Does it possibly mean the same as the unfamiliar word in question?

Understanding a Range of Words and Phrases to Improve Comprehension and Read at the College Level

Vocabulary

Vocabulary are the words that are found in any given language that are used to convey various meanings to others. A strong vocabulary and word recognition base enables students to access prior knowledge and experiences in order to make connections in written texts. A strong vocabulary also allows students to express ideas, learn new concepts, and decode the meanings of unfamiliar words by using context clues. Conversely, if a child's vocabulary knowledge is limited and does not steadily increase, reading comprehension will be negatively affected. If students become frustrated with their lack of understanding of written texts, they will likely choose only to read texts at their comfort level or refuse to read altogether. With direct instruction, educators introduce specific words to pre-teach before reading, or examine word roots, prefixes, and suffixes. Through indirect instruction, educators ensure that students are regularly exposed to new words. This engages students in high-quality conversations and social interactions and provides access to a wide variety of challenging and enjoyable reading material.

Morphology

Morphology is the study of the structure and the formation of words. A **phoneme** is the smallest unit of sound that does not necessarily carry meaning. Essentially, phonemes are combined to form words, and words are combined to form sentences. Morphology looks at the smallest meaningful part of a word, known as a morpheme. In contrast to a phoneme, a morpheme must carry a sound and a meaning. Free morphemes are those that can stand alone, carrying both sound and meaning, as in the following words: *girl, boy, man,* and *lady.* Just as the name suggests, bound morphemes are bound to other morphemes in order to carry meaning. Examples of bound morphemes include: ish, ness, ly, and dis.

Semantics

Semantics is the branch of linguistics that studies the meanings of words. Morphemes, words, phrases, and sentences all carry distinct meanings. The way these individual parts are arranged can have a significant effect on meaning. In order to construct language, students must be able to use semantics to arrange and rearrange words to achieve the particular meaning they are striving for. Activities that teach semantics revolve around teaching the arrangement of word parts (morphology) and root words, and then the teaching of vocabulary. Moving from vocabulary words into studying sentences and sentence structure leads students to learn how to use context clues

to determine meaning and to understand anomalies such as metaphors, idioms, and allusions. There are five types of semantic relationships that are critical to understand:

- **Hyponyms** refer to more-specific words that fall into the same category as a more general word (e.g., mare, stallion, foal, Appaloosa, and Clydesdale are all hyponyms of horse).

- **Meronyms** refer to a relationship between words where a whole word has multiple parts (meronyms) that comprise it (e.g., horse: tail, mane, hooves, ears).

- **Synonyms** refer to words that have the same meaning as another word (e.g., instructor/teacher/educator, canine/dog, feline/cat, herbivore/vegetarian).

- **Antonyms** refer to words that have the opposite meaning as another word (e.g., true/false, up/down, in/out, right/wrong).

- **Homonyms** refer to words that are spelled the same (homographs) or sound the same (homophones) but mean different things (e.g., there/their/they're, two/too/to, principal/principle, plain/plane, (kitchen) sink/sink (down as in water)).

Syntax

With its origins from the Greek word, "syntaxis," which means arrangement, **syntax** is the study of phrase and sentence formation. The study of syntax focuses on the ways in which specific words can be combined to create coherent meaning. For example: the simple rearrangement of the words, "I can run," is different from the question, "Can I run?" which is also different from the meaningless "Run I can."

The following methods can be used to teach syntax:

- **Proper Syntax Modeling**: Students don't need to be corrected for improper syntax. Instead, they should be shown ways to rephrase what they said with proper syntax. If a student says, "Run I can," then the teacher should say, "Oh, you can run how fast?" This puts syntax in place with conversational skills.

- **Open-Ended Sentences**: Students can complete open-ended sentences with proper syntax both orally and in written format, or they can correct sentences that have improper syntax so that they make sense.

- **Listening for Syntax**: Syntax is auditory. Students can often hear a syntax error before they can see it in writing. Teachers should have students use word cards or word magnets to arrange and rearrange simple sentences and read them aloud to check for syntax.

- **Repetition**: Syntax can be practiced by using songs, poems, and rhymes for repetitive automation.

Pragmatics

Pragmatics is the study of what words mean in certain situations. It helps to understand the intentions and interpretations of intentions through words used in human interaction. Different listeners and different situations call for different language and intonations of language. When people engage in a conversation, it is usually to convey a certain message, and the message (even using the same words) can change depending on the setting and the audience. The more fluent the speaker, the more success she or he will have in conveying the intended message.

The following methods can be used to teach pragmatics:

- When students state something incorrectly, respond to what they intended to say. For instance, if a student says, "That's how it didn't happen." Then the teacher might say, "Of course, that's not how it happened." Instead of putting students on defense by being corrected, this method puts them at ease and helps them learn.

40

- Role-playing conversations with different people in different situations can help teach pragmatics. For example, pretend playing can be used where a situation remains the same but the audience changes, or the audience stays the same but the situations change. This can be followed with a discussion about how language and intonations change too.

- Different ways to convey a message can be used, such as asking vs. persuading, or giving direct vs. indirect requests and polite vs. impolite messages.

- Various non-verbal signals can be used to see how they change pragmatics. For example, students can be encouraged to use mismatched words and facial expressions, such as angry words while smiling or happy words while pretending to cry.

Strategies to Help Read New and/or Difficult Words

Students who are developing reading fluency and comprehension skills can become frustrated when presented with unfamiliar words in a given text. With direct phonics instruction, educators can teach students to decode words and then use context clues to define the words while reading. If students have a strong enough understanding of language structures, including nouns and verbs, educators can ask them to consider what part of speech the unknown word might be based on and where it might fit into the sentence. Other useful strategies involve self-monitoring, in which students are asked to think as they read and ask themselves if what they have just read makes sense. Focusing on visual clues, such as drawings and photographs, may give students valuable insight into deciphering unknown words. Looking for the word in another section of the text to see how it relates to the overall meaning could give a clue to the new vocabulary word. Spelling the word out loud or looking for word chunks, prefixes, and suffixes, as well as demonstrating how to segment the unknown word into its individual syllables, may also be effective strategies to employ.

One of the most valuable strategies, however, for helping students to read and understand new words is pre-teaching. In this strategy, educators select what they evaluate to be the unfamiliar words in the text and then introduce them to the class before reading. Educators using this method should be careful not to simply ask the students to read the text and then spell the new words correctly. They should also provide clear definitions and give the students the opportunity to read these words in various sentences to decipher word meaning. This method can dramatically reduce how often students stop reading in order to reflect on unknown words. Educators are often unsure as to whether to correct every mispronounced word a child makes when reading. If the mispronounced word still makes sense, it is sometimes better to allow the child to continue to read, since the more the child stops, the more the child's reading comprehension and fluency are negatively affected.

Fact or Opinion

Discerning Fact Vs. Opinion in a Text

Teachers should educate and encourage students to view reading as an active process of discovering meaning in texts. Reading should not be passive. Readers should question what they read and apply their background knowledge to enhance their understanding and appreciation of written work. Teachers should bear in mind that the meaning derived from a given text for a student may depend on their background and experiences.

It's important to read any piece of writing critically. The goal is to discover the point and purpose of what the author is writing about through analysis. It's also crucial to establish the point or stance the author has taken on the topic of the piece. After determining the author's perspective, readers can then more effectively develop their own viewpoints on the subject of the piece.

It is important to distinguish between fact and opinion when reading a piece of writing. A **fact** is information that is true. If information can be disproven, it is not a fact. For example, water freezes at or below thirty-two degrees Fahrenheit. An argument stating that water freezes at seventy degrees Fahrenheit cannot be supported by data and is therefore not a fact. Facts tend to be associated with science, mathematics, and statistics. **Opinions** are

41

information open for debate. Opinions are often tied to concepts like equality, morality, and human rights. They can also be controversial.

Authors often use words like *think, feel, believe,* or *in my opinion* when expressing opinion, but these words won't always appear in an opinion piece, especially if it is formally written. An author's opinion may be backed up by facts, which gives it more credibility, but that opinion should not be taken as fact. A critical reader should be wary of an author's opinion, especially if it is only supported by other opinions.

Fact	Opinion
There are nine innings in a game of baseball.	Baseball games run too long.
James Garfield was assassinated on July 2, 1881.	James Garfield was a good president.
McDonalds has stores in 118 countries.	McDonalds has the best hamburgers.

Critical readers examine the facts used to support an author's argument. They check the facts against other sources to be sure those facts are correct. They also check the validity of the sources used to be sure those sources are credible, academic, and/or peer reviewed. Consider that when an author uses another person's opinion to support their argument, even if it is an expert's opinion, it is still only an opinion and should not be taken as fact. A strong argument uses valid, measurable facts to support ideas. Even then, the reader may disagree with the argument as it may be rooted in their personal beliefs.

An authoritative argument may use the facts to sway the reader. Because of this, a writer may choose to only use the information and expert opinion that supports their viewpoint.

If the argument is that wind energy is the best solution, the author will use facts that support this idea. That same author may leave out relevant facts on solar energy. The way the author uses facts can influence the reader, so it's important to consider the facts being used, how those facts are being presented, and what information might be left out.

Critical readers should also look for errors in the argument such as logical fallacies and bias. A **logical fallacy** is a flaw in the logic used to make the argument. Logical fallacies include slippery slope, straw man, and begging the question. Authors can also reflect **bias** if they ignore an opposing viewpoint or present their side in an unbalanced way. A strong argument considers the opposition and finds a way to refute it. Critical readers should look for an unfair or one-sided presentation of the argument and be skeptical, as a bias may be present. Even if this bias is unintentional, if it exists in the writing, the reader should be wary of the validity of the argument.

Readers should also look for the use of **stereotypes**. These are the overly simplified beliefs about a person, place, thing, etc. that is indiscriminately applied to a larger group. These can be positive but are usually negative in nature. When a reader comes across the use of stereotypes, they should take that into consideration as they analyze the author's argument. These should generally be avoided. Stereotypes reveal a flaw in the writer's thinking and may suggest a lack of knowledge or understanding about the subject.

Bias and Stereotypes

Not only can authors state facts or opinions in their writing, they sometimes intentionally or unintentionally show bias or portray a stereotype. A **bias** is when someone demonstrates a prejudice in favor of or against something or someone in an unfair manner. When an author is biased in their writing, readers should be skeptical despite the fact that the author's bias may be correct. For example, two athletes competed for the same position. One athlete is related to the coach and is a mediocre athlete, while the other player excels and deserves the position. The coach chose the less talented player who is related to him for the position. This is a biased decision because it favors someone in an unfair way.

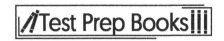

Similar to a bias, a **stereotype** shows favoritism or opposition but toward a specific group or place. Stereotypes create an oversimplified or overgeneralized idea about a certain group, person, or place. For example:

> Women are horrible drivers.

This statement basically labels *all* women as horrible drivers. While there may be some terrible female drivers, the stereotype implies that *all* women are bad drivers when, in fact, not *all* women are. While many readers are aware of several vile ethnic, religious, and cultural stereotypes, audiences should be cautious of authors' flawed assumptions because they can be less obvious than the despicable examples that are pervasive in society.

Integration of Knowledge and Ideas

Diverse Media and Formats

Interpreting Texts that Include Visual Formats

Literature refers to a collection of written works that are the distinctive voices of peoples, time periods, and cultures. The world has gained great insight into human thought, vices, virtues, and desires through the written word. As the work pertains to the author's approach to these insights, literature can be classified as fiction or non-fiction.

This study guide has primarily focused on the printed word for Praxis test takers; however, it's important to note media and non-print text. In the 21st century, rhetoric is evident in a variety of formats. Blogs, vlogs, videos, news footage, advertisements, and live video fill informational feeds, and readers see many shortened images and snapshot texts a day. It's important to note that the majority of these formats use images to appeal to emotion over factual information. Online visuals spread more quickly and are more easily adopted by consumers as fact than printed formats.

Critical readers should be aware that media and non-print text carries some societal weight to the population. In being inundated with pictures and live footage, readers often feel compelled to skip the task of critical reading analysis and accept truth at literal face value. Authors of non-print media are aware of this fact and frequently capitalize on it.

To critically address non-print media requires that the consumer address additional sources and not exclude printed text in order to reach sound conclusions. While it's tempting for consumers to get swept away in the latest viral media, it's important to remember that creators of such have an agenda, and unless the non-print media in question is backed up with sound supporting evidence, any thesis or message cannot be considered valid or factual. Memes, gifs, and looped video cannot tell the whole, truthful story although they may appeal to opinions with which readers already agree. Sharing such non-print media online can precipitate widespread misunderstanding.

When presented with non-print media, critical readers should consider these bits of information as teasers to be investigated for accuracy and veracity. Of course, certain non-print media exists solely for entertainment, but the critical reader should be able to separate out what's generalized for entertainment's sake and what's presented for further verification, before blindly accepting the message. Increasingly, this has become more difficult for readers to do, only because of the onslaught of information to which they are exposed.

If a reader is not to fall prey to strong imagery and non-print media, he or she will need to fact-check. This, of course, requires time and attention on the reader's part, and in current culture, taking the time to fact-check seems counterproductive. However, in order to maintain credibility themselves, readers must be able to evaluate multiple sources of information across media formats and be able to identify the emotional appeal used in the smaller sound bites of non-print media. Readers must view with a discerning eye, listen with a questioning ear, and think with a critical mind.

Informational Graphics

A test taker's ability to draw conclusions from an informational graphic is a sub-skill in displaying one's command of reading evidence. Drawing conclusions requires the reader to consider all information provided in the passage, then to use logic to piece it together to form a reasonably correct resolution. In this case, a test taker must look for facts as well as opinionated statements. Both should be considered in order to arrive at a conclusion. These types of questions test one's ability to conduct logical and analytical thinking.

Identifying data-driven evidence in informational graphics is very similar to analyzing factual information. However, it often involves the use of graphics in order to do so. In these types of questions, the test taker will be presented with a graph, or organizational tool, and asked questions regarding the information it contains.

Texts may have graphical representations to help illustrate and visually support assertions made. For example, graphs can be used to express samples or segments of a population or demonstrate growth or decay. Three of the most popular graphical formats include line graphs, bar graphs, and pie charts.

Line graphs rely on a horizontal X-axis and a vertical Y-axis to establish baseline values. Dots are plotted where the horizontal and vertical axes intersect, and those dots are connected with lines. Compared to bar graphs or pie charts, line graphs are more useful for looking at the past and present and predicting future outcomes. For instance, a potential investor would look for stocks that demonstrated steady growth over many decades when examining the stock market. Note that severe spikes up and down indicate instability, while line graphs that display a slow but steady increase may indicate good returns.

Here's an example of a bar graph:

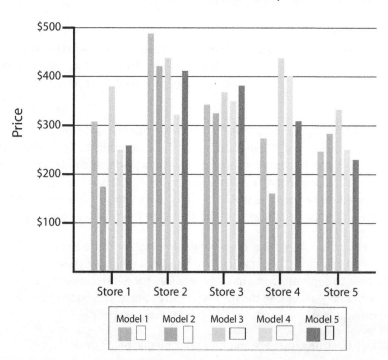

Tablet Model Price Comparison

Bar graphs are usually displayed on a vertical Y-axis. The bars themselves can be two- or three-dimensional, depending on the designer's tastes. Unlike a line graph, which shows the fluctuation of only one variable, the X-axis on a bar graph is excellent for making comparisons, because it shows differences between several variables. For instance, if a consumer wanted to buy a new tablet, she could narrow the selection down to a few choices by using

44

a bar graph to plot the prices side by side. The tallest bar would be the most expensive tablet, the shortest bar would be the cheapest.

A **pie chart** is divided into wedges that represent a numerical piece of the whole. Pie charts are useful for demonstrating how different categories add up to 100 percent. However, pie charts are not useful in comparing dissimilar items. High schools tend to use pie charts to track where students end up after graduation. Each wedge, for instance, might be labeled *vocational school*, *two-year college*, *four-year college*, *workforce*, or *unemployed*. By calculating the size of each wedge, schools can offer classes in the same ratios as where students will end up after high school. Pie charts are also useful for tracking finances. Items such as car payments, insurance, rent, credit cards, and entertainment would each get their own wedge proportional to the amount spent in a given time period. If one wedge is inordinately bigger than the rest, or if a wedge is expendable, it might be time to create a new financial strategy.

Evaluation of Arguments

Identifying the Relationships Among Ideas Presented in a Text

A reader must be able to evaluate the argument or point the author is trying to make and determine if it is adequately supported. The first step is to determine the main idea. The main idea is what the author wants to say about a specific topic. The next step is to locate the supporting details. An author uses supporting details to illustrate the main idea. These are the details that provide evidence or examples to help make a point. Supporting details often appear in the form of quotations, paraphrasing, or analysis. Test takers should then examine the text to make sure the author connects details and analysis to the main point. These steps are crucial to understanding the text and evaluating how well the author presents their argument and evidence. The following graphic demonstrates the connection between the main idea and the supporting details.

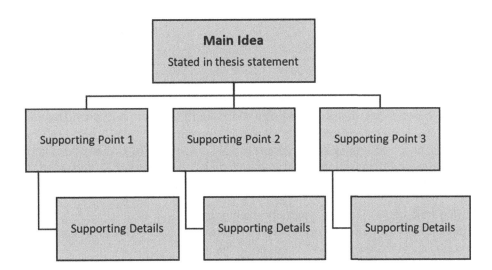

Determining Whether Evidence Strengthens, Weakens, or is Relevant to a Text

It is important to evaluate the author's supporting details to be sure that they are credible, provide evidence of the author's point, and directly support the main idea. Critical readers examine the facts used to support an author's argument and check those facts against other sources to make sure the facts are correct. They also check the validity of the sources used to make sure those sources are credible, academic, and/or peer-reviewed. A strong argument uses valid, measurable facts to support ideas.

Readers need to consider the evidence an author offers in support of their argument or conclusion. Evidence may strengthen or weaken an argument, or it may not be relevant. Additionally, test questions sometimes offer new

evidence or information in the question itself, and then as the test taker to choose a statement that, if true, strengthens or weakens the argument.

This is how these questions are often phrased:

- Which of the following statements, if true, strengthens (weakens) the argument?
- Which one of the following, if true, *most* strengthens (weakens) the argument?
- Each of the following, if true, weakens (strengthens) the argument, EXCEPT:

The first and third type of questions can be answered by finding the answer choice that goes in the opposite direction. For there to be a statement that strengthens or weakens an argument, the others necessarily must do the opposite. This is especially true for the questions with *except*. Although this analysis makes those questions much easier, the test taker should always check the answer with the argument.

For the second type, or the *most* questions, the answer choices could weaken, strengthen, or be completely irrelevant. All of the five answer choices could go in the same direction. For example, in a most weakens question, all five answer choices could weaken that argument. Or, three could be weakening choices, one a strengthening choice, and the other an irrelevant choice. Or, it could be some other combination. No matter what, the goal is to concentrate on the *most* part of the question. Weigh competing choices relative to each other, and always choose the one that does the *most*.

Follow these two preliminary steps when solving new information questions. Remember, practicing these skills will make them second nature. First, determine if it is something that weakens or strengthens. Second, determine the *most* strengthening or weakening answer. Always keep a look out for the *except* variety because the test makers always include deceiving and tricky choices. Finally, as with the Reading section in general, but particularly important for these question types, if the question says *if true*, then assume that it is true. No matter how ridiculous it seems or how strongly it generates disagreements, if it says true, then it is true.

Below are examples of the three different types:

Strengthens

> Countries that favor rehabilitation over retribution for crimes involving substance use, such as minor possession, have much lower rates of recidivism. Once countries commit to providing drug and alcohol rehabilitation, people who enter the criminal justice system are much less likely to return. Rehabilitation has been proven over and over again to cause crime rates to drop. The United States imprisons more drug parents who struggle with addiction and alcoholics than any other country in the world. The United States would greatly benefit by reconsidering its use of rehabilitation.

Which of the following statements, if true, strengthens the argument?
a. Fewer substance users live in the countries that have succeeded with increased rehabilitation.
b. The United States holds the second most prisoners in the world.
c. Rehabilitation is much cheaper than imprisonment.
d. Rehabilitation is much more expensive than imprisonment.
e. The United States currently favors retribution over rehabilitation more than any other country.

Since the answer wants the one answer choice that strengthens the argument, the other four answer choices will either weaken the argument or be irrelevant altogether.

Choice *A* is irrelevant. The argument does not say how a larger number of substance abusers impact the success of rehabilitation. According to the argument's logic, it does not matter how many substance abusers live in the countries that have succeeded at rehabilitation.

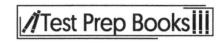

Choice *B* is also irrelevant. Like Choice *A*, the argument makes no mention as to whether an increased number of inmates would impact the effectiveness of transitioning to rehabilitation. Do not be tricked into selecting an answer just because two of the choices touch on the same irrelevant point.

Choice *C* is deceptive but irrelevant for the purposes of strengthening the argument. Rehabilitation's lower cost seems to be quite the benefit. However, the argument does not argue that rehabilitation would be cost-effective, or how these financial savings would make rehabilitation more appealing. It's making the argument that rehabilitation is better than retribution since it reduces recidivism, which lowers crime rates overall. It does not matter whether it is cheaper for purposes of this argument.

Choice *D* is also irrelevant for the same reasons as Choice *C*. In addition, even if it were relevant, it would weaken the argument. In this situation, pay special attention to the two *opposite* answer choices; however, one of them does not happen to be correct for this question.

Choice *E* strengthens the argument. If the United States currently uses an extreme amount of retribution and less rehabilitation than the rest of the world, then the benefits of a transition to rehabilitation would be enormous. The argument states that increased rehabilitation lowers crime rates. If the United States does not currently use any rehabilitation, then it would be in line for the biggest drop in crime rates. This is the correct answer since it is the only one that strengthens the argument.

Most Weakens

> Reading is the most important factor in academic achievement. Anyone who starts reading at a young age and continues reading throughout their schooling scores better on all levels of standardized tests. Mandatory reading requirements should be enforced in all grade levels from kindergarten through sixth grade.

Which one of the following, if true, most weakens the argument?
a. Some states already mandate required reading in their schools.
b. Anyone forced to read will actually read less overall.
c. The top 1% of Praxis scorers reported reading as their number one hobby.
d. Young readers usually stop reading for fun after graduating college.
e. Affluent students read more than their less wealthy peers.

This is a most weakens question, so it is possible for more than one answer choice to weaken the argument. The one that weakens the argument the *most* should be selected.

Choice *A* is irrelevant. It does not weaken the argument to say that some schools have already started what the author believes to be the most effective solution. Eliminate this choice.

Choice *B* definitely weakens the argument. The author's conclusion is that mandatory reading requirements should be enforced in early schooling. This will presumably increase reading, which is the most important factor in academic achievement according to the argument. If it is true that anyone forced to read would actually read less overall, then the argument makes no sense. If the goal is to increase reading and forcing reading decreases overall reading, then it makes no sense to make it a mandatory part of the curriculum. This certainly seems very forceful; however, review the other answers before making a choice. Look for the statement that would undermine the argument.

Choice *C* actually strengthens the argument. It proves one of the argument's premises that reading boosts standardized test performance. This is clearly incorrect and should be eliminated.

Choice *D* is irrelevant. The author wants to increase reading through mandatory requirements in order to increase academic achievement. If people stop reading after graduating college, it does not impact the argument.

Choice *E* is also irrelevant. It adds another factor that could be the reason for increased academic performance. It's saying that wealth directly contributes to increased reading, and therefore better performance. This choice is offering a competing theory. However, we need to evaluate it relative to our other option. Choice *B* totally destroys the logic's argument, while Choice *E* alters the discussion. Choice *B* is the better of the two.

Except Type

Football should be banned until the end of high school. Until completing puberty, at approximately sixteen years of age, the brain is still developing. High impact sports, such as football, are simply too damaging to developing brains. The risk of permanent injury is simply too great.

Each of the following, if true, strengthens the argument, EXCEPT:
a. Studies have shown that people who suffer concussions before puberty are three times as likely to drop out of high school.
b. The earlier in life someone suffers a concussion, the more concussions he or she will suffer throughout their life disproportionately increases.
c. The camaraderie and work ethic learned in youth football is invaluable.
d. Football cannot be made safe at the youth level.
e. Young athletes wishing to play college or professional football will not have more opportunities if they start playing young.

This an exception question. Notice that the wrong answer will always go in the opposite direction indicated in the question. The question states that the four remaining answers will strengthen the argument. In this instance, look for what weakens the argument.

Choice *A* strengthens the argument. This supports the argument's conclusion that the risk of permanent injury is too great to allow young people to play football. This statement says that people who suffer concussions before puberty are more likely to drop out of high school. It further justifies the author's desire to prohibit youth football.

Choice *B* strengthens the argument. If people suffer more concussions after suffering the first injury before puberty, then it further supports the prohibition.

Choice *C* weakens the argument. The choice attributes *invaluable* skills to youth football, which means that the risk might not be too great. If the skills learned could outweigh the risk, then it would not be reasonable to prohibit the sport at the youth level. This seems like the right choice; however, make sure that the remaining answer choices strengthen the argument.

Choice *D* strengthens the argument. If football cannot be made safe at the youth level, then a ban is the only solution. If there are no ways to reduce the harm, then it must be eliminated.

Choice *E* strengthens the argument. A reasonable suggestion is that the possibility of a college scholarship or professional career could outweigh the risk. This answer choice shuts down that potential counterargument. It definitely does not weaken the argument.

Therefore, Choice *C* is correct since it is the only answer choice that weakens the argument.

Determining the Assumptions on Which an Argument is Based

Assumptions can be thought of as unwritten premises. Although they never explicitly appear in the argument, the author is relying on it to defend the argument, just like a premise. Assumptions are the most important part of an argument that will never appear in an argument.

An argument in the abstract is: The author concludes Z based on W and X premises. But the W and X premises actually depend on the unmentioned assumption of Y. Therefore, the author is really saying that X, W, and Y make Z correct, but Y is assumed.

People assume all of the time. Assumptions and inferences allow the human mind to process the constant flow of information. Many assumptions underlie even the most basic arguments. However, readers must be able to identify underlying assumptions that a writer has made, as these weaken the credibility of the argument. One example is:

> Peyton Manning is the most over-rated quarterback of all time. He lost more big games than anyone else. Plus, he allegedly assaulted his female trainer in college. Peyton clearly shouldn't make the Hall of Fame.

The author certainly relies on a lot of assumptions. A few assumptions are:

- Peyton Manning plays quarterback.

- He is considered to be a great quarterback by at least some people.

- He played in many big games.

- Allegations and past settlements without any admission of guilt from over a decade ago can be relied upon as evidence against Hall of Fame acceptance.

- The Hall of Fame voters factor in off-the-field incidents, even if true.

- The best players should make the Hall of Fame.

- Losing big games negates, at least in part, the achievement of making it to those big games

- Peyton Manning is retired, and people will vote on whether he makes the Hall of Fame at some point in the future.

The author is relying on all of these assumptions. Some are clearly more important to his argument than others. In fact, disproving a necessary assumption can destroy a premise and possibly an entire conclusion. For example, what if the Hall of Fame did not factor in any of the off-the-field incidents? Then the alleged assault no longer factors into the argument. Even worse, what if making the big games actually was more important than losing those games in the eyes of the Hall of Fame voters? Then the whole conclusion falls apart and is no longer justified if that premise is disproven.

Assumption questions test this exact point by asking the test taker to identify which assumption the argument relies upon. If the author is making numerous assumptions, then the most important assumption must be chosen.

If the author truly relies on an assumption, then the argument will completely fall apart if the assumption isn't true. **Negating** a necessary assumption will *always* make the argument fall apart. This is a universal rule of logic and should be the first thing done in testing answer choices.

Here are some ways that underlying assumptions will appear as questions:

- Which of the following is a hidden assumption that the author makes to advance his argument?
- Which assumption, if true, would support the argument's conclusion (make it more logical)?
- The strength of the argument depends on which of the following?
- Upon which of the following assumptions does the author rely?
- Which assumption does the argument presuppose?

An example is:

> Frank Underwood is a terrible president. The man is a typical spend, spend, spend liberal. His employment program would exponentially increase the annual deficit and pile on the national debt. Not to mention, Underwood is also on the verge of starting a war with Russia.

Upon which of the following assumptions does the author's argument most rely?
   a. Frank Underwood is a terrible president.
   b. The United States cannot afford Frank Underwood's policy plans without spending more than the country raises in revenue.
   c. No spend, spend, spend liberal has ever succeeded as president.
   d. Starting a war with Russia is beneficial to the United States.
   e. Past presidents held drastically different policies and beliefs than the ones held by Underwood.

Use the negation rule to find the correct answer in the choices below.

Choice A is not an assumption—it is the author's conclusion. This type of restatement will never be the correct answer, but test it anyway. After negating the choice, what remains is: *Frank Underwood is a fantastic president.* Does this make the argument fall apart? No, it just becomes the new conclusion. The argument is certainly worse since it does not seem reasonable for someone to praise a president for being a spend, spend, spend liberal or raising the national debt; however, the argument still makes *logical* sense. Eliminate this choice.

Choice B is certainly an assumption. It underlies the premises that the country cannot afford Underwood's economic plans. When reversed to: *The United States can afford Frank Underwood's policy plans without spending more than the country raises in revenue.* This largely destroys the argument. If the United States can afford his plans, then the annual deficit and national debt won't increase; therefore, Underwood being a terrible president would only be based on the final premise. The argument is much weaker without the two sentences involving the financials. Keep it as a benchmark while working through the remaining choices.

Choice C is largely irrelevant. The author is not necessarily claiming that all loose-pocket liberals make for bad presidents. His argument specifically pertains to Underwood. Negate it— *Some spend, spend, spend liberals have succeeded as president.* This does not destroy the argument. Some other candidate could have succeeded as president. However, the author is pointing out that those policies would be disastrous considering the rising budget and debt. The author is not making an appeal to historical precedent. Although not a terrible choice, it is certainly weaker than *Choice B*. Eliminate this choice.

Choice D is definitely not an assumption made by the author. The author is assuming that a war with Russia is disastrous. Negate it anyway—*Starting a war with Russia is not beneficial for the United States.* This does not destroy the argument; it makes it stronger. Eliminate this choice.

Choice E is not integral to the argument. Whether past presidents held the same policies as Underwood is largely irrelevant. After reversing the choice, it reads: *Past presidents held the same policies and beliefs as the ones held by Underwood.* This makes the argument odd, like in the discussion of *Choice A*. The author's argument remains logically intact. He could mean that Underwood is continuing the same terrible policies. The argument is not broken, so it cannot be the answer. Eliminate this choice.

Related to assumptions, a reader must also be able to identify any *logical fallacies*—logically-flawed statements—that an author may make as those fallacies impact the validity and veracity of the author's claims.

Some of the more common fallacies are shown in the following chart.

Fallacy	Definition
Slippery Slope	A fallacy that is built on the idea that a particular action will lead to a series of events with negative results
Red Herring	The use of an observation or distraction to remove attention from the actual issue
Straw Man	An exaggeration or misrepresentation of an argument so that it is easier to refute
Post Hoc Ergo Propter Hoc	A fallacy that assumes an event to be the consequence of an earlier event merely because it came after it
Bandwagon	A fallacy that assumes because the majority of people feel or believe a certain way then it must be the right way
Ad Hominem	The use of a personal attack on the person or persons associated with a certain argument rather than focusing on the actual argument itself

Readers who are aware of the types of fallacious reasoning are able to weigh the credibility of the author's statements in terms of effective argument. Rhetorical text that contains a myriad of fallacious statements should be considered ineffectual and suspect.

Drawing Conclusions from a Text

Active readers should be able to draw conclusions from the text they are reading. When doing so, the reader should ask the following questions: What is this piece about? What does the author believe? Does this piece have merit? Do I believe the author? Would this piece support my argument? The reader should first determine the author's intent. Identify the author's viewpoint and connect relevant evidence to support it. Readers may then move to the most important step: deciding whether to agree and determining whether they are correct. Always read cautiously and critically. Interact with text, and record reactions in the margins. These active reading skills help determine not only what the author thinks, but what you think as the reader.

Determining conclusions requires being an active reader, as a reader must make a prediction and analyze facts to identify a conclusion. A reader should identify key words in a passage to determine the logical conclusion from the information presented. Consider the passage below:

> Lindsay, covered in flour, moved around the kitchen frantically. Her mom yelled from another room, "Lindsay, we're going to be late!"

Readers can conclude that Lindsay's next steps are to finish baking, clean herself up, and head off somewhere with her baked goods. It's important to note that the conclusion cannot be verified factually. Many conclusions are not spelled out specifically in the text; thus, they have to be inferred and deduced by the reader.

Readers draw **conclusions** about what an author has presented. This helps them better understand what the writer has intended to communicate and whether or not they agree with what the author has offered. There are a few ways to determine a logical conclusion, but careful reading is the most important. It's helpful to read a passage a few times, noting details that seem important to the piece. Sometimes, readers arrive at a conclusion that is different than what the writer intended or they may come up with more than one conclusion.

Textual evidence helps readers draw a conclusion about a passage. **Textual evidence** refers to information—facts and examples—that support the main point; it will likely come from outside sources and can be in the form of quoted or paraphrased material. In order to draw a conclusion from evidence, it's important to examine the credibility and validity of that evidence as well as how (and if) it relates to the main idea.

If an author presents a differing opinion or a **counterargument**, in order to refute it, the reader should consider how and why the information is being presented. It is meant to strengthen the original argument and shouldn't be confused with the author's intended conclusion, but it should also be considered in the reader's final evaluation.

Sometimes, authors explicitly state the conclusion that they want readers to understand. Alternatively, a conclusion may not be directly stated. In that case, readers must rely on the implications to form a logical conclusion:

> On the way to the bus stop, Michael realized his homework wasn't in his backpack. He ran back to the house to get it and made it back to the bus just in time.

In this example, although it's never explicitly stated, it can be inferred that Michael is a student on his way to school in the morning. When forming a conclusion from implied information, it's important to read the text carefully to find several pieces of evidence to support the conclusion.

Analysis and Comparison of Texts

Making Connections in Reading

Synthesis in reading involves the ability to fully comprehend text passages, and then going further by making new connections to see things in a new or different way. It involves a full thought process and requires readers to change the way they think about what they read.

Synthesis goes further than summary. When summarizing, a reader collects all of the information an author presents in a text passage and restates it in an effective manner. Synthesis requires that the test taker not only summarize reading material but be able to express new ideas based on the author's message. It is a full culmination of all reading comprehension strategies. It will require the test taker to order, recount, summarize, and recreate information into a whole new idea.

In utilizing synthesis, a reader must be able to form mental images about what they read, recall any background information they have about the topic, ask critical questions about the material, determine the importance of points an author makes, make inferences based on the reading, and finally be able to form new ideas based on all of the above skills. Synthesis requires the reader to make connections, visualize concepts, determine their importance, ask questions, make inferences, then fully synthesize all of this information into new thought.

There are three helpful thinking strategies to keep in mind when attempting to synthesize text passages:

- Think about how the content of a passage relates to life experience;
- Think about how the content of a passage relates to other text and;
- Think about how the content of a passage relates to the world in general.

When reading a given passage, the test taker should actively think about how the content relates to their life experience. While the author's message may express an opinion different from what the reader believes, or express

ideas with which the reader is unfamiliar, a good reader will try to relate any of the author's details to their own familiar ground. A reader should use context clues to understand unfamiliar terminology and recognize familiar information they have encountered in prior experience. Bringing prior life experience and knowledge to the test-taking situation is helpful in making connections. The ability to relate an unfamiliar idea to something the reader already knows is critical in understanding unique and new ideas.

When trying to make connections while reading, keep the following questions in mind:

- How does this feel familiar in personal experience?
- How is this similar to or different from other reading?
- How is this familiar in the real world?
- How does this relate to the world in general?

Reader should ask themselves these questions during the act of reading in order to actively make connections to past and present experiences. Utilizing the ability to make connections is an important step in achieving synthesis.

Applying Ideas Presented in a Text to Other Situations

A natural extension of being able to make an inference from a given set of information is also being able to apply that information to a new context. This is especially useful in nonfiction or informative writing. Considering the facts and details presented in the text, readers should consider how the same information might be relevant in a different situation. The following is an example of applying an inferential conclusion to a different context:

> Often, individuals behave differently in large groups than they do as individuals. One example of this is the psychological phenomenon known as the bystander effect. According to the bystander effect, the more people who witness an accident or crime occur, the less likely each individual bystander is to respond or offer assistance to the victim. A classic example of this is the murder of Kitty Genovese in New York City in the 1960s. Although there were over thirty witnesses to her killing by a stabber, none of them intervened to help Kitty or to contact the police.

Considering the phenomenon of the bystander effect, what would probably happen if somebody tripped on the stairs in a crowded subway station?
   a. Everybody would stop to help the person who tripped.
   b. Bystanders would point and laugh at the person who tripped.
   c. Someone would call the police after walking away from the station.
   d. Few, if any, bystanders would offer assistance to the person who tripped.
   e. Bystanders would quickly call the authorities

This question asks readers to apply the information they learned from the passage, which is an informative paragraph about the bystander effect. According to the passage, this is a concept in psychology that describes the way people in groups respond to an accident—the more people are present, the less likely any one person is to intervene. While the passage illustrates this effect with the example of a woman's murder, the question asks readers to apply it to a different context—in this case, someone falling down the stairs in front of many subway passengers. Although this specific situation is not discussed in the passage, readers should be able to apply the general concepts described in the paragraph. The definition of the bystander effect includes any instance of an accident or crime in front of a large group of people. The question asks about a situation that falls within the same definition, so the general concept should still hold true: in the midst of a large crowd, few individuals are likely to actually respond to an accident. In this case, answer Choice *D* is the best response.

Recognizing Points of Agreement and Disagreement Between Two Texts

When analyzing two or more texts, there are several different aspects that need to be considered, particularly the styles (or the artful way in which the authors use diction to deliver a theme), points of view, and types of argument. In order to do so, one should compare and contrast the following elements between the texts:

- **Style**: narrative, persuasive, descriptive, informative, etc.
- Tone: sarcastic, angry, somber, humorous, etc.
- Sentence structure: simple (1 clause) compound (2 clauses), complex-compound (3 clauses)
- Punctuation choice: question marks, exclamation points, periods, dashes, etc.
- Point of view: first person, second person, third person
- Paragraph structure: long, short, both, differences between the two
- Organizational structure: compare/contrast, problem/solution, chronological, etc.

The following two poems and the essay concern the theme of death and are presented to demonstrate how to evaluate the above elements:

Poem 1:

How wonderful is Death,
Death, and his brother Sleep!
One, pale as yonder waning moon
With lips of lurid blue;
The other, rosy as the morn
When throned on ocean's wave
It blushes o'er the world;
Yet both so passing wonderful!

"Queen Mab," Percy Bysshe Shelley

Poem 2:

After great pain, a formal feeling comes –
The Nerves sit ceremonious, like Tombs –
The stiff Heart questions 'was it He, that bore,'
And 'Yesterday, or Centuries before'?
The Feet, mechanical, go round –
A Wooden way
Of Ground, or Air, or Ought –
Regardless grown,
A Quartz contentment, like a stone –
This is the Hour of Lead –
Remembered, if outlived,
As Freezing persons, recollect the Snow –
First – Chill – then Stupor – then the letting go –

"After Great Pain, A Formal Feeling Comes," Emily Dickinson

Essay 1

The Process of Dying

Death occurs in several stages. The first stage is the pre-active stage, which occurs a few days to weeks before death, in which the desire to eat and drink decreases, and the person may feel restless, irritable, and

54

anxious. The second stage is the active stage, where the skin begins to cool, breathing becomes difficult as the lungs become congested (known as the "death rattle"), and the person loses control of their bodily fluids.

Once death occurs, there are also two stages. The first is clinical death, when the heart stops pumping blood and breathing ceases. This stage lasts approximately 4-6 minutes, and during this time, it is possible for a victim to be resuscitated via CPR or a defibrillator. After 6 minutes however, the oxygen stores within the brain begin to deplete, and the victim enters biological death. This is the point of no return, as the cells of the brain and vital organs begin to die, a process that is irreversible.

Now, using the outline above, the similarities and differences between the two passages are considered:

1. **Style**: The two poems are both descriptive as they focus on descriptions and sensations to convey their messages and do not follow any sort of timeline. The third selection is an expository style, presenting purely factual evidence on death, completely devoid of emotion.

2. **Tone**: Readers should notice the differences in the word choices between the two poems. Percy Shelley's word choices—"wonderful," "rosy," "blushes," "ocean"—surrounding death indicates that he views death in a welcoming manner as his words carry positive charges. The word choices by Dickinson, however, carry negative connotations—"pain," "wooden," "stone," "lead," "chill," "tombs"—which indicates an aversion to death. In contrast, the expository passage has no emotionally-charged words of any kind and seems to view death simply as a process that happens, neither welcoming nor fearing it. The tone in this passage, therefore, is neutral.

3. **Sentence structure**: Shelley's poem is composed mostly of compound sentences, which flow easily into one another. If read aloud, it sounds almost fluid, like the waves of the ocean he describes in his poem. His sentence structure mirrors the ease in which he views death. Dickinson's poem, on the other hand, is mostly simple sentences that are short and curt. They do not flow easily into one another, possibly representing her hesitancy and discomfort in her views of death. The expository passage contains many complex-compound sentences, which are used to accommodate lots of information. The structure of these sentences contributes to the overall informative nature of the selection.

4. **Punctuation choice**: Shelley uses commas, semicolons, and exclamation points in his poem, which, combined with his word choices and sentence structure, contributes to the overall positive tone of the poem. Dickinson uses lots of dashes, which make the poem feel almost cutting and jagged, which contributes to the overall negative tone of her poem. The expository text uses only commas and periods, which adds to the overall neutral tone of the selection.

5. **Point of view**: The point of view in all three selections is third person. In the two poems, there are no obvious pronouns; however, they both are presented in the third-person point of view, as Shelley speaks of Death in the third person, and Dickinson refers to "freezing persons." Generally, if there are no first- or second-person pronouns in a selection, the view is third person. The informational selection also uses third-person point of view, as it avoids any first- or second-person pronouns.

6. **Paragraph/stanza structure**: Shelley's poem is one stanza long, making it inherently simple in nature. The simplicity of the single stanza is representative (again) of the comfort in which the author finds the topic of death. Dickinson's poem is much lengthier, and comparatively, could signify the difficulty of letting go of the death of a loved one. The paragraph structure of the essay is much longer than the two and is used to fit in a lot more information than the poems, as the poems are trying to convey emotion, and the essay is presenting facts.

7. **Organizational structure**: Shelley's poem uses a compare and contrast method to illustrate the similarities between death and sleep: that death is merely a paler, bluer brother to the warm and rosy sleep. Dickinson's

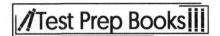

structure, however, is descriptive, focusing primarily on feelings and sensations. The expository passage, on the other hand, is chronologically-organized, as it follows a timeline of events that occur in stages.

When analyzing the different structures, it may be helpful to make a table and use single words to compare and contrast the texts:

Elements	Queen Mab	After Great Pain	Process of Dying
Style	Descriptive	Descriptive	Expository
Tone	Warm	Cold	Neutral
Sentence Structure	Fluid	Jagged	Long
Punctuation Choice	!	_	.
Point of View	Third	Third	Third
Paragraph Structure	Short	Longer	Longest
Organizational Structure	Compare-Contrast	Descriptive	Chronological

Using this table, the differences become very clear. Although the two poems are both about death, their word tone, sentence structure, punctuation choices, and organization depict differences in how the authors perceive death, while the elements in the expository text clearly indicate an objective view of death. It should be noted that these are only a handful of the endless possible interpretations the reader could make.

Practice Quiz

Questions 1 – 3 are based on the following passage.

Even though the rain can put a damper on the day, it can be helpful and fun, too. For one, the rain helps plants grow. Without rain, grass, flowers, and trees would be deprived of vital nutrients they need to develop. Not only does the rain help plants grow, but on days where there are brief spurts of sunshine, rainbows can appear. The rain reflects and refracts the light, creating beautiful rainbows in the sky. Finally, puddle jumping is another fun activity that can be done in or after the rain. Therefore, the rain can be helpful and fun.

1. What is the cause in this passage?
   a. Plants growing
   b. Rainbows
   c. Puddle jumping
   d. Rain

Read the following sentence and answer the question below.

"Without rain, grass, flowers, and trees would be deprived of vital nutrients they need to develop."

2. In this sentence, the author is using what literary device regarding the grass, flowers, and trees?
   a. Comparing
   b. Contrasting
   c. Describing
   d. Transitioning

3. What is an *effect* in this passage?
   a. Rain
   b. Brief spurts of sunshine
   c. Rainbows
   d. Weather

4. Read the following poem then choose which option best expresses the symbolic meaning of the "road" and the overall theme?

Two roads diverged in a yellow wood,
And sorry I could not travel both
And be one traveler, long I stood
And looked down one as far as I could
To where it bent in the undergrowth;

Then took the other, as just as fair,
And having perhaps the better claim,
Because it was grassy and wanted wear;
Though as for that the passing there
Had worn them really about the same,

And both that morning equally lay
In leaves no step had trodden black.
Oh, I kept the first for another day!

Yet knowing how way leads on to way,
I doubted if I should ever come back.

I shall be telling this with a sigh
Somewhere ages and ages hence:
Two roads diverged in a wood, and I—
I took the one less traveled by,
And that has made all the difference.

—Robert Frost, "The Road Not Taken"

a. A spot where the traveler had to choose between two paths
b. A choice between good and evil that the traveler needs to make
c. The traveler's feelings about a lost love and future prospects
d. Life's journey and the choices with which humans are faced

5. This work, published in 1922, was a modernist piece that was banned both in the United States and overseas for meeting the criteria of obscenity. Taking place in a single day (June 16th, 1904), the novel contains eighteen episodes reflecting the activities of character Leopold Bloom in Dublin, Ireland. Originally written as to portray an Odysseus figure for adults, the structure of the work is often viewed as convoluted and chaotic, as its author utilized the stream of consciousness technique. Its literary reception was vastly polarized and remains so to this day, although modern critics tend to hail the novel as addressing the vast panoramic of futility within contemporary history.

The above passage describes which famous literary work?
a. James Joyce's *Ulysses*
b. Anne Sexton's poem "45 Mercy Street"
c. F. Scott Fitzgerald's *Tender is the Night*
d. George Eliot's *Middlemarch: A Study of Provincial Life*

See answers on the next page.

Answer Explanations

1. D: Rain is the cause in this passage because it is why something happened. The effects are plants growing, rainbows, and puddle jumping.

2. A: The author is comparing the plants, trees, and flowers. The author is showing how these things react the same to rain. They all get important nutrients from rain. If the author described the differences, then it would be contrasting, Choice *B*.

3. C: Rainbows. This passage mentions several effects. Effects are the outcome of a certain cause. Remember that the cause here is rain, so Choice *A* is incorrect. Since the cause is rain, Choice *B*—brief spurts of sunshine—doesn't make sense because rain doesn't *cause* brief spurts of sunshine. Choice *C* makes the most sense because the effects of the rain in the passage are plants growing, rainbows, and puddle jumping. Lastly, Choice *D*, weather, is not an effect of rain but describes rain in a general sense.

4. D: Choice *A* is literal, not symbolic. Choice *B* is incorrect because the traveler deems both roads to be equally "fair" or pleasant. Choice *C* deals with the past and the future, but the traveler is considering two paths forward.

5. A: The correct answer is *A* as it is the only option that utilizes stream of consciousness technique in a novel format. Choice *B* is a poem by poet Anne Sexton, not a novel. Although Ms. Sexton's works were often criticized for their intimate content, this answer does not meet the question's criteria. Choices *C* and *D* are both incorrect. Both are novels, but not of the appropriate time period, country, or literary content.

Writing

Text Types, Purposes, and Production

Text Production: Writing Arguments

Producing an Argumentative Essay to Support a Claim Using Relevant and Sufficient Evidence

Before beginning any writing, it is imperative that a writer have a firm grasp on the message he or she wishes to convey and how he or she wants readers to be affected by the writing. For example, does the author want readers to be more informed about the subject? Does the writer want readers to agree with their opinion? Does the writer want readers to get caught up in an exciting narrative? The following steps are a guide to determining the appropriate type of writing for a task, purpose, and audience:

1. Identifying the purpose for writing the piece
2. Determining the audience
3. Adapting the writing mode, word choices, tone, and style to fit the audience and the purpose

It is important to distinguish between a work's purpose and its main idea. The essential difference between the two is that the **main idea** is what the author wants to communicate about the topic at hand whereas the **primary purpose** is why the author is writing in the first place. The primary purpose is what will determine the type of writing an author will choose to utilize, not the main idea, though the two are related. For example, if an author writes an article on the mistreatment of animals in factory farms and, at the end, suggests that people should convert to vegetarianism, the main idea is that vegetarianism would reduce the poor treatment of animals. The primary purpose is to convince the reader to stop eating animals. Since the primary purpose is to galvanize an audience into action, the author would choose the argumentative writing mode.

The next step is to consider to whom the author is appealing as this will determine the type of details to be included, the diction to be used, the tone to be employed, and the sentence structure to be used. An audience can be identified by considering the following questions:

- What is the purpose for writing the piece?
- To whom is it being written?
- What is their age range?
- Are they familiar with the material being presented, or are they just being newly introduced to it?
- Where are they from?
- Is the task at hand in a professional or casual setting?
- Is the task at hand for monetary gain?

These are just a few of the numerous considerations to keep in mind, but the main idea is to become as familiar with the audience as possible. Once the audience has been understood, the author can then adapt the writing style to align with the readers' education and interests. The audience is what determines the **rhetorical appeal** the author will use—ethos, pathos, or logos. **Ethos** is a rhetorical appeal to an audience's ethics and/or morals. Ethos is most often used in argumentative and informative writing modes. **Pathos** is an appeal to the audience's emotions and sympathies, and it is found in argumentative, descriptive, and narrative writing modes. **Logos** is an appeal to the audience's logic and reason and is used primarily in informative texts as well as in supporting details for argumentative pieces. Rhetorical appeals are discussed in depth in the informational texts and rhetoric section of the test.

If the author is trying to encourage global conversion to vegetarianism, he or she may choose to use all three rhetorical appeals to reach varying personality types. Those who are less interested in the welfare of animals but are

60

interested in facts and science would relate more to logos. Animal lovers would relate better to an emotional appeal. In general, the most effective works utilize all three appeals.

Finally, after determining the writing mode and rhetorical appeal, the author will consider word choice, sentence structure, and tone, depending on the purpose and audience. The author may choose words that convey sadness or anger when speaking about animal welfare if writing to persuade, or he or she will stick to dispassionate and matter-of-fact tones, if informing the public on the treatment of animals in factory farms. If the author is writing to a younger or less-educated audience, he or she may choose to shorten and simplify sentence structures and word choice. If appealing to an audience with more expert knowledge on a particular subject, writers will more likely employ a style of longer sentences and more complex vocabulary.

Depending on the task, the author may choose to use a first person, second person, or third person point of view. First person and second person perspectives are inherently more casual in tone, including the author and the reader in the rhetoric, while third person perspectives are often seen in more professional settings.

Argumentative essays—also called persuasive essays— are designed to change opinions and attitudes. The topic, stance, and arguments are found in the thesis, which is positioned near the end of the introduction. Later supporting paragraphs offer relevant quotations, paraphrases, and summaries from primary or secondary sources, which are then interpreted, analyzed, and evaluated. The goal of persuasive writers is not to stack quotes but to develop original ideas by using sources as a starting point. Good persuasive writing makes powerful arguments with valid sources and thoughtful analyses. Poor persuasive writing is riddled with bias and logical fallacies. Sometimes logical and illogical arguments are sandwiched together in the same text. Therefore, readers should employ skepticism when reading persuasive arguments.

Writing Clearly and Coherently
Addressing the Assigned Task Appropriately
An author's **writing style**—the way in which words, grammar, punctuation, and sentence fluidity are used—is the most influential element in a piece of writing, and it is dependent on the purpose and the audience for whom it is intended. Together, a writing style and mode of writing form the foundation of a written work, and a good writer will choose the most effective mode and style to convey a message to readers.

Writers should first determine what they are trying to say and then choose the most effective mode of writing to communicate that message. Different writing modes and word choices will affect the tone of a piece—that is, its underlying attitude, emotion, or character. The argumentative mode may utilize words that are earnest, angry, passionate, or excited whereas an informative piece may have a sterile, germane, or enthusiastic tone. The tones found in narratives vary greatly, depending on the purpose of the writing. Tone will also be affected by the audience—teaching science to children or those who may be uninterested would be most effective with enthusiastic language and exclamation points whereas teaching science to college students may take on a more serious and professional tone, with fewer charged words and punctuation choices that are inherent to academia.

Sentence fluidity—whether sentences are long and rhythmic or short and succinct—also affects a piece of writing as it determines the way in which a piece is read. Children or audiences unfamiliar with a subject do better with short, succinct sentence structures as these break difficult concepts up into shorter points. A period, question mark, or exclamation point is literally a signal for the reader to stop and takes more time to process. Thus, longer, more complex sentences are more appropriate for adults or educated audiences as they can fit more information in between processing time.

The amount of **supporting detail** provided is also tailored to the audience. A text that introduces a new subject to its readers will focus more on broad ideas without going into greater detail whereas a text that focuses on a more specific subject is likely to provide greater detail about the ideas discussed.

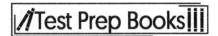

Writing styles, like modes, are most effective when tailored to their audiences. Having awareness of an audience's demographic is one of the most crucial aspects of properly communicating an argument, a story, or a set of information.

Organizing and Developing Ideas Logically

Almost all coherent written works contain three primary parts: a beginning, middle, and end. The organizational arrangements differ widely across distinct writing modes. Persuasive and expository texts utilize an introduction, body, and conclusion whereas narrative works use an orientation, series of events/conflict, and a resolution.

Every element within a written piece relates back to the main idea, and the beginning of a persuasive or expository text generally conveys the main idea or the purpose. For a narrative piece, the beginning is the section that acquaints the reader with the characters and setting, directing them to the purpose of the writing. The main idea in narrative may be implied or addressed at the end of the piece.

Depending on the primary purpose, the arrangement of the middle will adhere to one of the basic organizational structures described in the information texts and rhetoric section. They are cause and effect, problem and solution, compare and contrast, description/spatial, sequence, and order of importance.

The ending of a text is the metaphorical wrap-up of the writing. A solid ending is crucial for effective writing as it ties together loose ends, resolves the action, highlights the main points, or repeats the central idea. A conclusion ensures that readers come away from a text understanding the author's main idea. The table below highlights the important characteristics of each part of a piece of writing.

Structure	Argumentative/Informative	Narrative
Beginning	Introduction *Purpose, main idea*	Orientation *Introduces characters, setting, necessary background*
Middle	Body *Supporting details, reasons and evidence*	Events/Conflict *Story's events that revolve around a central conflict*
End	Conclusion *Highlights main points, summarizes and paraphrases ideas, reiterates the main idea*	Resolution *The solving of the central conflict*

Transitions are the glue that holds the writing together. They function to purposefully incorporate new topics and supporting details in a smooth and coherent way. Usually, transitions are found at the beginnings of sentences, but they can also be located in the middle as a way to link clauses together. There are two types of clauses: independent and dependent as discussed in the language use and vocabulary section.

Transition words connect clauses within and between sentences for smoother writing. "I dislike apples. They taste like garbage." is choppier than "I dislike apples because they taste like garbage." Transitions demonstrate the relationship between ideas, allow for more complex sentence structures, and can alert the reader to which type of organizational format the author is using. For example, the above selection on human evolution uses the words *first, another,* and *finally* to indicate that the writer will be listing the reasons why humans and apes are evolutionarily different.

Transition words can be categorized based on the relationships they create between ideas:

- **General order**: signaling elaboration of an idea to emphasize a point—e.g., *for example, for instance, to demonstrate, including, such as, in other words, that is, in fact, also, furthermore, likewise, and, truly, so, surely, certainly, obviously, doubtless*

- **Chronological order**: referencing the time frame in which the main event or idea occurs—e.g., *before, after, first, while, soon, shortly thereafter, meanwhile*

- **Numerical order/order of importance**: indicating that related ideas, supporting details, or events will be described in a sequence, possibly in order of importance—e.g., *first, second, also, finally, another, in addition, equally important, less importantly, most significantly, the main reason, last but not least*

- **Spatial order**: referring to the space and location of something or where things are located in relation to each other—e.g., *inside, outside, above, below, within, close, under, over, far, next to, adjacent to*

- **Cause and effect order**: signaling a causal relationship between events or ideas—e.g., *thus, therefore, since, resulted in, for this reason, as a result, consequently, hence, for, so*

- **Compare and contrast order**: identifying the similarities and differences between two or more objects, ideas, or lines of thought—e.g., *like, as, similarly, equally, just as, unlike, however, but, although, conversely, on the other hand, on the contrary*

- **Summary order**: indicating that a particular idea is coming to a close—e.g., *in conclusion, to sum up, in other words, ultimately, above all*

Sophisticated writing also aims to avoid overuse of transitions and ensure that those used are meaningful. Using a variety of transitions makes the writing appear livelier and more informed and helps readers follow the progression of ideas.

Providing and Sustaining a Clear Focus or Thesis

The main idea of a piece is the central topic or theme. To identify the main idea, a reader should consider these questions: "What's the point? What does the author want readers to take away from this text?" Everything within the selection should relate back to the main idea because it is the center of the organizational web of any written work. Particularly in articles and reports, the main idea often appears within the opening paragraphs to orient the reader to what the author wants to say about the subject. A sentence that expresses the main idea is known as a thesis sentence or **thesis statement**.

Using Supporting Reasons, Examples, and Details to Develop Ideas

After the main idea has been introduced, **supporting details** are what develop the main idea—they make up the bulk of the work. Without supporting details, the main idea would simply be a statement, so additional details are needed to give that statement weight and validity. Supporting details can often be identified by recognizing the key words that introduce them. The following example offers several supporting details, with key words underlined:

> Man did not evolve from apes. Though we share a common ancestor, humans and apes originated through very different evolutionary paths. There are several reasons why this is true. The <u>first</u> reason is that, logically, if humans evolved from apes, modern-day apes and humans would not coexist. Evolution occurs when a genetic mutation in a species ensures the survival over the rest of the species, allowing them to pass on their genes and create a new lineage of organisms. <u>Another</u> reason is that hominid fossils only fall into one of two categories—ape-like or human-like—and there are very strong differences between the two. Australopithecines, the hominid fossils originally believed to be ancestral to humans, are ape-like, indicated by their long arms, long and curved fingers, and funnel-shaped chests. Their hand bones suggest that they "knuckle-walked" like modern day chimpanzees and gorillas, something not found in *Homo sapien* fossils. <u>Finally</u>, there is no fossilized evidence to suggest a transition between the ape-like ancestor and the

Homo sapien, indicating that a sudden mutation may have been responsible. These and many other reasons are indicative that humans and ape-like creatures are evolutionarily different.

The underlined words—*first, another,* and *finally*—are the key words that identify the supporting details. These details can be summarized as follows:

- Humans and apes could not coexist.
- Human-like and ape-like fossils are very different.
- No transition is seen between humans and ape-like ancestors.

The supporting details all relate to the central idea that "Man did not evolve from apes," which is the first sentence of the paragraph.

Even though supporting details are more specific than the main idea, they should nevertheless all be directly related to the main idea. Without sufficient supporting details, the writer's main idea will be too weak to be effective.

Using Correct Language and Sentence Structures

All sentences contain the same basic elements: a subject and a verb. The **subject** is who or what the sentence is about; the **verb** describes the subject's action or condition. However, these elements, subjects and verbs, can be combined in different ways. The following graphic describes the different types of sentence structures.

Sentence Structure	Independent Clauses	Dependent Clauses
Simple	1	0
Compound	2 or more	0
Complex	1	1 or more
Compound-Complex	2 or more	1 or more

A **simple sentence** expresses a complete thought and consists of one subject and verb combination:

The children ate pizza.

The subject is *children*. The verb is *ate*.

Either the subject or the verb may be *compound*—that is, it could have more than one element:

The children and their parents ate pizza.

The children *ate pizza and watched a movie.*

All of these are still simple sentences. Despite having either compound subjects or compound verbs, each sentence still has only one subject and verb combination.

Compound sentences combine two or more simple sentences to form one sentence that has multiple subject-verb combinations:

The children ate pizza, and *their parents watched a movie.*

This structure is comprised of two independent clauses: (1) *the children ate pizza* and (2) *their parents watched a movie.* Compound sentences join different subject-verb combinations using a comma and a coordinating conjunction.

> I called my mom, *but* she didn't answer the phone.

> The weather was stormy, *so* we canceled our trip to the beach.

A **complex sentence** consists of an independent clause and one or more dependent clauses. Dependent clauses join a sentence using **subordinating conjunctions**. Some examples of subordinating conjunctions are *although, unless, as soon as, since, while, when, because, if,* and *before.*

> I missed class yesterday *because* my mother was ill.

> *Before* traveling to a new country, you need to exchange your money to the local currency.

The order of clauses determines their punctuation. If the dependent clause comes first, it should be separated from the independent clause with a comma. However, if the complex sentence consists of an independent clause followed by a dependent clause, then a comma is not always necessary.

A **compound-complex sentence** can be created by joining two or more independent clauses with at least one dependent clause:

> After the earthquake struck, thousands of homes were destroyed, and many families were left without a place to live.

The first independent clause in the compound structure includes a dependent clause—*after the earthquake struck.* Thus, the structure is both complex and compound.

Constructing Effective Sentences

There isn't an overabundance of absolutes in grammar, but here is one: every sentence in the English language falls into one of four categories.

- Declarative: a simple statement that ends with a period

    The price of milk per gallon is the same as the price of gasoline.

- Imperative: a command, instruction, or request that ends with a period

    Buy milk when you stop to fill up your car with gas.

- Interrogative: a question that ends with a question mark

    Will you buy the milk?

- Exclamatory: a statement or command that expresses emotions like anger, urgency, or surprise and ends with an exclamation mark

    Buy the milk now!

Declarative sentences are the most common type, probably because they are comprised of the most general content, without any of the bells and whistles that the other three types contain. They are, simply, declarations or statements of any degree of seriousness, importance, or information.

Imperative sentences often seem to be missing a subject. The subject is there, though; it is just not visible or audible because it is *implied*. Look at the imperative example sentence.

> Buy the milk when you fill up your car with gas.

You is the implied subject, the one to whom the command is issued. This is sometimes called *the understood you* because it is understood that *you* is the subject of the sentence.

Interrogative sentences—those that ask questions—are defined as such from the idea of the word *interrogation*, the action of questions being asked of suspects by investigators. Although that is serious business, interrogative sentences apply to all kinds of questions.

To exclaim is at the root of **exclamatory sentences**. These are made with strong emotions behind them. The only technical difference between a declarative or imperative sentence and an exclamatory one is the exclamation mark at the end. The example declarative and imperative sentences can both become an exclamatory one simply by putting an exclamation mark at the end of the sentences.

> The price of milk per gallon is the same as the price of gasoline!
> Buy milk when you stop to fill up your car with gas!

After all, someone might be really excited by the price of gas or milk, or they could be mad at the person that will be buying the milk! However, as stated before, exclamation marks in abundance defeat their own purpose! After a while, they begin to cause fatigue! When used only for their intended purpose, they can have their expected and desired effect.

Text Production: Writing Informative/Explanatory Texts

Producing an Informative/Explanatory Essay to Examine and Convey Complex Ideas and Information Clearly and Accurately

Informative writing tries to teach or inform. Workplace manuals, instructor lessons, statistical reports, and cookbooks are examples of informative texts. Informative writing is usually based on facts and does not use emotion and persuasion. Informative texts generally contain statistics, charts, and graphs. Although most informative texts lack a persuasive agenda, readers still must examine the text carefully to determine whether one exists within a given passage.

Drawing Evidence from Informational Texts to Support Analysis

Textual evidence within the details of an informative text helps readers draw a conclusion about a passage or text. **Textual evidence** refers to information—facts and examples—that support the main point; it will likely come from outside sources and can be in the form of quoted or paraphrased material. In order to draw a conclusion from evidence, it's important to examine the credibility and validity of that evidence as well as how (and if) it relates to the main idea.

With a wealth of information at people's fingertips in this digital age, it's important to know not only the type of information one is looking for, but also in what medium one is most likely to find it. Information needs to be specific and reliable. For example, if someone is repairing a car, an encyclopedia would be mostly useless. While an encyclopedia might include information about cars, an owner's manual will contain the specific information needed for repairs. Information must also be credible, or trustworthy. A well-known newspaper may have reliable information, but a peer-reviewed journal article will have likely gone through a more rigorous check for validity. Determining **bias** can be helpful in determining credibility. If the information source (person, organization, or company) has something to gain from the reader forming a certain view on a topic, it's likely the information is

66

skewed. For example, if trying to find the unemployment rate, the Bureau of Labor Statistics is a more credible source than a politician's speech.

Primary sources are best defined as records or items that serve as historical evidence. To be considered primary, the source documents or objects must have been created during the time period in which they reference. Examples include diaries, newspaper articles, speeches, government documents, photographs, and historical artifacts. In today's digital age, primary sources, which were once in print, are often embedded in secondary sources. **Secondary sources**—such as websites, history books, databases, or reviews—contain analysis or commentary on primary sources. Secondary sources borrow information from primary sources through the process of quoting, summarizing, or paraphrasing.

Today's students often complete research online through **electronic sources**. Electronic sources offer advantages over print and can be accessed on virtually any computer, while libraries or other research centers are limited to fixed locations and specific catalogs. Electronic sources are also efficient and yield massive amounts of data in seconds. The user can tailor a search based on key words, publication years, and article length. Lastly, many **databases** provide the user with instant citations, saving the user the trouble of manually assembling sources for a bibliography.

Although electronic sources yield powerful results, researchers must use caution. While there are many reputable and reliable sources on the internet, just as many are unreliable or biased sources. It's up to the researcher to examine and verify the reliability of sources. *Wikipedia*, for example, may or may not be accurate, depending on the contributor. Many databases, such as *EBSCO* or *SIRS*, offer peer-reviewed articles, meaning the publications have been reviewed for the quality and accuracy of their content.

The goal of most persuasive and informative texts is to make a claim and support it with evidence. A **claim** is a statement made as though it is fact. Many claims are opinions; for example, "stealing is wrong." While this is generally true, it is arguable, meaning it is capable of being challenged. An initial reaction to "stealing is wrong" might be to agree; however, there may be circumstances in which it is warranted. If it is necessary for the survival of an individual or their loved ones (e.g., if they are starving and cannot afford to eat), then this assertion becomes morally ambiguous. While it may still be illegal, whether it is "wrong" is unclear.

When an assertion is made within a text, it is typically reinforced with supporting details as is exemplified in the following passage:

> The extinction of the dinosaurs has been a hot debate amongst scientists since the discovery of fossils in the eighteenth century. Numerous theories were developed in explanation, including extreme climate change, an epidemic of disease, or changes in the atmosphere. It wasn't until the late 1970s that a young geochemist, named Walter Alvarez, noticed significant changes in the soil layers of limestone he was studying in Italy. The layers contained fossilized remains of millions of small organisms within the layer that corresponded with the same period in which the dinosaurs lived. He noticed that the soil layer directly above this layer was suddenly devoid of any trace of these organisms. The soil layer directly above *this* layer was filled with an entirely new species of organisms. It seemed the first species had disappeared at the exact same time as the dinosaurs!

> With the help of his father, Walter Alvarez analyzed the soil layer between the extinct species and the new species and realized this layer was filled with an abnormal amount of *iridium*—a substance that is abundant in meteorites but almost never found on Earth. Unlike other elements in the fossil record, which take a long time to deposit, the iridium had been laid down very abruptly. The layer also contained high levels of soot, enough to account for all of the earth's forests burning to the ground at the same time. This led scientists to create the best-supported theory that the tiny organisms, as well as the dinosaurs and countless other species, had been destroyed by a giant

asteroid that had slammed into Earth, raining tons of iridium down on the planet from a giant cosmic cloud.

Before beginning to answer questions, readers should summarize each. This will help in locating the supporting evidence. These summaries can be written down or completed mentally; full sentences are not necessary.

Paragraph 1: A layer of limestone shows that a species of organisms disappeared at the same time as the dinosaurs.

Paragraph 2: The layer had high amounts of iridium and soot—scientists believe the dinosaurs were destroyed by an asteroid.

Simply by summarizing the text, it has been plainly outlined where there will be answers to relevant questions. Although there are often claims already embedded within an educational text, a claim will most likely be given, but the evidence to support it will need to be located. Take this example question:

Q: What evidence within the text best supports the theory that the dinosaurs became extinct because of an asteroid?

The claim here is that the <u>dinosaurs went extinct because of an asteroid</u>. Because the text is already outlined in the summaries, it is easy to see that the evidence supporting this theory is in the second paragraph:

With the help of his father, they analyzed the soil layer between the extinct species and the new species and realized <u>this layer was filled with an abnormal amount of *iridium*</u>—a substance that is <u>abundant is meteorites</u> but almost never found on Earth. Unlike other elements in the fossil record, which takes a long time to deposit, the iridium had been laid down very abruptly. <u>The layer also contained high levels of soot</u>, enough to account for all of the earth's forests burning to the ground at the same time. <u>This led scientists to create the best-supported theory</u> that the tiny organisms, as well as the dinosaurs and countless other species, had been <u>destroyed by a giant asteroid</u> that had slammed into Earth, <u>raining tons of iridium down on the planet</u> from a giant cosmic cloud.

Now that the evidence within the text that best supports the theory has been located, the answer choices can be evaluated:
a. Changes in climate and atmosphere caused an asteroid to crash into Earth.
b. Walter and Luis Alvarez studied limestone with fossilized organisms.
c. A soil layer lacking organisms that existed at the same time as the dinosaurs showed low levels of iridium.
d. A soil layer lacking organisms that existed at the same time as the dinosaurs showed high levels of iridium.

Answer choice (a) is clearly false as there is nothing within the text that claims that climate changes caused an asteroid to crash into Earth.. This kind of answer choice displays an incorrect use of detail. Although the passage may have contained the words "change," "climate," and "atmosphere," these terms were manipulated to form an erroneous answer.

Answer choice (b) is incorrect because while the scientists did study limestone with fossilized organisms, and in doing so they discovered evidence that led to the formation of the theory, this is not the actual evidence itself. This is an example of an out-of-scope answer choice: a true statement that may or may not have been in the passage, but that isn't the whole answer or isn't the point.

Answer choice (c) is incorrect because it is the opposite of the correct answer. Assuming the second paragraph was summarized correctly, it is already known that the soil layer contained *high* levels of iridium, not low levels. Even if the paragraph was not summarized that way, the final sentence states that "tons of iridium rained down on the planet." So, answer choice (c) is false.

Answer choice (d) is correct because it matches the evidence found in the second paragraph.

Synthesizing Information from Multiple Sources on the Subject

It can be daunting to integrate so many sources into a research paper while still maintaining fluency and coherency. Most source material is incorporated in the form of quotations or paraphrases, while citing the source at the end of their respective references. There are several guidelines to consider when integrating a source into writing:

- The piece should be written in the author's voice. Quotations, especially long ones, should be limited and spaced evenly throughout the paper.

- All paragraphs should begin with the author's own words and end with their own words; quotations should never start or end a paragraph.

- Quotations and paraphrases should be used to emphasize a point, give weight to an idea, and validate a claim.

- Supporting evidence should be introduced in a sentence or paragraph, and then explained afterwards: According to Waters (1979) [signal phrase], "All in all, we're just another brick in the wall" (p.24). The wall suggests that people are becoming more alienated, and the bricks symbolize a paradoxical connection to that alienation [Explanation].

- When introducing a source for the first time, the author's name and a smooth transition should be included: In Pink Floyd's groundbreaking album *The Wall*, Roger Waters argues that society is causing people to become more alienated.

- There should be an even balance between quotations and paraphrases.

- Quotations or paraphrases should never be taken out of context in a way that alters the original author's intent.

- Quotations should be syntactically and grammatically integrated.

- Quotations should not simply be copied and pasted in the paper, rather, they should be introduced into a paper with natural transitions.

  o As argued in Johnson's article...
  o Evidence of this point can be found in Johnson's article, where she asserts that...
  o The central argument of John's article is...

Integrating and Attributing Information from Multiple Sources

The following information contains examples of the common types of sources used in research as well as the formats for each citation style. First lines of citation entries are presented flush to the left margin, and second/subsequent details are presented with a hanging indent. Some examples of bibliography entries are presented below:

Book

- MLA

  o *Format*: Last name, First name, Middle initial. Title of Source. Publisher, Publication Date.

  o E*xample*: Sampson, Maximus R. *Diaries from an Alien Invasion*. Campbell Press, 1989.

- APA

  o *Format*: Last name, First initial, Middle initial. (Year Published) Book Title. City, State: Publisher.

- o *Example*: Sampson, M. R. (1989). *Diaries from an Alien Invasion. Springfield, IL*: Campbell Press.

- Chicago/Turabian
  - o *Format*: Last name, First name, Middle initial. *Book Title*. City, State: Publisher, Year of publication.
  - o *Example*: Sampson, Maximus R. *Diaries from an Alien Invasion. Springfield, IL*: Campbell Press, 1989.

A Chapter in an Edited Book

- MLA
  - o *Format*: Last name, First name, Middle initial. "*Title* of Source." *Title of Container*, Other Contributors, Publisher, Publication Date, Location.
  - o *Example*: Sampson, Maximus R. "The Spaceship." *Diaries from an Alien Invasion*, edited by Allegra M. Brewer, Campbell Press, 1989, pp. 45-62.

- APA
  - o *Format*: Last name, First Initial, Middle initial. (Year Published) Chapter title. In First initial, Middle initial, Last Name (Ed.), *Book title* (pp. page numbers). City, State: Publisher.
  - o *Example*: Sampson, M. R. (1989). The Spaceship. In A. M. Brewer (Ed.), *Diaries from an Alien Invasion* (pp. 45-62). Springfield, IL: Campbell Press.

- Chicago/Turabian
  - o *Format*: Last name, First name, Middle initial. "Chapter Title." In Book Title, edited by Editor's Name (First, Middle In. Last), Page(s). City: Publisher, Year Published.
  - o *Example*: Sampson, Maximus R. "The Spaceship," in *Diaries from an Alien Invasion*, edited by Allegra M. Brewer, 45-62. Springfield: Campbell Press, 1989.

Article in a Journal

- MLA
  - o *Format*: Last name, First name, Middle initial. "Title of Source." *Title of Container*, Number, Publication Date, Location.
  - o *Example*: Rowe, Jason R. "The Grief Monster." *Strong Living*, vol. 9, no. 9, 2016, pp 25-31.

- APA
  - o *Format*: Last name, First initial, Middle initial. (Year Published). Title of article. *Name of Journal*, *volume*(issue), page(s).
  - o *Example*: Rowe, J. R. (2016). The grief monster. *Strong Living, 9*(9), 25-31.

- Chicago/Turabian
  - o *Format*: Last name, First name, Middle initial. "Title of Article." *Name of Journal* volume, issue (Year Published): Page(s).

70

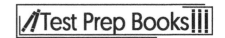

- o *Example*: Rowe, Jason, R. "The Grief Monster." Strong *Living* 9, no. 9 (2016): 25-31.

Page on a Website

- MLA
  - o *Format*: Last name, First name, Middle initial. "Title of Article." *Name of Website*, date published (Day Month Year), URL. Date accessed (Day Month Year).
  - o *Example*: Rowe, Jason. "The Grief Monster." *Strong Living Online*, 9 Sept. 2016. http://www.somanylosses.com/the-grief-monster/html. Accessed 13 Sept. 2016.

- APA
  - o *Format*: Last name, First initial. Middle initial. (Date Published—Year, Month Day). Page or article title. Retrieved from URL
  - o *Example*: Rowe, J. W. (2016, Sept. 9). The grief monster. Retrieved from http://www.somanylosses.com/ the-grief-monster/html

- Chicago/Turabian
  - o *Format*: Last Name, First Name, Middle initial. "Page Title." *Website Title*. Last modified Month day, year. Accessed month, day, year. URL.
  - o *Example: Rowe, Jason. "The Grief Monster." Strong Living Online. Last modified September 9, 2016. Acce*ssed September 13, 2016. http://www.somany losses.com/ the-grief-monster/html.

In-Text Citations

Most of the content found in a research paper will be supporting evidence that must be cited in-text, i.e., directly after the sentence that makes the statement. In-text citations contain details that correspond to the first detail in the bibliography entry—usually the author.

- MLA style - In-text citations will contain the author and the page number (if the source has page numbers) for direct quotations. Paraphrased source material may have just the author.
  - o According to Johnson, liver cancer treatment is "just beyond our reach" (976).
  - o The treatment of liver cancer is not within our reach, currently (Johnson).
  - o The narrator opens the story with a paradoxical description: "It was the best of times, it was the worst of times" (Dickens 1).

- APA Style - In text citations will contain the author, the year of publication, and a page marker—if the source is paginated—for direct quotations. Paraphrased source material will include the author and year of publication.
  - o According to Johnson (1986), liver cancer treatment is "just beyond our reach" (p. 976).
  - o The treatment of liver cancer is not within our reach, currently (Johnson, 1986).

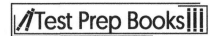

- Chicago Style - Chicago style has two approaches to in-text citation: notes and bibliography or author-date.
  - o Notes – There are two options for notes: endnotes—provided in a sequential list at the end of the paper and separate from bibliography—or footnotes provided at the bottom of a page. In either case, the use of superscript indicates the citation number.
    - Johnson states that treatment of liver cancer is "just beyond our reach."[1]
    - 1. Robert W. Johnson, Oncology in the Twenty-first Century (Kentville, Nova Scotia: Kentville Publishing, 1986), 159.
  - o Author-Date – The author-date system includes the author's name, publication year, and page number.
    - Johnson states that treatment of liver cancer is "just beyond our reach" (1986, 159).
    - Research shows that liver cancer treatment is not within our reach, currently (Johnson 1986, 159).

Text Production: Revision

Developing and Strengthening Writing by Revising and Editing
Choosing Words and Phrases for Effect

Stylistic choices refer to elements such as a writer's diction, sentence structure, and use of figurative language. A writer's **diction** is their word choice and may be elevated, academic, conversational, humorous, or any other style. The choice of diction depends on the purpose of a piece of writing. A textbook or a research paper is likely to use academic diction whereas a blog post will use more conversational expressions.

Sentence structure also affects an author's writing style. Will he or she use short, staccato sentences or longer sentences with complex structure? Effective writing tends to incorporate both styles to increase reader interest or to punctuate ideas.

Figurative language includes the use of simile, metaphor, hyperbole, or allusion, to name but a few examples. Creative or descriptive writing is likely to incorporate more non-literal expressions than academic or informative writing will. Instructors should allow students to experiment with different styles of writing and understand how style affects expression and understanding.

Choosing Words and Phrases to Convey Ideas Precisely

People often think of precision in terms of math, but precise word choice is another key to successful writing. Since language itself is imprecise, it's important for the writer to find the exact word or words to convey the full, intended meaning of a given situation. For example:

> The number of deaths has gone down since seat belt laws started.

There are several problems with this sentence. First, the word *deaths* is too general. From the context, it's assumed that the writer is referring only to deaths caused by car accidents. However, without clarification, the sentence lacks impact and is probably untrue. The phrase *gone down* might be accurate, but a more precise word would provide more information and greater accuracy. Did the numbers show a slow and steady decrease in highway fatalities or a sudden drop? If the latter is true, the writer is missing a chance to make their point more dramatically. Instead of *gone down* the author could substitute *plummeted*, *fallen drastically*, or *rapidly diminished* to bring the information to life. Also, the phrase *seat belt laws* is unclear. Does it refer to laws requiring cars to include seat belts or to laws requiring drivers and passengers to use them? Finally, *started* is not a strong verb. Words like *enacted* or *adopted*

72

are more direct and make the content more real. When put together, these changes create a far more powerful sentence:

> The number of highway fatalities has plummeted since laws requiring seat belt usage were enacted.

However, it's important to note that precise word choice can sometimes be taken too far. If the writer of the sentence above takes precision to an extreme, it might result in the following:

> The incidence of high-speed, automobile accident-related fatalities has decreased 75% and continued to remain at historical lows since the initial set of federal legislations requiring seat belt use were enacted in 1992.

This sentence is extremely precise, but it takes so long to achieve that precision that it suffers from a lack of clarity. Precise writing is about finding the right balance between information and flow. This is also an issue of conciseness (discussed in the next section).

The last thing for writers to consider with precision is a word choice that's not only unclear or uninteresting, but also confusing or misleading. For example:

> The number of highway fatalities has become hugely lower since laws requiring seat belt use were enacted.

In this case, the reader might be confused by the word *hugely*. Huge means large, but here the writer uses *hugely* in an incorrect and awkward manner. Although most readers can decipher this, doing so disconnects them from the flow of the writing and makes the writer's point less effective.

Maintaining Consistency in Style and Tone

Style and tone are often thought to be the same thing. Though they're closely related, there are important differences to keep in mind. The easiest way to do this is to remember that **style** creates and affects **tone**. More specifically, style is *how the writer uses words* to create the desired tone for their writing.

Style can include any number of technical writing choices, and some may have to be analyzed on the test. A few examples of style choices include:

- Sentence Construction: When presenting facts, does the writer use shorter sentences to create a quicker sense of the supporting evidence, or does he or she use longer sentences to elaborate and explain the information?

- Technical Language: Does the writer use jargon to demonstrate their expertise in the subject, or do the writer use ordinary language to help the reader understand things in simple terms?

- Formal Language: Does the writer refrain from using contractions such as *won't* or *can't* to create a more formal tone, or does he or she use a colloquial, conversational style to connect to the reader?

- Formatting: Does the writer use a series of shorter paragraphs to help the reader follow a line of argument, or does he or she use longer paragraphs to examine an issue in great detail and demonstrate their knowledge of the topic?

On the exam, test takers should examine the writer's style and how their writing choices affect the way the text comes across. The majority of writing assignments on the test will involve writing police reports and incident reports. These should use formal language, be succinct, direct, and carry and informative, tone.

Tone refers to the writer's attitude toward the subject matter. Tone conveys how the writer feels about characters, situations, events, ideas, etc.

73

A lot of nonfiction writing has a neutral tone, which is an important one for the writer to use. A neutral tone demonstrates that the writer is presenting a topic impartially and letting the information speak for itself. On the other hand, nonfiction writing can be just as effective and appropriate if the tone isn't neutral. The following short passage provides an example of tone in nonfiction writing:

> Seat belts save more lives than any other automobile safety feature. Many studies show that airbags save lives as well; however, not all cars have airbags. For instance, some older cars don't. Furthermore, air bags aren't entirely reliable. For example, studies show that in 15% of accidents airbags don't deploy as designed, but, on the other hand, seat belt malfunctions are extremely rare. The number of highway fatalities has plummeted since laws requiring seat belt usage were enacted.

In this passage, the writer mostly chooses to retain a neutral tone when presenting information. If instead, the author chose to include their own personal experience of losing a friend or family member in a car accident, the tone would change dramatically. Or, if the author used words and phrases such as, "Ever since the government required individuals to wear seat belts, the amount of hard working American lives that have been saved is extraordinary! Such a small task to undertake has changed the entire country." The tone would no longer be neutral and would show the reader the seriousness, joy, sadness, etc. of the situation. When analyzing tone, the reader should consider what the writer is trying to achieve in the text and how they *create* the tone using style.

Language and Research Skills for Writing

The Conventions of Standard English Grammar and Usage

Grammatical Relationships
Adjectives and Adverbs
An **adjective** modifies a noun, making it more precise or giving more information about it. Adjectives answer these questions: What kind? Which one?

> I just bought a *red* car.

> I don't like *cold* weather.

One special type of word that modifies a noun is a **determiner**. In fact, some grammarians classify determiners as a separate part of speech because whereas adjectives simply describe additional qualities of a noun, a determiner is often a necessary part of a noun phrase, without which the phrase is grammatically incomplete. A determiner indicates whether a noun is definite or indefinite and can identify which noun is being discussed. It also introduces context to the noun in terms of quantity and possession. The most commonly-used determiners are *articles—a, an, the*.

> I ordered *a* pizza.

> She lives in *the* city.

Possessive pronouns discussed above, such as *my, your*, and *our*, are also determiners, along with **demonstratives—** *this, that—*and **quantifiers—** *much, many, some*. These determiners can take the place of an article.

> Are you using *this* chair?

> I need *some* coffee!

Adverbs modify verbs, adjectives, and other adverbs. Words that end in –ly are usually adverbs. Adverbs answer these questions: When? Where? In what manner? To what degree?

> She talks *quickly*.
>
> The mountains are *incredibly* beautiful!
>
> The students arrived *early*.
>
> Please take your phone call *outside*.

Noun-Noun Agreement

Nouns can be a person, place, or thing. They can refer to concrete objects—e.g., *chair, apple, house*—or abstract things—love, knowledge, friendliness.

> Look at the *dog*!
>
> Where are my *keys*?

Some nouns are *countable*, meaning they can be counted as separate entities—*one chair, two chairs, three chairs*. They can be either singular or plural. Other nouns, usually substances or concepts, are *uncountable*—e.g., *air, information, wealth*—and some nouns can be both countable and uncountable depending on how they are used.

> I bought three *dresses*.
>
> *Respect* is important to me.
>
> I ate way too much *food* last night.
>
> At the international festival, you can sample *foods* from around the world.

Proper nouns are the specific names of people, places, or things and are almost always capitalized.

> *Marie Curie* studied at the *Flying University* in *Warsaw, Poland*.

Nouns that refer to other nouns must also match in number. Take the following example:

> John and Emily both served as an intern for Senator Wilson.

Two people are involved in this sentence: John and Emily. Therefore, the word *intern* should be plural to match. Here is how the sentence should read:

> John and Emily both served as interns for Senator Wilson.

Pronoun-Antecedent Agreement

Pronouns function as substitutes for nouns or noun phrases. Pronouns are often used to avoid constant repetition of a noun or to simplify sentences. **Personal pronouns** are used for people. Some pronouns are **subject pronouns**; they are used to replace the subject in a sentence—*I, we, he, she, they*.

> Is *he* your friend?
>
> *We* work together.

Object pronouns can function as the object of a sentence—*me, us, him, her, them*.

> Give the documents to *her*.

> Did you call *him* back yet?

Some pronouns can function as either the subject or the object—e.g., *you, it*. The subject of a sentence is the noun of the sentence that is doing or being something.

> *You* should try it.

> *It* tastes great.

Possessive pronouns indicate ownership. They can be used alone—*mine, yours, his, hers, theirs, ours*—or with a noun—*my, your, his, her, their, ours*. In the latter case, they function as a determiner, which is described in detail in the below section on adjectives.

> This table is *ours*.

> I can't find *my* phone!

Reflexive pronouns refer back to the person being spoken or written about. These pronouns end in *-self/ selves*.

> I've heard that New York City is gorgeous in the autumn, but I've never seen it for *myself*.

> After moving away from home, young people have to take care of *themselves*.

Indefinite pronouns are used for things that are unknown or unspecified. Some examples are *anybody, something,* and *everything*.

> I'm looking for *someone* who knows how to fix computers.

> I wanted to buy some shoes today, but I couldn't find *any* that I liked.

Pronouns are used to replace nouns so sentences don't have a lot of unnecessary repetition. This repetition can make a sentence seem awkward as in the following example:

> Seat belts are important because seat belts save lives, but seat belts can't do so unless seat belts are used.

Replacing some of the nouns (*seat belts*) with a pronoun (*they*) improves the flow of the sentence:

> Seat belts are important because they save lives, but they can't do so unless they are used.

A pronoun should agree in number (singular or plural) with the noun that precedes it. Another common writing error is the shift in *noun-pronoun agreement*. Here's an example:

> When people are getting in a car, he should always remember to buckle his seatbelt.

The first half of the sentence talks about a plural (*people*), while the second half refers to a singular person (*he* and *his*). These don't agree, so the sentence should be rewritten as:

> When people are getting in a car, they should always remember to buckle their seatbelt.

An *antecedent* is the noun to which a pronoun refers; it needs to be written or spoken before the pronoun is used. For many pronouns, antecedents are imperative for clarity. In particular, many of the personal, possessive, and

76

demonstrative pronouns need antecedents. Otherwise, it would be unclear who or what someone is referring to when they use a pronoun like *he* or *this*.

Pronoun reference means that the pronoun should refer clearly to one, clear, unmistakable noun (the antecedent).

Pronoun-antecedent agreement refers to the need for the antecedent and the corresponding pronoun to agree in gender, person, and number. Here are some examples:

The *kidneys* (plural antecedent) are part of the urinary system. *They* (plural pronoun) serve several roles.

The kidneys are part of the *urinary system* (singular antecedent). *It* (singular pronoun) is also known as the renal system.

Pronoun Case
The subjective pronouns —*I, you, he/she/it, we, they,* and *who*—are the subjects of the sentence.

> Example: *They* have a new house.

The objective pronouns—*me, you* (*singular*), *him/her, us, them,* and *whom*—are used when something is being done for or given to someone; they are objects of the action.

> Example: The teacher has an apple for *us*.

The possessive pronouns—*mine, my, your, yours, his, hers, its, their, theirs, our,* and *ours*—are used to denote that something (or someone) belongs to someone (or something).

> Example: It's *their* chocolate cake.
> Even Better Example: It's *my* chocolate cake!

One of the greatest challenges and worst abuses of pronouns concerns *who* and *whom*. Just knowing the following rule can eliminate confusion. *Who* is a subjective-case pronoun used only as a subject or subject complement. *Whom* is only objective-case and, therefore, the object of the verb or preposition.

> *Who* is going to the concert?

> You are going to the concert with *whom*?

Hint: When using *who* or *whom*, think of whether someone would say *he* or *him*. If the answer is *he*, use *who*. If the answer is *him*, use *whom*. This trick is easy to remember because *he* and *who* both end in vowels, and *him* and *whom* both end in the letter *M*.

Intensive Pronoun
Intensive pronouns end in "self" or "selves" and add emphasis to the antecedent of subject of the sentence. The singular intensive pronouns include *myself, yourself, himself, herself,* and *itself,* and the plural intensive pronouns include *ourselves, yourselves,* and *themselves.* These are the same as reflexive pronouns; however, unlike reflexive pronouns, intensive pronouns can be removed from a sentence and the sentence will still make sense. The following is an example of a sentence that uses an intensive pronoun:

> I saw the magician himself open the box.

The intensive pronoun *himself* adds emphasis that the speaker specifically saw the magician open the box, rather than anyone else.

When using intensive pronouns, it is important to ensure there is number agreement. The most common error in usage is putting a singular pronoun in place of what should be a plural one and vice versa. Using the same example from above, an error in agreement occurs in the following sentence:

I saw the magician themselves open the box.

Magician is singular and *themselves* is plural, so there is an error in number agreement.

Pronoun Number and Person

Pronouns need to agree in number and person. Writers make a grammatical mistake when they write a sentence that contains a shift in pronoun number or person. For example, a sentence might use a second person pronoun (*you*) initially, but then switch to a third person pronoun later in the sentence. The following sentence contains a pronoun shift in person:

If you weigh yourself weekly, most people will stay motivated to lose weight.

This example begins with second person (using the pronoun *you*), but switches to third person (*their*) after the dependent clause. Because the sentence must remain consistent in person one of the following two options could correct the error:

If you weigh yourself weekly, you will likely stay motivated to lose weight.

If they weigh yourself weekly, most people will stay motivated to lose weight.

Vague Pronouns

A pronoun shouldn't confuse the reader about whom or what it's describing, and it should clearly refer to its antecedent. For example:

Unclear: The shovel and the pail floated away in the ocean, and it was long gone.

In this sentence, it can't be determined if the pronoun *it* refers to *the shovel* or *the pail*.

Clear: The pail floated away in the ocean, and it was long gone.

In this sentence, the pronoun *it* clearly refers to its antecedent, *the pail*.

Subject-Verb Agreement

In English, verbs must agree with the subject. The form of a verb may change depending on whether the subject is singular or plural, or whether it is first, second, or third person. For example, the verb *to be* has various forms:

I <u>am</u> a student.

You <u>are</u> a student.

She <u>is</u> a student.

We <u>are</u> students.

They <u>are</u> students.

Errors occur when a verb does not agree with its subject. Sometimes, the error is readily apparent:

We is hungry.

Is is not the appropriate form of *to be* when used with the third person plural *we*.

> We are hungry.

This sentence now has correct subject-verb agreement.

However, some cases are trickier, particularly when the subject consists of a lengthy noun phrase with many modifiers:

> Students who are hoping to accompany the anthropology department on its annual summer trip to Ecuador needs to sign up by March 31st.

The verb in this sentence is *needs*. However, its subject is not the noun adjacent to it—Ecuador. The subject is the noun at the beginning of the sentence—students. Because *students* is plural, *needs* is the incorrect verb form.

> *Students* who are hoping to accompany the anthropology department on its annual summer trip to Ecuador *need* to sign up by March 31st.

This sentence now uses correct agreement between *students* and *need*.

Another case to be aware of is a *collective noun*. A collective noun refers to a group of many things or people but can be singular in itself—e.g., *family, committee, army, pair team, council, jury*. Whether or not a collective noun uses a singular or plural verb depends on how the noun is being used. If the noun refers to the group performing a collective action as one unit, it should use a singular verb conjugation:

> The family is moving to a new neighborhood.

The whole family is moving together in unison, so the singular verb form *is* is appropriate here.

> The committee has made its decision.

The verb *has* and the possessive pronoun *its* both reflect the word *committee* as a singular noun in the sentence above; however, when a collective noun refers to the group as individuals, it can take a plural verb:

> The newlywed pair spend every moment together.

This sentence emphasizes the love between two people in a pair, so it can use the plural verb *spend*.

> The council are all newly elected members.

The sentence refers to the council in terms of its individual members and uses the plural verb *are*.

Overall, though, American English is more likely to pair a collective noun with a singular verb, while British English is more likely to pair a collective noun with a plural verb.

Shifts in Verb Tense

Verb tense reflects when an action occurred or a state existed. For example, the tense known as **simple present** expresses something that is happening right now or that happens regularly:

> She *works* in a hospital.

Present continuous tense expresses something in progress. It is formed by to be + verb + -ing.

> Sorry, I can't go out right now. I *am doing* my homework.

79

Past tense is used to describe events that previously occurred. However, in conversational English, speakers often use present tense or a mix of past and present tense when relating past events because it gives the narrative a sense of immediacy. In formal written English, though, consistency in verb tense is necessary to avoid reader confusion.

> I traveled to Europe last summer. As soon as I stepped off the plane, I feel like I'm in a movie! I'm surrounded by quaint cafes and impressive architecture.

The passage above abruptly switches from past tense—*traveled*, *stepped*—to present tense—*feel*, *am surrounded*.

> I *traveled* to Europe last summer. As soon as I *stepped* off the plane, I *felt* like I was in a movie! I *was surrounded* by quaint cafes and impressive architecture.

All verbs are in past tense, so this passage now has consistent verb tense.

Split Infinitives

The **infinitive form** of a verb consists of "to + base verb"—e.g., to walk, to sleep, to approve. A **split infinitive** occurs when another word, usually an adverb, is placed between *to* and the verb:

> I decided *to simply walk* to work to get more exercise every day.

The infinitive *to walk* is split by the adverb *simply*.

> It was a mistake *to hastily approve* the project before conducting further preliminary research.

The infinitive *to approve* is split by *hastily*.

Although some grammarians still advise against split infinitives, this syntactic structure is common in both spoken and written English and is widely accepted in standard usage.

Structural Relationships

Placement of Phrases and Clauses Within a Sentence

Clauses contain a subject and a verb. An **independent clause** can function as a complete sentence on its own, but it might also be one component of a longer sentence. **Dependent clauses** cannot stand alone as complete sentences. They rely on independent clauses to complete their meaning. Dependent clauses usually begin with a subordinating conjunction. Independent and dependent clauses are sometimes also referred to as *main clauses* and *subordinate clauses*, respectively. The following structure highlights the differences:

> Apiculturists raise honeybees because they love insects.

Apiculturists raise honeybees is an independent or main clause. The subject is *apiculturists*, and the verb is *raise*. It expresses a complete thought and could be a standalone sentence.

Because they love insects is a dependent or subordinate clause. If it were not attached to the independent clause, it would be a sentence fragment. While it contains a subject and verb—*they love*—this clause is dependent because it begins with the subordinate conjunction *because*. Thus, it does not express a complete thought on its own.

Another type of clause is a **relative clause**, and it is sometimes referred to as an *adjective clause* because it gives further description about the noun. A relative clause begins with a **relative pronoun**: *that, which, who, whom,*

whichever, *whomever*, or *whoever*. It may also begin with a *relative adverb*: *where*, *why*, or *when*. Here's an example of a relative clause, functioning as an adjective:

> The strawberries that I bought yesterday are already beginning to spoil.

Here, the relative clause is *that I bought yesterday*; the relative pronoun is *that*. The subject is *I*, and the verb is *bought*. The clause modifies the subject *strawberries* by answering the question, "Which strawberries?" Here's an example of a relative clause with an adverb:

> The tutoring center is a place where students can get help with homework.

The relative clause is *where students can get help with homework*, and it gives more information about a place by describing what kind of place it is. It begins with the relative adverb *where* and contains the noun *students* along with its verb phrase *can get*.

Relative clauses may be further divided into two types: essential or nonessential. **Essential clauses** contain identifying information without which the sentence would lose significant meaning or not make sense. These are also sometimes referred to as **restrictive clauses**. The sentence above contains an example of an essential relative clause. Here is what happens when the clause is removed:

> The tutoring center is a place where students can get help with homework.

> The tutoring center is a place.

Without the relative clause, the sentence loses the majority of its meaning; thus, the clause is essential or restrictive.

Nonessential clauses—also referred to as **non-restrictive clauses**—offer additional information about a noun in the sentence, but they do not significantly control the overall meaning of the sentence. The following example indicates a nonessential clause:

> New York City, which is located in the northeastern part of the country, is the most populated city in America.

> New York City is the most populated city in America.

Even without the relative clause, the sentence is still understandable and continues to communicate its central message about New York City. Thus, it is a nonessential clause.

Punctuation differs between essential and nonessential relative clauses, too. Nonessential clauses are set apart from the sentence using commas whereas essential clauses are not separated with commas. Also, the relative pronoun *that* is generally used for essential clauses, while *which* is used for nonessential clauses. The following examples clarify this distinction:

> *Romeo and Juliet* is my favorite play *that Shakespeare wrote*.

The relative clause *that Shakespeare wrote* contains essential, controlling information about the noun *play*, limiting it to those plays by Shakespeare. Without it, it would seem that *Romeo and Juliet* is the speaker's favorite play out of every play ever written, not simply from Shakespeare's repertoire.

> *Romeo and Juliet, which Shakespeare wrote*, is my favorite play.

Here, the nonessential relative clause—"which Shakespeare wrote"—modifies *Romeo and Juliet*. It doesn't provide controlling information about the play, but simply offers further background details. Thus, commas are needed.

Phrases are groups of words that do not contain the subject-verb combination required for clauses. Phrases are classified by the part of speech that begins or controls the phrase.

A **noun phrase** consists of a noun and all its modifiers—adjectives, adverbs, and determiners. Noun phrases can serve many functions in a sentence, acting as subjects, objects, and object complements:

> *The shallow yellow bowl* sits on the top shelf.

> Nina just bought *some incredibly fresh organic produce*.

Prepositional phrases are made up of a preposition and its object. The object of a preposition might be a noun, noun phrase, pronoun, or gerund. Prepositional phrases may function as either an adjective or an adverb:

> Jack picked up the book *in front of him*.

The prepositional phrase *in front of him* acts as an adjective indicating which book Jack picked up.

> The dog ran into the back yard.

The phrase *into the backyard* describes where the dog ran, so it acts as an adverb.

Verb phrases include all of the words in a verb group, even if they are not directly adjacent to each other:

> I *should have woken up* earlier this morning.

> The company **is** now *offering* membership discounts for new enrollers.

This sentence's verb phrase is *is offering*. Even though they are separated by the word *now*, they function together as a single verb phrase.

Misplaced and Dangling Modifiers

Modifiers enhance meaning by clarifying or giving greater detail about another part of a sentence. However, incorrectly-placed modifiers have the opposite effect and can cause confusion. A **misplaced modifier** is a modifier that is not located appropriately in relation to the word or phrase that it modifies:

> Because he was one of the greatest thinkers of Renaissance Italy, John idolized Leonardo da Vinci.

In this sentence, the modifier is "because he was one of the greatest thinkers of Renaissance Italy," and the noun it is intended to modify is "Leonardo da Vinci." However, due to the placement of the modifier next to the subject, John, it seems as if the sentence is stating that John was a Renaissance genius, not Da Vinci.

> John idolized Leonard da Vinci because he was one of the greatest thinkers of Renaissance Italy.

The modifier is now adjacent to the appropriate noun, clarifying which of the two men in this sentence is the greatest thinker.

Dangling modifiers modify a word or phrase that is not readily apparent in the sentence. That is, they "dangle" because they are not clearly attached to anything:

> After getting accepted to college, Amir's parents were proud.

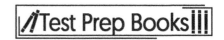

The modifier here, "after getting accepted to college," should modify who got accepted. The noun immediately following the modifier is "Amir's parents"—but they are probably not the ones who are going to college.

> After getting accepted to college, Amir made his parents proud.

The subject of the sentence has been changed to Amir himself, and now the subject and its modifier are appropriately matched.

Coordinating and Subordinating Conjunctions

Conjunctions are vital words that connect words, phrases, thoughts, and ideas. Conjunctions show relationships between components. There are two types:

Coordinating conjunctions are the primary class of conjunctions placed between words, phrases, clauses, and sentences that are of equal grammatical rank; the coordinating conjunctions are *for*, *and*, *nor*, *but*, *or*, *yet*, and *so*. A useful memorization trick is to remember that all the first letters of these conjunctions collectively spell the word fanboys.

> I need to go shopping, *but* I must be careful to leave enough money in the bank.
> She wore a black, red, *and* white shirt.

Subordinating conjunctions are the secondary class of conjunctions. They connect two unequal parts, one **main** (or **independent**) and the other **subordinate** (or **dependent**). I must go to the store *even though* I do not have enough money in the bank.

> *Because* I read the review, I do not want to go to the movie.

Notice that the presence of subordinating conjunctions makes clauses dependent. *I read the review* is an independent clause, but *because* makes the clause dependent. Thus, it needs an independent clause to complete the sentence.

Fragments and Run-Ons

A complete sentence requires a verb and a subject, and it must express a complete thought. Sometimes, the subject is omitted in the case of the implied *you*, used in sentences that are the command or imperative form—e.g., "Look!" or "Give me that." It is understood that the subject of the command is *you*, the listener or reader, so it is possible to have a structure without an explicit subject. Without these elements, though, the sentence is incomplete—it is a **sentence fragment**. While sentence fragments often occur in conversational English or creative writing, they are generally not appropriate in academic writing. Sentence fragments often occur when dependent clauses are not joined to an independent clause:

> *Sentence fragment*: Because the airline overbooked the flight.

The sentence above is a dependent clause that does not express a complete thought. What happened as a result of this cause? With the addition of an independent clause, this now becomes a complete sentence:

> *Complete sentence*: Because the airline overbooked the flight, several passengers were unable to board.

Sentences fragments may also occur through improper use of conjunctions:

> I'm going to the Bahamas for spring break. And to New York City for New Year's Eve.

While the first sentence above is a complete sentence, the second one is not because it is a prepositional phrase that lacks a subject [I] and a verb [am going]. Joining the two together with the coordinating conjunction forms one grammatically-correct sentence:

I'm going to the Bahamas for spring break and to New York City for New Year's Eve.

A **run-on** is a sentence with too many independent clauses that are improperly connected to each other:

This winter has been very cold some farmers have suffered damage to their crops.

The sentence above has two subject-verb combinations. The first is "this winter has been"; the second is "some farmers have suffered." However, they are simply stuck next to each other without any punctuation or conjunction. Therefore, the sentence is a run-on.

Another type of run-on occurs when writers use inappropriate punctuation:

This winter has been very cold, some farmers have suffered damage to their crops.

Though a comma has been added, this sentence is still not correct. When a comma alone is used to join two independent clauses, it is known as a **comma splice**. Without an appropriate conjunction, a comma cannot join two independent clauses by itself.

Run-on sentences can be corrected by either dividing the independent clauses into two or more separate sentences or inserting appropriate conjunctions and/or punctuation. The run-on sentence can be amended by separating each subject-verb pair into its own sentence:

This winter has been very cold. Some farmers have suffered damage to their crops.

The run-on can also be fixed by adding a comma and conjunction to join the two independent clauses with each other:

This winter has been very cold, so some farmers have suffered damage to their crops.

Correlative Conjunctions

Correlative conjunctions are distinct pairs of conjunctions that are used in tandem in a sentence. Although they appear at different spots in the sentence, both are required to maintain a grammatically correct sentence. Their function is to help tie together two different parts and thoughts in the sentence. Examples of these pairs of correlative conjunctions include *either/or, neither/nor, both/and, such/that, not/but, whether/or, as/as,* and *no sooner/than, rather/than.* Correlative conjunctions are typically more like coordinating conjunctions than subordinating conjunctions because they usually sentence fragments of the same weight.

Parallel Structure

Parallel structure occurs when phrases or clauses within a sentence contain the same structure. Parallelism increases readability and comprehensibility because it is easy to tell which sentence elements are paired with each other in meaning.

Jennifer enjoys cooking, knitting, and to spend time with her cat.

This sentence is not parallel because the items in the list appear in two different forms. Some are **gerunds**, which is the verb + ing: *cooking, knitting*. The other item uses the **infinitive** form, which is to + verb: *to spend*. To create parallelism, all items in the list may reflect the same form:

Jennifer enjoys cooking, knitting, and spending time with her cat.

84

All of the items in the list are now in gerund forms, so this sentence exhibits parallel structure. Here's another example:

The company is looking for employees who are responsible and with a lot of experience.

Again, the items that are listed in this sentence are not parallel. "Responsible" is an adjective, yet "with a lot of experience" is a prepositional phrase. The sentence elements do not utilize parallel parts of speech.

The company is looking for employees who are responsible and experienced.

"Responsible" and "experienced" are both adjectives, so this sentence now has parallel structure.

Word Choice

Idiomatic Expressions

An idiomatic expression is a phrase that has a distinct meaning that differs from the denotative meaning of the words on their own. For example, "it's raining cats and dogs" means that it is raining very hard, rather than insinuating that cats and dogs are falling from the sky. Errors in idiomatic expressions occur when a writer either uses the idiomatic expression incorrectly (perhaps by confusing its meaning), or when a writer uses an incorrect word in the expression. For example, a writer might do one of the following:

This pet adoption event has so many adoptable animals! It's raining cats and dogs here!

I wanted to go ride my bike, but it's raining cats and bats outside.

In the first sentence, the writer has confused the meaning of the phrase by thinking that a place with many cats and dogs bustling around is necessarily "raining cats and dogs." The idiomatic expression is misused. There is no indication in the previous sentence that the weather is wet and raining. In the second sentence, the writer has incorrectly swapped the word *bats* for *dogs*.

Recognizing errors in the use of idiomatic expressions can be difficult because it requires familiarity with the meaning, usage, and verbiage of the expression. There are websites dedicated to informing readers about these expressions, which can be helpful.

Frequently Confused Words

The following are some frequently confused words. Many are **homophones**, which are two or more words that have no particular relationship to one another except their identical pronunciations. Homophones make spelling English words fun and challenging like these:

Common Homophones		
allot, a lot	cell, sell	it's, its
barbecue, barbeque	do, due, dew	knew, new
bite, byte	dual, duel	principal, principle
brake, break	flew, flu, flue	their, there, they're
capital, capitol	gauge, gage	to, too, two
cash, cache	holy, wholly	yoke, yolk

- Its and It's: These pronouns are some of the most confused in the English language as most possessives contain the suffix –'s. However, for *it*, it is the opposite. *Its* is a possessive pronoun:

  The government is reassessing *its* spending plan.

It's is a contraction of the words *it is*:

  It's snowing outside.

- Saw and Seen: *Saw* and *seen* are both conjugations of the verb *to see*, but they express different verb tenses. *Saw* is used in the simple past tense. *Seen* is the past participle form of *to see* and can be used in all perfect tenses.

  I seen her yesterday.

This sentence is incorrect. Because it expresses a completed event from a specified point in time in the past, it should use simple past tense:

  I *saw* her yesterday.

This sentence uses the correct verb tense. Here's how the past participle is used correctly:

  I *have seen* her before.

The meaning in this sentence is slightly changed to indicate an event from an unspecific time in the past. In this case, present perfect is the appropriate verb tense to indicate an unspecified past experience. Present perfect conjugation is created by combining *to have* + past participle.

- Then and Than: *Then* is generally used as an adverb indicating something that happened next in a sequence or as the result of a conditional situation:

  We parked the car and *then* walked to the restaurant.

  If enough people register for the event, *then* we can begin planning.

Than is a conjunction indicating comparison:

  This watch is more expensive *than* that one.

  The bus departed later *than* I expected.

- They're, Their, and There: *They're* is a contraction of the words *they are*:

  They're moving to Ohio next week.

Their is a possessive pronoun:

  The baseball players are training for *their* upcoming season.

There can function as multiple parts of speech, but it is most commonly used as an adverb indicating a location:

  Let's go to the concert! Some great bands are playing *there*.

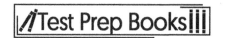
- Insure and Ensure: These terms are both verbs. *Insure* means to guarantee something against loss, harm, or damage, usually through an insurance policy that offers monetary compensation:

    The robbers made off with her prized diamond necklace, but luckily it was *insured* for one million dollars.

    Ensure means to make sure, to confirm, or to be certain:

    Ensure that you have your passport before entering the security checkpoint.

- Accept and Except: *Accept* is a verb meaning to take or agree to something:

    I would like to *accept* your offer of employment.

    Except is a preposition that indicates exclusion:

    I've been to every state in America *except* Hawaii.

- Affect and Effect: *Affect* is a verb meaning to influence or to have an impact on something:

    The amount of rainfall during the growing season *affects* the flavor of wine produced from these grapes.

    Effect can be used as either a noun or a verb. As a noun, *effect* is synonymous with a result:

    If we implement the changes, what will the *effect* be on our profits?

    As a verb, *effect* means to bring about or to make happen:

    In just a few short months, the healthy committee has *effected* real change in school nutrition.

Wrong Word Use

As with the case with many frequently confused words, wrong word use often occurs with homophones and homonyms. The following are some of the words that writers most often misuse:

- That/Which: The pronouns *that* and *which* are both used to refer to nouns—but they are not interchangeable. The rule is to use the word *that* in essential clauses and phrases that help convey the meaning of the sentence. Use the word *which* in nonessential (less important) clauses. Typically, *which* clauses are enclosed in commas.

    The morning <u>that I fell asleep in class</u> caused me a lot of trouble.

    This morning's coffee, <u>which had too much creamer</u>, woke me up.

- Who/Whom: We use the pronouns *who* and *whom* to refer to people. We always use *who* when it is the subject of the sentence or clause. *Whom* is always the object of a verb or preposition.

    <u>Who</u> hit the baseball for the home run? (subject)

    The baseball fell into the glove of <u>whom</u>? (object of the preposition of)

    The umpire called <u>whom</u> "out"? (object of the verb called)

- To/Too/Two

  to: a preposition or infinitive (*to walk, to run, walk to the store, run to the tree*)
  too: means also, as well, or very (*She likes cookies, too.; I ate too much.*)
  two: a number (*I have two cookies. She walked to the store two times.*)

- There/Their/They're

  there: an adjective, adverb, or pronoun used to start a sentence or indicate place (*There are four vintage cars over there.*)
  their: a possessive pronoun used to indicate belonging (*Their car is the blue and white one.*)
  they're: a contraction of the words "they are" (*They're going to enter the vintage car show.*)

- Your/You're

  your: a possessive pronoun (*Your artwork is terrific.*)
  you're: a contraction of the words "you are" (*You're a terrific artist.*)

- Its/It's

  its: a possessive pronoun (*The elephant had its trunk in the water.*)
  it's: a contraction of the words "it is" (*It's an impressive animal.*)

- Affect/Effect

  affect: as a verb means "to influence" (*How will the earthquake affect your home?*); as a noun means "emotion or mood" (*Her affect was somber.*)
  effect: as a verb means "to bring about" (*She will effect a change through philanthropy.*); as a noun means "a result of" (*The effect of the earthquake was devastating.*)

  Other mix-ups: Other pairs of words cause mix-ups but are not necessarily homonyms. Here are a few of those:

- Bring/Take

  bring: when the action is coming toward (*Bring me the money.*)
  take: when the action is going away from (*Take her the money.*)

- Can/May

  can: means "able to" (*The child can ride a bike.*)
  may: asks permission (*The child asked if he may ride his bike.*)

- Than/Then

  than: a conjunction used for comparison (*I like tacos better than pizza.*)
  then: an adverb telling when something happened (*I ate and then slept.*)

- Disinterested/Uninterested

  disinterested: used to mean "neutral" (*The jury remains disinterested during the trial.*)
  uninterested: used to mean "bored" (*I was uninterested during the lecture.*)

- Percent/Percentage

  percent: used when there is a number involved (*Five percent of us like tacos.*)
  percentage: used when there is no number (*That is a low percentage.*)

88

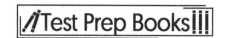

- Fewer/Less

  fewer: used for things you can count (*He has fewer playing cards.*)
  less: used for things you cannot count, as well as time (*He has less talent. You have less than a minute.*)

- Farther/Further

  farther: used when discussing distance (*His paper airplane flew farther than mine.*)
  further: used to mean "more" (*He needed further information.*)

- Lend/Loan

  lend: a verb used for borrowing (*Lend me your lawn mower. He will lend it to me.*)
  loan: a noun used for something borrowed (*She applied for a student loan.*)

Redundancy

Unfortunately, writers often include extra words and phrases that seem necessary at the time but add nothing to the main idea. This confuses the reader and creates unnecessary repetition. Writing that is redundant or lacks conciseness is usually guilty of excessive wordiness and redundant phrases. Here's an example containing both of these issues:

> When legislators decided to begin creating legislation making it mandatory for automobile drivers and passengers to make use of seat belts while in cars, a large number of them made those laws for reasons that were political reasons.

There are several empty or "fluff words" here that take up too much space. These can be eliminated while still maintaining the writer's meaning. For example:

- "Decided to begin" could be shortened to "began"
- "Making it mandatory for" could be shortened to "requiring"
- "Make use of" could be shortened to "use"
- "A large number" could be shortened to "many"

In addition, there are several examples of redundancy that can be eliminated:

- "Legislators decided to begin creating legislation" and "made those laws"
- "Automobile drivers and passengers" and "while in cars"
- "Reasons that were political reasons"

These changes are incorporated as follows:

> When legislators began requiring drivers and passengers to use seat belts, many of them did so for political reasons.

The Conventions of Standard English Capitalization and Punctuation

Capitalization

Here's a non-exhaustive list of things that should be capitalized:

- The first word of every sentence

- The first word of every line of poetry

- The first letter of proper nouns (World War II)

- Holidays (Valentine's Day)

- Days of the week and months of the year (Tuesday, March)

- The first word, last word, and all major words in the titles of books, movies, songs, and other creative works (*To Kill a Mockingbird,* note that *a* is lowercase since it's not a major word, but *to* is capitalized since it's the first word of the title.

- Titles when preceding a proper noun (President Roberto Gonzales, Aunt Judy)

When simply using a word such as president or secretary, though, the word is not capitalized.

> Officers of the new business must include a *president* and *treasurer*.

Seasons—spring, fall, etc.—are not capitalized.

North, *south*, *east*, and *west* are capitalized when referring to regions but are not when being used for directions. In general, if it's preceded by *the* it should be capitalized.

> I'm from the South.
> I drove south.

Punctuation
Commas
A **comma** (,) is the punctuation mark that signifies a pause—breath—between parts of a sentence. It denotes a break of flow. As with so many aspects of writing structure, authors will benefit by memorizing all of the different ways in which commas can be used so as not to abuse them.

In a complex sentence—one that contains a **subordinate** (**dependent**) clause or clauses—the use of a comma is dictated by where the subordinate clause is located. If the subordinate clause is located before the main clause, a comma is needed between the two clauses.

> Because I don't have enough money, I will not order steak.

Generally, if the subordinate clause is placed after the main clause, no punctuation is needed.

> I did well on my exam because I studied two hours the night before.

Notice how the last clause is dependent because it requires the earlier independent clauses to make sense.

Use a comma on both sides of an interrupting phrase.

> I will pay for the ice cream, *chocolate and vanilla*, and then will eat it all myself.

The words forming the phrase in italics are nonessential (extra) information. To determine if a phrase is nonessential, try reading the sentence without the phrase and see if it's still coherent.

A comma is not necessary in this next sentence because no interruption—nonessential or extra information—has occurred. Read sentences aloud when uncertain.

I will pay for his chocolate and vanilla ice cream and then will eat it all myself.

If the nonessential phrase comes at the beginning of a sentence, a comma should only go at the end of the phrase. If the phrase comes at the end of a sentence, a comma should only go at the beginning of the phrase.

90

Other types of interruptions include the following:

- interjections: Oh no, I am not going.
- abbreviations: Barry Potter, M.D., specializes in heart disorders.
- direct addresses: Yes, Claudia, I am tired and going to bed.
- parenthetical phrases: His wife, lovely as she was, was not helpful.
- transitional phrases: Also, it is not possible.

The second comma in the following sentence is called an Oxford comma.

> I will pay for ice cream, syrup, and pop.

It is a comma used after the second-to-last item in a series of three or more items. It comes before the word *or* or *and*. Not everyone uses the Oxford comma; it is optional, but many believe it is needed. The comma functions as a tool to reduce confusion in writing. So, if omitting the Oxford comma would cause confusion, then it's best to include it.

Commas are used in math to mark the place of thousands in numerals, breaking them up so they are easier to read. Other uses for commas are in dates (*March 19, 2016*), letter greetings (*Dear Sally,*), and in between cities and states (*Louisville, KY*).

Semicolons

In a sentence, **colons** are used before a list, a summary or elaboration, or an explanation related to the preceding information in the sentence:

> There are two ways to reserve tickets for the performance: by phone or in person.

> One thing is clear: students are spending more on tuition than ever before.

As these examples show, a colon must be preceded by an independent clause. However, the information after the colon may be in the form of an independent clause or in the form of a list.

Semicolons can be used in two different ways—to join ideas or to separate them. In some cases, semicolons can be used to connect what would otherwise be stand-alone sentences. Each part of the sentence joined by a semicolon must be an independent clause. The use of a semicolon indicates that these two independent clauses are closely related to each other:

> The rising cost of childcare is one major stressor for parents; healthcare expenses are another source of anxiety.

> Classes have been canceled due to the snowstorm; check the school website for updates.

Semicolons can also be used to divide elements of a sentence in a more distinct way than simply using a comma. This usage is particularly useful when the items in a list are especially long and complex and contain other internal punctuation.

> Retirees have many modes of income: some survive solely off their retirement checks; others supplement their income through part time jobs, like working in a supermarket or substitute teaching; and others are financially dependent on the support of family members, friends, and spouses.

Apostrophes

This punctuation mark, the apostrophe ('), is a versatile little mark. It has a few different functions:

- Quotes: Apostrophes are used when a second quote is needed within a quote.

    o In my letter to my friend, I wrote, "The girl had to get a new purse, and guess what Mary did? She said, 'I'd like to go with you to the store.' I knew Mary would buy it for her."

- Contractions: Another use for an apostrophe in the quote above is a contraction. I'd is used for I would.

- Possession: An apostrophe followed by the letter s shows possession (Mary's purse). If the possessive word is plural, the apostrophe generally just follows the word.

    o The trees' leaves are all over the ground.

Research Skills and Strategies

The Credibility and Relevance of Sources

There are several criteria that need to be examined before using a source for a research topic.

The following questions will help determine whether a source is credible:

- Author
    o Who is he or she?
    o Does he or she have the appropriate credentials—e.g., M.D, PhD?
    o Is this person authorized to write on the matter through their job or personal experiences?
    o Is he or she affiliated with any known credible individuals or organizations?
    o Has he or she written anything else?
- Publisher
    o Who published/produced the work? Is it a well-known journal, like National Geographic, or a tabloid, like The National Enquirer?
    o Is the publisher from a scholarly, commercial, or government association?
    o Do they publish works related to specific fields?
    o Have they published other works?
    o If a digital source, what kind of website hosts the text? Does it end in .edu, .org, or .com?
- Bias
    o Is the writing objective? Does it contain any loaded or emotional language?
    o Does the publisher/producer have a known bias, such as Fox News or CNN?
    o Does the work include diverse opinions or perspectives?
    o Does the author have any known bias—e.g., Michael Moore, Bill O'Reilly, or the Pope? Is he or she affiliated with any organizations or individuals that may have a known bias—e.g., Citizens United or the National Rifle Association?
    o Does the magazine, book, journal, or website contain any advertising?
- References
    o Are there any references?
    o Are the references credible? Do they follow the same criteria as stated above?
    o Are the references from a related field?
- Accuracy/reliability
    o Has the article, book, or digital source been peer reviewed?
    o Are all of the conclusions, supporting details, or ideas backed with published evidence?
    o If a digital source, is it free of grammatical errors, poor spelling, and improper English?
    o Do other published individuals have similar findings?

92

- Coverage
  - o Are the topic and related material both successfully addressed?
  - o Does the work add new information or theories to those of their sources?
  - o Is the target audience appropriate for the intended purpose?

Different Elements of a Citation

Citation styles vary according to which style guide is consulted. Examples of commonly-used styles include MLA, APA, and Chicago/Turabian. Each citation style includes similar components, although the order and formatting of these components varies.

MLA Style

For an MLA style citation, components must be included or excluded depending on the source, so writers should determine which components are applicable to the source being cited. Here are the basic components:

- Author—last name, first name
- Title of source
- Title of container—e.g., a journal title or website
- Other contributors—e.g., editor or translator
- Version
- Number
- Publisher
- Publication date
- Location—e.g., the URL or DOI
- Date of Access—optional

APA Style

The following components can be found in APA style citations. Components must be included or excluded depending on the source, so writers should determine which components are applicable to the source being cited.

The basic components are as follows:

- Author—last name, first initial, middle initial
- Publication date
- Title of chapter, article, or text
- Editor— last name, first initial, middle initial
- Version/volume
- Number/issue
- Page numbers
- DOI or URL
- Database—if article is difficult to locate
- City of publication
- State of publication, abbreviated
- Publisher

Chicago/Turabian Style

Chicago/Turabian style citations are also referred to as note systems and are used most frequently in the humanities and the arts. Components must be included or excluded depending on the source, so writers should determine which components are applicable to the source being cited. They contain the following elements:

- Author—last name, first name, middle initial

- Title of chapter or article—in quotation marks
- Title of source
- Editor—first name, last name
- Page numbers
- Version/volume
- Number/issue
- Page numbers
- Date of access
- DOI
- Publication location—city and state abbreviation/country
- Publisher
- Publication Date

Effective Research Strategies

The purpose of all research is to provide an answer to an unknown question. Therefore, all good research papers pose the topic in the form of a question, which they will then seek to answer with clear ideas, arguments, and supporting evidence.

A **research question** is the primary focus of the research piece, and it should be formulated on a unique topic. To formulate a research question, writers begin by choosing a general topic of interest and then research the literature to determine what sort of research has already been done—the *literature review*. This helps them narrow the topic into something original and determine what still needs to be asked and researched about the topic. A solid question is very specific and avoids generalizations. The following question is offered for evaluation:

What is most people's favorite kind of animal?

This research question is extremely broad without giving the paper any particular focus—it could go any direction and is not an exceptionally unique focus. To narrow it down, the question could consider a specific population:

What is the favorite animal of people in Ecuador?

While this question is better, it does not address exactly why this research is being conducted or why anyone would care about the answer. Here's another possibility:

What does the animal considered as the most favorite of people in different regions throughout Ecuador reveal about their socioeconomic status?

This question is extremely specific and gives a very clear direction of where the paper or project is going to go. However, sometimes the question can be too limited, where very little research has been conducted to create a solid paper, and the researcher most likely does not have the means to travel to Ecuador and travel door-to-door conducting a census on people's favorite animals. In this case, the research question would need to be broadened. Broadening a topic can mean introducing a wider range of criteria. Instead of people in Ecuador, the topic could be opened to include the population of South America or expanded to include more issues or considerations.

Information Relevant to a Particular Research Task

Relevant information is that which is pertinent to the topic at hand. Particularly when doing research online, it is easy for students to get overwhelmed with the wealth of information available to them. Before conducting research, then, students need to begin with a clear idea of the question they want to answer.

For example, a student may be interested in learning more about marriage practices in Jane Austen's England. If that student types "marriage" into a search engine, he or she will have to sift through thousands of unrelated sites

before finding anything related to that topic. Narrowing down search parameters can aid in locating relevant information.

When using a book, students can consult the table of contents, glossary, or index to discover whether the book contains relevant information before using it as a resource. If the student finds a hefty volume on Jane Austen, he or she can flip to the index in the back, look for the word marriage, and find out how many page references are listed in the book. If there are few or no references to the subject, it is probably not a relevant or useful source.

In evaluating research articles, students may also consult the title, abstract, and keywords before reading the article in its entirety. Referring to the date of publication will also determine whether the research contains up-to-date discoveries, theories, and ideas about the subject, or whether it is outdated.

Practice Quiz

Questions 1-5 are based on the following passage:

Flooding can result in severe devastation of nearby areas. Flash floods and tsunamis can result in sweeping waters that travel at destructive speeds. Fast-moving water has the power to demolish all obstacles in its path such as homes, trees, bridges, and buildings. Animals, plants, and humans may all lose their lives during a flood.

Floods can also cause pollution and infection. Sewage may seep from drains or septic tanks and contaminate drinking water or surrounding lands. Similarly, toxins, fuels, debris from annihilated buildings, and other hazardous materials can leave water unusable for consumption. (1) <u>As the water begins to drain, mold may begin to grow.</u> As a result, residents of flooded areas may be left without power, drinkable water, or be exposed to toxins and other diseases.

(2) <u>Although often associated with devastation, not all flooding results</u> in adverse circumstances. For thousands of years, people have inhabited floodplains of rivers. (3) <u>Examples include the Mississippi Valley of the United States, the Nile River in Egypt, and the Tigris River of the Middle East</u>. The flooding of such rivers (4) <u>caused</u> nutrient-rich silts to be deposited on the floodplains. Thus, after the floods recede, an extremely fertile soil is left behind. This soil is conducive to the agriculture of bountiful crops and has sustained the diets of humans for a millennium.

Technologies now allow scientists to predict where and when flooding is likely to occur. Such technologies can also be used (5) <u>to project</u> the severity of an anticipated flood. In this way, local inhabitants can be warned and take preventative measures such as boarding up their homes, gathering necessary provisions, and moving themselves and their possessions to higher grounds.

The picturesque views of coastal regions and rivers have long enticed people to build near such locations. Due to the costs associated with the repairs needed after the flooding of such residencies, many governments now require inhabitants of flood-prone areas to purchase flood insurance and build flood-resistant structures. Pictures of all items within a building or home should be taken so that proper reimbursement for losses can be made in the event that a flood does occur.

1. Which choice best maintains the pattern of the first sentence of the paragraph?
   a. NO CHANGE
   b. As the rain subsides and the water begins to drain, mold may begin to grow.
   c. Mold may begin to grow as the water begins to drain.
   d. The water will begin to drain and mold will begin to grow.

2. Which of the following would be the best replacement for the underlined portion of the sentence reproduced below?

   > (2) <u>Although often associated with devastation, not all flooding results</u> in adverse circumstances. For thousands of years, peoples have inhabited floodplains of rivers.

   a. NO CHANGE
   b. Although often associated with devastation not all flooding results
   c. Although often associated with devastation. Not all flooding results
   d. While often associated with devastation, not all flooding results

96

3. The author is considering deleting this sentence (reproduced below) from the tenth paragraph. Should the sentence be kept or deleted?

> (3) Examples include the Mississippi Valley of the United States, the Nile River in Egypt, and the Tigris River of the Middle East.

a. Kept, because it provides examples of floodplains that have been successfully inhabited by civilizations.
b. Kept, because it provides an example of how floods can be beneficial.
c. Deleted, because it blurs the paragraph's focus on the benefits of floods.
d. Deleted, because it distracts from the overall meaning of the paragraph.

4. Which of the following would be the best replacement for the underlined portion of the sentence reproduced below?

> The flooding of such rivers (4) <u>caused</u> nutrient-rich silts to be deposited on the floodplains.

a. NO CHANGE
b. Cause
c. Causing
d. Causes

5. Which of the following would be the best replacement for the underlined portion of the sentence reproduced below?

> Such technologies can also be used (5) <u>to project</u> the severity of an anticipated flood.

a. NO CHANGE
b. Projecting
c. Project
d. Projected

See answers on the next page.

Answer Explanations

1. C: Choice *C* is the best answer because it most closely maintains the sentence pattern of the first sentence of the paragraph, which begins with a noun and passive verb phrase. Choice *B* is incorrect because it does not maintain the sentence pattern of the first sentence of the paragraph. Instead, Choice *B* shifts the placement of the modifying prepositional phrase to the beginning of the sentence. Choice *D* is incorrect because it does not maintain the sentence pattern established by the first sentence of the paragraph. Instead, Choice *D* is an attempt to combine two independent clauses.

2. A: Choice *C* can be eliminated because creating a new sentence with *not* is grammatically incorrect and throws off the rest of the sentence. Choice *B* is wrong because a comma is definitely needed after *devastation* in the sentence. Choice *D* is also incorrect because "while" is a poor substitute for "although". *Although* in this context is meant to show contradiction with the idea that floods are associated with devastation. Therefore, none of these choices would be suitable revisions because the original was correct: NO CHANGE, Choice *A,* is the correct answer.

3. A: Idea and claims are best expressed and supported within a text through examples, evidence, and descriptions. Choice *A* is correct because it provides examples of rivers that support the tenth paragraph's claim that "not all flooding results in adverse circumstances." Choice *B* is incorrect because the sentence does not explain how floods are beneficial. Therefore, Choices *C* and *D* are incorrect.

4. D: In the sentence, *caused* is an incorrect tense, making Choice *A* wrong. Choice *B* is incorrect because *cause* is used as a noun or imperative verb form, we need *cause* in verb form. Choices *C* and *D* are very compelling. Choice *C,* *causing*, is a verb in the present continuous tense, which appears to agree with the verb flooding, but it is incorrectly used. This leaves Choice *D,* *causes*, which does fit because it is in the indefinite present tense. Fitting each choice into the sentence and reading it in your mind will also reveal that Choice *D,* *causes*, correctly completes the sentence. Apply this method to all the questions when possible.

5. A: To *project* means to anticipate or forecast. This goes very well with the sentence because it describes how new technology is trying to estimate flood activity in order to prevent damage and save lives. "Project" in this case needs to be assisted by "to" in order to function in the sentence. Therefore, Choice *A* is correct. Choices *B* and *D* are the incorrect tenses. Choice *C* is also wrong because it lacks *to*.

Mathematics

Number and Quantity

Solving Problems Involving Integers, Decimals, and Fractions

Basic Operations

Gaining more of something is related to addition, while taking something away relates to subtraction. Vocabulary words such as *total, more, less, left*, and *remain* are common when working with these problems. The + sign means *plus*. This shows that addition is happening. The − sign means *minus*. This shows that subtraction is happening. The symbols will be important when you write out equations.

Addition

Addition can also be defined in equation form. For example, $4 + 5 = 9$ shows that $4 + 5$ is the same as 9. Therefore, $9 = 9$, and "four plus five equals nine." When two quantities are being added together, the result is called the **sum**. Therefore, the sum of 4 and 5 is 9. The numbers being added, such as 4 and 5, are known as the **addends.**

Subtraction

Subtraction can also be in equation form. For example, $9 − 5 = 4$ shows that $9 − 5$ is the same as 4 and that "9 minus 5 is 4." The result of subtraction is known as a **difference.** The difference of $9 − 5$ is 4. 4 represents the amount that is left once the subtraction is done. The order in which subtraction is completed does matter. For example, $9 − 5$ and $5 − 9$ do not result in the same answer. $5 − 9$ results in a negative number. So, subtraction does not adhere to the commutative or associative property. The order in which subtraction is completed is important.

Adding and Subtracting Positive and Negative Numbers

Some problems require adding positive and negative numbers or subtracting positive and negative numbers. Adding a negative number to a positive one can be thought of a reducing or subtracting from the positive number, and the result should be less than the original positive number. For example, adding 8 and −3 is the same is subtracting 3 from 8; the result is 5. This can be visualized by imagining that the positive number (8) represents 8 apples that a student has in her basket. The negative number (−3) indicates the number of apples she is in debt or owes to her friend. In order to pay off her debt and "settle the score," she essentially is in possession of three fewer apples than in her basket ($8 − 3 = 5$), so she actually has five apples that are hers to keep.

Should the negative addend be of higher magnitude than the positive addend (for example $−9 + 3$), the result will be negative, but "less negative" or closer to zero than the large negative number. This is because adding a positive value, even if relatively smaller, to a negative value, reduces the magnitude of the negative in the total. Considering the apple example again, if the girl owed 9 apples to her friend (-9) but she picked 3 (+3) off a tree and gave them to her friend, she now would only owe him six apples (−6), which reduced her debt burden (her negative number of apples) by three.

Subtracting positive and negative numbers works the same way with one key distinction: subtracting a negative number from a negative number yields a "less negative" or more positive result because again, this can be considered as removing or alleviating some debt. For example, if the student with the apples owed 5 apples to her friend, she essentially has -5 applies. If her mom gives that friend 10 apples on behalf of the girl, she now has removed the need to pay back the 5 apples and surpassed neutral (no net apples owed) and now her friend owes *her* five apples (+5).

Stated mathematically: $-5 - (-10) = -5 + 10 = +5$

When subtracting integers and negative rational numbers, one has to change the problem to adding the opposite and then apply the rules of addition.

- Subtracting two positive numbers is the same as adding one positive and one negative number.

  For example, $4.9 - 7.1$ is the same as $4.9 + (-7.1)$. The solution is -2.2 since the absolute value of -7.1 is greater than 4.9. Another example is $8.5 - 6.4$ which is the same as $8.5 + (-6.4)$. The solution is 2.1 since the absolute value of 8.5 is greater than 6.4.

- Subtracting a positive number from a negative number results in negative value.

  For example, $(-12) - 7$ is the same as $(-12) + (-7)$ with a solution of -19.

- Subtracting a negative number from a positive number results in a positive value.

  For example, $12 - (-7)$ is the same as $12 + 7$ with a solution of 19.

- For multiplication and division of integers and rational numbers, if both numbers are positive or both numbers are negative, the result is a positive value.

  For example, $(-1.7) \times (-4)$ has a solution of 6.8 since both numbers are negative values.

- If one number is positive and another number is negative, the result is a negative value.

  For example, $(-15) \div 5$ has a solution of -3 since there is one negative number.

Adding one positive and one negative number requires taking the absolute values and finding the difference between them. Then, the sign of the number that has the higher absolute value for the final solution is used.

Multiplication

Multiplication is when we add equal amounts. The answer to a multiplication problem is called a **product**. Products stand for the total number of items within different groups. The symbol for multiplication is "×" or "·". We say 2×3 or $2 \cdot 3$ means "2 times 3."

As an example, there are three sets of four apples. The goal is to know how many apples there are in total. Three sets of four apples gives $4 + 4 + 4 = 12$. Also, three times four apples gives $3 \times 4 = 12$. Therefore, for any whole numbers a and b, where a is not equal to zero, $a \times b = b + b + \cdots b$, where b is added a times. Also, $a \times b$ can be thought of as the number of units in a rectangular block consisting of a rows and b columns.

For example, 3×7 is equal to the number of squares in the following rectangle:

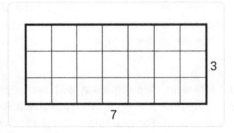

The answer is 21, and there are 21 squares in the rectangle.

When any number is multiplied by one (for example, $8 \times 1 = 8$), the value of original number does not change. Therefore, 1 is the **multiplicative identity**. For any whole number a, $1 \times a = a$. Also, any number multiplied by zero results in zero. Therefore, for any whole number a, $0 \times a = 0$.

Another method of multiplication can be done with the use of an **area model**. An area model is a rectangle that is divided into rows and columns that match up to the number of place values within each number. Take the example 29×65. These two numbers can be split into simpler numbers: $29 = 25 + 4$ and $65 = 60 + 5$. The products of those 4 numbers are found within the rectangle and then summed up to get the answer. The entire process is:

$$(60 \times 25) + (5 \times 25) + (60 \times 4) + (5 \times 4)$$

$$1,500 + 240 + 125 + 20 = 1,885$$

Here is the actual area model:

	25	**4**
60	60x25 1,500	60x4 240
5	5x25 125	5x4 20

```
      1 , 5 0 0
          2 4 0
          1 2 5
  +          2 0
      1 , 8 8 5
```

Division

Division is based on dividing a given number into parts. The simplest problem involves dividing a number into equal parts. For example, if a pack of 20 pencils is to be divided among 10 children, you would have to divide 20 by 10. In this example, each child would receive 2 pencils.

The symbol for division is "$\div$" or "$/$". The equation above is written as $20 \div 10 = 2$, or $20/10 = \frac{20}{10} = 2$. This means "20 divided by 10 is equal to 2." Division can be explained as the following: for any whole numbers a and b, where b is not equal to zero, $a \div b = c$ if—and only if—$a = b \times c$. This means, division can be thought of as a multiplication problem with a missing part. For instance, calculating $20 \div 10$ is the same as asking the following: "If there are 20 items in total with 10 in each group, how many are in each group?" Therefore, 20 is equal to ten times what value? This question is the same as asking, "If there are 20 items in total with 2 in each group, how many groups are there?" The answer to each question is 2.

In a division problem, a is known as the **dividend**, b is the **divisor**, and c is the **quotient**. Zero cannot be divided into parts. Therefore, for any nonzero whole number a, $0 \div a = 0$. Also, division by zero is undefined. Dividing an amount into zero parts is not possible.

More difficult division problems involve dividing a number into equal parts, but having some left over. An example is dividing a pack of 20 pencils among 8 friends so that each friend receives the same number of pencils. In this setting, each friend receives 2 pencils, but there are 4 pencils leftover. 20 is the dividend, 8 is the divisor, 2 is the quotient, and 4 is known as the **remainder**. Within this type of division problem, for whole numbers a, b, c, and d, $a \div b = c$ with a remainder of d. This is true if and only if $a = (b \times c) + d$. When calculating $a \div b$, if there is no remainder, a is said to be *divisible* by b. **Even numbers** are all divisible by the number 2. **Odd numbers** are not divisible by 2. An odd number of items cannot be paired up into groups of 2 without having one item leftover.

Dividing a number by a single digit or two digits can be turned into repeated subtraction problems. An area model can be used throughout the problem that represents multiples of the divisor. For example, the answer to $8580 \div 55$ can be found by subtracting 55 from 8,580 one at a time and counting the total number of subtractions necessary. However, a simpler process involves using larger multiples of 55. First, $100 \times 55 = 5,500$ is subtracted from 8,580, and 3,080 is leftover. Next, $50 \times 55 = 2,750$ is subtracted from 3,080 to obtain 380. $5 \times 55 = 275$ is subtracted from 330 to obtain 55, and finally, $1 \times 55 = 55$ is subtracted from 55 to obtain zero. Therefore, there is no remainder, and the answer is:

$$100 + 50 + 5 + 1 = 156$$

Here is a picture of the area model and the repeated subtraction process:

$$8580 \div 55$$

	55
100	5500
50	2750
5	275
1	55

```
55 ) 8580
    -5500   (100 x 55)
     3080
    -2750   (50 x 55)
      330
     -275   (5 x 55)
       55
      -55   (1 x 55)
        0
```

If you want to check the answer of a division problem, multiply the answer by the divisor. This will help you check to see if the dividend is obtained. If there is a remainder, the same process is done, but the remainder is added on at the end to try to match the dividend. In the previous example, $156 \times 55 = 8,580$ would be the checking procedure. Dividing decimals involves the same repeated subtraction process. The only difference would be that the subtractions would involve numbers that include values in the decimal places. Lining up decimal places is crucial in this type of problem.

Order of Operations

When reviewing calculations consisting of more than one operation, the order in which the operations are performed affects the resulting answer. Consider $5 \times 2 + 7$. Performing multiplication then addition results in an answer of 17 because ($5 \times 2 = 10$; $10 + 7 = 17$). However, if the problem is written $5 \times (2 + 7)$, the order of operations dictates that the operation inside the parentheses must be performed first. The resulting answer is 45:

$$2 + 7 = 9$$
$$5 \times 9 = 45$$

The order in which operations should be performed is remembered using the acronym PEMDAS. PEMDAS stands for parentheses, exponents, multiplication/division, addition/subtraction. Multiplication and division are performed in the same step, working from left to right with whichever comes first. Addition and subtraction are performed in the same step, working from left to right with whichever comes first.

Consider the following example:

$$8 \div 4 + 8(7 - 7)$$

Performing the operation inside the parentheses produces $8 \div 4 + 8(0)$ or $8 \div 4 + 8 \times 0$. There are no exponents, so multiplication and division are performed next from left to right resulting in: $2 + 8 \times 0$, then $2 + 0$. Finally, addition and subtraction are performed to obtain an answer of 2. Now consider the following example: $6 \times 3 + 3^2 - 6$. Parentheses are not applicable. Exponents are evaluated first, which brings us to $6 \times 3 + 9 - 6$. Then multiplication/division forms $18 + 9 - 6$. At last, addition/subtraction leads to the final answer of 21.

Fractions

A **fraction** is a part of something that is whole. Items such as apples can be cut into parts to help visualize fractions. If an apple is cut into 2 equal parts, each part represents ½ of the apple. If each half is then cut into two parts, the apple now is cut into quarters. Each piece now represents ¼ of the apple. In this example, each part is equal because they all have the same size. Geometric shapes, such as circles and squares, can also be utilized to help visualize the idea of fractions. For example, a circle can be drawn on the board and divided into 6 equal parts:

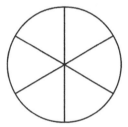

Shading can be used to represent parts of the circle that can be translated into fractions. The top of the fraction, the **numerator,** can represent how many segments are shaded. The bottom of the fraction, the **denominator,** can represent the number of segments that the circle is broken into. A pie is a good analogy to use in this example. If one piece of the circle is shaded, or one piece of pie is cut out, $\frac{1}{6}$ of the object is being referred to. An apple, a pie, or a circle can be utilized in order to compare simple fractions. For example, showing that $\frac{1}{2}$ is larger than $\frac{1}{4}$ and that $\frac{1}{4}$ is smaller than $\frac{1}{3}$ can be accomplished through shading. A **unit fraction** is a fraction in which the numerator is 1, and the denominator is a positive whole number. It represents one part of a whole—one piece of pie.

Imagine that an apple pie has been baked for a holiday party, and the full pie has eight slices. After the party, there are five slices left. How could the amount of the pie that remains be expressed as a fraction? The numerator is 5 since there are 5 pieces left, and the denominator is 8 since there were eight total slices in the whole pie. Thus, expressed as a fraction, the leftover pie totals $\frac{5}{8}$ of the original amount.

Fractions come in three different varieties: proper fractions, improper fractions, and mixed numbers. **Proper fractions** have a numerator less than the denominator, such as $\frac{3}{8}$, but **improper fractions** have a numerator greater than the denominator, such as $\frac{7}{2}$. **Mixed numbers** combine a whole number with a proper fraction, such as $3\frac{1}{2}$. Any

mixed number can be written as an improper fraction by multiplying the integer by the denominator, adding the product to the value of the numerator, and dividing the sum by the original denominator. For example:

$$3\frac{1}{2} = \frac{3 \times 2 + 1}{2} = \frac{7}{2}$$

Whole numbers can also be converted into fractions by placing the whole number as the numerator and making the denominator 1. For example, $3 = \frac{3}{1}$.

The bar in a fraction represents division. Therefore $\frac{6}{5}$ is the same as $6 \div 5$. In order to rewrite it as a mixed number, division is performed to obtain $6 \div 5 = 1 \text{ R } 1$. The remainder is then converted into fraction form. The actual remainder becomes the numerator of a fraction, and the divisor becomes the denominator. Therefore, 1 R 1 is written as $1\frac{1}{5}$, a mixed number. A mixed number can also decompose into the addition of a whole number and a fraction. For example,

$$1\frac{1}{5} = 1 + \frac{1}{5} \text{ and } 4\frac{5}{6} = 4 + \frac{1}{6} + \frac{1}{6} + \frac{1}{6} + \frac{1}{6} + \frac{1}{6}$$

Every fraction can be built from a combination of unit fractions.

One of the most fundamental concepts of fractions is their ability to be manipulated by multiplication or division. This is possible since $\frac{n}{n} = 1$ for any non-zero integer. As a result, multiplying or dividing by $\frac{n}{n}$ will not alter the original fraction since any number multiplied or divided by 1 doesn't change the value of that number. Fractions of the same value are known as equivalent fractions. For example, $\frac{2}{8}, \frac{25}{100}$, and $\frac{40}{160}$ are equivalent, as they are all equal to $\frac{1}{4}$.

Like fractions, or **equivalent fractions**, are the terms used to describe these fractions that are made up of different numbers but represent the same quantity. For example, the given fractions are $\frac{4}{8}$ and $\frac{3}{6}$. If a pie was cut into 8 pieces and 4 pieces were removed, half of the pie would remain. Also, if a pie was split into 6 pieces and 3 pieces were eaten, half of the pie would also remain. Therefore, both of the fractions represent half of a pie. These two fractions are referred to as like fractions. **Unlike fractions** are fractions that are different and do not represent equal quantities. When working with fractions in mathematical expressions, like fractions should be simplified. Both $\frac{4}{8}$ and $\frac{3}{6}$ can be simplified into $\frac{1}{2}$.

Comparing fractions can be completed through the use of a number line. For example, if $\frac{3}{5}$ and $\frac{6}{10}$ need to be compared, each fraction should be plotted on a number line. To plot $\frac{3}{5}$, the area from 0 to 1 should be broken into 5 equal segments, and the fraction represents 3 of them. To plot $\frac{6}{10}$, the area from 0 to 1 should be broken into 10 equal segments, and the fraction represents 6 of them.

It can be seen that $\frac{3}{5} = \frac{6}{10}$:

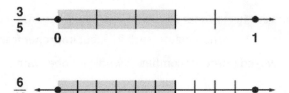

Like fractions are plotted at the same point on a number line. Unit fractions can also be used to compare fractions. For example, if it is known that $\frac{4}{5} > \frac{1}{2}$ and $\frac{1}{2} > \frac{4}{10}$, then it is also known that $\frac{4}{5} > \frac{4}{10}$.

Also, converting improper fractions to mixed numbers can be helpful in comparing fractions because the whole number portion of the number is more visible.

Adding and subtracting mixed numbers and fractions can be completed by decomposing fractions into a sum of whole numbers and unit fractions. For example, $5\frac{3}{7} + 2\frac{1}{7}$ decomposes into:

$$5 + \frac{1}{7} + \frac{1}{7} + \frac{1}{7} + 2 + \frac{1}{7}$$

This shows that the whole numbers can be added separately from the unit fractions. The answer is:

$$5 + 2 + \frac{1}{7} + \frac{1}{7} + \frac{1}{7} + \frac{1}{7} = 7 + \frac{4}{7} = 7\frac{4}{7}$$

Although many equivalent fractions exist, they are easier to compare and interpret when reduced or simplified. The numerator and denominator of a simple fraction will have no factors in common other than 1. When reducing or simplifying fractions, divide the numerator and denominator by the greatest common factor. A simple strategy is to divide the numerator and denominator by low numbers, like 2, 3, or 5 until arriving at a simple fraction, but the same thing could be achieved by determining the greatest common factor for both the numerator and denominator and dividing each by it. Using the first method is preferable when both the numerator and denominator are even, end in 5, or are obviously a multiple of another number. However, if no numbers seem to work, it will be necessary to factor the numerator and denominator to find the GCF. For example:

1) Simplify the fraction $\frac{6}{8}$:

Dividing the numerator and denominator by 2 results in $\frac{3}{4}$, which is a simple fraction.

2) Simplify the fraction $\frac{12}{36}$:

Dividing the numerator and denominator by 2 leaves $\frac{6}{18}$. This isn't a simple fraction, as both the numerator and denominator have factors in common. Dividing each by 3 results in $\frac{2}{6}$, but this can be further simplified by dividing by 2 to get $\frac{1}{3}$. This is the simplest fraction, as the numerator is 1. In cases like this, multiple division operations can be avoided by determining the greatest common factor (12, in this case) between the numerator and denominator.

3) Simplify the fraction $\frac{18}{54}$ by dividing by the greatest common factor:

First, determine the factors for the numerator and denominator. The factors of 18 are 1, 2, 3, 6, 9, and 18. The factors of 54 are 1, 2, 3, 6, 9, 18, 27, and 54. Thus, the greatest common factor is 18. Dividing $\frac{18}{54}$ by 18 leaves $\frac{1}{3}$, which is the simplest fraction. This method takes slightly more work, but it definitively arrives at the simplest fraction.

Adding and Subtracting Fractions
Adding and subtracting fractions that have the same denominators involves adding or subtracting the numerators. The denominator will stay the same. Therefore, the decomposition process can be made simpler, and the fractions do not have to be broken into unit fractions.

For example, the given problem is:

$$4\frac{7}{8} - 2\frac{6}{8}$$

The answer is found by adding the answers to both $4 - 2$ and $\frac{7}{8} - \frac{6}{8}$:

$$2 + \frac{1}{8} = 2\frac{1}{8}$$

A common mistake would be to add the denominators so that $\frac{1}{4} + \frac{1}{4} = \frac{1}{8}$ or to add numerators and denominators so that $\frac{1}{4} + \frac{1}{4} = \frac{2}{8}$. However, conceptually, it is known that two quarters make a half, so neither one of these are correct.

If two fractions have different denominators, equivalent fractions must be used to add or subtract them. The fractions must be converted into fractions that have common denominators. A **least common denominator** or the product of the two denominators can be used as the common denominator.

For example, in the problem $\frac{5}{6} + \frac{2}{3}$, either 6, which is the least common denominator, or 18, which is the product of the denominators, can be used. In order to use 6, $\frac{2}{3}$ must be converted to sixths. A number line can be used to show the equivalent fraction is $\frac{4}{6}$. What happens is that $\frac{2}{3}$ is multiplied by a fractional form of 1 to obtain a denominator of 6. Hence:

$$\frac{2}{3} \times \frac{2}{2} = \frac{4}{6}$$

Therefore, the problem is now $\frac{5}{6} + \frac{4}{6} = \frac{9}{6}$, which can be simplified into $\frac{3}{2}$. In order to use 18, both fractions must be converted into having 18 as their denominator. $\frac{5}{6}$ would have to be multiplied by $\frac{3}{3}$, and $\frac{2}{3}$ would need to be multiplied by $\frac{6}{6}$. The addition problem would be $\frac{15}{18} + \frac{12}{18} = \frac{27}{18}$, which reduces into $\frac{3}{2}$.

It is always possible to find a common denominator by multiplying the denominators. However, when the denominators are large numbers, this method is unwieldy, especially if the answer must be provided in its simplest form. Thus, it's beneficial to find the **least common denominator** of the fractions—the least common denominator is incidentally also the **least common multiple**.

Once equivalent fractions have been found with common denominators, simply add or subtract the numerators to arrive at the answer:

1) $\frac{1}{2} + \frac{3}{4} = \frac{2}{4} + \frac{3}{4} = \frac{5}{4}$

2) $\frac{3}{12} + \frac{11}{20} = \frac{15}{60} + \frac{33}{60} = \frac{48}{60} = \frac{4}{5}$

3) $\frac{7}{9} - \frac{4}{15} = \frac{35}{45} - \frac{12}{45} = \frac{23}{45}$

4) $\frac{5}{6} - \frac{7}{18} = \frac{15}{18} - \frac{7}{18} = \frac{8}{18} = \frac{4}{9}$

Multiplying and Dividing Fractions

Of the four basic operations that can be performed on fractions, the one that involves the least amount of work is multiplication. To multiply two fractions, simply multiply the numerators together, multiply the denominators together, and place the products of each as a fraction. Whole numbers and mixed numbers can also be expressed as a fraction, as described above, to multiply with a fraction.

Because multiplication is commutative, multiplying a fraction by a whole number is the same as multiplying a whole number by a fraction. The problem involves adding a fraction a specific number of times. The problem $3 \times \frac{1}{4}$ can be translated into adding the unit fraction three times:

$$\frac{1}{4} + \frac{1}{4} + \frac{1}{4} = \frac{3}{4}$$

In the problem $4 \times \frac{2}{5}$, the fraction can be decomposed into $\frac{1}{5} + \frac{1}{5}$ and then added four times to obtain $\frac{8}{5}$. Also, both of these answers can be found by just multiplying the whole number by the numerator of the fraction being multiplied.

The whole numbers can be written in fraction form as:

$$\frac{3}{1} \times \frac{1}{4} = \frac{3}{4}$$

$$\frac{4}{1} \times \frac{2}{5} = \frac{8}{5}$$

Multiplying a fraction by a fraction involves multiplying the numerators together separately and the denominators together separately. For example,

$$\frac{3}{8} \times \frac{2}{3} = \frac{3 \times 2}{8 \times 3} = \frac{6}{24}$$

This can then be reduced to $\frac{1}{4}$.

Dividing a fraction by a fraction is actually a multiplication problem. It involves flipping the divisor and then multiplying normally. For example,

$$\frac{22}{5} \div \frac{1}{2} = \frac{22}{5} \times \frac{2}{1} = \frac{44}{5}$$

The same procedure can be implemented for division problems involving fractions and whole numbers. The whole number can be rewritten as a fraction over a denominator of 1, and then division can be completed.

A common denominator approach can also be used in dividing fractions. Considering the same problem, $\frac{22}{5} \div \frac{1}{2}$, a common denominator between the two fractions is 10. $\frac{22}{5}$ would be rewritten as $\frac{22}{5} \times \frac{2}{2} = \frac{44}{10}$, and $\frac{1}{2}$ would be rewritten as:

$$\frac{1}{2} \times \frac{5}{5} = \frac{5}{10}$$

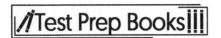

Dividing both numbers straight across results in:

$$\frac{44}{10} \div \frac{5}{10} = \frac{44/5}{10/10} = \frac{44/5}{1} = \frac{44}{5}$$

Many real-world problems will involve the use of fractions. Key words include actual fraction values, such as *half, quarter, third, fourth*, etc. The best approach to solving word problems involving fractions is to draw a picture or diagram that represents the scenario being discussed, while deciding which type of operation is necessary in order to solve the problem. A phrase such as "one fourth of 60 pounds of coal" creates a scenario in which multiplication should be used, and the mathematical form of the phrase is $\frac{1}{4} \times 60$.

Decimals

The **decimal system** is a way of writing out numbers that uses ten different numerals: 0, 1, 2, 3, 4, 5, 6, 7, 8, and 9. This is also called a "base ten" or "base 10" system. Other bases are also used. For example, computers work with a base of 2. This means they only use the numerals 0 and 1.

The **decimal place** denotes how far to the right of the decimal point a numeral is. The first digit to the right of the decimal point is in the **tenths'** place. The next is the **hundredths'** place. The third is the **thousandths'** place.

So, 3.142 has a 1 in the tenths place, a 4 in the hundredths place, and a 2 in the thousandths place.

The **decimal point** is a period used to separate the **ones'** place from the **tenths'** place when writing out a number as a decimal.

A **decimal number** is a number written out with a decimal point instead of as a fraction, for example, 1.25 instead of $\frac{5}{4}$. Depending on the situation, it may be easier to work with fractions, while other times, it may be easier to work with decimal numbers.

A decimal number is **terminating** if it stops at some point. It is called **repeating** if it never stops but repeats over and over. It is important to note that every rational number can be written as a terminating decimal or as a repeating decimal.

Addition with Decimals

To add decimal numbers, each number needs to be lined up by the decimal point in vertical columns. For each number being added, the zeros to the right of the last number need to be filled in so that each of the numbers has the same number of places to the right of the decimal. Then, the columns can be added together. Here is an example of $2.45 + 1.3 + 8.891$ written in column form:

$$\begin{array}{r} 2.450 \\ 1.300 \\ + \, 8.891 \end{array}$$

Zeros have been added in the columns so that each number has the same number of places to the right of the decimal.

Added together, the correct answer is 12.641:

$$\begin{array}{r} 2.450 \\ 1.300 \\ + \, 8.891 \\ \hline 12.641 \end{array}$$

Subtraction with Decimals

Subtracting decimal numbers is the same process as adding decimals. Here is 7.89 − 4.235 written in column form:

$$\begin{array}{r} 7.890 \\ -\ 4.235 \\ \hline 3.655 \end{array}$$

A zero has been added in the column so that each number has the same number of places to the right of the decimal.

Multiplication with Decimals

The simplest way to multiply decimals is to calculate the product as if the decimals are not there, then count the number of decimal places in the original problem. Use that total to place the decimal the same number of places over in your answer, counting from right to left. For example, 0.5×1.25 can be rewritten and multiplied as 5×125, which equals 625. Then the decimal is added three places from the right for 0.625.

The final answer will have the same number of decimal places as the total number of decimal places in the problem. The first number has one decimal place, and the second number has two decimal places. Therefore, the final answer will contain three decimal places:

$$0.5 \times 1.25 = 0.625$$

Division with Decimals

Dividing a decimal by a whole number entails using long division first by ignoring the decimal point. Then, the decimal point is moved the number of places given in the problem.

For example, $6.8 \div 4$ can be rewritten as $68 \div 4$, which is 17. There is one non-zero integer to the right of the decimal point, so the final solution would have one decimal place to the right of the solution. In this case, the solution is 1.7.

Dividing a decimal by another decimal requires changing the divisor to a whole number by moving its decimal point. The decimal place of the dividend should be moved by the same number of places as the divisor. Then, the problem is the same as dividing a decimal by a whole number.

For example, $5.72 \div 1.1$ has a divisor with one decimal point in the denominator. The expression can be rewritten as $57.2 \div 11$ by moving each number one decimal place to the right to eliminate the decimal. The long division can be completed as $572 \div 11$ with a result of 52. Since there is one non-zero integer to the right of the decimal point in the problem, the final solution is 5.2.

In another example, $8 \div 0.16$ has a divisor with two decimal points in the denominator. The expression can be rewritten as $800 \div 16$ by moving each number two decimal places to the right to eliminate the decimal in the divisor. The long division can be completed with a result of 50.

Conversions

Changing Fractions to Decimals

To change a fraction into a decimal, divide the denominator into the numerator until there are no remainders. There may be repeating decimals, so rounding is often acceptable. A straight line above the repeating portion denotes that the decimal repeats.

Example: Express $\frac{4}{5}$ as a decimal.

Set up the division problem.

$$5\overline{)4}$$

5 does not go into 4, so place the decimal and add a zero.

$$5\overline{)4\,.\,0}$$

5 goes into 40 eight times. There is no remainder.

$$\begin{array}{r} 0\,.\,8 \\ 5\overline{)4\,.\,0} \\ -\ 4\,.\,0 \\ \hline 0 \end{array}$$

The solution is 0.8.

Example: Express $\frac{1}{3}$ as a decimal.

Since the whole portion of the number is known, set it aside to calculate the decimal from the fraction portion.

Set up the division problem.

$$3\overline{)1}$$

3 does not go into 1, so place the decimal and add zeros. 3 goes into 10 three times.

$$\begin{array}{r} 0\,.\,3 \\ 3\overline{)1\,.\,0} \end{array}$$

This will repeat with a remainder of 1.

$$\begin{array}{r} 0\,.\,3\,3\,3 \\ 3\overline{)1\,.\,0\,0\,0} \\ -9 \\ \hline 1\,0 \\ -\ 9 \\ \hline 1\,0 \end{array}$$

So, we will place a line over the 3 to denote the repetition. The solution is written $0.\overline{3}$.

Changing Decimals to Fractions
To change decimals to fractions, place the decimal portion of the number—the numerator—over the respective place value—the denominator—then reduce, if possible.

Example: Express 0.25 as a fraction.

This is read as twenty-five hundredths, so put 25 over 100. Then reduce to find the solution.

$$\frac{25}{100} = \frac{1}{4}$$

Example: Express 0.455 as a fraction

110

This is read as four hundred fifty-five thousandths, so put 455 over 1,000. Then reduce to find the solution.

$$\frac{455}{1,000} = \frac{91}{200}$$

There are two types of problems that commonly involve percentages. The first is to calculate some percentage of a given quantity, where you convert the percentage to a decimal, and multiply the quantity by that decimal. Secondly, you are given a quantity and told it is a fixed percent of an unknown quantity. In this case, convert to a decimal, then divide the given quantity by that decimal.

Example: What is 30% of 760?

Convert the percent into a useable number. "Of" means to multiply.

$$30\% = 0.30$$

Set up the problem based on the givens, and solve.

$$0.30 \times 760 = 228$$

Example: 8.4 is 20% of what number?

Convert the percent into a useable number.

$$20\% = 0.20$$

The given number is a percent of the answer needed, so divide the given number by this decimal rather than multiplying it.

$$\frac{8.4}{0.20} = 42$$

Radicals and Exponents

Exponents are used in mathematics to express a number or variable multiplied by itself a certain number of times. For example, x^3 means x is multiplied by itself three times. In this expression, x is called the **base**, and 3 is the **exponent**. Exponents can be used in more complex problems when they contain fractions and negative numbers.

Fractional exponents can be explained by looking first at the inverse of exponents, which are **roots**. Given the expression x^2, the square root can be taken, $\sqrt{x^2}$, cancelling out the 2 and leaving x by itself, if x is positive. Cancellation occurs because $\sqrt{x}$ can be written with exponents, instead of roots, as $x^{\frac{1}{2}}$. The numerator of 1 is the exponent, and the denominator of 2 is called the root (which is why it's referred to as **square root**). Taking the square root of x^2 is the same as raising it to the $\frac{1}{2}$ power. Written out in mathematical form, it takes the following progression:

$$\sqrt{x^2} = (x^2)^{\frac{1}{2}} = x$$

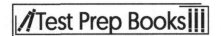

From properties of exponents, $2 \times \frac{1}{2} = 1$ is the actual exponent of x. Another example can be seen with $x^{\frac{4}{7}}$. The variable x, raised to four-sevenths, is equal to the seventh root of x to the fourth power: $\sqrt[7]{x^4}$. In general,

$$x^{\frac{1}{n}} = \sqrt[n]{x}$$

and

$$x^{\frac{m}{n}} = \sqrt[n]{x^m}$$

Negative exponents also involve fractions. Whereas y^3 can also be rewritten as $\frac{y^3}{1}$, y^{-3} can be rewritten as $\frac{1}{y^3}$. A negative exponent means the exponential expression must be moved to the opposite spot in a fraction to make the exponent positive. If the negative appears in the numerator, it moves to the denominator. If the negative appears in the denominator, it is moved to the numerator. In general, $a^{-n} = \frac{1}{a^n}$, and a^{-n} and a^n are reciprocals.

Take, for example, the following expression:

$$\frac{a^{-4}b^2}{c^{-5}}$$

Since a is raised to the negative fourth power, it can be moved to the denominator. Since c is raised to the negative fifth power, it can be moved to the numerator. The b variable is raised to the positive second power, so it does not move.

The simplified expression is as follows:

$$\frac{b^2 c^5}{a^4}$$

In mathematical expressions containing exponents and other operations, the order of operations must be followed. PEMDAS states that exponents are calculated after any parentheses and grouping symbols, but before any multiplication, division, addition, and subtraction.

There are a few rules for working with exponents. For any numbers a, b, m, n, the following hold true:

$$a^1 = a$$

$$1^a = 1$$

$$a^0 = 1$$

$$a^m \times a^n = a^{m+n}$$

$$a^m \div a^n = a^{m-n}$$

$$(a^m)^n = a^{m \times n}$$

$$(a \times b)^m = a^m \times b^m$$

$$(a \div b)^m = a^m \div b^m$$

Any number, including a fraction, can be an exponent. The same rules apply.

A **root** is a different way to write an exponent when the exponent is the reciprocal of a whole number. We use the **radical** symbol to write this in the following way:

$$\sqrt[n]{a} = a^{\frac{1}{n}}$$

This quantity is called the nth *root* of a. The n is called the **index** of the radical.

Note that if the nth root of a is multiplied by itself n times, the result will just be a. If no number n is written by the radical, it is assumed that n is 2:

$$\sqrt{5} = 5^{\frac{1}{2}}$$

The special case of the 2nd root is called the **square root**, and the third root is called the **cube root**.

A **perfect square** is a whole number that is the square of another whole number. For example, sixteen and 64 are perfect squares because 16 is the square of 4, and 64 is the square of 8.

Solving Problems Involving Ratios and Proportions

Ratios are used to show the relationship between two quantities. The ratio of oranges to apples in the grocery store may be 3 to 2. That means that for every 3 oranges, there are 2 apples. This comparison can be expanded to represent the actual number of oranges and apples, such as 36 oranges to 24 apples. Another example may be the number of boys to girls in a math class. If the ratio of boys to girls is given as 2 to 5, that means there are 2 boys to every 5 girls in the class. Ratios can also be compared if the units in each ratio are the same. The ratio of boys to girls in the math class can be compared to the ratio of boys to girls in a science class by stating which ratio is higher and which is lower.

The ratio between two similar geometric figures is called the **scale factor**. For example, a problem may depict two similar triangles, A and B. The scale factor from the smaller triangle A to the larger triangle B is given as 2 because the length of the corresponding side of the larger triangle, 16, is twice the corresponding side on the smaller triangle, 8. This scale factor can also be used to find the value of a missing side, x, in triangle A. Since the scale factor from the smaller triangle (A) to larger one (B) is 2, the larger corresponding side in triangle B (given as 25) can be divided by 2 to find the missing side in A ($x = 12.5$). The scale factor can also be represented in the equation $2A = B$ because two times the lengths of A gives the corresponding lengths of B. This is the idea behind similar triangles.

A **proportion** is a statement consisting of two equal ratios. Proportions will typically give three of four quantities and require solving for the missing value. The key to solving proportions is to set them up properly. Here's a sample problem:

If 7 gallons of gas costs $14.70, how many gallons can you get for $20?

The information should be written as equal ratios with a variable representing the missing quantity:

$$\left(\frac{\text{gallons}}{\text{cost}} = \frac{\text{gallons}}{\text{cost}}\right) : \frac{7 \text{ gallons}}{\$14.70} = \frac{x}{\$20}$$

To solve, cross-multiply (multiply the numerator of the first ratio by the denominator of the second and vice versa) is used, and the products are set equal to each other. Cross-multiplying results in:

$$(7)(20) = (14.7)(x)$$

113

After solving the equation for x, it can be determined that 9.5 gallons of gas can be purchased for $20.

For **direct proportions**, as one quantity increases, the other quantity also increases. For **indirect proportions** (also referred to as indirect variations, inverse proportions, or inverse variations), as one quantity increases, the other decreases. Direct proportions can be written:

$$\frac{y_1}{x_1} = \frac{y_2}{x_2}$$

Conversely, indirect proportions are written:

$$y_1 x_1 = y_2 x_2$$

Here's a sample problem:

It takes 3 carpenters 10 days to build the frame of a house. How long should it take 5 carpenters to build the same frame?

In this scenario, as one quantity increases (number of carpenters), the other decreases (number of days building); therefore, this is an inverse proportion. To solve, the products of the two variables (in this scenario, the total work performed) are set equal to each other ($y_1 x_1 = y_2 x_2$). Using y to represent carpenters and x to represent days, the resulting equation is:

$$(3)(10) = (5)(x_2)$$

Solving for x_2, it is determined that it should take 5 carpenters 6 days to build the frame of the house.

Much like a scale factor can be written using an equation like $2A = B$, a **relationship** is represented by the equation $Y = kX$. X and Y are proportional because as values of X increase, the values of Y also increase. A relationship that is inversely proportional can be represented by the equation $Y = \frac{k}{X}$, where the value of Y decreases as the value of X increases and vice versa.

Proportional reasoning can be used to solve problems involving ratios, percentages, and averages. Ratios can be used in setting up proportions and solving them to find unknowns. For example, if a student completes an average of 10 pages of math homework in 3 nights, how long would it take the student to complete 22 pages? Both ratios can be written as fractions. The second ratio would contain the unknown.

The following proportion represents this problem, where x is the unknown number of nights:

$$\frac{10 \text{ pages}}{3 \text{ nights}} = \frac{22 \text{ pages}}{x \text{ nights}}$$

Solving this proportion entails cross-multiplying and results in the following equation: $10x = 22 \times 3$. Simplifying and solving for x results in the exact solution: $x = 6.6$ nights. The result would be rounded up to 7 because the homework would actually be completed on the 7th night.

The following problem uses ratios involving percentages:

If 20% of the class is girls and 30 students are in the class, how many girls are in the class?

To set up this problem, it is helpful to use the common proportion:

$$\frac{\%}{100} = \frac{is}{of}$$

Within the proportion, % is the percentage of girls, 100 is the total percentage of the class, *is* is the number of girls, and *of* is the total number of students in the class. Most percentage problems can be written using this language. To solve this problem, the proportion should be set up as $\frac{20}{100} = \frac{x}{30}$, and then solved for x. Cross-multiplying results in the equation $20 \times 30 = 100x$, which results in the solution $x = 6$. There are 6 girls in the class.

Ratios can be used to solve problems that concern length, volume, and other units. For example, a problem may ask for the volume of a cone to be found that has a radius, $r = 7$ m and a height, $h = 16$ m. Referring to the formulas provided on the test, the volume of a cone is given as: $V = \pi r^2 \frac{h}{3}$, where r is the radius, and h is the height. Plugging $r = 7$ and $h = 16$ into the formula, the following is obtained:

$$V = \pi(7^2)\frac{16}{3}$$

Therefore, the volume of the cone is found to be approximately 821 m³. Sometimes, answers in different units are sought. If this problem wanted the answer in liters, 821 m³ would need to be converted. Using the equivalence statement 1 m³ = 1,000 L, the following ratio would be used to solve for liters:

$$821 \text{ m}^3 \times \frac{1,000 \text{ L}}{1 \text{ m}^3}$$

Cubic meters in the numerator and denominator cancel each other out, and the answer is converted to 821,000 liters, or 8.21×10^5 L.

Other conversions can also be made between different given and final units. If the temperature in a pool is 30°C, what is the temperature of the pool in degrees Fahrenheit? To convert these units, an equation is used relating Celsius to Fahrenheit. The following equation is used:

$$T_{°F} = 1.8 T_{°C} + 32$$

Plugging in the given temperature and solving the equation for T yields the result:

$$T_{°F} = 1.8(30) + 32 = 86°F$$

Units in both the metric system and U.S. customary system are widely used.

Here are some more examples of how to solve for proportions:

1) $\frac{75\%}{90\%} = \frac{25\%}{x}$

To solve for x, the fractions must be cross multiplied:

$$(75\% x = 90\% \times 25\%)$$

To make things easier, let's convert the percentages to decimals:

$$(0.9 \times 0.25 = 0.225 = 0.75x)$$

To get rid of x's coefficient, each side must be divided by that same coefficient to get the answer:

$$x = 0.3$$

The question could ask for the answer as a percentage or fraction in lowest terms, which are 30% and $\frac{3}{10}$, respectively.

2) $\frac{x}{12} = \frac{30}{96}$

Cross-multiply: $96x = 30 \times 12$

Multiply: $96x = 360$

Divide: $x = 360 \div 96$

Answer: $x = 3.75$

3) $\frac{0.5}{3} = \frac{x}{6}$

Cross-multiply: $3x = 0.5 \times 6$

Multiply: $3x = 3$

Divide: $x = 3 \div 3$

Answer: $x = 1$

You may have noticed there's a faster way to arrive at the answer. If there is an obvious operation being performed on the proportion, the same operation can be used on the other side of the proportion to solve for x. For example, in the first practice problem, 75% became 25% when divided by 3, and upon doing the same to 90%, the correct answer of 30% would have been found with much less legwork. However, these questions aren't always so intuitive, so it's a good idea to work through the steps, even if the answer seems apparent from the outset.

Solving Problems Involving Percent

Think of percentages as fractions with a denominator of 100. In fact, **percentage** means "per hundred." Problems often require converting numbers from percentages, fractions, and decimals.

The basic percent equation is the following:

$$\frac{is}{of} = \frac{\%}{100}$$

The placement of numbers in the equation depends on what the question asks.

Example 1
Find 40% of 80.

Basically, the problem is asking, "What is 40% of 80?" The 40% is the percent, and 80 is the number to find the percent "of." The equation is:

$$\frac{x}{80} = \frac{40}{100}$$

After cross-multiplying, the problem becomes $100x = 80(40)$. Solving for x produces the answer: $x = 32$.

This material is provided for exam preparation purposes only and does not indicate an endorsement of any specific scientific, political, or religious point of view. © TPB Publishing. You have been licensed one copy of this document for personal use only. Any other reproduction or redistribution is strictly prohibited. All rights reserved.

Example 2
What percent of 90 is 20?

The 20 fills in the "is" portion, while 90 fills in the "of." The question asks for the percent, so that will be x, the unknown. The following equation is set up:

$$\frac{20}{90} = \frac{x}{100}$$

Cross-multiplying yields the equation $90x = 20(100)$. Solving for x gives the answer: 22.2%.

Example 3
30% of what number is 30?

The following equation uses the clues and numbers in the problem:

$$\frac{30}{x} = \frac{30}{100}$$

Cross-multiplying results in the equation $30(100) = 30x$. Solving for x gives the answer: $x = 100$.

Conversions
Decimals and Percentages
Since a percentage is based on "per hundred," decimals and percentages can be converted by multiplying or dividing by 100. Practically speaking, this always involves moving the decimal point two places to the right or left, depending on the conversion. To convert a percentage to a decimal, move the decimal point two places to the left and remove the % sign. To convert a decimal to a percentage, move the decimal point two places to the right and add a % sign. Here are some examples:

$$65\% = 0.65$$
$$0.33 = 33\%$$
$$0.215 = 21.5\%$$
$$99.99\% = 0.9999$$
$$500\% = 5.00$$
$$7.55 = 755\%$$

Fractions and Percentages
Remember that a percentage is a number per one hundred. So, a percentage can be converted to a fraction by making the number in the percentage the numerator and putting 100 as the denominator:

$$43\% = \frac{43}{100}$$
$$97\% = \frac{97}{100}$$

Note that the percent symbol (%) kind of looks like a 0, a 1, and another 0. So, think of a percentage like 54% as 54 over 100.

To convert a fraction to a percent, follow the same logic. If the fraction happens to have 100 in the denominator, you're in luck. Just take the numerator and add a percent symbol:

$$\frac{28}{100} = 28\%$$

117

Otherwise, divide the numerator by the denominator to get a decimal:

$$\frac{9}{12} = 0.75$$

Then convert the decimal to a percentage:

$$0.75 = 75\%$$

Another option is to make the denominator equal to 100. Be sure to multiply the numerator and the denominator by the same number. For example:

$$\frac{3}{20} \times \frac{5}{5} = \frac{15}{100}$$

$$\frac{15}{100} = 15\%$$

Solving Problems Involving Constant Rates

Rates are used to compare two quantities with different units. **Unit rates** are the simplest form of rate. With unit rates, the denominator in the comparison of two units is one. For example, if someone can type at a rate of 1,000 words in 5 minutes, then their unit rate for typing is $\frac{1,000}{5} = 200$ words in one minute or 200 words per minute. Any rate can be converted into a unit rate by dividing to make the denominator one. 1,000 words in 5 minutes has been converted into the unit rate of 200 words per minute.

Ratios and rates can be used together to convert rates into different units. For example, if someone is driving 50 kilometers per hour, that rate can be converted into miles per hour by using a ratio known as the **conversion factor**. Since the given value contains kilometers and the final answer needs to be in miles, the ratio relating miles to kilometers needs to be used. There are 0.62 miles in 1 kilometer. This, written as a ratio and in fraction form, is:

$$\frac{0.62 \text{ miles}}{1 \text{ km}}$$

To convert 50km/hour into miles per hour, the following conversion needs to be set up:

$$\frac{50 \text{ km}}{\text{hour}} \times \frac{0.62 \text{ miles}}{1 \text{ km}} = 31 \text{ miles per hour}$$

Unit rate word problems will ask to calculate the rate or quantity of something in a different value. For example, a problem might say that a car drove a certain number of miles in a certain number of minutes and then ask how many miles per hour the car was traveling. These questions involve solving proportions. Consider the following examples:

1) Alexandra made $96 during the first 3 hours of her shift as a temporary worker at a law office. She will continue to earn money at this rate until she finishes in 5 more hours. How much does Alexandra make per hour? How much will Alexandra have made at the end of the day?

This problem can be solved in two ways. The first is to set up a proportion, as the rate of pay is constant. The second is to determine her hourly rate, multiply the 5 hours by that rate, and then add the $96.

To set up a proportion, put the money already earned over the hours already worked on one side of an equation. The other side has x over 8 hours (the total hours worked in the day). It looks like this:

$$\frac{96}{3} = \frac{x}{8}$$

Now, cross-multiply to get $768 = 3x$. To get x, divide by 3, which leaves $x = 256$. Alternatively, as x is the numerator of one of the proportions, multiplying by its denominator will reduce the solution by one step. Thus, Alexandra will make $256 at the end of the day. To calculate her hourly rate, divide the total by 8, giving $32 per hour.

Alternatively, it is possible to figure out the hourly rate by dividing $96 by 3 hours to get $32 per hour. Now her total pay can be figured by multiplying $32 per hour by 8 hours, which comes out to $256.

2) Jonathan is reading a novel. So far, he has read 215 of the 335 total pages. It takes Jonathan 25 minutes to read 10 pages, and the rate is constant. How long does it take Jonathan to read one page? How much longer will it take him to finish the novel? Express the answer in time.

To calculate how long it takes Jonathan to read one page, divide the 25 minutes by 10 pages to determine the page per minute rate. Thus, it takes 2.5 minutes to read one page.

Jonathan must read 120 more pages to complete the novel. (This is calculated by subtracting the pages already read from the total.) Now, multiply his rate per page by the number of pages. Thus, $120 \times 2.5 = 300$. Expressed in time, 300 minutes is equal to 5 hours.

3) At a hotel, $\frac{4}{5}$ of the 120 rooms are booked for Saturday. On Sunday, $\frac{3}{4}$ of the rooms are booked. On which day are more of the rooms booked, and by how many more?

The first step is to calculate the number of rooms booked for each day. Do this by multiplying the fraction of the rooms booked by the total number of rooms.

Saturday: $\frac{4}{5} \times 120 = \frac{4}{5} \times \frac{120}{1} = \frac{480}{5} = 96$ rooms

Sunday: $\frac{3}{4} \times 120 = \frac{3}{4} \times \frac{120}{1} = \frac{360}{4} = 90$ rooms

Thus, more rooms were booked on Saturday by 6 rooms.

4) In a veterinary hospital, the veterinarian-to-pet ratio is 1:9. The ratio is always constant. If there are 45 pets in the hospital, how many veterinarians are currently in the veterinary hospital?

Set up a proportion to solve for the number of veterinarians: $\frac{1}{9} = \frac{x}{45}$

Cross-multiplying results in $9x = 45$, which works out to 5 veterinarians.

Alternatively, as there are always 9 times as many pets as veterinarians, it is possible to divide the number of pets (45) by 9. This also arrives at the correct answer of 5 veterinarians.

5) At a general practice law firm, 30% of the lawyers work solely on tort cases. If 9 lawyers work solely on tort cases, how many lawyers work at the firm?

First, solve for the total number of lawyers working at the firm, which will be represented here with x. The problem states that 9 lawyers work solely on torts cases, and they make up 30% of the total lawyers at the firm. Thus, 30% multiplied by the total, x, will equal 9. Written as equation, this is:

$$30\% \times x = 9$$

It's easier to deal with the equation after converting the percentage to a decimal, leaving $0.3x = 9$. Thus, $x = \frac{9}{0.3} = 30$ lawyers working at the firm.

6) Xavier was hospitalized with pneumonia. He was originally given 35mg of antibiotics. Later, after his condition continued to worsen, Xavier's dosage was increased to 60mg. What was the percent increase of the antibiotics? Round the percentage to the nearest tenth.

An increase or decrease in percentage can be calculated by dividing the difference in amounts by the original amount and multiplying by 100. Written as an equation, the formula is:

$$\frac{new\ quantity - old\ quantity}{old\ quantity} \times 100$$

Here, the question states that the dosage was increased from 35mg to 60mg, so these are plugged into the formula to find the percentage increase.

$$\frac{60 - 35}{35} \times 100 = \frac{25}{35} \times 100$$

$$0.7142 \times 100 = 71.4\%$$

Place Value, Naming Decimals, and Ordering Numbers

Structure of the Number System

The mathematical number system is made up of two general types of numbers: real and complex. **Real numbers** are both irrational and rational numbers, while **complex numbers** are those composed of both a real number and an imaginary one. Imaginary numbers are the result of taking the square root of -1, and $\sqrt{-1} = i$.

The real number system is often explained using a Venn diagram similar to the one below. After a number has been labeled as a real number, further classification occurs when considering the other groups in this diagram. If a number is a never-ending, non-repeating decimal, it falls in the irrational category. Otherwise, it is rational. More information on these types of numbers is provided in the previous section. Furthermore, if a number does not have a fractional part, it is classified as an integer, such as -2, 75, or zero. Whole numbers are an even smaller group that

120

only includes positive integers and zero. The last group of natural numbers is made up of only positive integers, such as 2, 56, or 12.

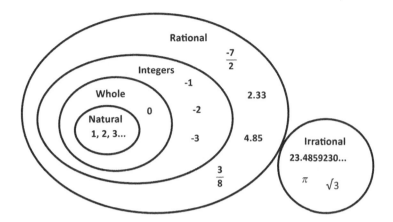

Real numbers can be compared and ordered using the number line. If a number falls to the left on the real number line, it is less than a number on the right. For example, $-2 < 5$ because -2 falls to the left of zero, and 5 falls to the right. Numbers to the left of zero are negative while those to the right are positive.

Complex numbers are made up of the sum of a real number and an imaginary number. Some examples of complex numbers include $6 + 2i$, $5 - 7i$, and $-3 + 12i$.

Adding and subtracting complex numbers is similar to collecting like terms. The real numbers are added together, and the imaginary numbers are added together.

For example, if the problem asks to simplify the expression $6 + 2i - 3 + 7i$, the 6 and (-3) are combined to make 3, and the $2i$ and $7i$ combine to make $9i$.

Multiplying and dividing complex numbers is similar to working with exponents. One rule to remember when multiplying is that:

$$i \times i = -1$$

For example, if a problem asks to simplify the expression $4i(3 + 7i)$, the $4i$ should be distributed throughout the 3 and the $7i$.

This leaves the final expression $12i - 28$.

The 28 is negative because $i \times i$ results in a negative number.

The last type of operation to consider with complex numbers is the conjugate. The **conjugate** of a complex number is a technique used to change the complex number into a real number.

For example, the conjugate of $4 - 3i$ is $4 + 3i$. Multiplying $(4 - 3i)(4 + 3i)$ results in $16 + 12i - 12i + 9$, which has a final answer of:

$$16 + 9 = 25$$

The order of operations—PEMDAS—simplifies longer expressions with real or imaginary numbers. Each operation is listed in the order of how they should be completed in a problem containing more than one operation. Parentheses can also mean grouping symbols, such as brackets and absolute value. Then, exponents are calculated. Multiplication and division should be completed from left to right, and addition and subtraction should be completed from left to right.

Simplification of another type of expression occurs when radicals are involved. Root is another word for radical. For example, the following expression is a radical that can be simplified: $\sqrt{24x^2}$. First, the number must be factored out to the highest perfect square. Any perfect square can be taken out of a radical. Twenty-four can be factored into 4 and 6, and 4 can be taken out of the radical. $\sqrt{4} = 2$ can be taken out, and 6 stays underneath. If $x > 0$, x can be taken out of the radical because it is a perfect square. The simplified radical is $2x\sqrt{6}$. An approximation can be found using a calculator.

There are also properties of numbers that are true for certain operations. The **commutative** property allows the order of the terms in an expression to change while keeping the same final answer. Both addition and multiplication can be completed in any order and still obtain the same result. However, order does matter in subtraction and division. The **associative** property allows any terms to be "associated" by parentheses and retain the same final answer.

For example,

$$(4 + 3) + 5 = 4 + (3 + 5)$$

Both addition and multiplication are associative; however, subtraction and division do not hold this property. The **distributive** property states that:

$$a(b + c) = ab + ac$$

It is a property that involves both addition and multiplication, and the a is distributed onto each term inside the parentheses.

Base-10 Numerals, Number Names, and Expanded Form
Numbers used in everyday life are constituted in a **base-10 system**. Each digit in a number, depending on its location, represents some multiple of 10, or quotient of 10 when dealing with decimals. Each digit to the left of the decimal point represents a higher multiple of 10. Each digit to the right of the decimal point represents a quotient of a higher multiple of 10 for the divisor. For example, consider the number 7,631.42. The digit one represents simply the number one. The digit 3 represents 3×10.

The digit 6 represents $6 \times 10 \times 10$ (or 6×100). The digit 7 represents $7 \times 10 \times 10 \times 10$ (or $7 \times 1,000$). The digit 4 represents $4 \div 10$. The digit 2 represents $(2 \div 10) \div 10$, or $2 \div (10 \times 10)$ or $2 \div 100$.

A number is written in **expanded form** by expressing it as the sum of the value of each of its digits. The expanded form in the example above, which is written with the highest value first down to the lowest value, is expressed as:
$$7,000 + 600 + 30 + 1 + 0.4 + 0.02$$

When verbally expressing a number, the integer part of the number (the numbers to the left of the decimal point) resembles the expanded form without the addition between values. In the above example, the numbers read "seven thousand six hundred thirty-one." When verbally expressing the decimal portion of a number, the number is read as a whole number, followed by the place value of the furthest digit (non-zero) to the right. In the above example, 0.42 is read "forty-two hundredths." Reading the number 7,631.42 in its entirety is expressed as "seven thousand six hundred thirty-one and forty-two hundredths." The word *and* is used between the integer and decimal parts of the number.

Composing and Decomposing Multi-Digit Numbers
Composing and decomposing numbers aids in conceptualizing what each digit of a multi-digit number represents. The standard, or typical, form in which numbers are written consists of a series of digits representing a given value

based on their place value. Consider the number 592.7. This number is composed of 5 hundreds, 9 tens, 2 ones, and 7 tenths.

Composing a number requires adding the given numbers for each place value and writing the numbers in standard form. For example, composing 4 thousands, 5 hundreds, 2 tens, and 8 ones consists of adding as follows: 4,000 + 500 + 20 + 8, to produce 4,528 (standard form).

Decomposing a number requires taking a number written in standard form and breaking it apart into the sum of each place value. For example, the number 83.17 is decomposed by breaking it into the sum of 4 values (for each of the 4 digits): 8 tens, 3 ones, 1 tenth, and 7 hundredths. The decomposed or "expanded" form of 83.17 is:

$$80 + 3 + 0.1 + 0.07$$

Place Value of a Given Digit

The number system that is used consists of only ten different digits or characters. However, this system is used to represent an infinite number of values. The place value system makes this infinite number of values possible. The position in which a digit is written corresponds to a given value. Starting from the decimal point (which is implied, if not physically present), each subsequent place value to the left represents a value greater than the one before it. Conversely, starting from the decimal point, each subsequent place value to the right represents a value less than the one before it.

The names for the place values to the left of the decimal point are as follows:

...	Billions	Hundred-Millions	Ten-Millions	Millions	Hundred-Thousands	Ten-Thousands	Thousands	Hundreds	Tens	Ones

*Note that this table can be extended infinitely further to the left.

The names for the place values to the right of the decimal point are as follows:

Decimal Point (.)	Tenths	Hundredths	Thousandths	Ten-Thousandths	...

*Note that this table can be extended infinitely further to the right.

When given a multi-digit number, the value of each digit depends on its place value. Consider the number 682,174.953. Referring to the chart above, it can be determined that the digit 8 is in the ten-thousands place. It is in the fifth place to the left of the decimal point. Its value is 8 ten-thousands or 80,000. The digit 5 is two places to the right of the decimal point. Therefore, the digit 5 is in the hundredths place. Its value is 5 hundredths or $\frac{5}{100}$ (equivalent to .05).

Value of Digits

In accordance with the base-10 system, the value of a digit increases by a factor of ten each place it moves to the left. For example, consider the number 7. Moving the digit one place to the left (70), increases its value by a factor of 10:

$$7 \times 10 = 70$$

Moving the digit two places to the left (700) increases its value by a factor of 10 twice ($7 \times 10 \times 10 = 700$). Moving the digit three places to the left (7,000) increases its value by a factor of 10 three times ($7 \times 10 \times 10 \times 10 = 7,000$), and so on.

Conversely, the value of a digit decreases by a factor of ten each place it moves to the right. (Note that multiplying by $\frac{1}{10}$ is equivalent to dividing by 10).

For example, consider the number 40. Moving the digit one place to the right (4) decreases its value by a factor of 10:

$$40 \div 10 = 4$$

Moving the digit two places to the right (0.4), decreases its value by a factor of 10 twice ($40 \div 10 \div 10 = 0.4$) or,

$$40 \times \frac{1}{10} \times \frac{1}{10} = 0.4$$

Moving the digit three places to the right (0.04) decreases its value by a factor of 10 three times ($40 \div 10 \div 10 \div 10 = 0.04$) or ($40 \times \frac{1}{10} \times \frac{1}{10} \times \frac{1}{10} = 0.04$), and so on.

Exponents to Denote Powers of 10
The value of a given digit of a number in the base-10 system can be expressed utilizing powers of 10. A power of 10 refers to 10 raised to a given exponent such as 10^0, 10^1, 10^2, 10^3, etc. For the number 10^3, 10 is the **base** and 3 is the **exponent**. A base raised by an exponent represents how many times the base is multiplied by itself. Therefore, $10^1 = 10$, $10^2 = 10 \times 10 = 100$, $10^3 = 10 \times 10 \times 10 = 1,000$, $10^4 = 10 \times 10 \times 10 \times 10 = 10,000$, etc. Any base with a zero exponent equals one.

Powers of 10 are utilized to decompose a multi-digit number without writing all the zeroes. Consider the number 872,349. This number is decomposed to:

$$800,000 + 70,000 + 2,000 + 300 + 40 + 9$$

When utilizing powers of 10, the number 872,349 is decomposed to:

$$(8 \times 10^5) + (7 \times 10^4) + (2 \times 10^3) + (3 \times 10^2) + (4 \times 10^1) + (9 \times 10^0)$$

The power of 10 by which the digit is multiplied corresponds to the number of zeroes following the digit when expressing its value in standard form. For example, 7×10^4 is equivalent to 70,000 or 7 followed by four zeros.

Ordering Numbers
A common question type on the Praxis Math section asks test takers to order rational numbers from least to greatest or greatest to least. The numbers will come in a variety of formats, including decimals, percentages, roots, fractions, and whole numbers. These questions test for knowledge of different types of numbers and the ability to determine their respective values.

Whether the question asks to order the numbers from greatest to least or least to greatest, the crux of the question is the same—convert the numbers into a common format. Generally, it's easiest to write the numbers as whole numbers and decimals so they can be placed on a number line. The following examples illustrate this strategy:

1. Order the following rational numbers from greatest to least:

$$\sqrt{36}, \ 0.65, \ 78\%, \ \frac{3}{4}, \ 7, \ 90\%, \ \frac{5}{2}$$

Of the seven numbers, the whole number (7) and decimal (0.65) are already in an accessible form, so test takers should concentrate on the other five.

First, the square root of 36 equals 6. (If the test asks for the root of a non-perfect root, determine which two whole numbers the root lies between.) Next, the percentages should be converted to decimals. A percentage means "per

124

hundred," so this conversion requires moving the decimal point two places to the left, leaving 0.78 and 0.9. Lastly, the fractions are evaluated:

$$\frac{3}{4} = \frac{75}{100} = 0.75$$

$$\frac{5}{2} = 2\frac{1}{2} = 2.5$$

Now, the only step left is to list the numbers in the requested order:

$7, \sqrt{36}, \frac{5}{2}, 90\%, 78\%, \frac{3}{4}, 0.65$

2. Order the following rational numbers from least to greatest:

$2.5, \sqrt{9}, -10.5, 0.853, 175\%, \sqrt{4}, \frac{4}{5}$

$\sqrt{9} = 3$

$175\% = 1.75$

$\sqrt{4} = 2$

$\frac{4}{5} = 0.8$

From least to greatest, the answer is: $-10.5, \frac{4}{5}, 0.853, 175\%, \sqrt{4}, 2.5, \sqrt{9}$

The Properties of Whole Numbers

Rational and Irrational Numbers

All real numbers can be separated into two groups: rational and irrational numbers. **Rational numbers** are any numbers that can be written as a fraction, such as $\frac{1}{3}, \frac{7}{4}$, and -25. Alternatively, **irrational numbers** are those that cannot be written as a fraction, such as numbers with never-ending, non-repeating decimal values. Many irrational numbers result from taking roots, such as $\sqrt{2}$ or $\sqrt{3}$. An irrational number may be written as:

$$34.5684952\ldots$$

The ellipsis (…) represents the line of numbers after the decimal that does not repeat and is never-ending.

When rational and irrational numbers interact, there are different types of number outcomes. For example, when adding or multiplying two rational numbers, the result is a rational number. No matter what two fractions are added or multiplied together, the result can always be written as a fraction. The following expression shows two rational numbers multiplied together:

$$\frac{3}{8} \times \frac{4}{7} = \frac{12}{56}$$

The product of these two fractions is another fraction that can be simplified to $\frac{3}{14}$.

As another interaction, rational numbers added to irrational numbers will always result in irrational numbers. No part of any fraction can be added to a never-ending, non-repeating decimal to make a rational number. The same

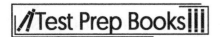

result is true when multiplying a rational and irrational number. Taking a fractional part of a never-ending, non-repeating decimal will always result in another never-ending, non-repeating decimal. An example of the product of rational and irrational numbers is shown in the following expression: $2 \times \sqrt{7}$.

The last type of interaction concerns two irrational numbers, where the sum or product may be rational or irrational depending on the numbers being used. The following expression shows a rational sum from two irrational numbers:

$$\sqrt{3} + (6 - \sqrt{3}) = 6$$

The product of two irrational numbers can be rational or irrational. A rational result can be seen in the following expression:

$$\sqrt{2} \times \sqrt{8} = \sqrt{2 \times 8} = \sqrt{16} = 4$$

An irrational result can be seen in the following:

$$\sqrt{3} \times \sqrt{2} = \sqrt{6}$$

Integers
An integer is any number that does not have a fractional part. This includes all positive and negative **whole numbers** and zero. Fractions and decimals—which aren't whole numbers—aren't integers.

Prime Numbers
A **prime** number cannot be divided except by 1 and itself. A prime number has no other factors, which means that no other combination of whole numbers can be multiplied to reach that number. For example, the set of prime numbers between 1 and 27 is {2, 3, 5, 7, 11, 13, 17, 19, 23}.

The number 7 is a prime number because its only factors are 1 and 7. In contrast, 12 isn't a prime number, as it can be divided by other numbers like 2, 3, 4, and 6. Because they are composed of multiple factors, numbers like 12 are called **composite** numbers. All numbers greater than 1 that aren't prime numbers are composite numbers.

Even and Odd Numbers
An integer is **even** if one of its factors is 2, while those integers without a factor of 2 are **odd**. No numbers except for integers can have either of these labels. For example, 2, 40, −16, and 108 are all even numbers, while −1, 13, 59, and 77 are all odd numbers since they are integers that cannot be divided by 2 without a remainder. Numbers like 0.4, $\frac{5}{9}$, π, and $\sqrt{7}$ are neither odd nor even because they are not integers.

Factorization
Factors are the numbers multiplied to achieve a product. Thus, every product in a multiplication equation has, at minimum, two factors. Of course, some products will have more than two factors. For the sake of most discussions, assume that factors are positive integers.

To find a number's factors, start with 1 and the number itself. Then divide the number by 2, 3, 4, and so on, seeing if any divisors can divide the number without a remainder, keeping a list of those that do. Stop upon reaching either the number itself or another factor.

Let's find the factors of 45. Start with 1 and 45. Then try to divide 45 by 2, which fails. Now divide 45 by 3. The answer is 15, so 3 and 15 are now factors. Dividing by 4 doesn't work and dividing by 5 leaves 9. Lastly, dividing 45 by 6, 7, and 8 all don't work. The next integer to try is 9, but this is already known to be a factor, so the factorization is complete. The factors of 45 are 1, 3, 5, 9, 15 and 45.

126

Prime Factorization

Prime factorization involves an additional step after breaking a number down to its factors: breaking down the factors until they are all prime numbers. A prime number is any number that can only be divided by 1 and itself. The prime numbers between 1 and 20 are 2, 3, 5, 7, 11, 13, 17, and 19. As a simple test, numbers that are even or end in 5 are not prime.

Let's break 129 down into its prime factors. First, the factors are 3 and 43. Both 3 and 43 are prime numbers, so we're done. But if 43 was not a prime number, then it would also need to be factorized until all of the factors are expressed as prime numbers.

Common Factor

A **common factor** is a factor shared by two numbers. Let's take 45 and 30 and find the common factors:

The factors of 45 are: 1, 3, 5, 9, 15, and 45.
The factors of 30 are: 1, 2, 3, 5, 6, 10, 15, and 30.
The common factors are 1, 3, 5, and 15.

Greatest Common Factor

The **greatest common factor** is the largest number among the shared, common factors. From the factors of 45 and 30, the common factors are 3, 5, and 15. Thus, 15 is the greatest common factor, as it's the largest number.

Least Common Multiple

The **least common multiple** is the smallest number that's a multiple of two numbers. Let's try to find the least common multiple of 4 and 9. The multiples of 4 are 4, 8, 12, 16, 20, 24, 28, 32, 36, and so on. For 9, the multiples are 9, 18, 27, 36, 45, 54, etc. Thus, the least common multiple of 4 and 9 is 36, the lowest number where 4 and 9 share multiples.

If two numbers share no factors besides 1 in common, then their least common multiple will be simply their product. If two numbers have common factors, then their least common multiple will be their product divided by their greatest common factor. This can be visualized by the formula $LCM = \frac{x \times y}{GCF}$, where x and y are some integers, and LCM and GCF are their least common multiple and greatest common factor, respectively.

Counterexamples

Examples are scenarios that support a statement, and counterexamples are scenarios that disprove propositions. For example, if the claim was made that all even numbers are positive, the number -2 would be a counterexample. Essentially, a counterexample is an example that shows a mathematical statement is false. Consider the following:

Which of the following is a counterexample that disproves the statement: *the product of two even numbers is an odd number?*

    a. $2 \times 3 = 6$
    b. $3 \times 5 = 15$
    c. $4 \times 6 = 24$
    d. $0 \times 1 = 0$

Remember that a counterexample is a specific example that shows the statement is not true. So $4 \times 6 = 24$ is an example of a product of two even numbers that is in an even number. Therefore, the answer is Choice *C.*

Let's try one more example:

Which of the following is a counterexample that disproves the statement "If one pair of opposite sides of a quadrilateral is parallel, then the quadrilateral is a parallelogram."
   a. Trapezoid
   b. Square
   c. Rhombus
   d. Rectangle

The correct answer is *A*. A trapezoid is a quadrilateral with only one set (a pair) of parallel sides, but it does not have two sets of parallel sides, which it would have to contain to be a parallelogram. Therefore, a trapezoid is a counterexample that shows why the statement is not true. It disproves the statement.

Solving Real-Life Problems Involving Rounding

Problem Situations for Operations

Addition and subtraction are **inverse operations**. Adding a number and then subtracting the same number will cancel each other out, resulting in the original number, and vice versa. For example, $8 + 7 - 7 = 8$ and $137 - 100 + 100 = 137$. Similarly, multiplication and division are inverse operations. Therefore, multiplying by a number and then dividing by the same number results in the original number, and vice versa.

For example, $8 \times 2 \div 2 = 8$ and $12 \div 4 \times 4 = 12$. Inverse operations are used to work backwards to solve problems. In the case that 7 and a number add to 18, the inverse operation of subtraction is used to find the unknown value ($18 - 7 = 11$). If a school's entire 4th grade was divided evenly into 3 classes each with 22 students, the inverse operation of multiplication is used to determine the total students in the grade ($22 \times 3 = 66$). Additional scenarios involving inverse operations are included in the tables below.

There are a variety of real-world situations in which one or more of the operators is used to solve a problem. The tables below display the most common scenarios.

Addition & Subtraction

	Unknown Result	Unknown Change	Unknown Start
Adding to	5 students were in class. 4 more students arrived. How many students are in class? $5 + 4 =?$	8 students were in class. More students arrived late. There are now 18 students in class. How many students arrived late? $8+? = 18$ Solved by inverse operations $18 - 8 =?$	Some students were in class early. 11 more students arrived. There are now 17 students in class. How many students were in class early? $? +11 = 17$ Solved by inverse operations $17- 11 =?$
Taking from	15 students were in class. 5 students left class. How many students are in class now? $15 - 5 =?$	12 students were in class. Some students left class. There are now 8 students in class. How many students left class? $12-? = 8$ Solved by inverse operations $8+? = 12 \;\to\; 12- 8 =?$	Some students were in class. 3 students left class. Then there were 13 students in class. How many students were in class before? $? -3 = 13$ Solved by inverse operations $13 + 3 =?$

	Unknown Total	Unknown Addends (Both)	Unknown Addends (One)
Putting together/ taking apart	The homework assignment is 10 addition problems and 8 subtraction problems. How many problems are in the homework assignment? $10 + 8 =?$	Bobby has \$9. How much can Bobby spend on candy and how much can Bobby spend on toys? $9 =? +?$	Bobby has 12 pairs of pants. 5 pairs of pants are shorts, and the rest are long. How many pairs of long pants does he have? $12 = 5+?$ Solved by inverse operations $12- 5 =?$

	Unknown Difference	Unknown Larger Value	Unknown Smaller Value
Comparing	Bobby has 5 toys. Tommy has 8 toys. How many more toys does Tommy have than Bobby? $$5 + ? = 8$$ Solved by inverse operations $8 - 5 = ?$ Bobby has \$6. Tommy has \$10. How many fewer dollars does Bobby have than Tommy? $$10 - 6 = ?$$	Tommy has 2 more toys than Bobby. Bobby has 4 toys. How many toys does Tommy have? $$2 + 4 = ?$$ Bobby has 3 fewer dollars than Tommy. Bobby has \$8. How many dollars does Tommy have? $$? - 3 = 8$$ Solved by inverse operations $8 + 3 = ?$	Tommy has 6 more toys than Bobby. Tommy has 10 toys. How many toys does Bobby have? $$? + 6 = 10$$ Solved by inverse operations $$10 - 6 = ?$$ Bobby has \$5 less than Tommy. Tommy has \$9. How many dollars does Bobby have? $$9 - 5 = ?$$

Multiplication and Division

	Unknown Product	Unknown Group Size	Unknown Number of Groups
Equal groups	There are 5 students, and each student has 4 pieces of candy. How many pieces of candy are there in all? $$5 \times 4 = ?$$	14 pieces of candy are shared equally by 7 students. How many pieces of candy does each student have? $$7 \times ? = 14$$ Solved by inverse operations $14 \div 7 = ?$	If 18 pieces of candy are to be given out 3 to each student, how many students will get candy? $$? \times 3 = 18$$ Solved by inverse operations $$18 \div 3 = ?$$

	Unknown Product	Unknown Factor	Unknown Factor
Arrays	There are 5 rows of students with 3 students in each row. How many students are there? $$5 \times 3 = ?$$	If 16 students are arranged into 4 equal rows, how many students will be in each row? $$4 \times ? = 16$$ Solved by inverse operations $$16 \div 4 = ?$$	If 24 students are arranged into an array with 6 columns, how many rows are there? $$? \times 6 = 24$$ Solved by inverse operations $24 \div 6 = ?$

	Larger Unknown	Smaller Unknown	Multiplier Unknown
	A small popcorn costs \$1.50. A large popcorn costs 3 times as	A large soda costs \$6 and that is 2 times as much as a	A large pretzel costs \$3 and a small pretzel costs \$2. How many

	Larger Unknown	Smaller Unknown	Multiplier Unknown
Comparing	much as a small popcorn. How much does a large popcorn cost? $1.50 \times 3 =?$	small soda costs. How much does a small soda cost? $2 \times ? = 6$ Solved by inverse operations $6 \div 2 =?$	times as much does the large pretzel cost as the small pretzel? $? \times 2 = 3$ Solved by inverse operations $3 \div 2 =?$

Estimation and Rounding

Estimation is finding a value that is close to a solution but is not the exact answer. For example, if there are values in the thousands to be multiplied, then each value can be estimated to the nearest thousand and the calculation performed. This value provides an approximate solution that can be determined very quickly.

Rounding is the process of either bumping a number up or leaving it the same, based on a specified place value. First, the place value is specified. Then, the digit to its right is looked at. For example, if rounding to the nearest hundreds place, the digit in the tens place is used. If it is a 0, 1, 2, 3, or 4, the digit being rounded to is left alone. If it is a 5, 6, 7, 8 or 9, the digit being rounded to is increased by one. All other digits before the decimal point are then changed to zeros, and the digits in decimal places are dropped. If a decimal place is being rounded to, all subsequent digits are just dropped. For example, if 845,231.45 was to be rounded to the nearest thousands place, the answer would be 845,000. The 5 would remain the same due to the 2 in the hundreds place. Also, if 4.567 was to be rounded to the nearest tenths place, the answer would be 4.6. The 5 increased to 6 due to the 6 in the hundredths place, and the rest of the decimal is dropped.

Sometimes when performing operations such as multiplying numbers, the result can be estimated by rounding. For example, to estimate the value of 11.2×2.01, each number can be rounded to the nearest integer. This will yield a result of 22.

Rounding numbers helps with estimation because it changes the given number to a simpler, although less accurate, number than the exact given number. Rounding allows for easier calculations, which estimate the results of using the exact given number. The accuracy of the estimate and ease of use depends on the place value to which the number is rounded. Rounding numbers consists of:

- Determining what place value the number is being rounded to
- Examining the digit to the right of the desired place value to decide whether to round up or keep the digit
- Replacing all digits to the right of the desired place value with zeros.

To round 746,311 to the nearest ten thousand, the digit in the ten thousands place should be located first. In this case, this digit is 4 (7<u>4</u>6,311). Then, the digit to its right is examined. If this digit is 5 or greater, the number will be rounded up by increasing the digit in the desired place by one. If the digit to the right of the place value being rounded is 4 or less, the number will be kept the same.

For the given example, the digit being examined is a 6, which means that the number will be rounded up by increasing the digit to the left by one. Therefore, the digit 4 is changed to a 5. Finally, to write the rounded number, any digits to the left of the place value being rounded remain the same and any to its right are replaced with zeros. For the given example, rounding 746,311 to the nearest ten thousand will produce 750,000. To round 746,311 to the nearest hundred, the digit to the right of the three in the hundreds place is examined to determine whether to round up or keep the same number. In this case, that digit is a 1, so the number will be kept the same and any digits to its right will be replaced with zeros. The resulting rounded number is 746,300.

Rounding place values to the right of the decimal follows the same procedure, but digits being replaced by zeros can simply be dropped. To round 3.752891 to the nearest thousandth, the desired place value is located (3.75<u>2</u>891) and the digit to the right is examined. In this case, the digit 8 indicates that the number will be rounded up, and the 2 in the thousandths place will increase to a 3. Rounding up and replacing the digits to the right of the thousandths place produces 3.753000 which is equivalent to 3.753. Therefore, the zeros are not necessary, and the rounded number should be written as 3.753.

When rounding up, if the digit to be increased is a 9, the digit to its left is increased by 1 and the digit in the desired place value is changed to a zero. For example, the number 1,598 rounded to the nearest ten is 1,600. Another example shows the number 43.72961 rounded to the nearest thousandth is 43.730 or 43.73.

Solving Problems Involving Units and Measurements

The United States customary system and the metric system each consist of distinct units to measure lengths and volume of liquids. The U.S. customary units for length, from smallest to largest, are: inch (in), foot (ft), yard (yd), and mile (mi). The metric units for length, from smallest to largest, are: millimeter (mm), centimeter (cm), decimeter (dm), meter (m), and kilometer (km). The relative size of each unit of length is shown below.

U.S. Customary	Metric	Conversion
12 in = 1 ft	10 mm = 1 cm	1 in = 254 cm
36 in = 3 ft = 1 yd	10 cm = 1 dm (decimeter)	1 m ≈ 3.28 ft ≈ 1.09 yd
5,280 ft = 1,760 yd = 1 mi	100 cm = 10 dm = 1 m	1 mi ≈ 1.6 km
	1,000 m = 1 km	

The U.S. customary units for volume of liquids, from smallest to largest, are: fluid ounces (fl oz), cup (c), pint (pt), quart (qt), and gallon (gal). The metric units for volume of liquids, from smallest to largest, are: milliliter (mL), centiliter (cL), deciliter (dL), liter (L), and kiloliter (kL). The relative size of each unit of liquid volume is shown below.

U.S. Customary	Metric	Conversion
8 fl oz = 1 c	10 mL = 1 cL	1 pt ≈ 0.473 L
2 c = 1 pt	10 cL = 1 dL	1 L ≈ 1.057 qt
4 c = 2 pt = 1 qt	1,000 mL = 100 cL = 10 dL = 1 L	1 gal ≈ 3,785 L
4 qt = 1 gal	1,000 L = 1 kL	

The U.S. customary system measures weight (how strongly Earth is pulling on an object) in the following units, from least to greatest: ounce (oz), pound (lb), and ton. The metric system measures mass (the quantity of matter within an object) in the following units, from least to greatest: milligram (mg), centigram (cg), gram (g), kilogram (kg), and metric ton (MT). The relative sizes of each unit of weight and mass are shown below.

U.S. Measures of Weight	Metric Measures of Mass
16 oz = 1 lb	10 mg = 1 cg
2,000 lb = 1 ton	100 cg = 1 g
	1,000 g = 1 kg
	1,000 kg = 1 MT

Note that weight and mass DO NOT measure the same thing.

Time is measured in the following units, from shortest to longest: second (sec), minute (min), hour (h), day (d), week (wk), month (mo), year (yr), decade, century, millennium. The relative sizes of each unit of time is shown below.

- $60 \sec = 1 \min$
- $60 \min = 1 \text{ h}$
- $24 \text{ hr} = 1 \text{ d}$
- $7 \text{ d} = 1 \text{ wk}$
- $52 \text{ wk} = 1 \text{ yr}$
- $12 \text{ mo} = 1 \text{ yr}$
- $10 \text{ yr} = 1 \text{ decade}$
- $100 \text{ yrs} = 1 \text{ century}$
- $1{,}000 \text{ yrs} = 1 \text{ millennium}$

When working with different systems of measurement, conversion from one unit to another may be necessary. The conversion rate must be known to convert units. One method for converting units is to write and solve a proportion. The arrangement of values in a proportion is extremely important. Suppose that a problem requires converting 20 fluid ounces to cups. To do so, a proportion can be written using the conversion rate of 8fl oz = 1c with x representing the missing value. The proportion can be written in any of the following ways:

$$\frac{1}{8} = \frac{x}{20} \left(\frac{\text{c for conversion}}{\text{fl oz for conversion}} = \frac{unknown \text{ c}}{\text{fl oz given}} \right)$$

$$\frac{8}{1} = \frac{20}{x} \left(\frac{\text{fl oz for conversion}}{\text{c for conversion}} = \frac{\text{fl oz given}}{unknown \text{ c}} \right)$$

$$\frac{1}{x} = \frac{8}{20} \left(\frac{\text{c for conversion}}{unknown \text{ c}} = \frac{\text{fl oz for conversion}}{\text{fl oz given}} \right)$$

$$\frac{x}{1} = \frac{20}{8} \left(\frac{unknown \text{ c}}{\text{c for conversion}} = \frac{\text{fl oz given}}{\text{fl oz for conversion}} \right)$$

To solve a proportion, the ratios are cross-multiplied and the resulting equation is solved. When cross-multiplying, all four proportions above will produce the same equation:

$$(8)(x) = (20)(1) \rightarrow 8x = 20$$

Divide by 8 to isolate the variable x, the result is $x = 2.5$. The variable x represented the unknown number of cups. Therefore, the conclusion is that 20 fluid ounces converts (is equal) to 2.5 cups.

Sometimes converting units requires writing and solving more than one proportion. Suppose an exam question asks to determine how many hours are in 2 weeks. Without knowing the conversion rate between hours and weeks, this can be determined knowing the conversion rates between weeks and days, and between days and hours. First, weeks are converted to days, then days are converted to hours. To convert from weeks to days, the following proportion can be written:

$$\frac{7}{1} = \frac{x}{2} \left(\frac{\text{days conversion}}{\text{weeks conversion}} = \frac{\text{days } unknown}{\text{weeks given}} \right)$$

Cross-multiplying produces:

$$(7)(2) = (x)(1) \rightarrow 14 = x$$

Therefore, 2 weeks is equal to 14 days. Next, a proportion is written to convert 14 days to hours:

$$\frac{24}{1} = \frac{x}{14} \left(\frac{\text{conversion hours}}{\text{conversion days}} = \frac{unknown \text{ hours}}{\text{given days}} \right)$$

Cross-multiplying produces:

$$(24)(14) = (x)(1) \rightarrow 336 = x$$

Therefore, the answer is that there are 336 hours in 2 weeks.

Dimensional analysis is the process of converting between different units using equivalent measurement statements. For instance, running 5 kilometers is approximately the same as running 3.1 miles. This conversion can be found by knowing that 1 kilometer is equal to approximately 0.62 miles.

When setting up the dimensional analysis calculations, the original units need to be opposite one another in each of the two fractions: one in the original amount (essentially in the numerator) and one in the denominator of the conversion factor. This enables them to cancel after multiplying, leaving the converted result.

Calculations involving formulas, such as determining volume and area, are a common situation in which units need to be interpreted and used. However, graphs can also carry meaning through units. The graph below is an example. It represents a graph of the position of an object over time. The y-axis represents the position or the number of meters the object is from the starting point at time s, in seconds. Interpreting this graph, the origin shows that at time zero seconds, the object is zero meters away from the starting point. As the time increases to one second, the position increases to five meters away.

This trend continues until 6 seconds, where the object is 30 meters away from the starting position. After this point in time—since the graph remains horizontal from 6 to 10 seconds—the object must have stopped moving.

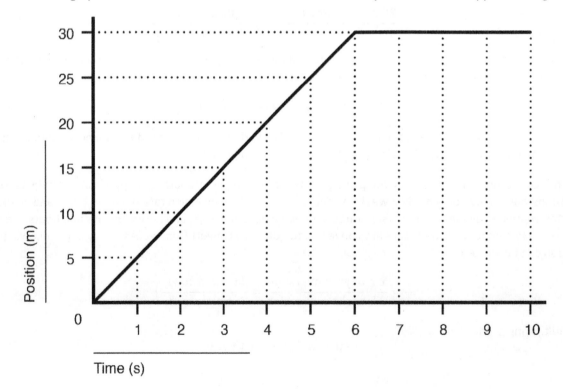

When solving problems with units, it's important to consider the reasonableness of the answer. If conversions are used, it's helpful to have an estimated value to compare the final answer to. This way, if the final answer is too distant from the estimate, it will be obvious that a mistake was made.

Data Interpretation and Representation, Statistics, and Probability

Working with Data and Data Representations to Solve Problems

Data Collection from Measurements on a Single Variable

Representing Data

Most statistics involve collecting a large amount of data, analyzing it, and then making decisions based on previously known information. These decisions also can be measured through additional data collection and then analyzed. Therefore, the cycle can repeat itself over and over. Representing the data visually is a large part of the process, and many plots on the real number line exist that allow this to be done. For example, a **dot plot** uses dots to represent data points above the number line. Also, a **histogram** represents a data set as a collection of rectangles, which illustrate the frequency distribution of the data. Finally, a **box plot** (also known as a **box and whisker plot**) plots a data set on the number line by segmenting the distribution into four quartiles that are divided equally in half by the median. Here's an example of a box plot, a histogram, and a dot plot for the same data set:

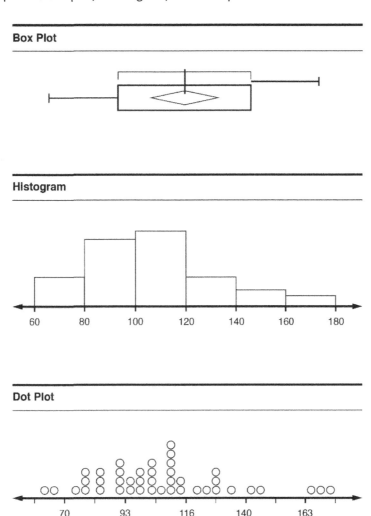

135

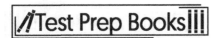
Normal Distribution

A **normal distribution** of data follows the shape of a bell curve and the data set's median, mean, and mode are equal. Therefore, 50% of its values are less than the mean and 50% are greater than the mean. Data sets that follow this shape can be generalized using normal distributions. Normal distributions are described as **frequency distributions** in which the data set is plotted as percentages rather than true data points. A **relative frequency distribution** is one where the y-axis is between zero and 1, which is the same as 0% to 100%.

Within a standard deviation, 68% of the values are within 1 standard deviation of the mean, 95% of the values are within 2 standard deviations of the mean, and 99.7% of the values are within 3 standard deviations of the mean. The number of standard deviations that a data point falls from the mean is called the **z-score**. The formula for the z-score is $Z = \frac{x-\mu}{\sigma}$, where μ is the mean, σ is the standard deviation, and x is the data point. This formula is used to fit any data set that resembles a normal distribution to a standard normal distribution in a process known as **standardizing**.

Here is a normal distribution with labelled z-scores:

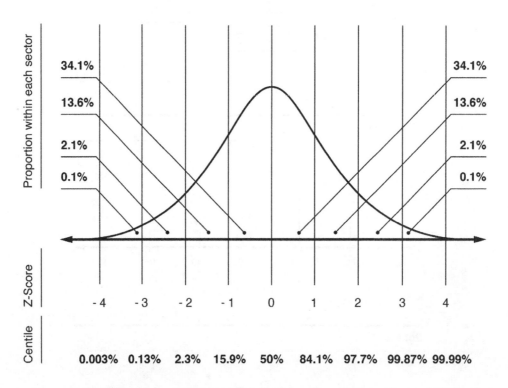

Normal Distribution with Labelled Z-Scores

Population percentages can be estimated using normal distributions. For example, the probability that a data point will be less than the mean, or that the z-score will be less than 0, is 50%. Similarly, the probability that a data point will be within 1 standard deviation of the mean, or that the z-score will be between -1 and 1, is about 68.2%. When using a z-table, the left column states how many standard deviations (to one decimal place) away from the

136

mean the point is, and the row heading states the second decimal place. The entries in the table corresponding to each column and row give the probability, which is equal to the area.

Areas Under the Curve

The area under the curve of a standard normal distribution is equal to 1. Areas under the curve can be estimated using the z-score and a table. The area is equal to the probability that a data point lies in that region in decimal form. For example, the area under the curve from $z = -1$ to $z = 1$ is 0.682.

Data Collection from Measurements on Two Variables

Two-Way Frequency Tables

Data that isn't described using numbers is known as **categorical data**. For example, age is numerical data but hair color is categorical data. Categorical data is summarized using two-way frequency tables. A **two-way frequency table** counts the relationship between two sets of categorical data. There are rows and columns for each category, and each cell represents frequency information that shows the actual data count between each combination.

For example, the graphic on the left-side below is a two-way frequency table showing the number of girls and boys taking language classes in school. Entries in the middle of the table are known as the **joint frequencies**. For example, the number of girls taking French class is 12, which is a joint frequency. The totals are the **marginal frequencies**. For example, the total number of boys is 20, which is a marginal frequency. If the frequencies are changed into percentages based on totals, the table is known as a **two-way relative frequency table**. Percentages can be calculated using the table total, the row totals, or the column totals. Here's the process of obtaining the two-way relative frequency table using the table total:

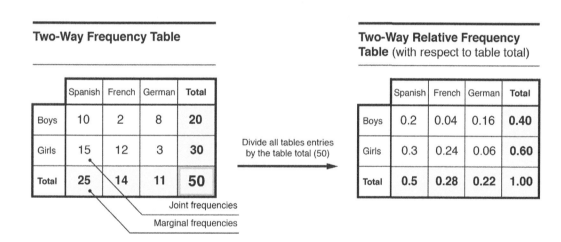

Two-Way Frequency Table

	Spanish	French	German	Total
Boys	10	2	8	**20**
Girls	15	12	3	**30**
Total	**25**	14	11	**50**

Joint frequencies
Marginal frequencies

Divide all tables entries by the table total (50) →

Two-Way Relative Frequency Table (with respect to table total)

	Spanish	French	German	Total
Boys	0.2	0.04	0.16	**0.40**
Girls	0.3	0.24	0.06	**0.60**
Total	**0.5**	**0.28**	**0.22**	**1.00**

The middle entries are known as **joint probabilities** and the totals are **marginal probabilities**. In this data set, it appears that more girls than boys take Spanish class. However, that might not be the case because more girls than boys were surveyed, and the results might be misleading. To avoid such errors, **conditional relative frequencies** are used. The relative frequencies are calculated based on a row or column.

137

Here are the conditional relative frequencies using column totals:

Two-Way Frequency Table

	Spanish	French	German	Total
Boys	10	2	8	**20**
Girls	15	12	3	**30**
Total	**25**	**14**	**11**	**50**

Divide each column entry by that column's total →

Two-Way Relative Frequency Table (with respect to table total)

	Spanish	French	German	Total
Boys	0.4	0.14	0.73	**0.4**
Girls	0.6	0.86	0.27	**0.6**
Total	**1.00**	**1.00**	**1.00**	**1.00**

Data Conclusions

Two-way frequency tables can help in making many conclusions about the data. If either the row or column of conditional relative frequencies differs between each row or column of the table, then an association exists between the two categories. If the frequencies are equal across the rows, there is no association, and the variables are labelled as independent. It's important to note that the association does exist in the above scenario, though these results may not occur the next semester when students are surveyed.

Plotting Variables

A **scatterplot** is a way to visually represent the relationship between two variables. Each variable has its own axis, and usually the independent variable is plotted on the horizontal axis while the dependent variable is plotted on the vertical axis. Data points are plotted in a process that's similar to how ordered pairs are plotted on an xy-plane. Once all points from the data set are plotted, the scatterplot is finished. Below is an example of a scatterplot that's plotting the quality and price of an item. Note that price is the independent variable and quality is the dependent variable:

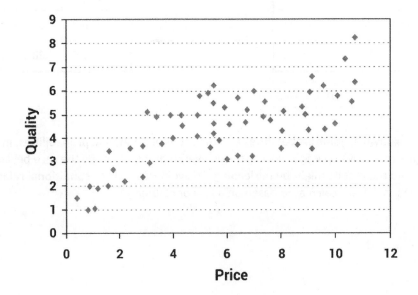

In this example, the quality of the item increases as the price increases.

Solving Problems Involving Measures of Central Tendency and Spread

Mean, Median, and Mode
The center of a set of data (statistical values) can be represented by its mean, median, or mode. These are sometimes referred to as measures of central tendency.

Mean
The first property that can be defined for this set of data is the **mean**. This is the same as the average. To find the mean, add up all the data points, then divide by the total number of data points. For example, suppose that in a class of 10 students, the scores on a test were 50, 60, 65, 65, 75, 80, 85, 85, 90, 100. Therefore, the average test score will be:

$$\frac{50 + 60 + 65 + 65 + 75 + 80 + 85 + 85 + 90 + 100}{10} = 75.5$$

The mean is a useful number if the distribution of data is normal (more on this later), which roughly means that the frequency of different outcomes has a single peak and is roughly equally distributed on both sides of that peak. However, it is less useful in some cases where the data might be split or where there are some outliers. **Outliers** are data points that are far from the rest of the data. For example, suppose there are 10 executives and 90 employees at a company. The executives make $1,000 per hour, and the employees make $10 per hour.

Therefore, the average pay rate will be:

$$\frac{\$1,000 \times 10 + \$10 \times 90}{100} = \$109 \text{ per hour}$$

In this case, this average is not very descriptive since it's not close to the actual pay of the executives or the employees.

Median
Another useful measurement is the **median**. In a data set, the median is the point in the middle. The middle refers to the point where half the data comes before it and half comes after, when the data is recorded in numerical order. For instance, these are the speeds of the fastball of a pitcher during the last inning that he pitched (in order from least to greatest):

$$90, 92, 93, 93, 95, 96, 97, 97, 97$$

There are nine total numbers, so the middle or *median* number is the 5th one, which is 95.

In cases where the number of data points is an even number, then the average of the two middle points is taken. In the previous example of test scores, the two middle points are 75 and 80. Since there is no single point, the average of these two scores needs to be found. The average is:

$$\frac{75 + 80}{2} = 77.5$$

The median is generally a good value to use if there are a few outliers in the data. It prevents those outliers from affecting the "middle" value as much as when using the mean.

Since an outlier is a data point that is far from most of the other data points in a data set, this means an outlier also is any point that is far from the median of the data set. The outliers can have a substantial effect on the mean of a data set, but they usually do not change the median or mode, or do not change them by a large quantity. For

example, consider the data set (3, 5, 6, 6, 6, 8). This has a median of 6 and a mode of 6, with a mean of $\frac{34}{6} \approx 5.67$. Now, suppose a new data point of 1,000 is added so that the data set is now (3, 5, 6, 6, 6, 8, 1,000). The median and mode, which are both still 6, remain unchanged. However, the average is now $\frac{1,034}{7}$, which is approximately 147.7. In this case, the median and mode will be better descriptions for most of the data points.

Outliers in a given data set are sometimes the result of an error by the experimenter, but oftentimes, they are perfectly valid data points that must be taken into consideration.

Mode
One additional measure to define for X is the **mode**. This is the data point that appears most frequently. If two or more data points all tie for the most frequent appearance, then each of them is considered a mode. In the case of the test scores, where the numbers were 50, 60, 65, 65, 75, 80, 85, 85, 90, 100, there are two modes: 65 and 85.

Quartiles and Percentiles
The **first quartile** of a set of data X refers to the largest value from the first $\frac{1}{4}$ of the data points. In practice, there are sometimes slightly different definitions that can be used, such as the median of the first half of the data points (excluding the median itself if there are an odd number of data points). The term also has a slightly different use: when it is said that a data point lies *in the first quartile*, it means it is less than or equal to the median of the first half of the data points. Conversely, if it lies *at* the first quartile, then it is equal to the first quartile.

When it is said that a data point lies in the **second quartile**, it means it is between the first quartile and the median.

The **third quartile** refers to data that lies between $\frac{1}{2}$ and $\frac{3}{4}$ of the way through the data set. Again, there are various methods for defining this precisely, but the simplest way is to include all of the data that lie between the median and the median of the top half of the data.

Data that lies in the **fourth quartile** refers to all of the data above the third quartile.

Percentiles may be defined in a similar manner to quartiles. Generally, this is defined in the following manner:

If a data point lies *in the nth percentile*, this means it lies in the range of the first *n%* of the data.

If a data point lies *at the nth percentile*, then it means that *n%* of the data lies below this data point.

Standard Deviation
Given a data set X consisting of data points $(x_1, x_2, x_3, \ldots x_n)$, the **variance** of X is defined to be:

$$\frac{\sum_{i=1}^{n}(x_i - \bar{X})^2}{n}$$

This means that the variance of X is the average of the squares of the differences between each data point and the mean of X.

Given a data set X consisting of data points $(x_1, x_2, x_3, \ldots x_n)$, the **standard deviation** of X is defined to be:

$$s_x = \sqrt{\frac{\sum_{i=1}^{n}(x_i - \bar{X})^2}{n}}$$

In other words, the standard deviation is the square root of the variance.

Both the variance and the standard deviation are measures of how much the data tend to be spread out. When the standard deviation is low, the data points are mostly clustered around the mean. When the standard deviation is high, this generally indicates that the data are quite spread out, or else that there are a few substantial outliers.

As a simple example, compute the standard deviation for the data set (1, 3, 3, 5). First, compute the mean, which will be:

$$\frac{1+3+3+5}{4} = \frac{12}{4} = 3$$

Now, find the variance of X with the formula:

$$\sum_{i=1}^{4}(x_i - \bar{X})^2 = (1-3)^2 + (3-3)^2 + (3-3)^2 + (5-3)^2$$

$$-2^2 + 0^2 + 0^2 + 2^2 = 8$$

Therefore, the variance is $\frac{8}{4} = 2$. Taking the square root, the standard deviation will be $\sqrt{2}$.

Note that the standard deviation only depends upon the mean, not upon the median or mode(s). Generally, if there are multiple modes that are far apart from one another, the standard deviation will be high. A high standard deviation does not always mean there are multiple modes, however.

Describing a Set of Data

A set of data can be described in terms of its center, spread, shape and any unusual features. The center of a data set can be measured by its mean, median, or mode. The spread of a data set refers to how far the data points are from the center (mean or median). A data set with all its data points clustered around the center will have a small spread. A data set covering a wide range of values will have a large spread.

When a data set is displayed as a graph like the one below, the shape indicates if a sample is normally distributed, symmetrical, or has measures of skewness. When graphed, a data set with a normal distribution will resemble a bell curve.

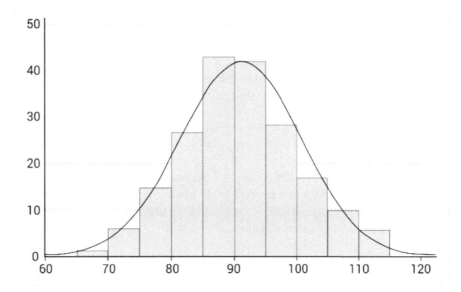

If the data set is symmetrical, each half of the graph when divided at the center is a mirror image of the other. If the graph has fewer data points to the right, the data is skewed right. If it has fewer data points to the left, the data is skewed left.

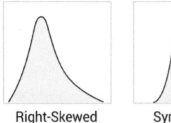

Right-Skewed

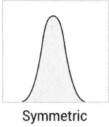

Symmetric

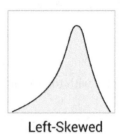

Left-Skewed

A description of a data set should include any unusual features such as gaps or outliers. A gap is a span within the range of the data set containing no data points. An outlier is a data point with a value either extremely large or extremely small when compared to the other values in the set.

The graphs above can be referred to as **unimodal** since they all have a single peak. In contrast, a bimodal graph has two peaks.

Using Data from a Random Sample to Draw Inferences About a Population

An **experiment** is the method by which a hypothesis is tested using a controlled process called the scientific method. A cause and the effect of that cause are measured, and the hypothesis is accepted or rejected. Experiments are usually completed in a controlled environment where the results of a control population are compared to the results of a test population. The groups are selected using a randomization process in which each group has a representative mix of the population being tested. Finally, an **observational study** is similar to an experiment. However, this design is used when circumstances prevent or do not allow for a designated control group and experimental group (e.g., lack of funding or unrealistic expectations). Instead, existing control and test populations must be used, so this method has a lack of randomization.

Data Gathering Techniques

The three most common types of data gathering techniques are sample surveys, experiments, and observational studies. **Sample surveys** involve collecting data from a random sample of people from a desired population. The measurement of the variable is only performed on this set of people. To have accurate data, the sampling must be unbiased and random. For example, surveying students in an advanced calculus class on how much they enjoy math classes is not a useful sample if the population should be all college students based on the research question. An **experiment** is the method by which a hypothesis is tested using a controlled process called the scientific method.

A cause and the effect of that cause are measured, and the hypothesis is accepted or rejected. Experiments are usually completed in a controlled environment where the results of a control population are compared to the results of a test population. The groups are selected using a randomization process in which each group has a representative mix of the population being tested. Finally, an **observational study** is similar to an experiment. However, this design is used when circumstances prevent or do not allow for a designated control group and experimental group (e.g., lack of funding or unrealistic expectations). Instead, existing control and test populations must be used, so this method has a lack of randomization.

Samples and Populations

Statistics involves making decisions and predictions about larger data sets based on smaller data sets. Basically, the information from one part or subset can help predict what happens in the entire data set or population at large. The

entire process involves guessing, and the predictions and decisions may not be 100% correct all of the time; however, there is some truth to these predictions, and the decisions do have mathematical support. The smaller data set is called a **sample** and the larger data set (in which the decision is being made) is called a **population**. A **random sample** is used as the sample, which is an unbiased collection of data points that represents the population as well as it can. There are many methods of forming a random sample, and all adhere to the fact that every potential data point has a predetermined probability of being chosen.

Population Mean and Proportion

Both the population mean and proportion can be calculated using data from a sample. The **population mean** (μ) is the average value of the parameter for the entire population. Due to size constraints, finding the exact value of μ is impossible, so the mean of the sample population is used as an estimate instead. The larger the sample size, the closer the sample mean gets to the population mean. An alternative to finding μ is to find the **proportion** of the population, which is the part of the population with the given characteristic. The proportion can be expressed as a decimal, a fraction, or a percentage, and can be given as a single value or a range of values. Because the population mean and proportion are both estimates, there's a **margin of error**, which is the difference between the actual value and the expected value.

T-Tests

A **randomized experiment** is used to compare two treatments by using statistics involving a *t-test*, which tests whether two data sets are significantly different from one another. To use a *t*-test, the test statistic must follow a normal distribution. The first step of the test involves calculating the *t*-value, which is given as:

$$t = \frac{\overline{x_1} - \overline{x_2}}{s_{\bar{x}_1 - \bar{x}_2}}$$

$\bar{x}_1$ and $\bar{x}_2$ are the averages of the two samples

Also,

$$s_{\bar{x}_1 - \bar{x}_2} = \sqrt{\frac{s_1^2}{n_1} + \frac{s_2^2}{n_2}}$$

s_1 and s_2 are the standard deviations of each sample and n_1 and n_2 are their respective sample sizes. The **degrees of freedom** for two samples are calculated as the following (rounded to the lowest whole number).

$$df = \frac{(n_1 - 1) + (n_2 - 1)}{2}$$

Also, a significance level α must be chosen, where a typical value is $\alpha = 0.05$. Once everything is compiled, the decision is made to use either a **one-tailed test** or a **two-tailed test**. If there's an assumed difference between the two treatments, a one-tailed test is used. If no difference is assumed, a two-tailed test is used.

Analyzing Test Results

Once the type of test is determined, the *t*-value, significance level, and degrees of freedom are applied to the published table showing the *t* distribution. The row is associated with degrees of freedom and each column corresponds to the probability. The *t*-value can be exactly equal to one entry or lie between two entries in a row. For example, consider a *t*-value of 1.7 with degrees of freedom equal to 30. This **test statistic** falls between the *p*-values of 0.05 and 0.025. For a one-tailed test, the corresponding *p*-value lies between 0.05 and 0.025. For a two-tailed test, the *p*-values need to be doubled so the corresponding *p*-value falls between 0.1 and 0.05. Once the probability is known, this range is compared to α. If $p < \alpha$, the hypothesis is rejected. If $p > \alpha$, the hypothesis isn't rejected. In a two-tailed test, this scenario means the hypothesis is accepted that there's no difference in the two

treatments. In a one-tailed test, the hypothesis is accepted, indicating that there's a difference in the two treatments.

Identifying Positive and Negative Linear Relationships in Scatterplots

In an experiment, variables are the key to analyzing data, especially when data is in a graph or table. Variables can represent anything, including objects, conditions, events, and amounts of time.

Covariance is a general term referring to how two variables move in relation to each other. Take for example an employee that gets paid by the hour. For them, hours worked and total pay have a positive covariance. As hours worked increases, so does pay.

Constant variables remain unchanged by the scientist across all trials. Because they are held constant for all groups in an experiment, they aren't being measured in the experiment, and they are usually ignored. Constants can either be controlled by the scientist directly like the nutrition, water, and sunlight given to plants, or they can be selected by the scientist specifically for an experiment like using a certain animal species or choosing to investigate only people of a certain age group.

Independent variables are also controlled by the scientist, but they are the same only for each group or trial in the experiment. Each group might be composed of students that all have the same color of car or each trial may be run on different soda brands. The independent variable of an experiment is what is being indirectly tested because it causes change in the dependent variables.

Dependent variables experience change caused by the independent variable and are what is being measured or observed. For example, college acceptance rates could be a dependent variable of an experiment that sorted a large sample of high school students by an independent variable such as test scores. In this experiment, the scientist groups the high school students by the independent variable (test scores) to see how it affects the dependent variable (their college acceptance rates).

Note that most variables can be held constant in one experiment, but also serve as the independent variable or a dependent variable in another. For example, when testing how well a fertilizer aids plant growth, its amount of sunlight should be held constant for each group of plants, but if the experiment is being done to determine the proper amount of sunlight a plant should have, the amount of sunlight is an independent variable because it is necessarily changed for each group of plants.

An *X-Y* **diagram**, also known as a scatter diagram, visually displays the relationship between two variables. The independent variable is placed on the *x*-**axis**, or horizontal axis, and the dependent variable is placed on the *y*-**axis**, or vertical axis.

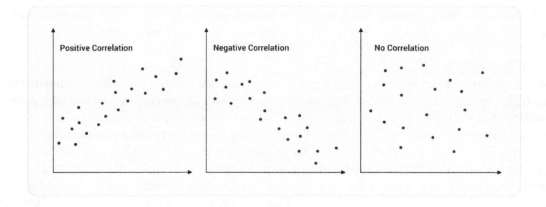

As shown in the figures above, an X-Y diagram may result in positive, negative, or no correlation between the two variables. So, in the first scatterplot as the Y factor increases the X factor increases as well. The opposite is true as well: as the X factor increases the Y factor also increases. Thus, there is a positive correlation because one factor appears to positively affect the other factor.

The **correlation coefficient** (r) measures the association between two variables. Its value is between -1 and 1, where -1 represents a perfect negative linear relationship, 0 represents no relationship, and 1 represents a perfect positive linear relationship. A **negative linear relationship** means that as x values increase, y values decrease. A **positive linear relationship** means that as x-values increase, y-values increase. The formula for computing the correlation coefficient is:

$$r = \frac{n(\sum xy) - (\sum x)(\sum y)}{\sqrt{n(\sum x^2) - (\sum x)^2}\sqrt{n(\sum y^2) - (\Sigma y)^2}}$$

n is the number of data points.

Both Microsoft Excel® and a graphing calculator can evaluate this easily once the data points are entered. A correlation greater than 0.8 or less than -0.8 is classified as "strong" while a correlation between -0.5 and 0.5 is classified as "weak."

Using a Linear Model for a Data Set to Make Predictions

Linear Regression
Regression lines are a way to calculate a relationship between the independent variable and the dependent variable. A straight line means that there's a linear trend in the data. Technology can be used to find the equation of this line (e.g., a graphing calculator or Microsoft Excel®). In either case, all of the data points are entered, and a line is "fit" that best represents the shape of the data. Other functions used to model data sets include quadratic and exponential models.

Estimating Data Points
Regression lines can be used to estimate data points not already given. For example, if an equation of a line is found that fit the temperature and beach visitor data set, its input is the average daily temperature and its output is the projected number of visitors. Thus, the number of beach visitors on a 100-degree day can be estimated. The output is a data point on the regression line, and the number of daily visitors is expected to be greater than on a 96-degree day because the regression line has a positive slope.

Plotting and Analyzing Residuals
Once the function is found that fits the data, its accuracy can be calculated. Therefore, how well the line fits the data can be determined. The difference between the actual dependent variable from the data set and the estimated value located on the regression line is known as a **residual**. Therefore, the residual is known as the predicted value $\hat{y}$ minus the actual value y. A residual is calculated for each data point and can be plotted on the scatterplot. If all the residuals appear to be approximately the same distance from the regression line, the line is a good fit. If the residuals seem to differ greatly across the board, the line isn't a good fit.

Interpreting the Regression Line
The formula for a regression line is $y = mx + b$, where m is the slope and b is the y-intercept. Both the slope and y-intercept are found in the **Method of Least Squares**, which is the process of finding the equation of the line through minimizing residuals. The slope represents the rate of change in y as x gets larger. Therefore, because y is the dependent variable, the slope actually provides the predicted values given the independent variable. The y-

145

intercept is the predicted value for when the independent variable equals zero. In the temperature example, the y-intercept is the expected number of beach visitors for a very cold average daily temperature of zero degrees.

Differentiating Between Correlation and Causation

Correlation and causation have two different meanings. If two values are correlated, there is an association between them. However, correlation doesn't necessarily mean that one variable causes the other. **Causation** (or "cause and effect") occurs when one variable causes the other. Average daily temperature and number of beachgoers are correlated and have causation. If the temperature increases, the change in weather causes more people to go to the beach. However, alcoholism and smoking are correlated but don't have causation. The more someone drinks the more likely they are to smoke, but drinking alcohol doesn't cause someone to smoke.

In other words, a positive correlation between two variables doesn't equate to a cause-and-effect relationship. For example, a positive correlation between labor hours and units produced may not equate to a cause-and-effect relationship between the two. Any instance of correlation only indicates how likely the presence of one variable is in the instance of another. The variables should be further analyzed to determine which, if any, other variables (i.e., quality of employee work) may contribute to the positive correlation.

Computing Simple Probabilities, and Using Probabilities to Solve Problems

Counting Techniques

There are many counting techniques that can help solve problems involving counting possibilities. For example, the **Addition Principle** states that if there are m choices from Group 1 and n choices from Group 2, then $n + m$ is the total number of choices possible from Groups 1 and 2. For this to be true, the groups can't have any choices in common. The **Multiplication Principle** states that if Process 1 can be completed n ways and Process 2 can be completed m ways, the total number of ways to complete both Process 1 and Process 2 is $n \times m$. For this rule to be used, both processes must be independent of each other. Counting techniques also involve permutations. A **permutation** is an arrangement of elements in a set for which order must be considered. For example, if three letters from the alphabet are chosen, ABC and BAC are two different permutations. The multiplication rule can be used to determine the total number of possibilities. If each letter can't be selected twice, the total number of possibilities is:

$$26 \times 25 \times 24 = 15{,}600$$

A formula can also be used to calculate this total. In general, the notation $P(n, r)$ represents the number of ways to arrange r objects from a set of n and, the formula is:

$$P(n, r) = \frac{n!}{(n - r)!}$$

In the previous example:

$$P(26, 3) = \frac{26!}{23!} = 15{,}600$$

Contrasting permutations, a **combination** is an arrangement of elements in which order doesn't matter. In this case, ABC and BAC are the same combination. In the previous scenario, there are six permutations that represent each single combination. Therefore, the total number of possible combinations is:

$$15{,}600 \div 6 = 2{,}600$$

In general, $C(n, r)$ represents the total number of combinations of n items selected r at a time where order doesn't matter. Another way to represent the combinations of r items selected out of a set of n items is $\binom{n}{r}$. The formula for select combinations of items is:

$$\binom{n}{r} = C(n, r) = \frac{n!}{(n - r)! \, r!}$$

Therefore, the following relationship exists between permutations and combinations:

$$C(n, r) = \frac{P(n, r)}{r!} = \frac{P(n, r)}{P(r, r)}$$

Fundamental Counting Principle

The **fundamental counting principle** states that if there are m potential ways an event can occur, and n potential ways a second event can occur, then there are $m \times n$ potential ways both events can occur. For example, there are two events that can occur after flipping a coin and six events that can occur after rolling a die, so there are $2 \times 6 = 12$ total possible event scenarios if both are done simultaneously. This principle can be used to find probabilities involving finite sample spaces and independent trials because it calculates the total number of possible outcomes. For this principle to work, the events must be independent of each other.

Independence and Conditional Probability

Sample Subsets

A sample can be broken up into subsets that are smaller parts of the whole. For example, consider a sample population of females. The sample can be divided into smaller subsets based on the characteristics of each female. There can be a group of females with brown hair and a group of females that wear glasses. There also can be a group of females that have brown hair *and* wear glasses. This "and" relates to the **intersection** of the two separate groups of brunettes and those with glasses. Every female in that intersection group has both characteristics. Similarly, there also can be a group of females that either have brown hair *or* wear glasses. The "or" relates to the union of the two separate groups of brunettes and glasses. Every female in this group has at least one of the characteristics. Finally, the group of females who do not wear glasses can be discussed. This "not" relates to the **complement** of the glass-wearing group. No one in the complement has glasses. **Venn diagrams** are useful in highlighting these ideas. When discussing statistical experiments, this idea can also relate to events instead of characteristics.

Verifying Independent Events

Two events aren't always independent. For example, females with glasses and brown hair aren't independent characteristics. There definitely can be overlap because people with brown hair can wear glasses. Also, two events that exist at the same time don't have to have a relationship. For example, even if everyone in a given sample is wearing glasses, the characteristics aren't related. In this case, the probability of a brunette wearing glasses is equal to the probability of a person being a brunette multiplied by the probability of a person wearing glasses. This mathematical test of $P(A \cap B) = P(A)P(B)$ verifies that two events are independent.

Conditional Probability

Conditional probability is the probability that event A will happen given that event B has already occurred. An example of this is calculating the probability that a person will eat dessert once they have eaten dinner. This is different than calculating the probability of a person just eating dessert. The formula for the conditional probability of event A occurring given B is $P(A|B) = \frac{P(A \text{ and } B)}{P(B)}$, and it's defined to be the probability of both A and B occurring divided by the probability of event B occurring. If A and B are independent, then the probability of both A and B occurring is equal to $P(A)P(B)$, so $P(A|B)$ reduces to just $P(A)$. This means that A and B have no relationship, and the probability of A occurring is the same as the conditional probability of A occurring given B. Similarly, $P(B|A) = \frac{P(B \text{ and } A)}{P(A)} = P(B)$ if A and B are independent.

Independent Versus Related Events

To summarize, conditional probability is the probability that an event occurs given that another event has happened. If the two events are related, the probability that the second event will occur changes if the other event has happened. However, if the two events aren't related and are therefore independent, the first event to occur won't impact the probability of the second event occurring.

Measuring Probabilities with Two-Way Frequency Tables

When measuring event probabilities, two-way frequency tables can be used to report the raw data and then used to calculate probabilities. If the frequency tables are translated into relative frequency tables, the probabilities presented in the table can be plugged directly into the formulas for conditional probabilities. By plugging in the correct frequencies, the data from the table can be used to determine if events are independent or dependent.

Differing Probabilities

The probability that event A occurs differs from the probability that event A occurs given B. When working within a given model, it's important to note the difference. $P(A|B)$ is determined using the formula $P(A|B) = \frac{P(A \text{ and } B)}{P(B)}$ and represents the total number of A's outcomes left that could occur after B occurs. $P(A)$ can be calculated without any regard for B. For example, the probability of a student finding a parking spot on a busy campus is different once class is in session.

The Addition Rule

The probability of event A or B occurring isn't equal to the sum of each individual probability. The probability that both events can occur at the same time must be subtracted from this total. This idea is shown in the **addition rule**:

$$P(A \text{ or } B) = P(A) + P(B) - P(A \text{ and } B)$$

The addition rule is another way to determine the probability of compound events that aren't mutually exclusive. If the events are mutually exclusive, the probability of both A and B occurring at the same time is 0.

Computing Probabilities

Simple and Compound Events

A **simple event** consists of only one outcome. The most popular simple event is flipping a coin, which results in either heads or tails. A **compound event** results in more than one outcome and consists of more than one simple event. An example of a compound event is flipping a coin while tossing a die. The result is either heads or tails on the coin and a number from one to six on the die. The probability of a simple event is calculated by dividing the number of possible outcomes by the total number of outcomes. Therefore, the probability of obtaining heads on a coin is $\frac{1}{2}$, and the probability of rolling a 6 on a die is $\frac{1}{6}$. The probability of compound events is calculated using the basic idea of the probability of simple events. If the two events are independent, the probability of one outcome is

equal to the product of the probabilities of each simple event. For example, the probability of obtaining heads on a coin and rolling a 6 is equal to:

$$\frac{1}{2} \times \frac{1}{6} = \frac{1}{12}$$

The probability of either A or B occurring is equal to the sum of the probabilities minus the probability that both A and B will occur. Therefore, the probability of obtaining either heads on a coin or rolling a 6 on a die is:

$$\frac{1}{2} + \frac{1}{6} - \frac{1}{12} = \frac{7}{12}$$

The two events aren't mutually exclusive because they can happen at the same time. If two events are mutually exclusive, and the probability of both events occurring at the same time is zero, the probability of event A or B occurring equals the sum of both probabilities. An example of calculating the probability of two mutually exclusive events is determining the probability of pulling a king or a queen from a deck of cards. The two events cannot occur at the same time.

Uniform and Non-Uniform Probability Models

A **uniform probability model** is one where each outcome has an equal chance of occurring, such as the probabilities of rolling each side of a die. A **non-uniform probability model** is one where each result has a different chance of taking place. In a uniform probability model, the conditional probability formulas for $P(B|A)$ and $P(A|B)$ can be multiplied by their respective denominators to obtain two formulas for $P(A$ and $B)$. Therefore, the multiplication rule is derived as:

$$P(A \text{ and } B) = P(A)P(B|A) = P(B)P(A|B)$$

In a model, if the probability of either individual event is known and the corresponding conditional probability is known, the multiplication rule allows the probability of the joint occurrence of A and B to be calculated.

Calculating Theoretical Probabilities

Given a statistical experiment, a theoretical probability distribution can be calculated if the theoretical probabilities are known. The theoretical probabilities are plugged into the formula for both the binomial probability and the expected value. An example of this is any scenario involving rolls of a die or flips of a coin. The theoretical probabilities are known without any observed experiments.

Determining Unknown Probabilities

Empirical data is defined as real data. If real data is known, approximations concerning samples and populations can be obtained by working backwards. This scenario is the case where theoretical probabilities are unknown, and experimental data must be used to make decisions. The sample data (including actual probabilities) must be plugged into the formulas for both binomial probability and the expected value. The actual probabilities are obtained using observation and can be seen in a probability distribution. An example of this scenario is determining a probability distribution for the number of televisions per household in the United States and determining the expected number of televisions per household as well.

Weighing Outcomes

Calculating if it's worth it to play a game or make a decision is a critical part of probability theory. Expected values can be calculated in terms of payoff values, and deciding whether to make a decision or play a game can be done based on the actual expected value. Applying this theory to gambling and card games is fairly typical. The payoff values in these instances are the actual monetary totals.

Algebra and Geometry

Algebra

The Properties of the Basic Operations

Properties of operations exist that make calculations easier and solve problems for missing values. The following table summarizes commonly used properties of real numbers.

Property	Addition	Multiplication
Commutative	$a + b = b + a$	$a \times b = b \times a$
Associative	$(a + b) + c = a + (b + c)$	$(a \times b) \times c = a \times (b \times c)$
Identity	$a + 0 = a; 0 + a = a$	$a \times 1 = a; 1 \times a = a$
Inverse	$a + (-a) = 0$	$a \times \frac{1}{a} = 1; a \neq 0$
Distributive	$a(b + c) = ab + ac$	

The **commutative property of addition** states that the order in which numbers are added does not change the sum. Similarly, the **commutative property of multiplication** states that the order in which numbers are multiplied does not change the product. The **associative property** of addition and multiplication state that the grouping of numbers being added or multiplied does not change the sum or product, respectively. The commutative and associative properties are useful for performing calculations. For example, $(47 + 25) + 3$ is equivalent to $(47 + 3) + 25$, which is easier to calculate.

The **identity property of addition** states that adding zero to any number does not change its value. The **identity property of multiplication** states that multiplying a number by 1 does not change its value. The **inverse property of addition** states that the sum of a number and its opposite equals zero. Opposites are numbers that are the same with different signs (ex. 5 and -5; $-\frac{1}{2}$ and $\frac{1}{2}$).

The **inverse property of multiplication** states that the product of a number (other than 0) and its reciprocal equals 1. **Reciprocal numbers** have numerators and denominators that are inverted (ex. $\frac{2}{5}$ and $\frac{5}{2}$). Inverse properties are useful for canceling quantities to find missing values (see algebra content). For example, $a + 7 = 12$ is solved by adding the inverse of 7 (which is -7) to both sides in order to isolate a.

The **distributive property** states that multiplying a sum (or difference) by a number produces the same result as multiplying each value in the sum (or difference) by the number and adding (or subtracting) the products. Consider the following scenario: You are buying three tickets for a baseball game. Each ticket costs $18. You are also charged a fee of $2 per ticket for purchasing the tickets online. The cost is calculated: $3 \times 18 + 3 \times 2$. Using the distributive property, the cost can also be calculated $3(18 + 2)$.

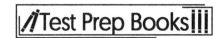

Following an Arithmetic or Algebraic Procedure

Evaluating and Simplifying Algebraic Expressions

Given an algebraic expression, students may be asked to evaluate for given values of variable(s). In doing so, students will arrive at a numerical value as an answer. For example:

$$\text{Evaluate } a - 2b + ab \text{ for } a = 3 \text{ and } b = -1$$

To evaluate an expression, the given values should be substituted for the variables and simplified using the order of operations. In this case:

$$(3) - 2(-1) + (3)(-1)$$

Parentheses are used when substituting.

Given an algebraic expression, students may be asked to simplify the expression. For example:

$$\text{Simplify } 5x^2 - 10x + 2 - 8x^2 + x - 1.$$

Simplifying algebraic expressions requires combining like terms. A term is a number, variable, or product of a number and variables separated by addition and subtraction. The terms in the above expression are: $5x^2$, $-10x$, 2, $-8x^2$, x, and -1. Like terms have the same variables raised to the same powers (exponents). To combine like terms, the coefficients (numerical factor of the term including sign) are added, while the variables and their powers are kept the same. The example above simplifies to

$$-3x^2 - 9x + 1$$

Use of Formulas

Formulas are mathematical expressions that define the value of one quantity, given the value of one or more different quantities. Formulas look like equations because they contain variables, numbers, operators, and an equal sign. All formulas are equations, but not all equations are formulas. A formula must have more than one variable. For example, $2x + 7 = y$ is an equation and a formula (it relates the unknown quantities x and y). However, $2x + 7 = 3$ is an equation but not a formula (it only expresses the value of the unknown quantity x).

Formulas are typically written with one variable alone (or isolated) on one side of the equal sign. This variable can be thought of as the *subject* in that the formula is stating the value of the *subject* in terms of the relationship between the other variables. Consider the distance formula: $distance = rate \times time$ or $d = rt$. The value of the subject variable d (distance) is the product of the variable r and t (rate and time). Given the rate and time, the distance traveled can easily be determined by substituting the values into the formula and evaluating.

The formula $P = 2l + 2w$ expresses how to calculate the perimeter of a rectangle (P) given its length (l) and width (w). To find the perimeter of a rectangle with a length of 3 ft and a width of 2 ft, these values are substituted into the formula for l and w:

$$P = 2(3ft) + 2(2ft)$$

Following the order of operations, the perimeter is determined to be 10 ft. When working with formulas such as these, including units is an important step.

Given a formula expressed in terms of one variable, the formula can be manipulated to express the relationship in terms of any other variable. In other words, the formula can be rearranged to change which variable is the **subject.** To solve for a variable of interest by manipulating a formula, the equation may be solved as if all other variables were numbers. The same steps for solving are followed, leaving operations in terms of the variables instead of calculating numerical values. For the formula $P = 2l + 2w$, the perimeter is the subject expressed in terms of the

length and width. To write a formula to calculate the width of a rectangle, given its length and perimeter, the previous formula relating the three variables is solved for the variable w. If P and l were numerical values, this is a two-step linear equation solved by subtraction and division. To solve the equation $P = 2l + 2w$ for w, $2l$ is first subtracted from both sides:

$$P - 2l = 2w$$

Then both sides are divided by 2:

$$\frac{P - 2l}{2} = w$$

Applying Understanding of Arithmetic to Algebraic Expressions

A fraction, or ratio, wherein each part is a polynomial, defines **rational expressions**. Some examples include $\frac{2x+6}{x}$, $\frac{1}{x^2-4x+8}$, and $\frac{z^2}{x+5}$. Exponents on the variables are restricted to whole numbers, which means roots and negative exponents are not included in rational expressions.

Rational expressions can be transformed by factoring. For example, the expression $\frac{x^2-5x+6}{(x-3)}$ can be rewritten by factoring the numerator to obtain:

$$\frac{(x-3)(x-2)}{(x-3)}$$

Therefore, the common binomial $(x-3)$ can cancel so that the simplified expression is:

$$\frac{(x-2)}{1} = (x-2)$$

Additionally, other rational expressions can be rewritten to take on different forms. Some may be factorable in themselves, while others can be transformed through arithmetic operations. Rational expressions are closed under addition, subtraction, multiplication, and division by a nonzero expression. **Closed** means that if any one of these operations is performed on a rational expression, the result will still be a rational expression. The set of all real numbers is another example of a set closed under all four operations.

Adding and subtracting rational expressions is based on the same concepts as adding and subtracting simple fractions. For both concepts, the denominators must be the same for the operation to take place. For example, here are two rational expressions:

$$\frac{x^3 - 4}{(x-3)} + \frac{x+8}{(x-3)}$$

Since the denominators are both $(x-3)$, the numerators can be combined by collecting like terms to form:

$$\frac{x^3 + x + 4}{(x-3)}$$

If the denominators are different, they need to be made common (the same) by using the Least Common Denominator (LCD). Each denominator needs to be factored, and the LCD contains each factor that appears in any one denominator the greatest number of times it appears in any denominator. The original expressions need to be multiplied times a form of 1, which will turn each denominator into the LCD. This process is like adding fractions with unlike denominators. It is also important when working with rational expressions to define what value of the variable makes the denominator zero. For this particular value, the expression is undefined.

152

Multiplication of rational expressions is performed like multiplication of fractions. The numerators are multiplied; then, the denominators are multiplied. The final fraction is then simplified. The expressions are simplified by factoring and cancelling out common terms. In the following example, the numerator of the second expression can be factored first to simplify the expression before multiplying:

$$\frac{x^2}{(x-4)} \times \frac{x^2 - x - 12}{2}$$

$$\frac{x^2}{(x-4)} \times \frac{(x-4)(x+3)}{2}$$

The $(x-4)$ on the top and bottom cancel out:

$$\frac{x^2}{1} \times \frac{(x+3)}{2}$$

Then multiplication is performed, resulting in:

$$\frac{x^3 + 3x^2}{2}$$

Dividing rational expressions is similar to the division of fractions, where division turns into multiplying by a reciprocal. So, the following expression can be rewritten as a multiplication problem:

$$\frac{x^2 - 3x + 7}{x - 4} \div \frac{x^2 - 5x + 3}{x - 4}$$

$$\frac{x^2 - 3x + 7}{x - 4} \times \frac{x - 4}{x^2 - 5x + 3}$$

The $x - 4$ cancels out, leaving:

$$\frac{x^2 - 3x + 7}{x^2 - 5x + 3}$$

The final answers should always be completely simplified. If a function is composed of a rational expression, the zeros of the graph can be found from setting the polynomial in the numerator as equal to zero and solving. The values that make the denominator equal to zero will either exist on the graph as a hole or a vertical asymptote.

Using Properties of Operations to Identify or Generate Equivalent Algebraic Expressions

Algebraic expressions are made up of numbers, variables, and combinations of the two, using mathematical operations. Expressions can be rewritten based on their factors. For example, the expression $6x + 4$ can be rewritten as $2(3x + 2)$ because 2 is a factor of both $6x$ and 4. More complex expressions can also be rewritten based on their factors. The expression $x^4 - 16$ can be rewritten as $(x^2 - 4)(x^2 + 4)$. This is a different type of factoring, where a difference of squares is factored into a sum and difference of the same two terms. With some expressions, the factoring process is simple and only leads to a different way to represent the expression. With others, factoring and rewriting the expression leads to more information about the given problem.

In the following quadratic equation, factoring the binomial leads to finding the zeros of the function:

$$x^2 - 5x + 6 = y$$

This equation factors into $(x - 3)(x - 2) = y$, where 2 and 3 are found to be the zeros of the function when y is set equal to zero. The zeros of any function are the x-values where the graph of the function on the coordinate plane crosses the x-axis.

Factoring an equation is a simple way to rewrite the equation and find the zeros, but factoring is not possible for every quadratic. Completing the square is one way to find zeros when factoring is not an option. The following equation cannot be factored:

$$x^2 + 10x - 9 = 0$$

The first step in this method is to move the constant to the right side of the equation, making it:

$$x^2 + 10x = 9$$

Then, the coefficient of x is divided by 2 and squared. This number is then added to both sides of the equation, to make the equation still true. For this example, $\left(\frac{10}{2}\right)^2 = 25$ is added to both sides of the equation to obtain:

$$x^2 + 10x + 25 = 9 + 25$$

This expression simplifies to $x^2 + 10x + 25 = 34$, which can then be factored into:

$$(x + 5)^2 = 34$$

Solving for x then involves taking the square root of both sides and subtracting 5. This leads to two zeros of the function:

$$x = \pm\sqrt{34} - 5$$

Depending on the type of answer the question seeks, a calculator may be used to find exact numbers.

Given a quadratic equation in standard form—$ax^2 + bx + c = 0$—the sign of a tells whether the function has a minimum value or a maximum value. If $a > 0$, the graph opens up and has a minimum value. If $a < 0$, the graph opens down and has a maximum value. Depending on the way the quadratic equation is written, multiplication may need to occur before a max/min value is determined.

Exponential expressions can also be rewritten, just as quadratic equations. Properties of exponents must be understood.

Distributive Property

The distributive property states that multiplying a sum (or difference) by a number produces the same result as multiplying each value in the sum (or difference) by the number and adding (or subtracting) the products. Using mathematical symbols, the distributive property states $a(b + c) = ab + ac$. The expression $4(3 + 2)$ is simplified using the order of operations. Simplifying inside the parentheses first produces 4×5, which equals 20. The expression $4(3 + 2)$ can also be simplified using the distributive property:

$$4(3 + 2)$$
$$4 \times 3 + 4 \times 2$$
$$12 + 8 = 20$$

Consider the following example: $4(3x - 2)$. The expression cannot be simplified inside the parentheses because $3x$ and -2 are not like terms, and therefore cannot be combined. However, the expression can be simplified by using the distributive property and multiplying each term inside of the parentheses by the term outside of the parentheses: $12x - 8$. The resulting equivalent expression contains no like terms, so it cannot be further simplified.

Consider the expression:

$$(3x + 2y + 1) - (5x - 3) + 2(3y + 4)$$

Again, there are no like terms, but the distributive property is used to simplify the expression. Note there is an implied one in front of the first set of parentheses and an implied -1 in front of the second set of parentheses.

Distributing the 1, -1, and 2 produces:

$$1(3x) + 1(2y) + 1(1) - 1(5x) - 1(-3) + 2(3y) + 2(4)$$

$$3x + 2y + 1 - 5x + 3 + 6y + 8$$

This expression contains like terms that are combined to produce the simplified expression:

$$-2x + 8y + 12$$

Algebraic expressions are tested to be equivalent by choosing values for the variables and evaluating both expressions. For example, $4(3x - 2)$ and $12x - 8$ are tested by substituting 3 for the variable x and calculating to determine if equivalent values result.

Writing Linear Expressions and Equations

Linear relationships describe the way two quantities change with respect to each other. The relationship is defined as linear because a line is produced if all the sets of corresponding values are graphed on a coordinate grid. When expressing the linear relationship as an equation, the equation is often written in the form $y = mx + b$ (slope-intercept form) where m and b are numerical values and x and y are variables (for example, $y = 5x + 10$). Given a linear equation and the value of either variable (x or y), the value of the other variable can be determined.

Suppose a teacher is grading a test containing 20 questions with 5 points given for each correct answer, adding a curve of 10 points to each test. This linear relationship can be expressed as the equation $y = 5x + 10$ where x represents the number of correct answers, and y represents the test score. To determine the score of a test with a given number of correct answers, the number of correct answers is substituted into the equation for x and evaluated. For example, for 10 correct answers, 10 is substituted for x:
$$y = 5(10) + 10 \rightarrow y = 60$$

Therefore, 10 correct answers will result in a score of 60. The number of correct answers needed to obtain a certain score can also be determined. To determine the number of correct answers needed to score a 90, 90 is substituted for y in the equation (y represents the test score) and solved:

$$90 = 5x + 10 \rightarrow 80 = 5x \rightarrow 16 = x$$

Therefore, 16 correct answers are needed to score a 90.

Linear relationships may be represented by a table of 2 corresponding values. Certain tables may determine the relationship between the values and predict other corresponding sets. Consider the table below, which displays the money in a checking account that charges a monthly fee:

Month	0	1	2	3	4
Balance	$210	$195	$180	$165	$150

155

An examination of the values reveals that the account loses $15 every month (the month increases by one and the balance decreases by 15). This information can be used to predict future values. To determine what the value will be in month 6, the pattern can be continued, and it can be concluded that the balance will be $120. To determine which month the balance will be $0, $210 is divided by $15 (since the balance decreases $15 every month), resulting in month 14.

Similar to a table, a graph can display corresponding values of a linear relationship.

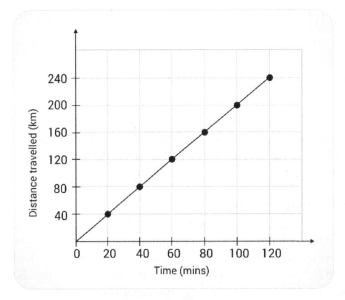

The graph above represents the relationship between distance traveled and time. To find the distance traveled in 80 minutes, the mark for 80 minutes is located at the bottom of the graph. By following this mark directly up on the graph, the corresponding point for 80 minutes is directly across from the 160-kilometer mark. This information indicates that the distance travelled in 80 minutes is 160 kilometers. To predict information not displayed on the graph, the way in which the variables change with respect to one another is determined. In this case, distance increases by 40 kilometers as time increases by 20 minutes. This information can be used to continue the data in the graph or convert the values to a table.

Writing Linear Expressions and Equations

A linear expression is a statement about an unknown quantity expressed in mathematical symbols. The statement "five times a number added to forty" can be expressed as $5x + 40$. A linear equation is a statement in which two expressions (at least one containing a variable) are equal to each other. The statement "five times a number added to forty is equal to ten" can be expressed as $5x + 40 = 10$. Real-world scenarios can also be expressed mathematically. Consider the following:

Bob had $20 and Tom had $4. After selling 4 ice cream cones to Bob, Tom has as much money as Bob.

The cost of an ice cream cone is an unknown quantity and can be represented by a variable. The amount of money Bob has after his purchase is four times the cost of an ice cream cone subtracted from his original $20. The amount of money Tom has after his sale is four times the cost of an ice cream cone added to his original $4. This can be expressed as: $20 - 4x = 4x + 4$, where x represents the cost of an ice cream cone.

When expressing a verbal or written statement mathematically, it is key to understand words or phrases that can be represented with symbols. The following are examples:

Symbol	Phrase
$+$	added to, increased by, sum of, more than
$-$	decreased by, difference between, less than, take away
x	multiplied by, 3 (4, 5 ...) times as large, product of
$\div$	divided by, quotient of, half (third, etc.) of
$=$	is, the same as, results in, as much as
x, t, n, etc.	a number, unknown quantity, value of

Identifying Variables for Linear Models

The first step to writing a linear model is to identify what the variables represent. A **variable** represents an unknown quantity, and in the case of a linear equation, a specific relationship exists between the two variables (usually x and y). Within a given scenario, the variables are the two quantities that are changing. The variable x is considered the independent variable and represents the inputs of a function. The variable y is considered the dependent variable and represents the outputs of a function. For example, if a scenario describes distance traveled and time traveled, distance would be represented by y and time represented by x. The distance traveled depends on the time spent traveling (time is independent). If a scenario describes the cost of a cab ride and the distance traveled, the cost would be represented by y and the distance represented by x. The cost of a cab ride depends on the distance traveled.

Identifying the Slope and Y-Intercept for Linear Models

The **slope of the graph of a line** represents the rate of change between the variables of an equation. In the context of a real-world scenario, the slope will tell the way in which the unknown quantities (variables) change with respect to each other. A scenario involving distance and time might state that someone is traveling at a rate of 45 miles per hour. The slope of the linear model would be 45. A scenario involving the cost of a cab ride and distance traveled might state that the person is charged $3 for each mile. The slope of the linear model would be 3.

The y-**intercept of a linear function** is the value of y when $x = 0$ (the point where the line intercepts the y-axis on the graph of the equation). It is sometimes helpful to think of this as a "starting point" for a linear function. Suppose for the scenario about the cab ride that the person is told that the cab company charges a flat fee of $5 plus $3 for each mile. Before traveling any distance ($x = 0$), the cost is $5. The y-intercept for the linear model would be 5.

Identifying Ordered Pairs for Linear Models

A linear equation with two variables can be written given a point (ordered pair) and the slope or given two points on a line. An ordered pair gives a set of corresponding values for the two variables (x and y). As an example, for a scenario involving distance and time, it is given that the person traveled 112.5 miles in 2 ½ hours. Knowing that x represents time and y represents distance, this information can be written as the ordered pair $(2.5, 112.5)$.

Writing Linear Functions

Linear relationships between two quantities can be expressed in two ways: function notation or as a linear equation with two variables. The relationship is referred to as linear because its graph is represented by a line. For a relationship to be linear, both variables must be raised to the first power only.

A **relation** is a set of input and output values that can be written as ordered pairs. A function is a relation in which each input is paired with exactly one output. The domain of a function consists of all inputs, and the range consists of all outputs. Graphing the ordered pairs of a linear function produces a straight line. An example of a function would be $f(x) = 4x + 4$, read "f of x is equal to four times x plus four." In this example, the input would be x and the output would be $f(x)$. Ordered pairs would be represented as $(x, f(x))$. To find the output for an input value of 3, 3 would be substituted for x into the function as follows: $f(3) = 4(3) + 4$, resulting in $f(3) = 16$. Therefore, the ordered pair $(3, f(3)) = (3, 16)$. Note $f(x)$ is a function of x denoted by f. Functions of x could be named $g(x)$, read "g of x"; $p(x)$, read "p of x"; etc.

A linear function could also be written in the form of an equation with two variables. Typically, the variable x represents the inputs and the variable y represents the outputs. The variable x is considered the independent variable and y the dependent variable. The above function would be written as $y = 4x + 4$. Ordered pairs are written in the form (x, y).

Writing Linear Equations in Two Variables

When writing linear equations in two variables, the process depends on the information given. Questions will typically provide the slope of the line and its y-intercept, an ordered pair and the slope, or two ordered pairs.

Linear equations are commonly written in slope-intercept form, $y = mx + b$, where m represents the slope of the line and b represents the y-intercept. The slope is the rate of change between the variables, usually expressed as a whole number or fraction. The y-intercept is the value of y when $x = 0$ (the point where the line intercepts the y-axis on a graph). Given the slope and y-intercept of a line, the values are substituted for m and b into the equation. A line with a slope of $\frac{1}{2}$ and y-intercept of -2 would have an equation:

$$y = \frac{1}{2}x - 2$$

The point-slope form of a line, $y - y_1 = m(x - x_1)$, is used to write an equation when given an ordered pair (point on the equation's graph) for the function and its rate of change (slope of the line). The values for the slope, m, and the point (x_1, y_1) are substituted into the point-slope form to obtain the equation of the line. A line with a slope of 3 and an ordered pair $(4, -2)$ would have an equation:

$$y - (-2) = 3(x - 4)$$

If a question specifies that the equation be written in slope-intercept form, the equation should be manipulated to isolate y:

Solve: $y - (-2) = 3(x - 4)$

Distribute: $y + 2 = 3x - 12$

Subtract 2 from both sides: $y = 3x - 14$

Given two ordered pairs for a function, (x_1, y_1) and (x_2, y_2), it is possible to determine the rate of change between the variables (slope of the line). To calculate the slope of the line, m, the values for the ordered pairs should be substituted into the formula:

$$m = \frac{y_2 - y_1}{x_2 - x_1}$$

The expression is substituted to obtain a whole number or fraction for the slope. Once the slope is calculated, the slope and either of the ordered pairs should be substituted into the point-slope form to obtain the equation of the line.

Writing Linear Inequalities

Linear inequalities are a concise mathematical way to express the relationship between unequal values. More specifically, they describe in what way the values are unequal. A value could be greater than (>); less than (<); greater than or equal to (≥); or less than or equal to (≤) another value. The statement "five times a number added to forty is more than sixty-five" can be expressed as $5x + 40 > 65$. Common words and phrases that express inequalities are:

Symbol	Phrase
<	is under, is below, smaller than, beneath
>	is above, is over, bigger than, exceeds
≤	no more than, at most, maximum
≥	no less than, at least, minimum

Solving Word Problems

Word problems can appear daunting, but prepared test takers shouldn't let the verbiage psyche them out. No matter the scenario or specifics, the key to answering them is to translate the words into a math problem. It is critical to keep in mind what the question is asking and what operations could lead to that answer. The following word problem resembles one of the question types most frequently encountered on the exam.

Working with Money

Walter's Coffee Shop sells a variety of drinks and breakfast treats.

Price List	
Hot Coffee	$2.00
Slow Drip Iced Coffee	$3.00
Latte	$4.00
Muffins	$2.00
Crepe	$4.00
Egg Sandwich	$5.00

Costs	
Hot Coffee	$0.25
Slow Drip Iced Coffee	$0.75
Latte	$1.00
Muffins	$1.00
Crepe	$2.00
Egg Sandwich	$3.00

Walter's utilities, rent, and labor costs him $500 per day. Today, Walter sold 200 hot coffees, 100 slow drip iced coffees, 50 lattes, 75 muffins, 45 crepes, and 60 egg sandwiches. What was Walter's total profit today?

To accurately answer this type of question, the first step is to determine the total cost of making his drinks and treats, then determine how much revenue he earned from selling those products. After arriving at these two totals, the profit is measured by deducting the total cost from the total revenue.

Walter's costs for today:

200 hot coffees	× $0.25	= $50
100 slow drip iced coffees	× $0.75	= $75
50 lattes	× $1.00	= $50
75 muffins	× $1.00	= $75
45 crepes	× $2.00	= $90
60 egg sandwiches	× $3.00	= $180
Utilities, Rent, and Labor		= $500
Total costs		= $1,020

Walter's revenue for today:

200 hot coffees	× $2.00	= $400
100 slow drip iced coffees	× $3.00	= $300
50 lattes	× $4.00	= $200
75 muffins	× $2.00	= $150
45 crepes	× $4.00	= $180
60 egg sandwiches	× $5.00	= $300
Total revenue		= $1,530

The formula for Walter's profits is:

$$Profit = Revenue - Costs = \$1,530 - \$1,020 = \$510$$

This strategy can be applied to other question types. For example, calculating salary after deductions, balancing a checkbook, and calculating a dinner bill are common word problems similar to business planning. In all cases, the most important step is remembering to use the correct operations. When a balance is increased, addition is used. When a balance is decreased, the problem requires subtraction. Common sense and organization are one's greatest assets when answering word problems.

Solving Linear Equations in One Variable Algebraically

Solving equations in one variable is the process of isolating that variable on one side of the equation. The letters in an equation are variables as they stand for unknown quantities that you are trying to solve for. The numbers attached to the variables by multiplication are called coefficients. X is commonly used as a variable, though any letter can be used. For example, in $3x - 7 = 20$, the variable is $3x$, and it needs to be isolated. The numbers (also called constants) are -7 and 20. That means $3x$ needs to be on one side of the equals sign (either side is fine), and all the numbers need to be on the other side of the equals sign.

To accomplish this, the equation must be manipulated by performing opposite operations of what already exists. Remember that addition and subtraction are opposites and that multiplication and division are opposites. Any action taken to one side of the equation must be taken on the other side to maintain equality.

So, since the 7 is being subtracted, it can be moved to the right side of the equation by adding seven to both sides:

$$3x - 7 = 20$$

$$3x - 7 + 7 = 20 + 7$$

$$3x = 27$$

Now that the variable $3x$ is on one side and the constants (now combined into one constant) are on the other side, the 3 needs to be moved to the right side. 3 and x are being multiplied together, so 3 then needs to be divided from each side.

$$\frac{3x}{3} = \frac{27}{3}$$

$$x = 9$$

Now x has been completely isolated, and thus we know its value.

The solution is found to be $x = 9$. This solution can be checked for accuracy by plugging $x = 9$ in the original equation. After simplifying the equation, $20 = 20$ is found, which is a true statement:

$$3 \times 9 - 7 = 20$$

$$27 - 7 = 20$$

$$20 = 20$$

Equations that require solving for a variable (**algebraic equations**) come in many forms. Here are some more examples:

No coefficient attached to the variable:

$$x + 8 = 20$$

$$x + 8 - 8 = 20 - 8$$

$$x = 12$$

A fractional coefficient:

$$\frac{1}{2}z + 24 = 36$$

$$\frac{1}{2}z + 24 - 24 = 36 - 24$$

$$\frac{1}{2}z = 12$$

Now we multiply the fraction by its inverse:

$$\frac{2}{1} \times \frac{1}{2}z = 12 \times \frac{2}{1}$$

$$z = 24$$

Multiple instances of x:

$$14x + x - 4 = 3x + 2$$

All instances of x can be combined.

$$15x - 4 = 3x + 2$$

$$15x - 4 + 4 = 3x + 2 + 4$$

$$15x = 3x + 6$$

$$15x - 3x = 3x + 6 - 3x$$

$$12x = 6$$

Then simply divide by 12.

$$\frac{12x}{12} = \frac{6}{12}$$

$$x = \frac{1}{2}$$

Methods for Solving Equations

Equations with one variable can be solved using the addition principle and multiplication principle. If $a = b$, then $a + c = b + c$, and $ac = bc$. Given the equation $2x - 3 = 5x + 7$, the first step is to combine the variable terms and the constant terms. Using the principles, expressions can be added and subtracted onto and off both sides of the equals sign, so the equation turns into $-10 = 3x$. Dividing by 3 on both sides through the multiplication principle with $c = \frac{1}{3}$ results in the final answer of:

$$x = \frac{-10}{3}$$

Some equations have a higher degree and are not solved by simply using opposite operations. When an equation has a degree of 2, completing the square is an option. For example, the quadratic equation $x^2 - 6x + 2 = 0$ can be rewritten by completing the square. The goal of completing the square is to get the equation into the form:

$$(x - p)^2 = q$$

Using the example, the constant term 2 first needs to be moved over to the opposite side by subtracting. Then, the square can be completed by adding 9 to both sides, which is the square of half of the coefficient of the middle term $-6x$. The current equation is:

$$x^2 - 6x + 9 = 7$$

The left side can be factored into a square of a binomial, resulting in:

$$(x - 3)^2 = 7$$

To solve for x, the square root of both sides should be taken, resulting in:

$$(x - 3) = \pm\sqrt{7}$$

$$x = 3 \pm \sqrt{7}$$

Other ways of solving quadratic equations include graphing, factoring, and using the quadratic formula. The equation $y = x^2 - 4x + 3$ can be graphed on the coordinate plane, and the solutions can be observed where it crosses the x-axis. The graph will be a parabola that opens up with two solutions at 1 and 3.

The equation can also be factored to find the solutions. The original equation, $y = x^2 - 4x + 3$ can be factored into:

$$y = (x - 1)(x - 3)$$

Setting this equal to zero, the x-values are found to be 1 and 3, just as on the graph. Solving by factoring and graphing are not always possible. The quadratic formula is a method of solving quadratic equations that always results in exact solutions.

The formula is:

$$x = \frac{-b \pm \sqrt{b^2 - 4ac}}{2a}$$

where a, b, and c are the coefficients in the original equation in standard form:

$$y = ax^2 + bx + c$$

For this example,

$$x = \frac{4 \pm \sqrt{(-4)^2 - 4(1)(3)}}{2(1)} = \frac{4 \pm \sqrt{16 - 12}}{2} = \frac{4 \pm 2}{2} = 1, 3$$

The expression underneath the radical is called the **discriminant**. Without working out the entire formula, the value of the discriminant can reveal the nature of the solutions. If the value of the discriminant $b^2 - 4ac$ is positive, then there will be two real solutions. If the value is zero, there will be one real solution. If the value is negative, the two solutions will be imaginary or complex. If the solutions are complex, it means that the parabola never touches the x-axis. An example of a complex solution can be found by solving the following quadratic:

$$y = x^2 - 4x + 8$$

By using the quadratic formula, the solutions are found to be:

$$x = \frac{4 \pm \sqrt{(-4)^2 - 4(1)(8)}}{2(1)}$$

$$\frac{4 \pm \sqrt{16 - 32}}{2} \frac{4 \pm \sqrt{-16}}{2} = 2 \pm 2i$$

The solutions both have a real part, 2, and an imaginary part, $2i$.

Solving Linear Inequalities

Linear equations and linear inequalities are both comparisons of two algebraic expressions. However, unlike equations in which the expressions are equal, linear inequalities compare expressions that may be unequal. Linear equations typically have one value for the variable that makes the statement true. Linear inequalities generally have an infinite number of values that make the statement true.

When solving a linear equation, the desired result requires determining a numerical value for the unknown variable. If given a linear equation involving addition, subtraction, multiplication, or division, working backwards isolates the variable. Addition and subtraction are inverse operations, as are multiplication and division. Therefore, they can be used to cancel each other out.

For example, solve:
$$4(t-2) + 2t - 4 = 2(9 - 2t)$$

Distributing:
$$4t - 8 + 2t - 4 = 18 - 4t$$

Combining like terms:

$$6t - 12 = 18 - 4t$$

Adding $4t$ to each side to move the variable:

$$10t - 12 = 18$$

Adding 12 to each side to isolate the variable:
$$10t = 30$$

Dividing each side by 10 to isolate the variable: $t = 3$

The answer can be checked by substituting the value for the variable into the original equation, ensuring that both sides calculate to be equal.

Linear inequalities express the relationship between unequal values. More specifically, they describe in what way the values are unequal. A value can be greater than (>), less than (<), greater than or equal to (≥), or less than or equal to (≤) another value. $5x + 40 > 65$ is read as *five times a number added to forty is greater than sixty-five.*

When solving a linear inequality, the solution is the set of all numbers that make the statement true. The inequality $x + 2 \geq 6$ has a solution set of 4 and every number greater than 4 (4.01; 5; 12; 107; etc.). Adding 2 to 4 or any number greater than 4 results in a value that is greater than or equal to 6. Therefore, $x \geq 4$ is the solution set.

To algebraically solve a linear inequality, follow the same steps as those for solving a linear equation. The inequality symbol stays the same for all operations *except* when multiplying or dividing by a negative number. If multiplying or dividing by a negative number while solving an inequality, the relationship reverses (the sign flips). In other words, > switches to < and vice versa. Multiplying or dividing by a positive number does not change the relationship, so the sign stays the same. An example is shown below.

Solve $-2(x + 4) \leq 22$ for the value of x.

First, distribute -2 to the binomial by multiplying:

$$-2x - 8 \leq 22$$

Next, add 8 to both sides to isolate the variable:

$$-2x \leq 30$$

Divide both sides by -2 to solve for x:

$$x \geq -15$$

Solutions of a linear equation or a linear inequality are the values of the variable that make a statement true. In the case of a linear equation, the solution set (list of all possible solutions) typically consists of a single numerical value. To find the solution, the equation is solved by isolating the variable. For example, solving the equation $3x - 7 = -13$ produces the solution $x = -2$. The only value for x which produces a true statement is -2. This can be checked by substituting -2 into the original equation to check that both sides are equal. In this case, $3(-2) - 7 = -13 \rightarrow -13 = -13$; therefore, -2 is a solution.

164

Although linear equations generally have one solution, this is not always the case. If there is no value for the variable that makes the statement true, there is no solution to the equation. Consider the equation $x + 3 = x - 1$. There is no value for x in which adding 3 to the value produces the same result as subtracting one from the value. Conversely, if any value for the variable makes a true statement, the equation has an infinite number of solutions. Consider the equation:

$$3x + 6 = 3(x + 2)$$

Any number substituted for x will result in a true statement (both sides of the equation are equal).

By manipulating equations like the two above, the variable of the equation will cancel out completely. If the remaining constants express a true statement (ex. $6 = 6$), then all real numbers are solutions to the equation. If the constants left express a false statement (ex. $3 = -1$), then no solution exists for the equation.

Solving a linear inequality requires all values that make the statement true to be determined. For example, solving $3x - 7 \geq -13$ produces the solution $x \geq -2$. This means that -2 and any number greater than -2 produces a true statement. Solution sets for linear inequalities will often be displayed using a number line. If a value is included in the set ($\geq$ or $\leq$), a shaded dot is placed on that value and an arrow extending in the direction of the solutions. For a variable $>$ or $\geq$ a number, the arrow will point right on a number line, the direction where the numbers increase. If a variable is $<$ or $\leq$ a number, the arrow will point left on a number line, which is the direction where the numbers decrease. If the value is not included in the set ($>$ or $<$), an open (unshaded) circle on that value is used with an arrow in the appropriate direction.

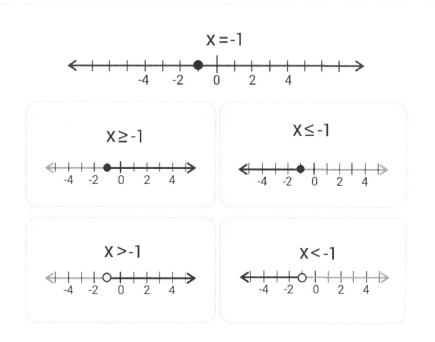

Similar to linear equations, a linear inequality may have a solution set consisting of all real numbers or can contain no solution. When solved algebraically, a linear inequality in which the variable cancels out and results in a true statement (ex. $7 \geq 2$) has a solution set of all real numbers. A linear inequality in which the variable cancels out and results in a false statement (ex. $7 \leq 2$) has no solution.

Solving Simple Quadratic Equations

A **quadratic equation** is an equation in the form:

$$ax^2 + bx + c = 0$$

There are several methods to solve such equations. The easiest method will depend on the quadratic equation in question.

Sometimes, it is possible to solve quadratic equations by manually *factoring* them. This means rewriting them in the form:

$$(x + A)(x + B) = 0$$

If this is done, then they can be solved by remembering that when $ab = 0$, either a or b must be equal to zero.

Therefore, to have $(x + A)(x + B) = 0$, $(x + A) = 0$ or $(x + B) = 0$ is needed. These equations have the solutions $x = -A$ and $x = -B$, respectively.

In order to factor a quadratic equation, note that:

$$(x + A)(x + B) = x^2 + (A + B)x + AB$$

So, if an equation is in the form $x^2 + bx + c$, two numbers, A and B, need to be found that will add up to give us b, and multiply together to give us c.

As an example, consider solving the equation:

$$-3x^2 + 6x + 9 = 0$$

Start by dividing both sides by -3, leaving:

$$x^2 - 2x - 3 = 0$$

Now, notice that $1 - 3 = -2$, and also that $(1)(-3) = -3$. This means the equation can be factored into:
$$(x + 1)(x - 3) = 0$$

Now, solve $(x + 1) = 0$ and $(x - 3) = 0$ to get $x = -1$ and $x = 3$ as the solutions.

It is useful when trying to factor to remember these three things:

$$x^2 + 2xy + y^2 = (x + y)^2$$

$$x^2 - 2xy + y^2 = (x - y)^2$$

and

$$x^2 - y^2 = (x + y)(x - y)$$

However, factoring by hand is often hard to do. If there are no obvious ways to factor the quadratic equation, solutions can still be found by using the **quadratic formula**.

The quadratic formula is:

$$x = \frac{-b \pm \sqrt{b^2 - 4ac}}{2a}$$

166

This method will always work, although it sometimes can take longer than factoring by hand, if the factors are easy to guess. Using the standard form $ax^2 + bx + c = 0$, plug the values of a, b, and c from the equation into the formula and solve for x. There will either be two answers, one answer, or no real answer. No real answer comes when the value of the discriminant, the number under the square root, is a negative number. Since there are no real numbers that square to get a negative, the answer will be no real roots.

Here is an example of solving a quadratic equation using the quadratic formula. Suppose the equation to solve is:
$$-2x^2 + 3x + 1 = 0$$

There is no obvious way to factor this, so the quadratic formula is used, with $a = -2$, $b = 3$, $c = 1$. After substituting these values into the quadratic formula, it yields this:

$$x = \frac{-3 \pm \sqrt{3^2 - 4(-2)(1)}}{2(-2)}$$

This can be simplified to obtain:

$$\frac{3 \pm \sqrt{9 + 8}}{4}$$

or

$$\frac{3 \pm \sqrt{17}}{4}$$

Challenges can be encountered when asked to find a quadratic equation with specific roots. Given roots A and B, a quadratic function can be constructed with those roots by taking:

$$(x - A)(x - B)$$

So, in constructing a quadratic equation with roots $x = -2, 3$, it would result in:

$$(x + 2)(x - 3) = x^2 - x - 6$$

Multiplying this by a constant also could be done without changing the roots.

Geometry

Utilizing Basic Properties of Common Two-Dimensional Shapes to Solve Problems

A **polygon** is a closed geometric figure in a plane (flat surface) consisting of at least 3 sides formed by line segments. These are often defined as two-dimensional shapes. Common two-dimensional shapes include circles, triangles, squares, rectangles, pentagons, and hexagons. Note that a circle is a two-dimensional shape without sides.

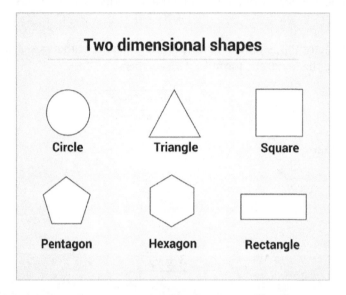

Polygons can be either convex or concave. A polygon that has interior angles all measuring less than 180° is convex. A concave polygon has one or more interior angles measuring greater than 180°. Examples are shown below.

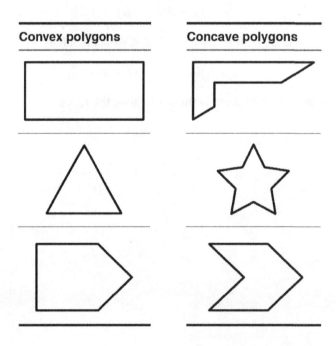

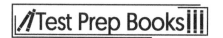

Polygons can be classified by the number of sides (also equal to the number of angles) they have. The following are the names of polygons with a given number of sides or angles:

# of Sides	Name of Polygon
3	Triangle
4	Quadrilateral
5	Pentagon
6	Hexagon
7	Septagon (or heptagon)
8	Octagon
9	Nonagon
10	Decagon

Equiangular polygons are polygons in which the measure of every interior angle is the same. The sides of equilateral polygons are always the same length. If a polygon is both equiangular and equilateral, the polygon is defined as a regular polygon.

Triangles can be further classified by their sides and angles. A triangle with its largest angle measuring 90° is a right triangle. A triangle with the largest angle less than 90° is an acute triangle. A triangle with the largest angle greater than 90° is an obtuse triangle. Below is an example of a right triangle.

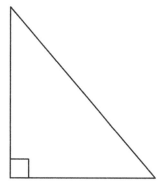

A triangle consisting of two equal sides and two equal angles is an isosceles triangle. A triangle with three equal sides and three equal angles is an equilateral triangle. A triangle with no equal sides or angles is a scalene triangle.

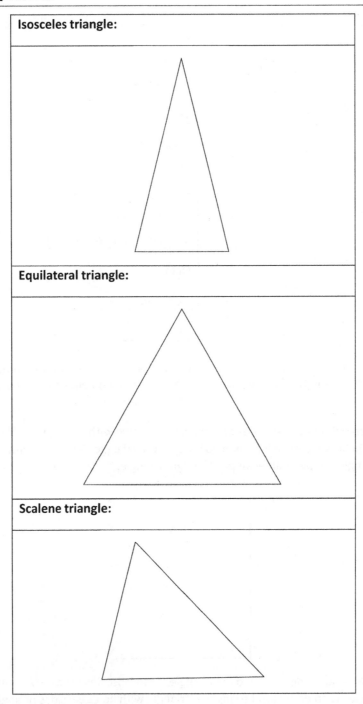

Quadrilaterals can be further classified according to their sides and angles. A quadrilateral with exactly one pair of parallel sides is called a trapezoid. A quadrilateral that shows both pairs of opposite sides parallel is a parallelogram. Parallelograms include rhombuses, rectangles, and squares. A rhombus has four equal sides. A rectangle has four equal angles (90° each). A square has four 90° angles and four equal sides. Therefore, a square is both a rhombus and a rectangle.

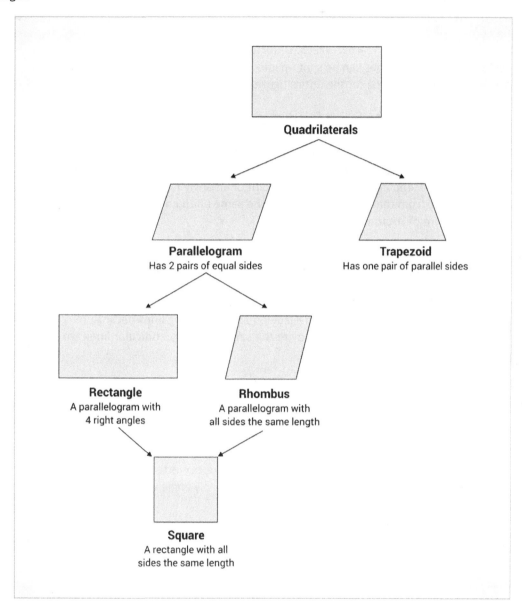

Angles and Diagonals

Diagonals are lines (excluding sides) that connect two vertices within a polygon. **Mutually bisecting diagonals** intersect at their midpoints. Parallelograms, rectangles, squares, and rhombuses have mutually bisecting diagonals. However, trapezoids don't have such lines. **Perpendicular diagonals** occur when they form four right triangles at their point of intersection. Squares and rhombuses have perpendicular diagonals, but trapezoids, rectangles, and parallelograms do not. Finally, **perpendicular bisecting diagonals** (also known as **perpendicular bisectors**) form four right triangles at their point of intersection, but this intersection is also the midpoint of the two lines. Both rhombuses and squares have perpendicular bisecting angles, but trapezoids, rectangles, and parallelograms do not. Knowing these definitions can help tremendously in problems that involve both angles and diagonals.

171

Polygons with More than Four Sides

A **pentagon** is a five-sided figure. A six-sided shape is a **hexagon**. A seven-sided figure is classified as a **heptagon**, and an eight-sided figure is called an **octagon**. An important characteristic is whether a polygon is regular or irregular. If it's **regular,** the side lengths and angle measurements are all equal. An **irregular** polygon has unequal side lengths and angle measurements. Mathematical problems involving polygons with more than four sides usually involve side length and angle measurements. The sum of all internal angles in a polygon $= 180(n - 2)$ degrees, where n is the number of sides. Therefore, the total of all internal angles in a pentagon is 540 degrees because there are five sides so $180(5 - 2) = 540$ degrees. Unfortunately, area formulas don't exist for polygons with more than four sides. However, their shapes can be split up into triangles, and the formula for area of a triangle can be applied and totaled to obtain the area for the entire figure.

Utilizing Facts About Angles to Solve Problems

In geometry, a **line** connects two points, has no thickness, and extends indefinitely in both directions beyond each point. If the length is finite, it's known as a **line segment** and has two **endpoints**. A **ray** is the straight portion of a line that has one endpoint and extends indefinitely in the other direction. An **angle** is formed when two rays begin at the same endpoint and extend indefinitely. The endpoint of an angle is called a **vertex**. **Adjacent angles** are two side-by-side angles formed from the same ray that have the same endpoint. Angles are measured in **degrees** or **radians**, which is a measure of **rotation**.

A **full rotation** equals 360 degrees or 2π radians, which represents a circle. Half a rotation equals 180 degrees or π radians and represents a half-circle. Angle measurement is additive. When an angle is broken into two non-overlapping angles, the total measure of the larger angle equals the sum of the two smaller angles. Lines are **coplanar** if they're located in the same plane. Two lines are **parallel** if they are coplanar, extend in the same direction, and never cross. If lines do cross, they're labeled as **intersecting lines** because they "intersect" at one point. If they intersect at more than one point, they're the same line. **Perpendicular lines** are coplanar lines that form a right angle at their point of intersection.

Classification of Angles

An angle consists of two rays that have a common endpoint. This common endpoint is called the **vertex of the angle**. The two rays can be called sides of the angle. The angle below has a vertex at point B and the sides consist of ray BA and ray BC. An angle can be named in three ways:

1. Using the vertex and a point from each side, with the vertex letter in the middle.
2. Using only the vertex. This can only be used if it is the only angle with that vertex.
3. Using a number that is written inside the angle.

The angle below can be written $\angle ABC$ (read angle ABC), $\angle CBA$, $\angle B$, or $\angle 1$.

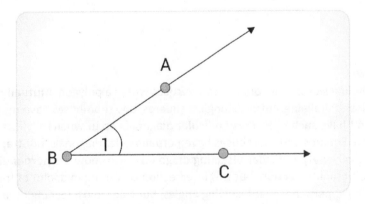

An angle divides a plane, or flat surface, into three parts: the angle itself, the interior (inside) of the angle, and the exterior (outside) of the angle. The figure below shows point *M* on the interior of the angle and point *N* on the exterior of the angle.

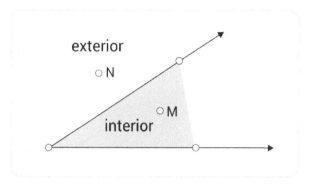

Angles can be measured in units called degrees, with the symbol °. The degree measure of an angle is between 0° and 180° and can be obtained by using a protractor.

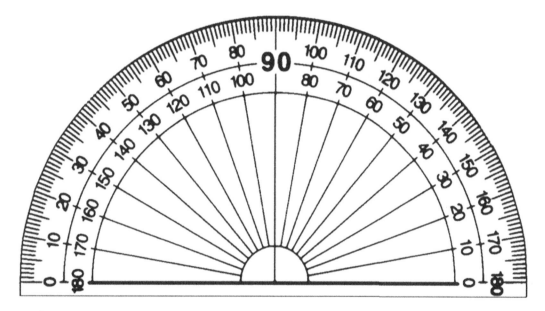

A straight angle (or simply a line) measures exactly 180°. A right angle's sides meet at the vertex to create a square corner. A right angle measures exactly 90° and is typically indicated by a box drawn in the interior of the angle. An acute angle has an interior that is narrower than a right angle. The measure of an acute angle is any value less than 90° and greater than 0°. For example, 89.9°, 47°, 12°, and 1°. An obtuse angle has an interior that is wider than a

right angle. The measure of an obtuse angle is any value greater than 90° but less than 180°. For example, 90.1°, 110°, 150°, and 179.9°.

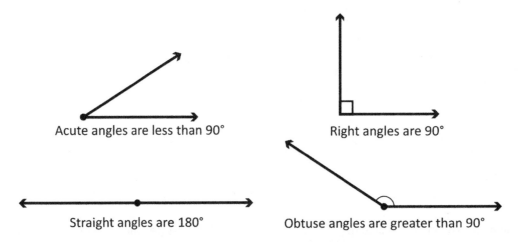

Acute angles are less than 90°

Right angles are 90°

Straight angles are 180°

Obtuse angles are greater than 90°

Solving Line Problems

Two lines are parallel if they have the same slope and a different intercept. Two lines are perpendicular if the product of their slope equals −1. Parallel lines never intersect unless they are the same line, and perpendicular lines intersect at a right angle. If two lines aren't parallel, they must intersect at one point. Determining equations of lines based on properties of parallel and perpendicular lines appears in word problems. To find an equation of a line, both the slope and a point the line goes through are necessary.

Therefore, if an equation of a line is needed that's parallel to a given line and runs through a specified point, the slope of the given line and the point are plugged into the point-slope form of an equation of a line. Secondly, if an equation of a line is needed that's perpendicular to a given line running through a specified point, the negative reciprocal of the slope of the given line and the point are plugged into the point-slope form. Also, if the point of intersection of two lines is known, that point will be used to solve the set of equations. Therefore, to solve a system of equations, the point of intersection must be found. If a set of two equations with two unknown variables has no solution, the lines are parallel.

Trigonometric Functions

Within similar triangles, corresponding sides are proportional, and angles are congruent. In addition, within similar triangles, the ratio of the side lengths is the same. This property is true even if side lengths are different. Within right triangles, trigonometric ratios can be defined for the acute angles within the triangle. The functions are defined through ratios in a right triangle. Sine of acute angle, A, is opposite over hypotenuse, cosine is adjacent over hypotenuse, and tangent is opposite over adjacent. Note that expanding or shrinking the triangle won't change the ratios. However, changing the angle measurements will alter the calculations.

Complementary Angles

Angles that add up to 90 degrees are **complementary**. Within a right triangle, two complementary angles exist because the third angle is always 90 degrees. In this scenario, the **sine** of one of the complementary angles is equal to the **cosine** of the other angle. The opposite is also true. This relationship exists because sine and cosine will be calculated as the ratios of the same side lengths.

The Pythagorean Theorem

The Pythagorean theorem is an important concept in geometry. It states that for right triangles, the sum of the squares of the two shorter sides will be equal to the square of the longest side (also called the **hypotenuse**). The

longest side will always be the side opposite to the 90° angle. If this side is called c, and the other two sides are a and b, then the Pythagorean theorem states that:

$$c^2 = a^2 + b^2$$

Since lengths are always positive, this also can be written as:

$$c = \sqrt{a^2 + b^2}$$

A diagram to show the parts of a triangle using the Pythagorean theorem is below.

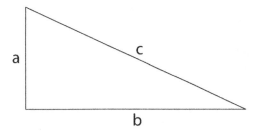

As an example of the theorem, suppose that Shirley has a rectangular field that is 5 feet wide and 12 feet long, and she wants to split it in half using a fence that goes from one corner to the opposite corner. How long will this fence need to be? To figure this out, note that this makes the field into two right triangles, whose hypotenuse will be the fence dividing it in half. Therefore, the fence length will be given by:

$$\sqrt{5^2 + 12^2} = \sqrt{169} = 13 \text{ feet long}$$

Utilizing Facts About Congruency and Similarity of Geometric Figures to Solve Problems
Similarity

Sometimes, two figures are similar, meaning they have the same basic shape and the same interior angles, but they have different dimensions. If the ratio of two corresponding sides is known, then that ratio, or scale factor, holds true for all of the dimensions of the new figure.

Here is an example of applying this principle. Suppose that Lara is 5 feet tall and is standing 30 feet from the base of a light pole, and her shadow is 6 feet long. How high is the light on the pole? To figure this, it helps to make a sketch of the situation:

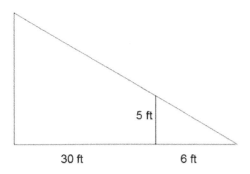

The light pole is the left side of the triangle. Lara is the 5-foot vertical line. Notice that there are two right triangles here, and that they have all the same angles as one another. Therefore, they form similar triangles. So, the ratio of proportionality between them must be determined.

The bases of these triangles are known. The small triangle, formed by Lara and her shadow, has a base of 6 feet. The large triangle formed by the light pole along with the line from the base of the pole out to the end of Lara's shadow is $30 + 6 = 36$ feet long. So, the ratio of the big triangle to the little triangle will be $\frac{36}{6} = 6$. The height of the little triangle is 5 feet. Therefore, the height of the big triangle will be $6 \times 5 = 30$ feet, meaning that the light is 30 feet up the pole.

Notice that the perimeter of a figure changes by the ratio of proportionality between two similar figures, but the area changes by the *square* of the ratio. This is because if the length of one side is doubled, the area is quadrupled.

As an example, suppose two rectangles are similar, but the edges of the second rectangle are three times longer than the edges of the first rectangle. The area of the first rectangle is 10 square inches. How much more area does the second rectangle have than the first?

To answer this, note that the area of the second rectangle is $3^2 = 9$ times the area of the first rectangle, which is 10 square inches. Therefore, the area of the second rectangle is going to be $9 \times 10 = 90$ square inches. This means it has $90 - 10 = 80$ square inches more area than the first rectangle.

As a second example, suppose X and Y are similar right triangles. The hypotenuse of X is 4 inches. The area of Y is $\frac{1}{4}$ the area of X. What is the hypotenuse of Y?

First, realize the area has changed by a factor of $\frac{1}{4}$. The area changes by a factor that is the *square* of the ratio of changes in lengths, so the ratio of the lengths is the square root of the ratio of areas. That means that the ratio of lengths must be is $\sqrt{\frac{1}{4}} = \frac{1}{2}$, and the hypotenuse of Y must be,

$$\frac{1}{2} \times 4 = 2 \text{ inches}$$

Volumes between similar solids change like the cube of the change in the lengths of their edges. Likewise, if the ratio of the volumes between similar solids is known, the ratio between their lengths is known by finding the cube root of the ratio of their volumes.

For example, suppose there are two similar rectangular pyramids X and Y. The base of X is 1 inch by 2 inches, and the volume of X is 8 inches. The volume of Y is 64 inches. What are the dimensions of the base of Y?

To answer this, first find the ratio of the volume of Y to the volume of X. This will be given by $\frac{64}{8} = 8$. Now the ratio of lengths is the cube root of the ratio of volumes, or $\sqrt[3]{8} = 2$. So, the dimensions of the base of Y must be 2 inches by 4 inches.

Transformations

Given a figure drawn on a plane, many changes can be made to that figure, including rotation, translation, and reflection. **Rotations** turn the figure about a point, **translations** slide the figure, and **reflections** flip the figure over a specified line. When performing these transformations, the original figure is called the **pre-image**, and the figure after transformation is called the **image**.

More specifically, **translation** means that all points in the figure are moved in the same direction by the same distance. In other words, the figure is slid in some fixed direction. Of course, while the entire figure is slid by the same distance, this does not change any of the measurements of the figures involved. The result will have the same distances and angles as the original figure.

In terms of Cartesian coordinates, a translation means a shift of each of the original points (x, y) by a fixed amount in the x and y directions, to become $(x + a, y + b)$.

Another procedure that can be performed is called **reflection**. To do this, a line in the plane is specified, called the **line of reflection**. Then, take each point and flip it over the line so that it is the same distance from the line but on the opposite side of it. This does not change any of the distances or angles involved, but it does reverse the order in which everything appears.

To reflect something over the x-axis, the points (x, y) are sent to $(x, -y)$. To reflect something over the y-axis, the points (x, y) are sent to the points $(-x, y)$. Flipping over other lines is not something easy to express in Cartesian coordinates. However, by drawing the figure and the line of reflection, the distance to the line and the original points can be used to find the reflected figure.

Example: Reflect this triangle with vertices $(-1, 0)$, $(2, 1)$, and $(2, 0)$ over the y-axis. The pre-image is shown below.

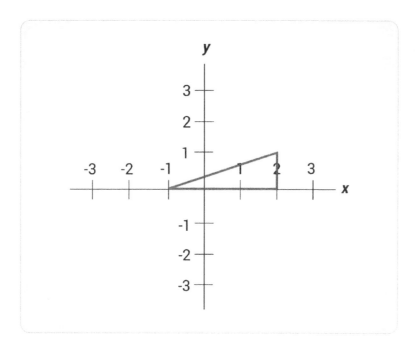

To do this, flip the x-values of the points involved to the negatives of themselves, while keeping the y-values the same. The image is shown here.

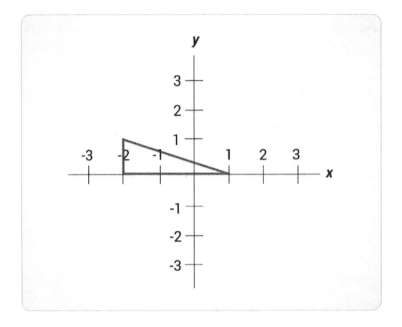

The new vertices will be $(1, 0)$, $(-2, 1)$, and $(-2, 0)$.

Another procedure that does not change the distances and angles in a figure is **rotation**. In this procedure, pick a center point, then rotate every vertex along a circle around that point by the same angle. This procedure is also not easy to express in Cartesian coordinates, and this is not a requirement on this test. However, as with reflections, it's helpful to draw the figures and see what the result of the rotation would look like. This transformation can be performed using a compass and protractor.

Each one of these transformations can be performed on the coordinate plane without changes to the original dimensions or angles.

If two figures in the plane involve the same distances and angles, they are called **congruent figures**. In other words, two figures are congruent when they go from one form to another through reflection, rotation, and translation, or a combination of these.

Remember that rotation and translation will give back a new figure that is identical to the original figure, but reflection will give back a mirror image of it.

To recognize that a figure has undergone a rotation, check to see that the figure has not been changed into a mirror image, but that its orientation has changed (that is, whether the parts of the figure now form different angles with the x and y axes).

To recognize that a figure has undergone a translation, check to see that the figure has not been changed into a mirror image, and that the orientation remains the same.

To recognize that a figure has undergone a reflection, check to see that the new figure is a mirror image of the old figure.

Keep in mind that sometimes a combination of translations, reflections, and rotations may be performed on a figure.

Dilation

A **dilation** is a transformation that preserves angles, but not distances. This can be thought of as stretching or shrinking a figure. If a dilation makes figures larger, it is called an **enlargement**. If a dilation makes figures smaller, it is called a **reduction**. The easiest example is to dilate around the origin. In this case, multiply the x and y coordinates by a **scale factor**, k, sending points (x, y) to (kx, ky).

As an example, draw a dilation of the following triangle, whose vertices will be the points $(-1, 0)$, $(1, 0)$, and $(1, 1)$.

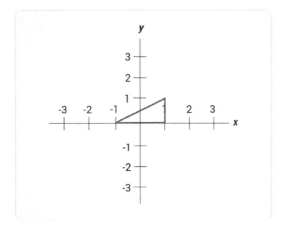

For this problem, dilate by a scale factor of 2, so the new vertices will be $(-2, 0)$, $(2, 0)$, and $(2, 2)$.

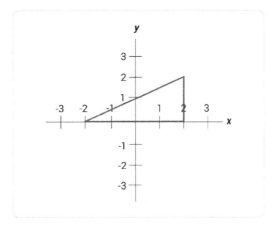

Note that after a dilation, the distances between the vertices of the figure will have changed, but the angles will remain the same. The two figures that are obtained by dilation, along with possibly translation, rotation, and reflection, are all *similar* to one another. Another way to think of this is that similar figures have the same number of vertices and edges, and their angles are all the same. Similar figures have the same basic shape but are different in size.

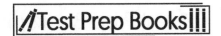

Symmetry

Using the types of transformations above, if an object can undergo these changes and not appear to have changed, then the figure is symmetrical. If an object can be split in half by a line and flipped over that line to lie directly on top of itself, it is said to have **line symmetry**. An example of both types of figures is seen below.

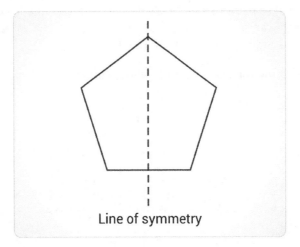

Line of symmetry

If an object can be rotated about its center to any degree smaller than 360, and it lies directly on top of itself, the object is said to have **rotational symmetry**. An example of this type of symmetry is shown below. The pentagon has an order of 5.

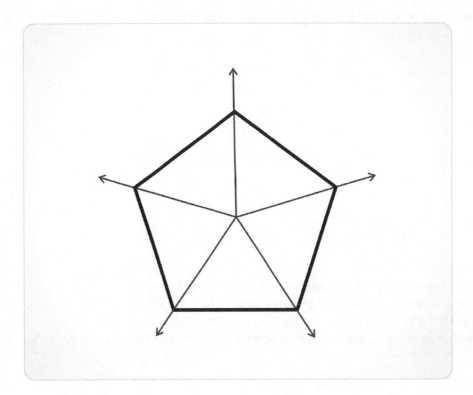

The rotational symmetry lines in the figure above can be used to find the angles formed at the center of the pentagon. Knowing that all of the angles together form a full circle, at 360 degrees, the figure can be split into 5 angles equally. By dividing the 360° by 5, each angle is 72°.

180

Given the length of one side of the figure, the perimeter of the pentagon can also be found using rotational symmetry. If one side length was 3 cm, that side length can be rotated onto each other side length four times. This would give a total of 5 side lengths equal to 3 cm. To find the perimeter, or distance around the figure, multiply 3 by 5. The perimeter of the figure would be 15 cm.

If a line cannot be drawn anywhere on the object to flip the figure onto itself or rotated less than or equal to 180 degrees to lay on top of itself, the object is asymmetrical. Examples of these types of figures are shown below.

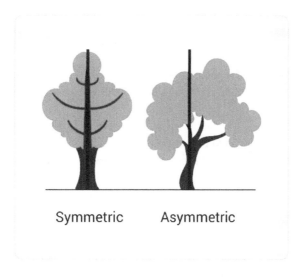

Symmetric   Asymmetric

No line of symmetry

Using Formulas for the Area and Circumference of a Circle to Solve Problems

A circle's perimeter—also known as its circumference—is measured by multiplying the diameter by π.

Diameter is the straight line measured from a point on one side of the circle to a point directly across on the opposite side of the circle.

π is referred to as pi and is equal to 3.14 (with rounding).

So, the formula is $\pi \times d$.

This is sometimes expressed by the formula $C = 2 \times \pi \times r$, where r is the radius of the circle. These formulas are equivalent, as the radius equals half of the diameter.

The area of a circle is calculated through the formula $A = \pi \times r^2$. The test will indicate either to leave the answer with π attached or to calculate to the nearest decimal place, which means multiplying by 3.14 for π.

Arc

The **arc of a circle** is the distance between two points on the circle. The length of the arc of a circle in terms of **degrees** is easily determined if the value of the central angle is known. The length of the arc is simply the value of the central angle. In this example, the length of the arc of the circle in degrees is 75°.

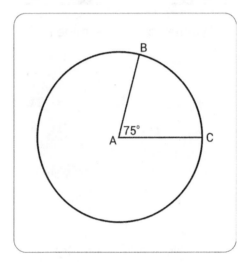

To determine the length of the arc of a circle in distance, the values for both the central angle and the radius must be known. This formula is:

$$\frac{central\ angle}{360°} = \frac{arc\ length}{2\pi r}$$

The equation is simplified by cross-multiplying to solve for the arc length.

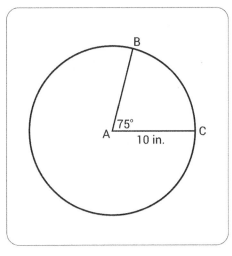
In the following example, to solve for arc length, substitute the values of the central angle (75°) and the radius (10 inches) into the equation above.

$$\frac{75°}{360°} = \frac{arc\ length}{2(3.14)(10in.)}$$

To solve the equation, first cross-multiply: $4,710 = 360(arc\ length)$. Next, divide each side of the equation by 360. The result of the formula is that the arc length is 13.1 (rounded).

Circle Angles

The distance from the middle of a circle to any other point on the circle is known as the **radius**. A **chord** of a circle is a straight line formed when its endpoints are allowed to be any two points on the circle. Many angles exist within a circle. A **central angle** is formed by using two radii as its rays and the center of the circle as its vertex. An inscribed angle is formed by using two chords as its rays, and its vertex is a point on the circle itself. Finally, a **circumscribed angle** has a vertex that is a point outside the circle and rays that are tangent to circle.

Some relationships exist between these types of angles, and, in order to define these relationships, arc measure must be understood. An **arc** of a circle is a portion of the circumference. Finding the **arc measure** is the same as finding the degree measure of the central angle that intersects the circle to form the arc. The measure of an inscribed angle is half the measure of its intercepted arc. It's also true that the measure of a circumscribed angle is equal to 180 degrees minus the measure of the central angle that forms the arc in the angle.

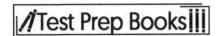

Quadrilateral Angles

If a quadrilateral is inscribed in a circle, the sum of its opposite angles is 180 degrees. Consider the quadrilateral $ABCD$ centered at the point O:

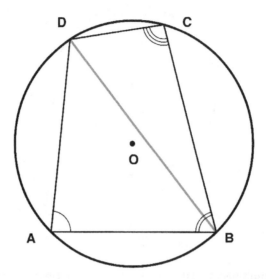

Each of the four-line segments within the quadrilateral is a chord of the circle. Consider the diagonal DB. Angle DAB is an inscribed angle leaning on the arc DCB. Therefore, angle DAB is half the measure of the arc DCB. Conversely, angle DCB is an inscribed angle leaning on the arc DAB. Therefore, angle DCB is half the measure of the arc DAB. The sum of arcs DCB and DAB is 360 degrees because they make up the entire circle. Therefore, the sum of angles DAB and DCB equals half of 360 degrees, which is 180 degrees.

Circle Lines

A **tangent line** is a line that touches a curve at a single point without going through it. A **compass** and a **straight edge** are the tools necessary to construct a tangent line from a point P outside the circle to the circle. A tangent line is constructed by drawing a line segment from the center of the circle O to the point P, and then finding its midpoint M by bisecting the line segment. By using M as the center, a compass is used to draw a circle through points O and P. N is defined as the intersection of the two circles. Finally, a line segment is drawn through P and N. This is the tangent line. Each point on a circle has only one tangent line, which is perpendicular to the radius at that point. A line similar to a tangent line is a **secant line**. Instead of intersecting the circle at one point, a secant line intersects the circle at two points. A **chord** is a smaller portion of a secant line.

Here's an example:

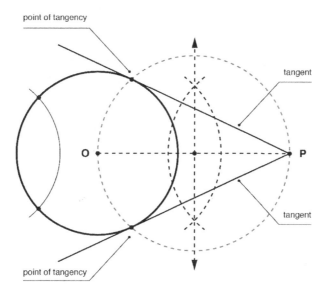

Using Formulas for the Perimeter and Area of Shapes and the Volume of Rectangular Prisms to Solve Problems

Perimeter and Area of Shapes

Perimeter is the measurement of a distance around something or the sum of all sides of a polygon. Think of perimeter as the length of the boundary, like a fence. In contrast, **area** is the space occupied by a defined enclosure, like a field enclosed by a fence.

When thinking about perimeter, think about walking around the outside of something. When thinking about area, think about the amount of space or **surface area** something takes up.

The perimeter of a square is measured by adding together all of the sides. Since a square has four equal sides, its perimeter can be calculated by multiplying the length of one side by 4. Thus, the formula is $P = 4 \times s$, where s equals one side. For example, the following square has side lengths of 5 meters:

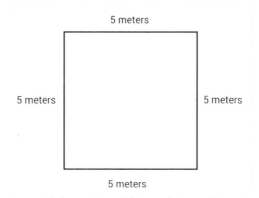

The perimeter is 20 meters because 4 times 5 is 20.

The area of a square is the length of a side squared. For example, if a side of a square is 7 centimeters, then the area is 49 square centimeters. The formula for this example is:

$$A = s^2 = 7^2 = 49 \text{ square centimeters}$$

An example is if the rectangle has a length of 6 inches and a width of 7 inches, then the area is 42 square inches:
$$A = lw = 6(7) = 42 \text{ square inches}$$

Like a square, a rectangle's perimeter is measured by adding together all of the sides. But as the sides are unequal, the formula is different. A rectangle has equal values for its lengths (long sides) and equal values for its widths (short sides), so the perimeter formula for a rectangle is:

$$P = l + l + w + w = 2l + 2w$$

l equals length.
w equals width.

The area is found by multiplying the length by the width, so the formula is $A = l \times w$.

For example, if the length of a rectangle is 10 inches and the width 8 inches, then the perimeter is 36 inches because:
$$P = 2l + 2w = 2(10) + 2(8) = 20 + 16 = 36 \text{ inches}$$

A triangle's perimeter is measured by adding together the three sides, so the formula is $P = a + b + c$, where a, b, and c are the values of the three sides. The area is the product of one-half the base and height so the formula is:
$$A = \frac{1}{2} \times b \times h$$

It can be simplified to:

$$A = \frac{bh}{2}$$

The base is the bottom of the triangle, and the height is the distance from the base to the peak. If a problem asks to calculate the area of a triangle, it will provide the base and height.

For example, if the base of the triangle is 2 feet and the height 4 feet, then the area is 4 square feet. The following equation shows the formula used to calculate the area of the triangle:

$$A = \frac{1}{2}bh = \frac{1}{2}(2)(4) = 4 \text{ square feet}$$

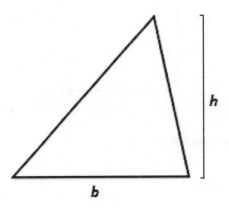

The perimeter of an irregular polygon is found by adding the lengths of all of the sides. In cases where all of the sides are given, this will be very straightforward, as it will simply involve finding the sum of the provided lengths. Other times, a side length may be missing and must be determined before the perimeter can be calculated. Consider the example below:

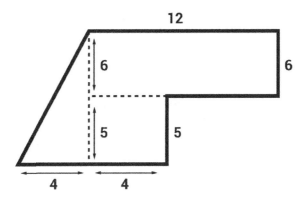

All of the side lengths are provided except for the angled side on the left. Test takers should notice that this is the hypotenuse of a right triangle. The other two sides of the triangle are provided (the base is 4 and the height is $6 + 5 = 11$). The Pythagorean Theorem can be used to find the length of the hypotenuse, remembering that $a^2 + b^2 = c^2$.

Substituting the side values provided yields:

$$(4)^2 + (11)^2 = c^2$$

Therefore,

$$c = \sqrt{16 + 121} = 11.7$$

Finally, the perimeter can be found by adding this new side length with the other provided lengths to get the total length around the figure:

$$4 + 4 + 5 + 8 + 6 + 12 + 11.7 = 50.7$$

Although units are not provided in this figure, remember that reporting units with a measurement is important.

The area of an irregular polygon is found by decomposing, or breaking apart, the figure into smaller shapes. When the area of the smaller shapes is determined, these areas are added together to produce the total area of the area of the original figure. Consider the same example provided before:

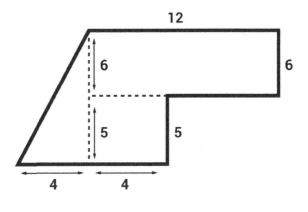

The irregular polygon is decomposed into two rectangles and a triangle. The area of the large rectangle:

$$A = l \times w \rightarrow A = 12 \times 6 = 72 \text{ square units}$$

The area of the small rectangle is 20 square units:

$$A = 4 \times 5$$

The area of the triangle ($A = \frac{1}{2} \times b \times h \rightarrow A = \frac{1}{2} \times 4 \times 11$) is 22 square units. The sum of the areas of these figures produces the total area of the original polygon:

$$A = 72 + 20 + 22 \rightarrow A = 114 \text{ square units}$$

Surface Area and Volume

Many real-world objects are a combination of prisms, cylinders, pyramids, and spheres. **Surface area** problems relate to quantifying the outside area of such a three-dimensional object, and **volume** problems involve quantifying how much the three-dimensional object can hold. For example, when calculating how much paint is needed to paint an entire house, surface area is used. Conversely, when calculating how much water a cylindrical tank can hold, volume is used. The surface area of a **prism** is the sum of all the areas, which simplifies into $SA = 2A + Bh$ where A is the area of the base, B is the perimeter of the base, and h is the height of the prism. The volume of the same prism is:

$$V = Ah$$

The surface area of a **cylinder** is the sum of the areas of both ends and the side, which is:

$$SA = 2\pi rh + 2\pi r^2$$

The surface area of a **pyramid** is calculated by adding known area formulas. It is equal to the area of the base (which is rectangular) plus the area of the four triangles that form the sides. The surface area of a **cone** is equal to the area of the base plus the area of the top, which is:

$$SA = \pi r^2 + \pi \pi r \sqrt{h^2 + r^2}$$

Finally, the formula for surface area of a sphere is $SA = 4\pi r^2$ and its volume is:

$$V = \frac{4}{3}\pi r^3$$

The **cube** is the simplest figure for which volume can be determined because all dimensions in a cube are equal. In the following example, the length, width, and height of the cube are all represented by the variable a because these measurements are equal lengths.

The volume of any rectangular, three-dimensional object is found by multiplying its length by its width by its height. In the case of a cube, the length, width, and height are all equal lengths, represented by the variable a. Therefore, the equation used to calculate the volume is ($a \times a \times a$) or a^3. In a real-world example of this situation, if the length of a side of the cube is 3 centimeters, the volume is calculated by utilizing the formula:

$$3 \times 3 \times 3 = 27 \text{cm}^3$$

The dimensions of a **rectangular prism** are not necessarily equal as those of a cube. Therefore, the formula for a rectangular prism recognizes that the dimensions vary and use different variables to represent these lengths. The length, width, and height of a rectangular prism can be represented with the variables a, b, and c.

The equation used to calculate volume is length times width times height. In a real-world application of this situation, if $a = 3$ cm, $b = 4$ cm, and $c = 5$ cm, the volume is calculated by utilizing the formula:

$$3 \times 4 \times 5 = 60 \text{ cm}^3$$

Discovering a **cylinder**'s volume requires the measurement of the cylinder's base, length of the radius, and height. The height of the cylinder can be represented with variable h, and the radius can be represented with variable r.

The formula to find the volume of a cylinder is $\pi r^2 h$. For example, if the radius is 5 feet and the height of the cylinder is 10 feet, the cylinder's volume is calculated by using the following equation: $\pi 5^2 \times 10$. Substituting 3.14 for π, the volume is 785 ft^3.

The formula to calculate the volume of a circular cone is similar to the formula for the volume of a pyramid. The primary difference in determining the area of a cone is that a circle serves as the base of a cone. Therefore, the area of a circle is used for the cone's base.

The variable r represents the radius, and the variable h represents the height of the cone. The formula used to calculate the volume of a cone is:

$$\frac{1}{3}\pi r^2 h$$

In a real-life example where the radius of a cone is 2 meters and the height of a cone is 5 meters, the volume of the cone is calculated by utilizing the formula:

$$\frac{1}{3}\pi 2^2 \times 5 = 21$$

After substituting 3.14 for π, the volume is 20.9 m^3.

The volume of a **sphere** uses π due to its circular shape. The length of the radius, r, is the only variable needed to determine the sphere's volume. The formula to calculate the volume of a sphere is:

$$\frac{4}{3}\pi r^3$$

Therefore, if the radius of a sphere is 8 centimeters, the volume of the sphere is calculated by utilizing the formula:

$$\frac{4}{3}\pi(8)^3 = 2,143.6 \text{ cm}^3$$

Surface Area of Three-Dimensional Figures

The area of a two-dimensional figure refers to the number of square units needed to cover the interior region of the figure. This concept is similar to wallpaper covering the flat surface of a wall. For example, if a rectangle has an area of 8 square inches (written 8 in^2), it will take 8 squares, each with sides one inch in length, to cover the interior region of the rectangle. Note that area is measured in square units such as: square feet or ft^2; square yards or yd^2; square miles or mi^2.

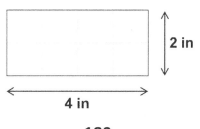

4 in

2 in

189

The surface area of a three-dimensional figure refers to the number of square units needed to cover the entire surface of the figure. This concept is similar to using wrapping paper to completely cover the outside of a box. For example, if a triangular pyramid has a surface area of 17 square inches (written 17 in^2), it will take 17 squares, each with sides one inch in length, to cover the entire surface of the pyramid. Surface area is also measured in square units.

Many three-dimensional figures (solid figures) can be represented by nets consisting of rectangles and triangles. The surface area of such solids can be determined by adding the areas of each of its faces and bases. Finding the surface area using this method requires calculating the areas of rectangles and triangles. To find the area (A) of a rectangle, the length (l) is multiplied by the width:

$$(w) \rightarrow A = l \times w$$

The area of a rectangle with a length of 8 cm and a width of 4 cm is calculated:

$$A = (8 \text{ cm}) \times (4 \text{ cm}) \rightarrow A = 32 \text{ cm}^2$$

To calculate the area (A) of a triangle, the product of $\frac{1}{2}$, the base (b), and the height (h) is found:

$$A = \frac{1}{2} \times b \times h$$

Note that the height of a triangle is measured from the base to the vertex opposite of it forming a right angle with the base. The area of a triangle with a base of 11 cm and a height of 6 cm is calculated:

$$A = \frac{1}{2} \times (11 \text{ cm}) \times (6 \text{ cm}) \rightarrow A = 33 \text{ cm}^2$$

Consider the following triangular prism, which is represented by a net consisting of two triangles and three rectangles.

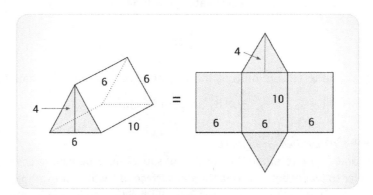

The surface area of the prism can be determined by adding the areas of each of its faces and bases.

$$Surface\ Area\ (SA) = area\ of\ triangle + area\ of\ triangle + \\ area\ of\ rectangle + area\ of\ rectangle + area\ of\ rectangle.$$

$$SA = \left(\frac{1}{2} \times b \times h\right) + \left(\frac{1}{2} \times b \times h\right) + (l \times w) + (l \times w) + (l \times w)$$

$$SA = \left(\frac{1}{2} \times 6 \times 4\right) + \left(\frac{1}{2} \times 6 \times 4\right) + (6 \times 10) + (6 \times 10) + (6 \times 10)$$

$$SA = (12) + (12) + (60) + (60) + (60)$$

$$SA = 204\ \text{square units}$$

Volume is the measurement of how much space an object occupies, like how much space is in the cube. Volume questions will ask how much of something is needed to completely fill the object. The most common surface area and volume questions deal with spheres, cubes, and rectangular prisms.

The **volume** of a cylinder is then found by adding a third dimension onto the circle. Volume of a cylinder is calculated by multiplying the area of the base (which is a circle) by the height of the cylinder. Doing so results in the equation:

$$V = \pi r^2 h$$

Next, consider the *volume of a rectangular box = lwh* , where l is length, w is width, and h is height. This can be simplified into $V = Ah$, where A is the area of the base. The **volume** of a pyramid with the same dimensions is $\frac{1}{3}$ of this quantity because it fills up $\frac{1}{3}$ of the space. Therefore, the volume of a pyramid is:

$$V = \frac{1}{3}Ah$$

In a similar fashion, the volume of a cone is $\frac{1}{3}$ of the volume of a cylinder. Therefore, the formula for the volume of a cylinder is:

$$\frac{1}{3}\pi r^2 h$$

Practice Quiz

1. What is the solution to $9 \times 9 \div 9 + 9 - 9 \div 9$?
   a. 0
   b. 17
   c. 81
   d. 9

2. Using the following diagram, calculate the total circumference, rounding to the nearest tenth:

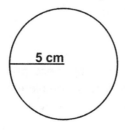

   a. 25.0 cm
   b. 15.7 cm
   c. 78.5 cm
   d. 31.4 cm

3. A couple buys a house for $150,000. They sell it for $165,000. By what percentage did the house's value increase?
   a. 10%
   b. 13%
   c. 15%
   d. 17%

4. What is the volume of a sphere with a radius of 3 inches, in terms of π?
   a. $36\pi \text{ in}^3$
   b. $27\pi \text{ in}^3$
   c. $9\pi \text{ in}^3$
   d. $72\pi \text{ in}^3$

5. Marty wishes to save $150 over a 4-day period. How much must Marty save each day on average?
   a. $37.50
   b. $35
   c. $45.50
   d. $41

See answers on the next page.

Answer Explanations

1. B: According to the order of operations, multiplication and division must be completed first from left to right. Then, addition and subtraction are completed from left to right. Therefore,

$$9 \times 9 \div 9 + 9 - 9 \div 9$$

$$81 \div 9 + 9 - 9 \div 9$$

$$9 + 9 - 9 \div 9$$

$$9 + 9 - 1 = 18 - 1 = 17$$

2. D: To calculate the circumference of a circle, use the formula $2\pi r$, where r equals the radius (half of the diameter) of the circle and $\pi \approx 3.14$. Substitute the given information to get:

$$2 \times 3.14 \times 5 = 31.4$$

3. A: The value went up by $165,000 - $150,000 = $15,000. Out of $150,000, this is $\frac{15,000}{150,000} = \frac{1}{10}$. If we multiply the top and bottom by 10 to give us a denominator of 100, the result is $\frac{10}{100}$, or 10%.

4. A: The formula for the volume of a sphere is $\frac{4}{3}\pi r^3$, and $\frac{4}{3} \times \pi \times 3^3$ is 36π in^3.

5. A: Divide the total amount by the number of days: $\frac{150}{4} = 37.5$. She needs to save an average of $37.50 per day.

193

Practice Test #1

Reading

Questions 1-6 are based upon the following passage:

My gentleness and good behaviour had gained so far on the emperor and his court, and indeed upon the army and people in general, that I began to conceive hopes of getting my liberty in a short time. I took all possible methods to cultivate this favourable disposition. The natives came, by degrees, to be less apprehensive of any danger from me. I would sometimes lie down, and let five or six of them dance on my hand; and at last the boys and girls would venture to come and play at hide-and-seek in my hair. I had now made a good progress in understanding and speaking the language. The emperor had a mind one day to entertain me with several of the country shows, wherein they exceed all nations I have known, both for dexterity and magnificence. I was diverted with none so much as that of the rope-dancers, performed upon a slender white thread, extended about two feet, and twelve inches from the ground. Upon which I shall desire liberty, with the reader's patience, to enlarge a little.

This diversion is only practised by those persons who are candidates for great employments, and high favour at court. They are trained in this art from their youth, and are not always of noble birth, or liberal education. When a great office is vacant, either by death or disgrace (which often happens), five or six of those candidates petition the emperor to entertain his majesty and the court with a dance on the rope; and whoever jumps the highest, without falling, succeeds in the office. Very often the chief ministers themselves are commanded to show their skill, and to convince the emperor that they have not lost their faculty. Flimnap, the treasurer, is allowed to cut a caper on the straight rope, at least an inch higher than any other lord in the whole empire. I have seen him do the summerset several times together, upon a trencher fixed on a rope which is no thicker than a common packthread in England. My friend Reldresal, principal secretary for private affairs, is, in my opinion, if I am not partial, the second after the treasurer; the rest of the great officers are much upon a par.

Excerpt from an adaptation of Gulliver's Travels into Several Remote Nations of the World by Jonathan Swift

1. Which of the following statements best summarizes the central purpose of this text?
    a. Gulliver details his fondness for the archaic, yet interesting, practices of his captors.
    b. Gulliver conjectures about the intentions of the aristocratic sector of society.
    c. Gulliver becomes acquainted with the people and practices of his new surroundings.
    d. Gulliver's differences cause him to become penitent around new acquaintances.

2. What is the word *principal* referring to in the following text?

    My friend Reldresal, principal secretary for private affairs, is, in my opinion, if I am not partial, the second after the treasurer; the rest of the great officers are much upon a par.

    a. Primary or chief
    b. An acolyte
    c. An individual who provides nurturing
    d. One in a subordinate position

194

3. What can the reader infer from the following text?

> I would sometimes lie down, and let five or six of them dance on my hand; and at last the boys and girls would venture to come and play at hide-and-seek in my hair.

  a.   The children tortured Gulliver.
  b.   Gulliver traveled because he wanted to meet new people.
  c.   Gulliver is considerably larger than the children who are playing around him.
  d.   Gulliver has a genuine love and enthusiasm for people of all sizes.

4. What is the significance of the word *mind* in the following passage?

> The emperor had a mind one day to entertain me with several of the country shows, wherein they exceed all nations I have known, both for dexterity and magnificence.

  a.   The ability to think
  b.   A collective vote
  c.   A definitive decision
  d.   A mythological question

5. Which of the following assertions does NOT support the fact that games are a commonplace event in this culture?
  a.   My gentleness and good behavior ... short time.
  b.   They are trained in this art from their youth ... liberal education.
  c.   Very often the chief ministers themselves are commanded to show their skill ... not lost their faculty.
  d.   Flimnap, the treasurer, is allowed to cut a caper on the straight rope ... higher than any other lord in the whole empire.

6. How do Flimnap and Reldresal demonstrate the community's emphasis on physical strength and leadership abilities?
  a.   Only children used Gulliver's hands as a playground.
  b.   The two men who exhibited superior abilities held prominent positions in the community.
  c.   Only common townspeople, not leaders, walk the straight rope.
  d.   No one could jump higher than Gulliver.

Questions 7-12 are based upon the following passage:

> "Did you ever come across a protégé of his—one Hyde?" he asked.

> "Hyde?" repeated Lanyon. "No. Never heard of him. Since my time."

> That was the amount of information that the lawyer carried back with him to the great, dark bed on which he tossed to and fro until the small hours of the morning began to grow large. It was a night of little ease to his toiling mind, toiling in mere darkness and besieged by questions.

> Six o'clock struck on the bells of the church that was so conveniently near to Mr. Utterson's dwelling, and still he was digging at the problem. Hitherto it had touched him on the intellectual side alone; but now his imagination also was engaged, or rather enslaved; and as he lay and tossed in the gross darkness of the night in the curtained room, Mr. Enfield's tale went by before his mind in a scroll of lighted pictures. He would be aware of the great field of lamps in a nocturnal city; then of the figure of a man walking swiftly; then of a child running from the doctor's; and then these met, and that human Juggernaut trod the child down and passed on regardless of her screams. Or else he would see a room in a rich house, where his friend lay asleep, dreaming and smiling at his

dreams; and then the door of that room would be opened, the curtains of the bed plucked apart, the sleeper recalled, and, lo! There would stand by his side a figure to whom power was given, and even at that dead hour he must rise and do its bidding. The figure in these two phases haunted the lawyer all night; and if at anytime he dozed over, it was but to see it glide more stealthily through sleeping houses, or move the more swiftly, and still the more smoothly, even to dizziness, through wider labyrinths of lamplighted city, and at every street corner crush a child and leave her screaming. And still the figure had no face by which he might know it; even in his dreams it had no face, or one that baffled him and melted before his eyes; and thus it was that there sprung up and grew apace in the lawyer's mind a singularly strong, almost an inordinate, curiosity to behold the features of the real Mr. Hyde. If he could but once set eyes on him, he thought the mystery would lighten and perhaps roll altogether away, as was the habit of mysterious things when well examined. He might see a reason for his friend's strange preference or bondage, and even for the startling clauses of the will. And at least it would be a face worth seeing: the face of a man who was without bowels of mercy: a face which had but to show itself to raise up, in the mind of the unimpressionable Enfield, a spirit of enduring hatred.

From that time forward, Mr. Utterson began to haunt the door in the by-street of shops. In the morning before office hours, at noon when business was plenty and time scarce, at night under the face of the fogged city moon, by all lights and at all hours of solitude or concourse, the lawyer was to be found on his chosen post.

"If he be Mr. Hyde," he had thought, "I should be Mr. Seek."

Excerpt from The Strange Case of Dr. Jekyll and Mr. Hyde *by Robert Louis Stevenson*

7. What is the purpose of the use of repetition in the following passage?

   It was a night of little ease to his toiling mind, toiling in mere darkness and besieged by questions.

   a.   It serves as a demonstration of the mental state of Mr. Lanyon.
   b.   It is reminiscent of the church bells that are mentioned in the story.
   c.   It mimics Mr. Utterson's ambivalence.
   d.   It emphasizes Mr. Utterson's anguish in failing to identify Hyde's whereabouts.

8. What is the setting of the story in this passage?
   a.   In the city
   b.   On the countryside
   c.   In a jail
   d.   In a mental health facility

9. What can one infer about the meaning of the word *Juggernaut* from the author's use of it in the passage?
   a.   It is an apparition that appears at daybreak.
   b.   It scares children.
   c.   It is associated with space travel.
   d.   Mr. Utterson finds it soothing.

10. What is the definition of the word *haunt* in the following passage?

    From that time forward, Mr. Utterson began to haunt the door in the by-street of shops. In the morning before office hours, at noon when business was plenty and time scarce, at night under the face of the

fogged city moon, by all lights and at all hours of solitude or concourse, the lawyer was to be found on his chosen post.

a. To levitate
b. To constantly visit
c. To terrorize
d. To daunt

11. The phrase *labyrinths of lamplighted city* contains an example of what?
    a. Hyperbole
    b. Simile
    c. Juxtaposition
    d. Alliteration

12. What can one reasonably conclude from the final comment of this passage?

"If he be Mr. Hyde," he had thought, "I should be Mr. Seek."

a. The speaker is considering a name change.
b. The speaker is experiencing an identity crisis.
c. The speaker has mistakenly been looking for the wrong person.
d. The speaker intends to continue to look for Hyde.

Questions 13-18 are based on the following passage:

Fellow citizens—Pardon me, and allow me to ask, why am I called upon to speak here today? What have I, or those I represent, to do with your national independence? Are the great principles of political freedom and of natural justice, embodied in that Declaration of Independence, extended to us? And am I, therefore, called upon to bring our humble offering to the national altar, and to confess the benefits and express devout gratitude for the blessings resulting from your independence to us?

Would to God, both for your sakes and ours, that an affirmative answer could be truthfully returned to these questions! Then would my task be light, and my burden easy and delightful. For who is there so cold, that a nation's sympathy could not warm him? Who so obdurate and dead to the claims of gratitude, that would not thankfully acknowledge such priceless benefits? Who so stolid and selfish, that would not give his voice to swell the hallelujahs of a nation's jubilee, when the chains of servitude had been torn from his limbs? I am not that man. In a case like that, the dumb may eloquently speak, and the lame man leap as an hart.

But, such is not the state of the case. I say it with a sad sense of the disparity between us. I am not included within the pale of this glorious anniversary. Oh pity! Your high independence only reveals the immeasurable distance between us. The blessings in which you, this day, rejoice, are not enjoyed in common. The rich inheritance of justice, liberty, prosperity, and independence, bequeathed by your fathers, is shared by you, not by me. The sunlight that brought life and healing to you, has brought stripes and death to me. This Fourth [of] July is yours, not mine. You may rejoice, I must mourn. To drag a man in fetters into the grand illuminated temple of liberty, and call upon him to join you in joyous anthems, were inhuman mockery and sacrilegious irony. Do you mean, citizens, to mock me, by asking me to speak to-day? If so, there is a parallel to your conduct. And let me warn you that it is dangerous to copy the example of a nation whose crimes, towering up to heaven, were thrown down by the breath of the Almighty, burying that nation in irrecoverable ruin! I can to-day take up the plaintive lament of a peeled and woe-smitten people!

"By the rivers of Babylon, there we sat down. Yea! We wept when we remembered Zion. We hanged our harps upon the willows in the midst thereof. For there, they that carried us away captive, required of us a song; and they who wasted us required of us mirth, saying, 'Sing us one of the songs of Zion.' How can we sing the Lord's song in a strange land? If I forget thee, O Jerusalem, let my right hand forget her cunning. If I do not remember thee, let my tongue cleave to the roof of my mouth."

Excerpt from speech *What to the Slave is the Fourth of July?* by Frederick Douglass written in 1852

13. What is the tone of the first paragraph of this passage?
    a. Exasperated
    b. Inclusive
    c. Contemplative
    d. Nonchalant

14. Which word is NOT a synonym for "obdurate" as it is used in the sentence below?

    Who so obdurate and dead to the claims of gratitude, that would not thankfully acknowledge such priceless benefits?

    a. Callous
    b. Stubborn
    c. Contented
    d. Hardened

15. What is the central purpose of this text?
    a. To demonstrate the author's extensive knowledge of the Bible
    b. To address the hypocrisy of the Fourth of July holiday
    c. To convince wealthy landowners to adopt new holiday rituals
    d. To explain why minorities often relished the notion of segregation in government institutions

16. What statement shows the central purpose of this text?
    a. By the rivers of Babylon, there we sat down.
    b. Fellow citizens —Pardon me, and allow me to ask, why am I called upon to speak here today?
    c. I can today take up the plaintive lament of a peeled and woe-smitten people.
    d. The rich inheritance of justice, liberty, prosperity, and independence, bequeathed by your fathers, is shared by you, not by me.

17. The statement below features an example of which of the following literary devices:

    Your high independence only reveals the immeasurable distance between us.

    a. Assonance
    b. Parallelism
    c. Amplification
    d. Hyperbole

18. The speaker's use of the quote from the Bible helps the audience to do all of the following EXCEPT:
   a. Identify with the speaker through the use of common text.
   b. Draw a connection between another group of people who have been affected by slavery and American slaves.
   c. The speaker's use of biblical references does not help the reader recognize the equivocation of the speaker and those that he represents.
   d. Appeal to the listener's sense of humanity.

19. Which organizational style is used in the following passage?

   There are several reasons why the new student café has not been as successful as expected. One factor is that prices are higher than originally advertised, so many students cannot afford to buy food and beverages there. Also, the café closes rather early; as a result, students go out into town to other late-night gathering places rather than meeting friends at the café on campus.

   a. Cause and effect order
   b. Compare and contrast order
   c. Spatial order
   d. Time order

20. Hank is a professional writer. He submits regular columns at two blogs and self-publishes romance novels. Hank recently signed with an agent based in New York. To date, Hank has never made any money off his writing. The strength of the argument depends on which of the following?
   a. Hank's agent works at the biggest firm in New York.
   b. Being a professional writer requires representation by an agent.
   c. Hank's self-published novels and blogs have received generally positive reviews.
   d. Being a professional writer does not require earning money.

21. David Foster Wallace's *Infinite Jest* is the holy grail of modern literature. It will stand the test of time in its relevance. Every single person who starts reading *Infinite Jest* cannot physically put down the book until completing it.
Which of the following is the main point of the passage?
   a. David Foster Wallace's *Infinite Jest* is the holy grail of modern literature.
   b. *Infinite Jest* is a page-turner.
   c. David Foster Wallace wrote *Infinite Jest*.
   d. *Infinite Jest* is a modern classic for good reason, and everybody should read it.

22. The assassination of Archduke Franz Ferdinand of Austria is often ascribed as the cause of World War I. However, the assassination merely lit the fuse in a combustible situation since many of the world powers were in complicated and convoluted military alliances. For example, England, France, and Russia entered into a mutual defense treaty seven years prior to World War I. Even without Franz Ferdinand's assassination,

_____

Which of the following most logically completes the passage?
   a. a war between the world powers was extremely likely.
   b. World War I never would have happened.
   c. England, France, and Russia would have started the war.
   d. Austria would have started the war.

Questions 23–30 are based on the following passages.

   Passage I

199

Lethal force, or deadly force, is defined as the physical means to cause death or serious harm to another individual. The law holds that lethal force is only acceptable when you or another person are in immediate and unavoidable danger of death or severe bodily harm. For example, a person could be beating someone in such a way that the victim is suffering severe trauma that could result in death or serious harm. This would be an instance where lethal force would be acceptable and possibly the only way to save the victim from irrevocable damage.

Another example of when to use lethal force would be when someone enters your home with a deadly weapon. The intruder's presence and possession of the weapon indicate malicious intent and the ability to inflict death or severe injury upon you and your loved ones. Again, lethal force can be used in this situation. Lethal force can also be applied to prevent the harm of another individual. If a woman is being brutally assaulted and is unable to fend off an attacker, lethal force can be used to defend her as a last-ditch effort. If she is in immediate jeopardy of rape, harm, and/or death, lethal force could be the only response that could effectively deter the assailant.

The key to understanding the concept of lethal force is the term *last resort*. Deadly force cannot be taken back; it should be used only to prevent severe harm or death. The law does distinguish whether the means of one's self-defense is fully warranted or if the individual goes out of control in the process. If you continually attack the assailant after they are rendered incapacitated, this would be causing unnecessary harm, and the law can bring charges against you. Likewise, if you kill an attacker unnecessarily after defending yourself, you can be charged with murder. This would move lethal force beyond necessary defense, making it no longer a last resort but rather a use of excessive force.

Passage II

Assault is an unlawful and intentional act that causes reasonable apprehension in another individual, either by an imminent threat or by initiating offensive contact. Assaults can vary, encompassing physical strikes, threatening body language, and even provocative language. In the case of the latter, even if a hand has not been laid, it is still considered an assault because of its threatening nature.

Let's look at an example. A homeowner is angered because his neighbor blows fallen leaves onto his freshly mowed lawn. Irate, the homeowner gestures a fist to his neighbor and threatens to bash his head in for littering on his lawn. The homeowner's physical motions and verbal threats herald a physical threat against the other neighbor. These factors classify the homeowner's reaction as an assault. If the angry neighbor hits the threatening homeowner in retaliation, that would constitute an assault as well because he physically hit the homeowner.

Assault also centers on the involvement of weapons in a conflict. If someone fired a gun at another person, it could be interpreted as an assault, unless the shooter acted in self-defense. If an individual drew a gun or a knife on someone with the intent to harm them, it would be considered assault. However, it's also considered an assault if someone simply aims a weapon, loaded or not, at another person in a threatening manner.

23. What is the purpose of the second passage?
    a. To inform the reader about what assault is and how it is committed
    b. To inform the reader about how assault is a minor example of lethal force
    c. To argue that the use of assault is more common than the use of lethal force
    d. To recount an incident in which the author was assaulted

24. According to the passages, using lethal force would be legal in which of the following situations?
    a. A disgruntled cashier yells obscenities at a customer.
    b. A thief is seen running away with stolen cash.
    c. A man is attacked in an alley by another man with a knife.
    d. A woman punches another woman in a bar.

25. Given the information in the passages, which of the following must be true about assault?
    a. All assault is considered an expression of lethal force.
    b. There are various forms of assault.
    c. Assault is justified only as a last resort.
    d. Assault charges are more severe than unnecessary use of force charges.

26. Which of the following, if true, would most seriously undermine the explanation proposed by the author in the third paragraph of Passage I?
    a. An instance of lethal force in self-defense is not absolutely absolved from blame. The law takes into account the necessary use of force at the time it is committed.
    b. An individual who uses lethal force only in necessary defense is in direct compliance with the law under most circumstances.
    c. Lethal force in self-defense should be forgiven in all cases for the peace of mind of the primary victim.
    d. The use of lethal force is only evaluated on the severity of the primary attack that warranted self-defense and not based on intent at all.

27. Based on the passages, what can we infer about the relationship between assault and lethal force?
    a. An act of lethal force always leads to a type of assault.
    b. Assault and lethal force have no conceivable connection.
    c. An assault with deadly intent can lead to an individual using lethal force to preserve their well-being.
    d. If someone uses self-defense in a conflict, it is called deadly force; if actions or threats are intended, it is called assault.

28. Which of the following best describes the way the passages are structured?
    a. Both passages open by defining a legal concept and then continue to describe situations in order to further explain the concept.
    b. Both passages begin with situations, introduce accepted definitions, and then cite legal ramifications.
    c. Both cite specific legal doctrines and proceed to explain the rulings.
    d. The first passage explains both concepts and then focuses on lethal force. The second passage picks up with assault and explains the concept in depth.

29. What can we infer about the role of intent in lethal force and assault?
    a. Intent is very important for determining both lethal force and assault; intent is examined in both parties and helps determine the severity of the issue.
    b. Intent is vital for determining the lawfulness of using lethal force but not for assault.
    c. Intent is only taken into account for assault charges.
    d. The intent of the assailant is the main focus for determining legal ramifications; it is used to determine if the defender was justified in using force to respond.

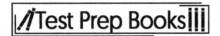
30. The author uses the example in the second paragraph of Passage II in order to do what?
   a. To demonstrate two different types of assault by showing how each specifically relates to the other.
   b. To demonstrate a single example of two different types of assault, then adding in the third type of assault in the example's conclusion.
   c. To prove that the definition of lethal force is altered when the victim in question is a homeowner and his property is threatened.
   d. To suggest that verbal assault can be an exaggerated crime by the law and does not necessarily lead to physical violence.
   e. To demonstrate that threatening body language is only considered a type of assault if it leads to physical violence.

Questions 31-36 are based on the following passage:

> Three years ago, I think there were not many bird-lovers in the United States who believed it possible to prevent the total extinction of both egrets from our fauna. All the known rookeries accessible to plume-hunters had been totally destroyed. Two years ago, the secret discovery of several small, hidden colonies prompted William Dutcher, President of the National Association of Audubon Societies, and Mr. T. Gilbert Pearson, Secretary, to attempt the protection of those colonies. With a fund contributed for the purpose, wardens were hired and duly commissioned. As previously stated, one of those wardens was shot dead in cold blood by a plume hunter. The task of guarding swamp rookeries from the attacks of money-hungry desperadoes, to whom the accursed plumes were worth their weight in gold, is a very chancy proceeding. There is now one warden in Florida who says that "before they get my rookery they will first have to get me."

> Thus far, the protective work of the Audubon Association has been successful. Now there are 20 colonies, which contain, all told, about 5,000 egrets and about 120,000 herons and ibises which are guarded by the Audubon wardens. One of the most important is on Bird Island, a mile out in Orange Lake, Central Florida, and it is ably defended by Oscar E. Baynard. To-day, the plume hunters who do not dare to raid the guarded rookeries are trying to study out the lines of flight of the birds, to and from their feeding-grounds, and shoot them in transit. Their motto is "Anything to beat the law, and get the plumes." It is there that the state of Florida should take part in the war.

> The success of this campaign is attested by the fact that last year a number of egrets were seen in eastern Massachusetts—for the first time in many years. And so to-day the question is, can the wardens continue to hold the plume-hunters at bay?

> Excerpt from *Our Vanishing Wildlife*, by William T. Hornaday

31. The author's use of first-person pronouns in the following text does NOT have which of the following effects?

> Three years ago, I think there were not many bird-lovers in the United States who believed it possible to prevent the total extinction of both egrets from our fauna.

   a. The phrase "I think" acts as a sort of hedging, where the author's tone is less direct and absolute.
   b. It allows the reader to more easily connect with the author.
   c. It encourages the reader to empathize with the egrets.
   d. It distances the reader from the text by overemphasizing the story.

32. What purpose does the quote serve at the end of the first paragraph?
    a. The quote shows proof of a hunter threatening one of the wardens.
    b. The quote lightens the mood by illustrating the colloquial language of the region.
    c. The quote provides an example of a warden protecting one of the colonies.
    d. The quote provides much needed comic relief in the form of a joke.

33. What is the meaning of the word *rookeries* in the following text?

> To-day, the plume hunters who do not dare to raid the guarded rookeries are trying to study out the lines of flight of the birds, to and from their feeding-grounds, and shoot them in transit.

    a. Houses in a slum area
    b. A place where hunters gather to trade tools
    c. A place where wardens go to trade stories
    d. A colony of breeding birds

34. What is on Bird Island?
    a. Hunters selling plumes
    b. An important bird colony
    c. Bird Island Battle between the hunters and the wardens
    d. An important egret with unique plumes

35. What is the main purpose of the passage?
    a. To persuade the audience to act in preservation of the bird colonies
    b. To show the effect hunting egrets has had on the environment
    c. To argue that the preservation of bird colonies has had a negative impact on the environment
    d. To demonstrate the success of the protective work of the Audubon Association

36. Why are hunters trying to study the lines of flight of the birds?
    a. To further their studies of ornithology
    b. To help wardens preserve the lives of the birds
    c. To have a better opportunity to hunt the birds
    d. To build their homes under the lines of flight because they believe it brings good luck

Questions 37-42 are from the following passage:

> Insects as a whole are preeminently creatures of the land and the air. This is shown not only by the possession of wings by a vast majority of the class, but by the mode of breathing to which reference has already been made, a system of branching air-tubes carrying atmospheric air with its combustion-supporting oxygen to all the insect's tissues. The air gains access to these tubes through a number of paired air-holes or spiracles, arranged segmentally in series.

> It is of great interest to find that, nevertheless, a number of insects spend much of their time under water. This is true of not a few in the perfect winged state, as for example aquatic beetles and water-bugs ('boatmen' and 'scorpions') which have some way of protecting their spiracles when submerged, and, possessing usually the power of flight, can pass on occasion from pond or stream to upper air. But it is advisable in connection with our present subject to dwell especially on some insects that remain continually under water till they are ready to undergo their final moult and attain the winged state, which they pass entirely in the air. The preparatory instars of such insects are aquatic; the adult instar is aerial. All may-flies, dragon-flies, and caddis-flies, many beetles and two-winged flies, and a few moths thus divide their life-story between the water and the air. For

the present we confine attention to the Stone-flies, the May-flies, and the Dragon-flies, three well-known orders of insects respectively called by systematists the Plecoptera, the Ephemeroptera, and the Odonata.

In the case of many insects that have aquatic larvae, the latter are provided with some arrangement for enabling them to reach atmospheric air through the surface-film of the water. But the larva of a stone-fly, a dragon-fly, or a may-fly is adapted more completely than these for aquatic life; it can, by means of gills of some kind, breathe the air dissolved in water.

This excerpt is adapted from The Life-Story of Insects by Geo H. Carpenter

37. Which statement best details the central idea in this passage?
   a. It introduces certain insects that transition from water to air.
   b. It delves into entomology, especially where gills are concerned.
   c. It defines what constitutes as insects' breathing.
   d. It invites readers to have a hand in the preservation of insects.

38. Which definition most closely relates to the usage of the word *moult* in the passage?
   a. An adventure of sorts, especially underwater
   b. Mating act between two insects
   c. The act of shedding part or all of the outer shell
   d. Death of an organism that ends in a revival of life

39. What is the purpose of the first paragraph in relation to the second paragraph?
   a. The first paragraph serves as a cause, and the second paragraph serves as an effect.
   b. The first paragraph serves as a contrast to the second.
   c. The first paragraph is a description for the argument in the second paragraph.
   d. The first and second paragraphs are merely presented in a sequence.

40. What does the following sentence most nearly mean?

   The preparatory instars of such insects are aquatic; the adult instar is aerial.

   a. The volume of water is necessary to prep the insect for transition rather than the volume of the air.
   b. The abdomen of the insect is designed like a star in the water as well as the air.
   c. The early stages in between periods of molting are acted out in the water, while the last stage is in the air.
   d. These insects breathe first in the water through gills, yet continue to use the same organs to breathe in the air.

41. Which of the statements reflects information that one could reasonably infer based on the author's tone?
   a. The author's tone is persuasive and attempts to call the audience to action.
   b. The author's tone is passionate due to excitement over the subject and personal narrative.
   c. The author's tone is informative and exhibits interest in the subject of the study.
   d. The author's tone is somber, depicting some anger at the state of insect larvae.

42. Which statement best describes stoneflies, mayflies, and dragonflies?
   a. They are creatures of the land and the air.
   b. They have a way of protecting their spiracles when submerged.
   c. Their larvae can breathe the air dissolved in water through gills of some kind.
   d. The preparatory instars of these insects are aerial.

43. Which of the following statements least supports the argument that the American economy is healthy?
    a. The gross domestic product (GDP), which is the measure of all the goods and services produced in a country, increased by two percent last year.
    b. Unemployment is the lowest it's been in over a decade due to a spike in job creation.
    c. Average household income just hit a historical high point for the twentieth consecutive quarter.
    d. Last year, the output of the manufacturing sector decreased despite repeated massive investments by both the private and public sectors.

44. Which of these descriptions would give the most detailed and objective support for the claim that drinking and driving is unsafe?
    a. A dramatized television commercial reenacting a fatal drinking and driving accident, including heart-wrenching testimonials from loved ones
    b. The Department of Transportation's press release noting the additional drinking and driving special patrol units that will be on the road during the holiday season
    c. Congressional written testimony on the number of drinking and driving incidents across the country and their relationship to underage drinking statistics, according to experts
    d. A highway bulletin warning drivers of penalties associated with drinking and driving

Question 45 is based on the following passage.

A famous children's author recently published a historical fiction novel under a pseudonym; however, it did not sell as many copies as her children's books. In her earlier years, she had majored in history and earned a graduate degree in Antebellum American History, which is the time frame of her new novel. Critics praised this newest work far more than the children's series that made her famous. In fact, her new novel was nominated for the prestigious Albert J. Beveridge Award but still isn't selling like her children's books, which fly off the shelves because of her name alone.

45. Which one of the following statements might be accurately inferred based on the above passage?
    a. The famous children's author produced an inferior book under her pseudonym.
    b. The famous children's author is the foremost expert on Antebellum America.
    c. The famous children's author did not receive the bump in publicity for her historical novel that it would have received if it were written under her given name.
    d. People generally prefer to read children's series over historical fiction.

Question 46 is based on the following passage.

In 2015, 28 countries, including Estonia, Portugal, Slovenia, and Latvia, scored significantly higher than the United States on standardized high school math tests. In the 1960s, the United States consistently ranked first in the world. Today, the United States spends more than $800 billion on education, which exceeds the next highest country by more than $600 billion. The United States also leads the world in spending per school-aged child by an enormous margin.

46. If the statements above are true, which of the following statements must be correct?
    a. Outspending other countries on education has benefits beyond standardized math tests.
    b. The United States' education system is corrupt and broken.
    c. The standardized math tests are not representative of American academic prowess.
    d. Spending more money does not guarantee success on standardized math tests.

Question 47 is based on the following conversation between a scientist and a politician.

Scientist: Last year was the warmest ever recorded in the last 134 years. During that time period, the 10 warmest years have all occurred since 2000. This correlates directly with the recent increases in carbon dioxide as large countries like China, India, and Brazil continue developing and industrializing. No longer do just a handful of countries burn massive amounts of carbon-based fossil fuels; it is quickly becoming the case throughout the whole world as technology and industry spread.

Politician: Yes, but there is no causal link between increases in carbon emissions and increasing temperatures. The link is tenuous and nothing close to certain. We need to wait for all of the data before drawing hasty conclusions. For all we know, the temperature increase could be entirely natural. I believe the temperatures also rose dramatically during the dinosaurs' time, and I do not think they were burning any fossil fuels back then.

47. What is one point on which the scientist and politician agree?
    a. Burning fossil fuels causes global temperatures to rise.
    b. Global temperatures are increasing.
    c. Countries must revisit their energy policies before it's too late.
    d. Earth's climate naturally goes through warming and cooling periods.

Questions 48–54 are based on the following passage.

In the quest to understand existence, modern philosophers must question if humans can fully comprehend the world. Classical Western approaches to philosophy tend to hold that one can understand something, be it an event or object, by standing outside of the phenomenon and observing it. It is then by unbiased observation that one can grasp the details of the world. This seems to hold true for many things. Scientists conduct experiments and record their findings, and thus many natural phenomena become comprehensible. However, many of these observations were possible because humans used tools in order to make these discoveries.

This may seem like an extraneous matter. After all, people invented things like microscopes and telescopes in order to enhance their capacity to view cells or the movement of stars. While humans are still capable of seeing things, the question remains if human beings have the capacity to fully observe and see the world in order to understand it. It would not be an impossible stretch to argue that what humans see through a microscope is not the exact thing itself but rather a human interpretation of it.

This would seem to be the case in the "Business of the Holes" experiment conducted by Richard Feynman. To study the way electrons behave, Feynman set up a barrier with two holes and a plate. The plate was there to indicate how many times the electrons would pass through the hole(s). Rather than casually observing the electrons acting under normal circumstances, Feynman discovered that electrons behave in two totally different ways depending on whether or not they are observed. The electrons that were observed had passed through either one of the holes or were caught on the plate as particles. However, electrons that weren't observed acted as waves instead of particles and passed through both holes. This indicated that electrons have a dual nature. Electrons seen by the human eye act like particles, while unseen electrons act like waves of energy.

This dual nature of the electrons presents a conundrum. While humans now have a better understanding of electrons, the fact remains that people cannot entirely perceive how electrons

206

behave without the use of instruments. We can only observe one of the mentioned behaviors, which only provides a partial understanding of the entire function of electrons. Therefore, we're forced to ask ourselves whether the world we observe is objective or if it is subjectively perceived by humans. Or, an alternative question: can humans understand the world only through machines that will allow them to observe natural phenomena?

Both questions humble humanity's capacity to grasp the world. However, those ideas don't take into account that many phenomena have been proven by human beings without the use of machines, such as the discovery of gravity. Like all philosophical questions, whether humanity's reason and observation alone can understand the universe can be approached from many angles.

48. What is the author's motivation for writing the passage?
  a. Bring to light an alternative view on human perception by examining the role of technology in human understanding.
  b. Educate the reader on the latest astroparticle physics discovery and offer terms that may be unfamiliar to the reader.
  c. Argue that humans are totally blind to the realities of the world by presenting an experiment that proves that electrons are not what they seem on the surface.
  d. Reflect on opposing views of human understanding.

49. Which of the following best describes how paragraph four is structured?
  a. It offers one solution, questions the solution, and then ends with an alternative solution.
  b. It presents an inquiry, explains the details of that inquiry, and then offers a solution.
  c. It presents a problem, explains the details of that problem, and then ends with more inquiries.
  d. It gives a definition, offers an explanation, and then ends with an inquiry.

50. For the classical approach of understanding to hold true, which of the following is required?
  a. A telescope is needed.
  b. The person observing must prove their theory beyond a doubt.
  c. Multiple witnesses must be present.
  d. The person observing must be unbiased.

51. Which best describes how the electrons in the experiment behaved like waves?
  a. The electrons moved up and down like ocean waves.
  b. The electrons passed through both holes and then onto the plate.
  c. The electrons converted to photons upon touching the plate.
  d. Electrons were seen passing through one hole or the other.

52. The author mentions gravity in the last paragraph in order to do what?
  a. In order to show that different natural phenomena test man's ability to grasp the world
  b. To prove that since man has not measured it with the use of tools or machines, humans cannot know the true nature of gravity
  c. To demonstrate an example of natural phenomena humans discovered and understood without the use of tools or machines
  d. To show an alternative solution to the nature of electrons that humans have not thought of yet

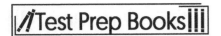

53. Which situation best parallels the revelation of the dual nature of electrons discovered in Feynman's experiment?
    a. A man is born color-blind and grows up observing everything in lighter or darker shades. With the invention of special goggles he puts on, he discovers that there are other colors in addition to different shades.
    b. The coelacanth was thought to be extinct, but a live specimen was just recently discovered. There are now two living species of coelacanth known, and both are believed to be endangered.
    c. In the Middle Ages, blacksmiths added carbon to iron, thus inventing steel. This important discovery would have its biggest effects during the industrial revolution.
    d. The x-ray machine was invented to help doctors better examine and treat broken bones. It was put to use in hospitals and medical centers.

54. Which statement about technology would the author likely disagree with?
    a. Technology can help expand the field of human vision.
    b. Technology renders human observation irrelevant.
    c. Developing tools used in observation and research indicates growing understanding of our world in itself.
    d. Studying certain phenomena necessitates the use of tools and machines.

55. The following exchange occurred after the baseball coach's team suffered a heartbreaking loss in the final inning:

Reporter: The team clearly did not rise to the challenge. I'm sure that getting zero hits in 20 at-bats with runners in scoring position hurt the team's chances at winning the game. What are your thoughts on this devastating loss?

Baseball Coach: Hitting with runners in scoring position was not the reason we lost this game. We made numerous errors in the field, and our pitchers gave out too many free passes. Also, we did not even need a hit with runners in scoring position. Many of those at-bats could have driven in the run by simply making contact. Our team did not deserve to win the game.

Which of the following best describes the main point of dispute between the reporter and baseball coach?
    a. The loss was heartbreaking.
    b. Getting zero hits in 20 at-bats with runners in scoring position caused the loss.
    c. Numerous errors in the field and pitchers giving too many free passes caused the loss.
    d. The team deserved to win the game.

56. Conservative politician: Social welfare programs are destroying our country. These programs are not only adding to the annual deficit, which increases the national debt, but they also discourage hard work. Our country must continue producing leaders who bootstrap their way to the top. None of our country's citizens truly need assistance from the government; rather, the assistance just makes things easier.

Liberal politician: Our great country is founded on the principle of hope. The country is built on the backs of immigrants who came here with nothing, except for the hope of a better life. Our country is too wealthy not to provide basic necessities for the less fortunate. Recent immigrants, single mothers, and people who are elderly, disabled, or have historically been disenfranchised all require an ample safety net.

What is the main point of dispute between the politicians?
  a. Spending on social welfare programs increases the national debt.
  b. Certain classes of people rely on social welfare programs to meet their basic needs.
  c. Certain classes of people would be irreparably harmed if the country failed to provide a social welfare program.
  d. All of the country's leaders have bootstrapped their way to the top.
  e. Immigrants founded the country

Writing

Usage

Which part of the sentence contains an error?

1. (A) It has recently been brought to my attention that most people believe that 75% (B) of your body heat is lost through your head. (C) I had certainly heard this before, and (D) am not going to attempt to say I didn't believe it when I first heard it. (E) No error.

2. (A) It is natural to be gullible (B) too anything said with enough authority. (C) But the "fact" that the majority of your body heat is (D) lost through your head is a lie. (E) No error.

3. (A) Heat loss is proportional (B) to surface area exposed. (C) An elephant loses a great deal more heat than an (D) anteater because it has a much greater surface area than an anteater. (E) No error.

4. (A) Our modern society would actually look down (B) on some of Platos ideas in *The Republic.* (C) But why? (D) Certainly, his ideas could help create a more orderly system, but at what cost? (E) No error.

5. (A) In many of his examples (B) Plato takes the individual completely (C) out of the equation. (D) Plato's ideal society is one that places human desire aside. (E) No error.

6. (A) To enforce these ideas, (B) Plato seeks to use government (C) to regulate and mandate rules. (D) This is the greatest breech of freedom. (E) No error.

7. (A) Today, (B) people would think Plato's suggestion to confiscate citizens' children (C) and place them in diferent homes is utterly barbaric. (D) We cannot imagine the pain of losing one's own child to be raised by others. (E) No error.

8. Quantum mechanics, (A) which describes how the universe works on its smallest scale, (B) is inherently weird. (C) Even the founders of the field (D) are unsettled by it's implications. (E) No error.

9. (A) In our everyday lives, determinism, is (B) actually expressed in the thought experiment of Schrödinger's cat. (C) Devised by Erwin Schrödinger, one of the founders of quantum mechanics, (D) its purpose is to show how truly strange the framework is. (E) No error.

10. (A) Picture a box containing a cat, (B) a radioactive element, (C) and a vial of poison. (D) If the radioactive element decay, it will release the poison and kill the cat. (E) No error.

11. (A) The box is closed. (B) So there is no way for anyone outside to know (C) what's happening inside. (D) Since the cat's status—alive and dead—are mutually exclusive, only one state can exist. (E) No error.

12. (A) What quantum mechanics says, however, (B) is that the cat is simultaneously alive and dead, (C) existing in both states until (D) the box's lid is removed and one outcome is chosen. (E) No error.

209

13. During (A) <u>their time</u> in present-day Newfoundland, (B) <u>Leif's expedition</u> made contact with the natives (C) <u>whom they referred to as Skraelings</u> (which translates (D) <u>to 'wretched ones' in Norse</u>). There are several secondhand accounts (E) <u>of their meetings</u>.

Sentence Correction

Directions for questions 14–22:

Choose the best version of the underlined segment of the sentence. If you feel the original sentence is correct, then choose the first answer choice. The following sentences are based on an excerpt from *Perelandra* by C.S. Lewis.

14. Which of the following would be the best replacement for the underlined portion of the sentence reproduced below?

    Everyone has heard the (14) <u>idea of the end justifying the means; that would be Weston's philosophy.</u>

   a. NO CHANGE
   b. idea of the end justifying the means; this is Weston's philosophy.
   c. idea of the end justifying the means, this is the philosophy of Weston.
   d. idea of the end justifying the means. That would be Weston's philosophy.

15. Which of the following would be the best replacement for the underlined portion of the sentence reproduced below?

    (15) <u>Ransom is repulsed by this fact, seeing total evil in Weston's plan.</u>

   a. NO CHANGE
   b. Ransom is reviled by this fact; seeing total evil in Weston's plan.
   c. Ransom, is reviled by this fact, seeing total evil in Weston's plan.
   d. Ransom reviled by this, sees total evil in Weston's plan.

16. Which of the following would be the best replacement for the underlined portion of the sentence reproduced below?

    To do an evil act in order (16) <u>to gain a result that's supposedly good would ultimately warp the final act.</u>

   a. NO CHANGE
   b. for an outcome that's for a greater good would ultimately warp the final act.
   c. to gain a final act would warp its goodness.
   d. to achieve something that's supposedly good would ultimately warp the final result.

17. Which of the following would be the best replacement for the underlined portion of the sentence reproduced below?

    (17) <u>This opposing viewpoints immediately distinguishes Ransom as the hero.</u>

   a. NO CHANGE
   b. This opposing viewpoints immediately distinguishes Ransom, as the hero.
   c. This opposing viewpoint immediately distinguishes Ransom as the hero.
   d. Those opposing viewpoints immediately distinguishes Ransom as the hero.

18. Which of the following would be the best replacement for the underlined portion of the sentence reproduced below?

> Instead, Ransom makes it clear that by allowing such processes as murder and lying dictate how one attains a positive outcome, (18) the righteous goal becomes corrupted.

a. NO CHANGE
b. the goal becomes corrupted and no longer righteous.
c. the righteous goal becomes, corrupted.
d. the goal becomes corrupted, when once it was righteous.

19. Which of the following would be the best replacement for the underlined portion of the sentence reproduced below?

> (19) This idea of allowing necessary evils to happen, is very tempting, it is what Weston fell prey to.

a. NO CHANGE
b. This idea of allowing necessary evils to happen, is very tempting. This is what Weston fell prey to.
c. This idea, allowing necessary evils to happen, is very tempting, it is what Weston fell prey to.
d. This tempting idea of allowing necessary evils to happen is what Weston fell prey to.

20. Which of the following would be the best replacement for the underlined portion of the sentence reproduced below?

> (20) The temptation of the evil spirit Un-man ultimately takes over Weston and he is possessed.

a. NO CHANGE
b. Weston gives into the temptation of the evil spirit Un-man and becomes possessed.
c. Weston is possessed as a result of the temptation of the evil spirit Un-man ultimately, who takes over.
d. The temptation of the evil spirit Un-man takes over Weston and he is possessed ultimately.

21. Which of the following would be the best replacement for the underlined portion of the sentence reproduced below?

> Just as Weston was corrupted by the Un-man, (21) Un-man after this seeks to tempt the Queen of Perelandra to darkness.

a. NO CHANGE
b. Un-man, after this, would tempt the Queen of Perelandra
c. Un-man, after this, seeks to tempt the Queen of Perelandra
d. Un-man then seeks to tempt the Queen of Perelandra

22. Which of the following would be the best replacement for the underlined portion of the sentence reproduced below?

Ransom must literally (22) show her the right path, to accomplish this, he does this based on the same principle as the "means to an end" argument—that good follows good, and evil follows evil.

a. show her the right path, to accomplish this, he does this based on the same principle as the "means to an end" argument
b. show her the right path. To accomplish this, he uses the same principle as the "means to an end" argument
c. show her the right path; to accomplish this he uses the same principle as the "means to an end" argument
d. show her the right path, to accomplish this, the same principle as the "means to an end" argument is applied

Revision in Context

Read the selection about traveling in an RV and answer Questions 23–29.

I have to admit that when my father bought a recreational vehicle (RV), I thought he was making a huge mistake. I didn't really know anything about RVs, but I knew that my dad was as big a "city slicker" as there was. (23) In fact, I even thought he might have gone a little bit crazy. On trips to the beach, he preferred to swim at the pool, and whenever he went hiking, he avoided touching any plants for fear that they might be poison ivy. Why would this man, with an almost irrational fear of the outdoors, want a 40-foot camping behemoth?

(24) The RV was a great purchase for our family and brought us all closer together. Every morning (25) we would wake up, eat breakfast, and broke camp. We laughed at our own comical attempts to back The Beast into spaces that seemed impossibly small. (26) We rejoiced as "hackers." When things inevitably went wrong and we couldn't solve the problems on our own, we discovered the incredible helpfulness and friendliness of the RV community. (27) We even made some new friends in the process.

(28) Above all, it allowed us to share adventures. While traveling across America, which we could not have experienced in cars and hotels. Enjoying a campfire on a chilly summer evening with the mountains of Glacier National Park in the background, or waking up early in the morning to see the sun rising over the distant spires of Arches National Park are memories that will always stay with me and our entire family. (29) Those are also memories that my siblings and me have now shared with our own children.

23. Which of the following would be the best replacement for the underlined portion of the sentence reproduced below?

(23) In fact, I even thought he might have gone a little bit crazy.

a. (as it is now)
b. Move the sentence so that it comes before the preceding sentence.
c. Move the sentence to the end of the first paragraph.
d. Omit the sentence.
e. Move the sentence so that it comes after the next sentence.

212

24. Choose the best replacement for the underlined text (reproduced below).

   (24) <u>The RV</u> was a great purchase for our family and brought us all closer together.

   a. (as it is now)
   b. Not surprisingly, the RV
   c. Furthermore, the RV
   d. As it turns out, the RV
   e. In addition, the RV

25. Which is the best version of the underlined portion of this sentence (reproduced below)?

   Every morning (25) <u>we would wake up, eat breakfast, and broke camp.</u>

   a. (as it is now)
   b. we would wake up, eating breakfast and breaking camp.
   c. would we wake up, eat breakfast, and break camp?
   d. we are waking up, eating breakfast, and breaking camp.
   e. we would wake up, eat breakfast, and break camp.

26. Which is the best version of the underlined portion of this sentence (reproduced below)?

   (26) <u>We rejoiced as "hackers."</u>

   a. (as it is now)
   b. To a nagging problem of technology, we rejoiced as "hackers."
   c. We rejoiced when we figured out how to "hack" a solution to a nagging technological problem.
   d. To "hack" our way to a solution, we had to rejoice.
   e. There was a nagging problem of technology that we rejoiced to as "hackers."

27. Which is the best version of the underlined portion of this sentence (reproduced below)?

   (27) <u>We even made some new friends in the process.</u>

   a. (as it is now)
   b. In the process was the friends we were making.
   c. We are even making some new friends in the process.
   d. We will make new friends in the process.
   e. We even make some new friends in the process.

28. Which is the best version of the underlined portion of these sentences (reproduced below)?

   (28) <u>Above all, it allowed us to share adventures. While traveling across America</u>, which we could not have experienced in cars and hotels.

   a. (as it is now)
   b. Above all, it allowed us to share adventures while traveling across America,
   c. Above all, it allowed us to share adventures; while traveling across America,
   d. Above all, it allowed us to share adventures—while traveling across America,
   e. Above all it allowed us to share adventures while travelling across America

213

29. Which is the best version of the underlined portion of this sentence (reproduced below)?

(29) <u>Those are also memories that my siblings and me</u> have now shared with our own children.

a. (as it is now)
b. Those are also memories that me and my siblings
c. Those are also memories that my siblings and I
d. Those are also memories that I and my siblings
e. This is also memories that my siblings and I

Questions 30-35 are based on the following passage:

Fred Hampton desired to see lasting social change for African American people through nonviolent means and community recognition. (30) <u>In the meantime,</u> he became an African American activist during the American Civil Rights Movement and led the Chicago chapter of the Black Panther Party.

Hampton's Education

Hampton was born and raised (31) <u>in the Maywood neighborhood of Chicago, Illinois in 1948.</u> Gifted academically and a natural athlete, he became a stellar baseball player in high school. (32) <u>Hampton graduated from Proviso East High School in 1966. He later went on to study law at Triton Junior College. While studying at Triton, Hampton joined and became a leader of the National Association for the Advancement of Colored People (NAACP). As a result of his leadership, the NAACP gained more than 500 members.</u> Hampton worked relentlessly to establish recreational facilities in the Maywood neighborhood and improve the educational resources provided to the impoverished black community.

The Black Panthers

The Black Panther Party (BPP) (33) <u>was another that</u> formed around the same time as and was similar in function to the NAACP. Hampton was quickly attracted to the (34) <u>Black Panther Party's approach</u> to the fight for equal rights for African Americans. Hampton eventually joined the chapter and relocated to downtown Chicago to be closer to its headquarters.

His charismatic personality, organizational abilities, sheer determination, and rhetorical skills (35) <u>enable him to quickly rise</u> through the chapter's ranks. Hampton soon became the leader of the Chicago chapter of the BPP where he organized rallies, taught political education classes, and established a free medical clinic. He also took part in the community police supervision project and played an instrumental role in the BPP breakfast program for impoverished African American children.

30. Choose the best replacement for the underlined text (reproduced below).

(30) <u>In the meantime,</u> he became an African American activist during the American Civil Rights Movement and led the Chicago chapter of the Black Panther Party.

a. (as it is now)
b. Unfortunately,
c. Finally,
d. As a result,
e. In hindsight,

31. Which is the best version of the underlined portion of this sentence (reproduced below)?

Hampton was born and raised (31) <u>in the Maywood neighborhood of Chicago, Illinois in 1948.</u>

a. (as it is now)
b. in the Maywood neighborhood, of Chicago, Illinois in 1948.
c. in the Maywood neighborhood of Chicago, Illinois, in 1948.
d. in Chicago, Illinois of Maywood neighborhood in 1948.
e. in Chicago Illinois of Maywood in 1948.

32. Which of the following sentences, if any, should begin a new paragraph?

(32) <u>Hampton graduated from Proviso East High School in 1966. He later went on to study law at Triton Junior College. While studying at Triton, Hampton joined and became a leader of the National Association for the Advancement of Colored People (NAACP). As a result of his leadership, the NAACP gained more than 500 members.</u>

a. (as it is now)
b. Hampton graduated from Proviso East High School in 1966.
c. He later went on to study law at Triton Junior College.
d. While studying at Triton, Hampton joined and became a leader of the National Association for the Advancement of Colored People (NAACP).
e. As a result of his leadership, the NAACP gained more than 500 members.

33. Choose the best replacement for the underlined text (reproduced below).

The Black Panther Party (BPP) (33) <u>was another that</u> formed around the same time as and was similar in function to the NAACP.

a. (as it is now)
b. had lost all its members that
c. had a lot of members that
d. was another school that
e. was another activist group that

34. Which is the best version of the underlined portion of this sentence (reproduced below)?

Hampton was quickly attracted to the (34) <u>Black Panther Party's approach</u> to the fight for equal rights for African Americans.

a. (as it is now)
b. Black Panther Parties approach
c. Black Panther Partys' approach
d. Black Panther Parties' approach
e. Black Panther Partys approach

215

35. Which is the best version of the underlined portion of this sentence (reproduced below)?

His charismatic personality, organizational abilities, sheer determination, and rhetorical skills (35) <u>enable him to quickly rise</u> through the chapter's ranks.

    a.   (as it is now)
    b.   are enabling him to quickly rise
    c.   enabled him to quickly rise
    d.   will enable him to quickly rise
    e.   enables him to quickly rise

Research Skills

36. A student is starting a research assignment on Japanese American internment camps during World War II, but she is unsure of how to gather relevant resources. Which of the following would be the most helpful advice for the student?
    a.   Conduct a broad internet search to get a wide view of the subject.
    b.   Consult an American history textbook.
    c.   Find websites about Japanese culture such as fashion and politics.
    d.   Locate texts in the library related to World War II in America and look for references to internment camps in the index.
    e.   Find a historical fiction novel about Japanese American internment camps.

37. Which of the following should be evaluated to ensure the credibility of a source?
    a.   The publisher, the author, and the references
    b.   The subject, the title, and the audience
    c.   The organization, stylistic choices, and transition words
    d.   The length, the tone, and the contributions of multiple authors
    e.   The author's purpose, the audience, and the syntax

38. Which of the following is true of using citations in a research paper?
    a.   If a source is cited in the bibliography, it is not necessary to cite it in the text as well.
    b.   In-text citations differ in format from bibliographic citations.
    c.   Students should learn one standard method of citing sources.
    d.   Books and articles need to be cited, but websites and multimedia sources do not.
    e.   Websites and multimedia sources need to be cited, but not books or articles.

39. Which of the following is true regarding the integration of source material to maintain the flow of ideas in a paper?
    a.   There should be at least one quotation in every paragraph.
    b.   If a source is paraphrased instead of being directly quoted, it is not necessary to include a citation.
    c.   An author's full name must be used in every signal phrase.
    d.   In-text citations should be used to support the paper's argument without overwhelming the student's writing.
    e.   There should be at least one paraphrase in every paragraph.

40. Guerin, Wilfred L., et al. *A Handbook of Critical Approaches to Literature*. Oxford University Press, 2011.

In the above citation, the abbreviation "et al." indicates that the book
   a.   has an author who is deceased.
   b.   has more than one author.
   c.   has more than one publication date.
   d.   was published before the presented date.
   e.   is both a book and a journal.

Mathematics

1. Simplify:

$$\frac{4a^{-1}b^3}{a^4b^{-2}} \times \frac{3a}{b}$$

   a. $12a^3b^5$
   b. $12\frac{b^4}{a^4}$
   c. $\frac{12}{a^4}$
   d. $7\frac{b^4}{a}$

2. What is the product of two irrational numbers?
   a.   Irrational
   b.   Rational
   c.   Irrational or rational
   d.   Complex and imaginary

3. The graph shows the position of a car over a 10-second time interval. Which of the following is the correct interpretation of the graph for the interval 1 to 3 seconds?

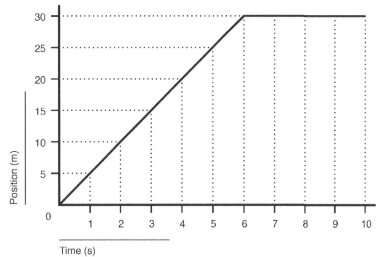

   a.   The car remains in the same position.
   b.   The car is traveling at a speed of 5 m/s.
   c.   The car is traveling up a hill.
   d.   The car is traveling at 5 mph.

217

4. The number −4 can be classified as which of the following?
   a.   Real, rational, integer, whole, natural
   b.   Real, rational, integer, natural
   c.   Real, rational, integer
   d.   Real, irrational

5. Which of the following is NOT a way to write 40% of N?
   a. $(0.4)N$

   b. $\frac{2}{5}N$

   c. $40N$

   d. $\frac{4}{10}N$

6. A student gets an 85% on a test with 20 questions. How many questions did the student solve correctly?
   a.   15 questions
   b.   16 questions
   c.   17 questions
   d.   18 questions

7. Four people split a bill. The first person pays for $\frac{1}{5}$, the second person pays for $\frac{1}{4}$, and the third person pays for $\frac{1}{3}$. What fraction of the bill does the fourth person pay?
   a. $\frac{13}{60}$

   b. $\frac{47}{60}$

   c. $\frac{1}{4}$

   d. $\frac{4}{15}$

8. Karen gets paid a weekly salary and a commission for every sale that she makes. The table below shows the number of sales and her pay for different weeks.

Sales	2	7	4	8
Pay	$380	$580	$460	$620

Which of the following equations represents Karen's weekly pay?
   a. $y = 90x + 200$
   b. $y = 90x - 200$
   c. $y = 40x + 300$
   d. $y = 40x - 300$

9. What is the simplified form of the expression: $(7n + 3n^3 + 3) + (8n + 5n^3 + 2n^4)$
   a. $9n^4 + 15n - 2$
   b. $2n^4 + 5n^3 + 15n - 2$
   c. $9n^4 + 8n^3 + 15n$
   d. $2n^4 + 8n^3 + 15n + 3$

10. What is the product of the following expressions?

$$(4x - 8)(5x^2 + x + 6)$$

a. $20x^3 - 36x^2 + 16x - 48$
b. $6x^3 - 41x^2 + 12x + 15$
c. $20x^3 + 11x^2 - 37x - 12$
d. $2x^3 - 11x^2 - 32x + 20$

11. Alan currently weighs 200 pounds, but he wants to lose weight to get down to 175 pounds. What is this difference in kilograms? (1 pound is approximately equal to 0.45 kilograms.)

a. 9 kg
b. 11.25 kg
c. 78.75 kg
d. 90 kg

12. What is the simplified quotient of the following expression?

$$\frac{5x^3}{3x^2y} \div \frac{25}{3y^9}$$

a. $\frac{125x}{9y^{10}}$

b. $\frac{x}{5y^8}$

c. $\frac{5}{xy^8}$

d. $\frac{xy^8}{5}$

13. What is the solution for the following equation?

$$\frac{x^2 + x - 30}{x - 5} = 11$$

a. $x = -6$
b. There is no solution.
c. $x = 16$
d. $x = 5$

14. $3\frac{2}{3} - 1\frac{4}{5} =$

a. $1\frac{13}{15}$

b. $\frac{14}{15}$

c. $2\frac{2}{3}$

d. $\frac{4}{5}$

15. How do you solve $V = lwh$ for h?
    a. $lwV = h$

    b. $h = \dfrac{V}{lw}$

    c. $h = \dfrac{Vl}{w}$

    d. $h = \dfrac{Vw}{l}$

16. The total perimeter of a rectangle is 36 cm. If the length is 12 cm, what is the width?
    a. 3 cm
    b. 12 cm
    c. 6 cm
    d. 8 cm

17. If Sarah reads at an average rate of 21 pages in 4 nights, how long will it take her to read 140 pages?
    a. 6 nights
    b. 26 nights
    c. 8 nights
    d. 27 nights

18. The phone bill is calculated each month using the equation $c = 50g + 75$. The cost of the phone bill per month is represented by c, and g represents the gigabytes of data used that month. What is the value and interpretation of the slope of this equation?
    a. 75 dollars per day
    b. 75 gigabytes per day
    c. 50 dollars per day
    d. 50 dollars per gigabyte

19. If $\dfrac{5}{2} \div \dfrac{1}{3} = n$, then n is between:
    a. 5 and 7
    b. 7 and 9
    c. 9 and 11
    d. 3 and 5

20. A closet is filled with red, blue, and green shirts. If $\dfrac{1}{3}$ of the shirts are green and $\dfrac{2}{5}$ are red, what fraction of the shirts are blue?

    a. $\dfrac{4}{15}$

    b. $\dfrac{1}{5}$

    c. $\dfrac{7}{15}$

    d. $\dfrac{1}{2}$

21. Shawna buys $2\frac{1}{2}$ gallons of paint. If she uses $\frac{1}{3}$ of it on the first day, how much does she have left?

    a. $1\frac{5}{6}$ gallons

    b. $1\frac{1}{2}$ gallons

    c. $1\frac{2}{3}$ gallons

    d.   2 gallons

22. What are all the factors of 12?
    a.   12, 24, 36
    b.   1, 2, 4, 6, 12
    c.   12, 24, 36, 48
    d.   1, 2, 3, 4, 6, 12

23. 20 is 40% of what number?
    a.   50
    b.   8
    c.   200
    d.   5,000

24. Divide and reduce: $\frac{4}{13} \div \frac{27}{169}$

    a. $\frac{52}{27}$

    b. $\frac{51}{27}$

    c. $\frac{52}{29}$

    d. $\frac{51}{29}$

25. You measure the width of your door to be 36 inches. The true width of the door is 35.75 inches. What is the relative error in your measurement?
    a.   0.7%
    b.   0.007%
    c.   0.99%
    d.   0.1%

26. What is the y-intercept for $y = x^2 + 3x - 4$?
    a. $y = 1$
    b. $y = -4$
    c. $y = 3$
    d. $y = 4$

27. Is the following function even, odd, neither, or both?

$$y = \frac{1}{2}x^4 + 2x^2 - 6$$

a. Even
b. Odd
c. Neither
d. Both

28. Which equation is NOT a function of x?
   a. $y = |x|$
   b. $y = x^2$
   c. $x = 3$
   d. $y = 4$

29. What type of function is modeled by the values in the following table?

x	$f(x)$
1	2
2	4
3	8
4	16
5	32

a. Linear
b. Exponential
c. Quadratic
d. Cubic

30. If $a \neq b$, solve for x if $\frac{1}{x} + \frac{2}{a} = \frac{2}{b}$

a. $\frac{a-b}{ab}$

b. $\frac{ab}{2(a-b)}$

c. $\frac{2(a-b)}{ab}$

d. $\frac{a-b}{2ab}$

31. If $x^2 - x - 3 = 0$, what is the value of $\left(x - \frac{1}{2}\right)^2$?

a. $\frac{13}{2}$

b. $\frac{13}{4}$

c. 13

d. $\frac{169}{4}$

32. What is an equation for the line passing through the origin and the point $(2, 1)$?
  a. $y = 2x$
  b. $y = \frac{1}{2}x$
  c. $y = x - 2$
  d. $2y = x + 1$

33. Jessica buys 10 cans of paint. Red paint costs $1 per can, and blue paint costs $2 per can. In total, she spends $16. How many red cans did she buy?
  a. 2
  b. 3
  c. 4
  d. 5

34. A farmer owns two (non-adjacent) square plots of land, which he wishes to fence. The area of one is 1,000 square feet, while the area of the other is 10 square feet. How much fencing does he need, in feet?
  a. 44
  b. $40\sqrt{10}$
  c. $440\sqrt{10}$
  d. $44\sqrt{10}$

35. $2x(3x + 1) - 5(3x + 1) =$
  a. $10x(3x + 1)$
  b. $10x^2(3x + 1)$
  c. $(2x - 5)(3x + 1)$
  d. $(2x + 1)(3x - 5)$

36. For which real numbers x is $-3x^2 + x - 8 > 0$?
  a. For all real numbers x

  b. $-2\sqrt{\frac{2}{3}} < x < 2\sqrt{\frac{2}{3}}$

  c. $1 - 2\sqrt{\frac{2}{3}} < x < 1 + 2\sqrt{\frac{2}{3}}$

  d. For no real numbers x

37. Which of the following is a root of $x^2 - 2x - 2$?
  a. $1 + \sqrt{3}$
  b. $1 + 2\sqrt{2}$
  c. $2 + 2\sqrt{3}$
  d. $2 - 2\sqrt{3}$

38. In the xy-plane, the graph of $y = x^2 + 2$ and the circle with center $(0,1)$ and radius 1 have how many points of intersection?
  a. 0
  b. 1
  c. 2
  d. 3

39. A line goes through the point $(-4, 0)$ and the point $(0, 2)$. What is the slope of the line?

    a. 2

    b. 4

    c. $\frac{3}{2}$

    d. $\frac{1}{2}$

40. Six people apply to work for Janice's company, but she only needs four workers. How many different groups of four employees can Janice choose?

    a. 6
    b. 10
    c. 15
    d. 36

41. Which of the following shows a line of symmetry?

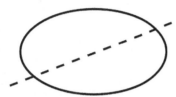

    a.

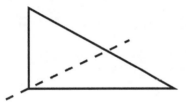

    b.

    c.

    d.

224

42. If $4x - 3 = 5$, what is the value of x?
   a. 1
   b. 2
   c. 3
   d. 4

43. A ball is drawn at random from a ball pit containing 8 red balls, 7 yellow balls, 6 green balls, and 5 purple balls. What's the probability that the ball drawn is yellow?
   a. $\frac{1}{26}$
   b. $\frac{19}{26}$
   c. $\frac{7}{26}$
   d. 1

44. A shuffled deck of 52 cards contains 4 kings. One card is drawn and is not put back in the deck. Then, a second card is drawn. What's the probability that both cards are kings?
   a. $\frac{1}{169}$
   b. $\frac{1}{221}$
   c. $\frac{1}{13}$
   d. $\frac{4}{13}$

45. What's the probability of rolling a 6 at least once in two rolls of a die?
   a. $\frac{1}{3}$
   b. $\frac{1}{36}$
   c. $\frac{1}{6}$
   d. $\frac{5}{18}$

46. For a group of 20 men, the median weight is 180 pounds, and the range is 30 pounds. If each man gains 10 pounds, which of the following would be true?
   a. The median weight will increase, and the range will remain the same.
   b. The median weight and range will both remain the same.
   c. The median weight will stay the same, and the range will increase.
   d. The median weight and range will both increase.

47. For the following similar triangles, what are the values of x and y (rounded to one decimal place)?

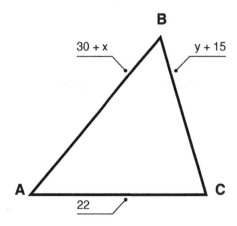 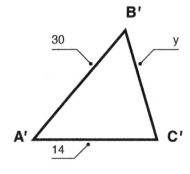

    a. $x = 16.5, y = 25.1$
    b. $x = 19.5, y = 24.1$
    c. $x = 17.1, y = 26.3$
    d. $x = 26.3, y = 17.1$

48. What are the center and radius of a circle with equation $4x^2 + 4y^2 - 16x - 24y + 51 = 0$?
    a.   Center $(3, 2)$ and radius $\frac{1}{2}$
    b.   Center $(2, 3)$ and radius $\frac{1}{2}$
    c.   Center $(3, 2)$ and radius $\frac{1}{4}$
    d.   Center $(2, 3)$ and radius $\frac{1}{4}$

49. If the point $(-3, -4)$ is reflected over the x-axis, what new point does it make?
    a. $(-3, -4)$
    b. $(3, -4)$
    c. $(3, 4)$
    d. $(-3, 4)$

50. A company invests $50,000 in a building where they can produce saws. If the cost of producing one saw is $40, then which function expresses the total amount of money the company spends on producing saws? The variable y is the money paid, and x is the number of saws produced.
    a. $y = 50{,}000x + 40$
    b. $y + 40 = x - 50{,}000$
    c. $y = 40x - 50{,}000$
    d. $y = 40x + 50{,}000$

51. The triangle shown below is a right triangle. What's the value of x?

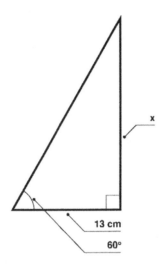

13 cm

60°

a. $x = 1.73$
b. $x = 0.57$
c. $x = 13$
d. $x = 22.52$

52. Apples cost $2 each, while bananas cost $3 each. Maria purchased a total of 10 pieces of fruit and spent $22. How many apples did she buy?
a. 5
b. 6
c. 7
d. 8

53. A sample data set contains the following values: 1, 3, 5, 7. What's the standard deviation of the set?
a. 2.58
b. 4
c. 6.23
d. 1.1

54. A pair of dice is thrown, and the sum of the two scores is calculated. What's the expected value of the roll?
a. 5
b. 6
c. 7
d. 8

55. What is the sum of $(2.6 \times 10^5) + (1.3 \times 10^4)$? Enter your answer in the answer box below.

56. What would the equation be for the following problem? Enter your answer in the answer box below.

Three times the sum of a number and seven is greater than or equal to 32.

227

Essay Prompts #1

Directions: Please read the prompts below and answer in an essay format.

Essay 1

Some people feel that sharing their lives on social media sites such as Facebook, Instagram, and Snapchat is fine. They share every aspect of their lives, including pictures of themselves and their families, what they ate for lunch, who they are dating, and when they are going on vacation. They even say that if it's not on social media, it didn't happen. Other people believe that sharing so much personal information is an invasion of privacy and could prove dangerous. They think sharing personal pictures and details invites predators, cyberbullying, and identity theft.

Write an essay to someone who is considering whether to participate in social media. Take a side on the issue and argue whether or not he/she should join a social media network. Use specific examples to support your argument.

Essay 2

Read the two articles below. Then, write a 500-word essay in which you synthesize the two articles with your own opinion of the topic. That is, you must develop a position of the topic then use both sources to draw upon your knowledge of the topic and appeal to your audience. Refer to each source by the author's last name or title.

Passage A

From such verses the Poems in these volumes will be found distinguished at least by one mark of difference, that each of them has a worthy *purpose*. Not that I always began to write with a distinct purpose formerly conceived; but habits of meditation have, I trust, so prompted and regulated my feelings, that my descriptions of such objects as strongly excite those feelings, will be found to carry along with them a *purpose*. If this opinion be erroneous, I can have little right to the name of a Poet. For all good poetry is the spontaneous overflow of powerful feelings: and though this be true, Poems to which any value can be attached were never produced on any variety of subjects but by a man who, being possessed of more than usual organic sensibility, had also thought long and deeply. For our continued influxes of feeling are modified and directed by our thoughts, which are indeed the representatives of all our past feelings; and, as by contemplating the relation of these general representatives to each other, we discover what is really important to men, so, by the repetition and continuance of this act, our feelings will be connected with important subjects, till at length, if we be originally possessed of much sensibility, such habits of mind will be produced, that, by obeying blindly and mechanically the impulses of those habits, we shall describe objects, and utter sentiments, of such a nature, and in such connexion with each other, that the understanding of the Reader must necessarily be in some degree enlightened, and his affections strengthened and purified.

Excerpt from Preface to Lyrical Ballads by William Wordsworth, written in 1800

Passage B

If you compare several representative passages of the greatest poetry you see how great is the variety of types of combination, and also how completely any semi-ethical criterion of "sublimity" misses the mark. For it is not the "greatness," the intensity, of the emotions, the components, but the intensity of the artistic process, the pressure, so to speak, under which the fusion takes place,

228

that counts. The episode of Paolo and Francesca employs a definite emotion, but the intensity of the poetry is something quite different from whatever intensity in the supposed experience it may give the impression of. It is no more intense, furthermore, than Canto XXVI, the voyage of Ulysses, which has not the direct dependence upon an emotion. Great variety is possible in the process of transmution of emotion: the murder of Agamemnon, or the agony of Othello, gives an artistic effect apparently closer to a possible original than the scenes from Dante. In the *Agamemnon,* the artistic emotion approximates to the emotion of an actual spectator; in *Othello* to the emotion of the protagonist himself. But the difference between art and the event is always absolute; the combination which is the murder of Agamemnon is probably as complex as that which is the voyage of Ulysses. In either case there has been a fusion of elements. The ode of Keats contains a number of feelings which have nothing particular to do with the nightingale, but which the nightingale, partly, perhaps, because of its attractive name, and partly because of its reputation, served to bring together.

Excerpt from *Tradition and the Individual Talent* by T.S. Eliot, written in 1919

The following pages are provided for writing your essays.

Write Your Essay

_____

_____

_____

_____

_____

_____

_____

_____

_____

_____

_____

_____

_____

229

Answer Explanations #1

Reading

1. C: Choice *C* is the correct answer because it most extensively summarizes the entire passage. While Choices *A* and *B* are reasonable possibilities, they reference portions of Gulliver's experience, not the whole. Choice *D* is incorrect because Gulliver doesn't express repentance or sorrow in this particular passage.

2. A: Principal refers to *chief* or *primary* within the context of this text. Choice *A* is the answer that most closely aligns with this definition. Choices *B* and *D* refer to a helper or follower, while Choice *C* doesn't meet the description of Reldresal from the passage.

3. C: One can reasonably infer that Gulliver is considerably larger than the children who were playing around him because multiple children could fit into his hand. Choice *A* is incorrect because there is no indication of stress in Gulliver's tone. Choices *B* and *D* aren't the best answers because, though Gulliver seems fond of his new acquaintances, he didn't travel there with the intentions of meeting new people, nor does he express a definite love for them in this particular portion of the text.

4. C: The emperor made a definitive decision to expose Gulliver to their native customs. In this instance, the word *mind* was not related to a vote, question, or cognitive ability.

5. A: The assertion in Choice *A* does not support the fact that games are a commonplace event in this culture because it mentions conduct, not games. Choices *B*, *C*, and *D* are incorrect because these do support the fact that games are a commonplace event.

6. B: Choice *B* is the only option that mentions the correlation between physical ability and leadership positions. Choices *A* and *D* are unrelated to physical strength and leadership abilities. Choice *C* does not make a deduction that would lead to the correct answer—it only comments upon the abilities of common townspeople.

7. D: Context clues indicate that Choice *D* is correct because the passage provides great detail on Mr. Utterson's feelings about locating Hyde. Choice *A* does not fit because there is no mention of Mr. Lanyon's mental state. Choice *B* is incorrect; although the text does make mention of bells, Choice *B* is not the *best* answer overall. Choice *C* is incorrect because the passage states that Mr. Utterson was determined, not unsure.

8. A: The word *city* appears in the passage several times, thus establishing the location for the reader.

9. B: The passage states that the Juggernaut causes the children to scream. Choices *A* and *D* don't apply because the text doesn't mention either of these instances specifically. Choice *C* is incorrect because there is nothing in the text that mentions space travel.

10. B: The mention of *morning, noon,* and *night* make it clear that the word *haunt* refers to frequent appearances at various times. Choice *A* doesn't work because the text makes no mention of levitating. Choices *C* and *D* are not correct because the text mentions Mr. Utterson's anguish and disheartenment because of his failure to find Hyde but does not mention Mr. Utterson's feelings negatively affecting anyone else.

11. D: Choice *D* is the correct answer because of the repetition of the *L*-words. Hyperbole is an exaggeration, so Choice *A* doesn't work. No comparison is being made, so no simile or juxtaposition is being used, thus eliminating Choices *B* and *C*.

12. D: The speaker invokes the game of hide and seek to indicate they will continue their search for Hyde. Choices *A* and *B* are not possible answers because the text doesn't refer to any name changes or an identity crisis, despite Mr.

Utterson's extreme obsession with finding Hyde. The text also makes no mention of a mistaken identity when referring to Hyde, so Choice *C* is also incorrect.

13. A: The tone is exasperated. While contemplative might seem like an option because of the thoughtful nature of the text, Choice *A* is correct because the speaker is annoyed by the thought of being included when he felt that the fellow members of his race were being excluded. The speaker is not nonchalant, nor accepting of the circumstances which he describes.

14. C: Choice *C*, *contented*, is the only word that has the opposite meaning of *obdurate*.

15. B: While the speaker makes biblical references, it is not the main focus of the passage, thus eliminating Choice *A* as an answer. The passage also makes no mention of wealthy landowners and doesn't speak of any positive response to the historical events, so Choices *C* and *D* are not correct.

16. D: Choice *D* is the correct answer because it clearly references the disparity between slaves and free people in the United States.

17. D: It is an example of hyperbole; the physical distance between Frederick Douglass and his audience was not, in fact, immeasurable. However, it clearly demonstrated the differences in the lives and situations of free men and slaves in the United States. Choice *A* is incorrect because assonance is the repetition of sounds and commonly occurs in poetry. Choice *B* is incorrect because parallelism refers to two statements that correlate, or parallel each other, in some manner.

18. C: Choice *C* is correct because the speaker is clear about his intention and stance throughout the text; he does not equivocate. Choice *A* is incorrect because knowledge of the Bible would have been common at the time, creating a common ground between Frederick Douglass and his audience. Choice *B* is incorrect because another group of people affected by slavery is being referenced, and Douglass is clearly drawing a connection between that group of people and American slaves. Choice *D* is incorrect because the quoted passage describes the sorrow of other people in a similar situation.

19. A: The passage describes a situation and then explains the causes that led to it. Also, it utilizes cause and effect signal words, such as *reasons*, *factors*, *so*, and *as a result*. Choice *B* is incorrect because a compare and contrast order considers the similarities and differences of two or more things. Choice *C* is incorrect because spatial order describes where things are located in relation to each other. Finally, Choice *D* is incorrect because time order describes when things occurred chronologically.

20. D: Choice *A* is irrelevant. The argument's conclusion is that Hank is a professional writer. The argument does not depend on whether Hank's agent is the best or worst in the business. Eliminate this choice. Choice *B* seems fairly strong at first glance. It feels reasonable to say that being a professional writer requires representation. However, the argument would still be strong if being a professional writer did not require an agent. Hank would still be a professional writer. Eliminate this choice. Choice *C* is irrelevant. Whether Hank is a professional writer does not depend on his reviews. Eliminate this choice. Choice *D* is strong. Negate it to determine if the argument falls apart. If being a professional writer requires earning money, then Hank would not be a professional writer. The argument falls apart. This is almost definitely the correct answer. Therefore, Choice *D* is the correct answer.

21. D: Choice *D* looks like a strong answer. This answer choice references the argument's main points—*Infinite Jest* is a modern classic, the book deserves its praise, and everybody should read it. In contrast, Choice *A* restates the author's conclusion. The correct answer to main point questions will often be closely related to the conclusion. Choice *B* restates a premise. Is the author's main point that *Infinite Jest* is a page-turner? No, he uses readers' obsession with the book as a premise. Eliminate this choice. Choice *C* is definitely not the main point of the passage. It's a simple fact underlying the argument. It certainly cannot be considered the main point. Eliminate this choice.

234

22. A: Choice *A* is consistent with the argument's logic. The argument asserts that the world powers' military alliances amounted to a delicate fuse, and the assassination merely lit it. The main point of the argument is that any event involving the military alliances would have led to a world war. Choice *B* runs counter to the argument's tone and reasoning. It can immediately be eliminated. Choice *C* is also clearly incorrect. At no point does the argument blame any single or group of countries for starting World War I. Choice *D* is incorrect for the same reason as Choice *C*. Eliminate this choice.

23. A: The purpose is to inform the reader about what assault is and how it is committed. Choice *B* is incorrect because the passage does not state that assault is a lesser form of lethal force, only that an assault can use lethal force, or alternatively, lethal force can be utilized to counter a dangerous assault. Choice *C* is incorrect because the passage is informative and does not have a set agenda. Finally, Choice *D* is incorrect because although the author uses an example in order to explain assault, it is not indicated that this is the author's personal account.

24. C: The situation of the man who is attacked in an alley by another man with a knife would most merit the use of lethal force. If the man being attacked used lethal force in self-defense, it would not be considered illegal. The presence of a deadly weapon indicates malicious intent, and because the individual is isolated in an alley, lethal force in self-defense may be the only way to preserve his life. Choices *A* and *B* can be ruled out because in these situations no one is in danger of immediate death or bodily harm by someone else. Choice *D* is an assault that does exhibit intent to harm, but this situation isn't severe enough to merit lethal force; there is no intent to kill.

25. B: As discussed in the second passage, there are several forms of assault, like assault with a deadly weapon, verbal assault, or threatening posture or language. Choice *A* is incorrect because lethal force and assault are separate, as indicated by the passages. Choice *C* is incorrect because assault is never justified. Self-defense resulting in lethal force can be justified. Choice *D* is incorrect because the author does not mention what the charges are on assaults; therefore, we cannot assume that they are more or less than unnecessary use of force charges.

26. D: If true, the statement in Choice *D* would most undermine the last part of the passage because it directly contradicts how the law evaluates the use of lethal force. Choices *A* and *B* are stated in the paragraph, and therefore do not undermine the explanation from the author. Choice *C* does not necessarily undermine the passage, but it does not support the passage either. It is more of an opinion that does not strengthen or weaken the explanation.

27. C: Choice *C* is correct because it clearly establishes what both assault and lethal force are and gives the specific way in which the two concepts meet. Choice *A* is incorrect because lethal force doesn't necessarily result in assault. Choice *B* is incorrect because it contradicts the information in the passage (that assault with deadly intent can lead to an individual using lethal force). Choice *D* is compelling but ultimately too vague; the statement touches on aspects of the two ideas but fails to present the concrete way in which the two are connected to each other.

28. A: Both passages open by defining a legal concept and then describing situations in order to further explain the concept. Choice *C* is incorrect because while the passages utilize examples to help explain the concepts discussed, the author doesn't indicate that they are specific court cases. It's also clear that the passages don't open with examples but instead begin by defining the terms addressed in each passage. This eliminates Choice *B* and ultimately reveals Choice *A* to be the correct answer. Choice *A* accurately outlines the way both passages are structured. Because the passages follow a nearly identical structure, the rest of the choices can be ruled out.

29. A: Intent is very important for determining both lethal force and assault; intent is examined in both parties and helps determine the severity of the issue. Choices *B* and *C* are incorrect because it is clear in both passages that intent is a prevailing theme in both lethal force and assault. Choice *D* is compelling, but if a person uses lethal force to defend themselves, the intent of the defender is also examined in order to help determine if there was excessive force used. Choice *A* is correct because it states that intent is important for determining both lethal force and

assault and that intent is used to gauge the severity of the issues. Remember, just as lethal force can escalate to excessive use of force, there are different kinds of assault. Intent dictates several different forms of assault.

30. B: To demonstrate a single example of two different types of assault, then adding in a third type of assault to the example's conclusion. The example mainly serves to show an instance of "threatening body language" and "provocative language" with the homeowner gesturing threats to his neighbor. It ends the example by adding a third type of assault: physical strikes. This example is used to show the variant nature of assaults. Choice *A* is incorrect because it doesn't mention the "physical strike" assault at the end and is not specific enough. Choice *C* is incorrect because the example does not say anything about the definition of lethal force or how it might be altered. Choice *D* is incorrect, as the example mentions nothing of cause and effect.

31. D: The use of "I" could serve to have a "hedging" effect, allow the reader to connect with the author in a more personal way and cause the reader to empathize more with the egrets. However, it doesn't distance the reader from the text, making Choice *D* the answer to this question.

32. C: The quote gives the warden's direct statement regarding his dedication to the rookery. Choice *A* is incorrect because the speaker of the quote is a warden, not a hunter. Choice *B* is incorrect because the quote does not lighten the mood, but shows the danger of the situation between the wardens and the hunters. Choice *D* is incorrect because there is no humor found in the quote.

33. D: A *rookery* is a colony of breeding birds. Although *rookery* could mean Choice *A*, *houses in a slum area*, it does not make sense in this context. Choices *B* and *C* are both incorrect, as this is not a place for hunters to trade tools or for wardens to trade stories.

34. B: The previous sentence is describing "20 colonies" of birds, so what follows should be a bird colony. Choice *A* may be true, but we have no evidence of this in the text. Choice *C* does touch on the tension between the hunters and wardens, but there is no official "Bird Island Battle" mentioned in the text. Choice *D* does not exist in the text.

35. D: The text mentions several different times how and why the association has been successful and gives examples to back this fact. Choice *A* is incorrect because although the article, in some instances, calls certain people to act, it is not the purpose of the entire passage. There is no way to tell if Choices *B* and *C* are correct, as they are not mentioned in the text.

36. C: Choice *A* might be true in a general sense, but it is not relevant to the context of the text. Choice *B* is incorrect because the hunters are not studying lines of flight to help wardens, but to hunt birds. Choice *D* is incorrect because nothing in the text mentions that hunters are trying to build homes underneath lines of flight of birds for good luck.

37. A: The passage's purpose is to introduce certain insects that transition from water to air. Choice *B* is incorrect because although the passage talks about gills, it is not the central idea of the passage. Choices *C* and *D* are incorrect because the passage does not define insect breathing or invite readers to participate in insect preservation. Rather, the passage serves as an introduction to stoneflies, dragonflies, and mayflies and their transition from water to air.

38. C: To *moult* is to shed part or all of the outer shell, as noted in Choice *C*. Choices *A*, *B*, and *D* are incorrect.

39. B: Notice how the first paragraph goes into detail describing how insects are able to breathe air. The second paragraph acts as a contrast to the first by stating, "[i]t is of great interest to find that, nevertheless, a number of insects spend much of their time under water." Watch for transition words such as *nevertheless* to help find what type of passage you're dealing with.

236

40: C: *Instars* are the phases between two periods of molting, and the text explains when these transitions occur. The preparatory stages are acted out in the water, while the last stage is in the air. Choices *A*, *B*, and *D* are all incorrect.

41. C: Overall, the author presents us with information on the subject. One moment where personal interest is depicted is when the author states, "It is of great interest to find that, nevertheless, a number of insects spend much of their time under water."

42. C: Their larvae can breathe the air dissolved in water through gills of some kind. This is stated in the last paragraph. Choice *A* is incorrect because the text mentions this in a general way at the beginning of the passage concerning "insects as a whole." Choice *B* is incorrect because this is stated of beetles and water-bugs, and not the insects in question. Choice *D* is incorrect because this is the opposite of what the text says of instars.

43. D: Choice *A* says that the GDP increased by 2% last year, which supports a claim of health. Choice *B* relays that unemployment is the lowest it's been in over a decade, a sign of a strong economy. Choice *C* states that average household income is at a historical high point, also a sign of a strong economy. In contrast, a declining manufacturing sector is a sign of an unhealthy economy, making Choice *D* is the correct answer.

44. C: The answer we seek has both the most detailed and objective information; thus, Choice *C* is the correct answer. The number of incidents and their relationship to a possible cause are both detailed and objective information. Choice *A* describing a television commercial with a dramatized reenactment is not particularly detailed. Choice *B*, a notice to the public informing them of additional drinking and driving units on patrol, is not detailed and objective information. Choice *D*, a highway bulletin, does not present the type of information required.

45. C: We are looking for an inference—a conclusion that is reached on the basis of evidence and reasoning—from the passage that will likely explain why the famous children's author did not achieve her usual success with the new genre (despite the book's acclaim). Choice *A* is wrong because the statement is false according to the passage. Choice *B* is wrong because, although the passage says the author has a graduate degree on the subject, it would be an unrealistic leap to infer that she is the foremost expert on Antebellum America. Choice *D* is wrong because there is nothing in the passage to lead us to infer that people generally prefer a children's series to historical fiction. In contrast, Choice *C* can be logically inferred since the passage speaks of the great success of the children's series and the declaration that the fame of the author's name causes the children's books to "fly off the shelves." Thus, we can infer that she did not receive any bump from her name since she published the historical novel under a pseudonym, which makes Choice *C* correct.

46. D: Outspending other countries on education could have other benefits, but there is no reference to this in the passage, so Choice *A* is incorrect. Choice *B* is incorrect because the author does not mention corruption. Choice *C* is incorrect because there is nothing in the passage stating that the tests are not genuinely representative. Choice *D* is accurate because spending more money has not brought success. The United States already spends the most money, and the country is not excelling on these tests. Choice *D* is the correct answer.

47. B: The scientist and politician largely disagree, but the question asks for a point where the two are in agreement. The politician would not concur that burning fossil fuels causes global temperatures to rise; thus, Choice *A* is wrong. He would not agree with Choice *C* suggesting that countries must revisit their energy policies. By inference from the given information, the scientist would likely not concur that earth's climate naturally goes through warming and cooling cycles; so Choice *D* is incorrect. However, both the scientist and politician would agree that global temperatures are increasing. The reason for this is in dispute. The politician thinks it is part of the earth's natural cycle; the scientist thinks it is from the burning of fossil fuels. However, both acknowledge an increase, so Choice *B* is the correct answer.

48. A: This is a challenging question because the author's purpose is somewhat open-ended. The author concludes by stating that the questions regarding human perception and observation can be approached from many angles. Thus, they do not seem to be attempting to prove one thing or another. Choice *B* is incorrect because nothing suggests that the electron experiment is related to astroparticle physics, or that the discovery is recent. Choice *C* is a broad generalization that does not reflect accurately on the writer's views. While the author does appear to reflect on opposing views of human understanding, Choice *D*, the best answer is Choice *A*.

49. C: The beginning of this paragraph literally "presents a conundrum," explains the problem of partial understanding, and then ends with more questions, or inquiries. There is no solution offered in this paragraph, making Choices *A* and *B* incorrect. Choice *D* is incorrect because the paragraph does not begin with a definition.

50. D: Looking back in the text, the author describes that classical philosophy holds that understanding can be reached by careful observation. This will not work if they are overly invested or biased in their pursuit. Choices *A* and *C* are in no way related and are completely unnecessary. A specific theory is not necessary to understanding, according to classical philosophy mentioned by the author. Again, the key to understanding is observing the phenomena outside of it, without bias or predisposition. Thus, Choice *B* is wrong.

51. B: Choices *A* and *C* are incorrect because such behavior is not mentioned at all in the text. In the passage, the author says that electrons that were physically observed appeared to pass through one hole or another. Remember, the electrons that were observed doing this were described as acting like particles. Therefore, Choice *D* is incorrect. Recall that the plate actually recorded electrons passing through both holes simultaneously and hitting the plate. This behavior, the electron activity that wasn't seen by humans, was characteristic of waves. Thus, Choice *B* is the correct answer.

52. C: Choice *A* mirrors the language in the beginning of the paragraph but is incorrect in its intent. Choice *B* is incorrect; the paragraph mentions nothing of not knowing the true nature of gravity. Choice *D* is incorrect as well. There is no mention of an "alternative solution" in this paragraph.

53. A: The important thing to keep in mind is that we must choose a scenario that best parallels, or is most similar to, the discovery of the experiment mentioned in the passage. The important aspects of the experiment can be summed up like so: humans directly observed one behavior of electrons, and then, through analyzing a tool (the plate that recorded electron hits), discovered that there was another electron behavior that could not be physically seen by human eyes. This best parallels the scenario in Choice *A*. Like Feynman, the color-blind person is able to observe one aspect of the world, but through the special goggles (a tool), he is able to see a natural phenomenon that he could not physically see on his own. While Choice *D* is compelling, the x-ray does not necessarily reveal that a bone is broken. Usually, the x-ray helps to see a bone that is already known to be broken. The other choices do not parallel the scenario in question. Therefore, Choice *A* is the best choice.

54. B: The author would not agree that technology renders human observation irrelevant. Choice *A* is incorrect because much of the passage discusses how technology helps humans observe what cannot be seen with the naked eye, therefore the author would agree with this statement. This line of reasoning is also why the author would agree with Choice *D*, making it incorrect as well. As indicated in the second paragraph, the author seems to think that humans create inventions and tools with the goal of studying phenomena more precisely. This indicates increased understanding as people recognize limitations and develop items to help bypass the limitations and learn. Therefore, Choice *C* is incorrect as well.

55. B: Choice *A* uses similar language, but it is not the main point of disagreement. The reporter calls the loss devastating, and there's no reason to believe that the coach would disagree with this assessment. Eliminate this choice.

Choice *B* is strong since both passages mention the at-bats with runners in scoring position. The reporter asserts that the team lost due to the team failing to get such a hit. In contrast, the coach identifies several other reasons for the loss, including fielding and pitching errors. Additionally, the coach disagrees that the team even needed a hit in those situations.

Choice *C* is mentioned by the coach but not by the reporter. It is unclear whether the reporter would agree with this assessment. Eliminate this choice.

Choice *D* is mentioned by the coach but not by the reporter. It is not stated whether the reporter believes that the team deserved to win. Eliminate this choice.

Therefore, Choice *B* is the correct answer.

56. C: Choice *A* is incorrect. The Conservative Politician definitely believes that spending on social welfare programs increases the national debt. However, the Liberal Politician does not address the cost of those programs. Choice *B* is a strong answer choice. The Liberal politician explicitly agrees that certain classes of people rely on social welfare programs. The Conservative politician does agree that people rely on the programs but thinks this reliance is detrimental. This answer choice is slightly off base. Eliminate this choice. Choice *C* improves on Choice *B*. The Liberal Politician definitely believes that certain classes of people would be irreparably harmed. In contrast, the Conservative Politician asserts that the programs are actually harmful since people become dependent on the programs. The Conservative Politician concludes that people don't need the assistance and would be better off if left to fend for themselves. This is definitely the main point of disagreement. Choice *D* is not the main point of dispute. Neither of the politicians discusses whether *all* of the nation's leaders have bootstrapped their way to the top. Eliminate this choice.

Writing

Usage

1. D: Choice *D* is followed by the use of a comma and the conjunction *and*. This indicates that Choices *C* and *D* make up a compound sentence. Choice *D*, however, does not contain a subject, such as *I*, to indicate who is not going to attempt to say something.

2. B: Choice *B* uses the word *too* where the word *to* should be used instead. *Too* means *also* or an excessive amount.

3. E: There are no errors in this sentence.

4. B: Choice *B* contains the phrase "Platos ideas." Since Plato is the possessor of these ideas, *Platos* should contain and apostrophe before the *s* to indicate possession: *Plato's*.

5. A: Choice *A* should contain a comma after the word *examples* since there is an introductory phrase.

6. E: There are no errors in this sentence.

7. C: Choice *C* contains a misspelled word. The word used here is *diferent*. The proper spelling is *different*.

8. D: Choice *D* uses the conjunction *it's* even though it is referring to *implications*. If *it's* were spelled out, the sentence would read, "Even the founders of the field are unsettled by *it is* implications."

9. A: Choice *A* places commas around the word *determinisms*. The use of commas in this way is to separate relevant or clarifying information that is not pertinent to the sentence. For this sentence, the word *determinism* is essential

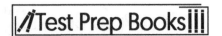

for the sentence to function. If *determinism* was removed, the sentence would read, "In our everyday lives is actually expressed in the thought experiment of Schrodinger's cat."

10. D: Choice *D* contains in error in the word *decay*. This verb, in this context, should be future tense, making the word *decays*.

11. B: Choice *B* begins with the word *so*. This needs to be followed by a comma since *so* is an introductory clause.

12. E: There are no errors in this sentence.

13. D: The single quotes should be double quotes. Single quotes are used for quotes within a quote.

Sentence Correction

14. B: Choices *A* and *D* use the wrong verb tense in the second clause. Choice *C* uses a comma where a semicolon is needed and rephrases the second clause awkwardly.

15. A: Choices *B* and *C* employ unnecessary semicolons and commas. Choice *D* would be an ideal revision, but it lacks the comma that would be needed after *Ransom*.

16. D: It is the result, not an action, that would be warped.

17. C: Choice *C* fixes the disagreement between the singular *this* and the plural *viewpoints*. Choice *B* introduces an unnecessary comma. In Choice *D*, *those* agrees with *viewpoints*, but neither agrees with *distinguishes*.

18. A: Choice *A* is direct and clear, without any punctuation errors. Choice *B* is well written but too wordy. Choice *C* adds an unnecessary comma. Choice *D* is also well written but much less concise than Choice *A*.

19. D: Choice *D* rearranges the sentence to improve clarity and impact, with *tempting* directly describing *idea*. On its own, Choice *A* is a run-on sentence. Choice *B* is better because it separates the clauses, but it keeps the unnecessary comma. Choice *C* is also an improvement but still a run-on sentence.

20. B: Choice *B* improves the sentence structure and includes the required comma before *and*. The sentence structure and punctuation in Choices *C* and *D* are grammatically incorrect.

21. D: Changing the phrase *after this* to *then* makes the sentence less complicated and captures the writer's intent, making Choice *D* correct. Choice *A* is awkwardly constructed. Choices *B* and *C* misuse their commas and do not adequately improve the clarity.

22. B: By starting a new sentence, the run-on issue is eliminated, and a new line of reasoning can be seamlessly introduced, making Choice *B* correct. While Choice *C* fixes the run-on issue via a semicolon, a comma is still needed after *this*. Choice *D* contains a comma splice. The independent clauses must be separated by more than just a comma, even with the rearrangement of the second half of the sentence.

Revision in Context

23. B: For this question, place the underlined sentence in each prospective choice's position. Leaving the sentence in place is incorrect because the father "going crazy" doesn't logically follow the fact that he was a "city slicker." Choice *C* is incorrect because the sentence in question is not a concluding sentence and does not transition smoothly into the second paragraph. Choice *D* is incorrect because the sentence doesn't necessarily need to be omitted since it logically follows the very first sentence in the passage. Choice *E* is incorrect because the "In fact" transition does not logically follow the sentence that begins with "On trips to the beach."

24. D: Choice *D* is correct because "As it turns out" indicates a contrast from the previous sentiment, that the RV was a great purchase. Choice *A* is incorrect because the sentence needs an effective transition from the paragraph before. Choice *B* is incorrect because the text indicates it *is* surprising that the RV was a great purchase because the author was skeptical beforehand. Choices *C* and *E* are incorrect because the transitions "furthermore" and "in addition" do not indicate a contrast.

25. E: This sentence calls for parallel structure. Choice *E* is correct because the verbs "wake," "eat," and "break" are consistent in tense and parts of speech. Choice *A* is incorrect because the words "wake" and "eat" are present tense while the word "broke" is in past tense. Choice *C* is incorrect because this turns the sentence into a question, which doesn't make sense within the context. Choice *D* is incorrect because it breaks tense with the rest of the passage. "Waking," "eating," and "breaking" are all present participles, and the context around the sentence is in past tense. Choice *E* is incorrect because it does not display parallel structure in verb form.

26. C: Choice *C* is correct because it is clear and fits within the context of the passage. Choice *A* is incorrect because "We rejoiced as 'hackers'" does not explain what was meant by "hackers" or why it was a cause for rejoicing. Choices *B* and *E* are incorrect because they do not mention a solution being found and are therefore not specific enough. Choice *D* is incorrect because the meaning is eschewed by the helping verb "had to rejoice," and the sentence suggests that rejoicing was necessary to "hack" a solution.

27. A: The original sentence is correct because the verb tense and the meaning both align with the rest of the passage. Choice *B* is incorrect because the order of the words makes the sentence more confusing than it otherwise would be. Choices *C* and *E* are incorrect because "We are even making" and "We even make" are in present tense. Choice *D* is incorrect because "We will make" is future tense. The surrounding text of the sentence is in past tense.

28. B: Choice *B* is correct because there is no punctuation needed if a dependent clause ("while traveling across America") is located behind the independent clause ("it allowed us to share adventures"). Choice *A* is incorrect because there are two dependent clauses connected and no independent clause, and a complete sentence requires at least one independent clause. Choice *C* is incorrect because of the same reason as Choice *A*. Semicolons have the same function as periods; therefore, there must be an independent clause on either side of the semicolon. Choice *D* is incorrect because the dash simply interrupts the complete sentence. Choice *E* is incorrect because it omits all commas; there is a comma needed after the introductory phrase "above all" as well as after the independent clause after "across America."

29. C: The rule for *me* and *I* is that one should use *I* when it is the subject pronoun of a sentence and me when it is the object pronoun of the sentence. Break the sentence up to see if *I* or *me* should be used. To say "Those are memories that I have now shared" is correct, rather than "Those are memories that me have now shared." Choice D is incorrect because *my siblings* should come before *I*.

30. D: Choice *D* is correct because Fred Hampton becoming an activist was a direct result of him wanting to see lasting social change for Black people. Choice *A* doesn't make sense because "In the meantime" denotes something happening at the same time as another thing. Choice *B* is incorrect because the text's tone does not indicate that becoming a civil rights activist is an unfortunate path. Choice *C* is incorrect because "Finally" indicates something that comes last in a series but the sentence comes at the beginning of the introductory paragraph.

31. C: Choice *C* is correct because there should be a comma between the city and state, as well as after the word "Illinois." Commas should be used to separate all geographical items within a sentence. Choice *A* is incorrect because it does not include the comma after "Illinois." Choice *B* is incorrect because the comma after "neighborhood" interrupts the phrase, "the Maywood neighborhood of Chicago." Finally, Choice *D* is incorrect because the order of the sentence designates that Chicago, Illinois is in Maywood, which is incorrect.

241

32. D: The paragraph is incorrect as-is because it is too long and thus loses the reader as it changes focus halfway through. Choice *D* is correct because if the new paragraph began with "While studying at Triton," we would see a smooth transition from one paragraph to the next. We can also see how the two paragraphs are logically split in two. The first half of the paragraph talks about where he studied. The second half of the paragraph talks about the NAACP and the result of his leadership in the association. If we look at the passage as a whole, we can see that there are two main topics that should be broken into two separate paragraphs.

33. E: We can determine this answer by using context clues. We know that the BPP is "similar in function" to the NAACP. Previous sentences describe the function of the NAACP as an activist group, so we can assume that the BPP is also an activist group.

34. A: Choice *C* is incorrect because it misplaces the apostrophe. While Choice *D* contains proper construction of a possessive, it changes the name of the organization from the *Black Panther Party* to the *Black Panther Parties*. Choice *B* also changes the name of the organization, and it doesn't use a possessive form. Choice *D* is incorrect because, again, the word "parties" should not be plural; instead, it is one unified party. Choice *E* is incorrect because it is missing the apostrophe before the "s."

35. C: Choice *C* is correct because the passage is in the past tense and "enabled" is a past tense verb. Choices *A* and *E*, "enable" and "enables," are present tense. Choice *B*, "are enabling," is a present participle, which suggests a continuing action. Choice *D*, "will enable," is future tense.

Research Skills

36. D: Relevant information refers to information that is closely related to the subject being researched. Students might get overwhelmed by information when they first begin researching, so they should learn how to narrow down search terms for their field of study. Choices *A* and *B* are incorrect because they start with a range that is far too wide; the student will spend too much time sifting through unrelated information to gather only a few related facts. Choice *C* introduces a more limited range, but it is not closely related to the topic that is being researched. Choice *E* would not be a credible enough source, since it is in part fiction. Finally, Choice *D* is correct because the student is choosing books that are more closely related to the topic and is using the index or table of contents to evaluate whether the source contains the necessary information.

37. A: The publisher, author, and references are elements of a resource that determine credibility. If the publisher has published more than one work, the author has written more than one piece on the subject, or the work references other recognized research, the credibility of a source will be stronger. Choice *B* is incorrect because the subject and title may be used to determine relevancy, not credibility, and the audience does not have much to do with the credibility of a source. Choice *C* is incorrect because the organization, stylistic choices, and transition words are all components of an effectively written piece, but they have less to do with credibility, other than to ensure that the author knows how to write. The length and tone of a piece are a matter of author's preference, and a work does not have to be written by multiple people to be considered a credible source. Choice *E* is incorrect; although the syntax helps with the credibility of a source, this is not the best answer.

38. B: In-text citations are much shorter and usually only include the author's last name, page numbers being referenced, and for some styles, the publication year. Bibliographic citations contain much more detailed reference information. Choice *A* is incorrect because citations are necessary both in the text and in a bibliography. Choice *C* is incorrect because there are several different citation styles depending on the type of paper or article being written. Rather, students should learn when it is appropriate to apply each different style. *D* and *E* are incorrect because all sources need to be cited regardless of medium.

39. D: The purpose of integrating research is to add support and credibility to the student's ideas, not to replace the student's own ideas altogether. Choices *A* and *E* are incorrect as the bulk of the paper or project should be

242

comprised of the author's own words, and quotations and paraphrases should be used to support them. Outside sources should be included when they enhance the writer's argument, but they are not required in every single paragraph. Choice *B* is also incorrect because regardless of whether ideas are directly quoted or paraphrased, it is essential to always credit authors for their ideas. The use of the author's full name in every signal phrase is unnecessary, so Choice *C* is also incorrect.

40. B: Choice *B* is the best answer choice. The abbreviation "et al." indicates that the book has more than one author. The main author is listed in the citation while the others are left off to keep the citation brief.

Mathematics

1. B: The first step is to make all exponents positive by moving the terms with negative exponents to the opposite side of the fraction. This expression becomes:

$$\frac{4b^3b^2}{a^1a^4} \times \frac{3a}{b}$$

Then the rules for exponents can be used to simplify. Multiplying the same bases means the exponents can be added. Dividing the same bases means the exponents are subtracted. Thus, after multiplying the exponents in the first fraction, the expression becomes:

$$\frac{4b^5}{a^5} \times \frac{3a}{b}$$

Therefore, we can first multiply to get:

$$\frac{12ab^5}{a^5b}$$

Then, simplifying yields:

$$12\frac{b^4}{a^4}$$

2. C: The product of two irrational numbers can be rational or irrational. Sometimes the irrational parts of the two numbers cancel each other out, leaving a rational number. For example, $\sqrt{2} \times \sqrt{2} = 2$ because the roots cancel each other out. Technically, the product of two irrational numbers is a complex number, because real numbers are a type of complex number. However, Choice *D* is incorrect because the product of two irrational numbers is not an imaginary number.

3. B: The car is traveling at a speed of 5 meters per second. On the interval from 1 to 3 seconds, the position changes by 10 meters. This is 10 meters in 2 seconds, or 5 meters in each second.

4. C: The terms "whole numbers" and "natural numbers" include all the ordinary counting numbers (1, 2, 3, 4, 5, ...), and sometimes zero depending on the definition used, but no negative numbers. The term "integers" includes all those numbers, their negatives, and zero. So −4 is not a whole number or a natural number, but it is an integer. It is also rational because it can be written as a ratio of two integers ($-\frac{4}{1}$); all integers are rational. It is a real number because it does not have an imaginary component (symbolized by the letter i); all integers are real numbers.

5. C: $40N$ would be 4,000% of N. All of the other coefficients are equivalent to $\frac{40}{100}$ or 40%.

This material is provided for exam preparation purposes only and does not indicate an endorsement of any specific scientific, political, or religious point of view. © TPB Publishing. You have been licensed one copy of this document for personal use only. Any other reproduction or redistribution is strictly prohibited. All rights reserved.

6. C: To get 85% of a number, multiply it by 0.85

$$0.85 \times 20 = \frac{85}{100} \times \frac{20}{1}$$

This can be simplified to:

$$\frac{17}{20} \times \frac{20}{1} = 17$$

7. A: To find the fraction of the bill that the first three people pay, the fractions need to be added, which means finding the common denominator. The common denominator is 60.

$$\frac{1}{5} + \frac{1}{4} + \frac{1}{3} = \frac{12}{60} + \frac{15}{60} + \frac{20}{60} = \frac{47}{60}$$

The remainder of the bill is:

$$1 - \frac{47}{60} = \frac{60}{60} - \frac{47}{60} = \frac{13}{60}$$

8. C: In this scenario, the variables are the number of sales and Karen's weekly pay. The weekly pay depends on the number of sales. Therefore, weekly pay is the dependent variable (y), and the number of sales is the independent variable (x). All four answer choices are in slope-intercept form, $y = mx + b$, so we just need to find m (the slope) and b (the y-intercept). We can calculate both by picking any two points, for example, (2, 380) and (4, 460).

The slope is given by $m = \frac{y_2 - y_1}{x_2 - x_1}$, so $m = \frac{460 - 380}{4 - 2} = 40$. This gives us the equation $y = 40x + b$. Now we can plug in the x and y values from our first point to find b. Since $380 = 40(2) + b$, we find $b = 300$. This means the equation is $y = 40x + 300$.

9. D: The expression is simplified by collecting like terms. Terms with the same variable and exponent are like terms, and their coefficients can be added.

10. A: Finding the product means distributing one polynomial to the other so that each term in the first is multiplied by each term in the second. Then, like terms can be collected. Multiplying the factors yields the expression:

$$20x^3 + 4x^2 + 24x - 40x^2 - 8x - 48$$

Collecting like terms means adding the x^2 terms and adding the x terms. The final answer after simplifying the expression is:

$$20x^3 - 36x^2 + 16x - 48$$

11. B: Using the conversion rate, multiply the projected weight loss of 25 lbs by $0.45 \frac{\text{kg}}{\text{lb}}$ to get the amount in kilograms (11.25 kg).

12. D: Dividing rational expressions follows the same rule as dividing fractions. The division is changed to multiplication by the reciprocal of the second fraction. This turns the expression into:

$$\frac{5x^3}{3x^2y} \times \frac{3y^9}{25}$$

This can be simplified by finding common factors in the numerators and denominators of the two fractions.

$$\frac{x^3}{x^2 y} \times \frac{y^9}{5}$$

Multiplying across creates:

$$\frac{x^3 y^9}{5x^2 y}$$

Simplifying leads to the final expression of:

$$\frac{xy^8}{5}$$

13. B: We can try to solve the equation by factoring the numerator into:

$$(x + 6)(x - 5)$$

Since $(x - 5)$ is on the top and bottom, that factor cancels out. This leaves the equation $x + 6 = 11$. Solving the equation gives the answer $x = 5$. When this value is plugged into the equation, it yields a zero in the denominator of the fraction. Since this is undefined, there is no solution.

14. A: First, convert the mixed numbers to improper fractions: $\frac{11}{3} - \frac{9}{5}$. Then, use 15 as a common denominator:

$$\frac{11}{3} - \frac{9}{5} = \frac{55}{15} - \frac{27}{15} = \frac{28}{15} = 1\frac{13}{15}$$

15. B: The formula can be manipulated by dividing both sides by the length, l, and the width, w. The length and width will cancel on the right, leaving height, h, by itself.

16. C: The formula for the perimeter of a rectangle is $P = 2L + 2W$, where P is the perimeter, L is the length, and W is the width. The first step is to substitute all of the data into the formula:

$$36 = 2(12) + 2W$$

Simplify by multiplying 2×12:

$$36 = 24 + 2W$$

Simplifying this further by subtracting 24 on each side gives:

$$36 - 24 = 24 - 24 + 2W$$

$$12 = 2W$$

Divide by 2:

$$6 = W$$

The width is 6 cm. Remember to test this answer by substituting this value into the original formula:

$$36 = 2(12) + 2(6)$$

245

17. D: This problem can be solved by setting up a proportion involving the given information and the unknown value. The proportion is:

$$\frac{21 \text{ pages}}{4 \text{ nights}} = \frac{140 \text{ pages}}{x \text{ nights}}$$

We can cross-multiply to get $21x = 4 \times 140$. Solving this, we find $x \approx 26.67$. Since this is not an integer, we round up to 27 nights because 26 nights would not give Sarah enough time to finish.

18. D: The slope from this equation is 50, and it is interpreted as the cost per gigabyte used. Since the g-value represents the number of gigabytes and the equation is set equal to the cost in dollars, the slope relates these two values. For every gigabyte used on the phone, the bill goes up 50 dollars.

19. B: $\frac{5}{2} \div \frac{1}{3} = \frac{5}{2} \times \frac{3}{1} = \frac{15}{2} = 7.5$.

20. A: The total fraction taken up by green and red shirts will be:

$$\frac{1}{3} + \frac{2}{5} = \frac{5}{15} + \frac{6}{15} = \frac{11}{15}$$

The remaining fraction is:

$$1 - \frac{11}{15} = \frac{15}{15} - \frac{11}{15} = \frac{4}{15}$$

21. C: If Shawna has used $\frac{1}{3}$ of the paint, she has $\frac{2}{3}$ remaining. The mixed fraction can be converted because $2\frac{1}{2}$ gallons is the same as $\frac{5}{2}$ gallons. The calculation is:

$$\frac{2}{3} \times \frac{5}{2} = \frac{10}{6} = \frac{5}{3} = 1\frac{2}{3} \text{ gallons}$$

22. D: A given number divides evenly by each of its factors to produce an integer (no decimals). To find the factors of 12, determine what whole numbers when multiplied equal 12. 1×12, 2×6, and 3×4 are all the ways to multiply to 12 using whole numbers, so the factors of 12 are: 1, 2, 3, 4, 6, 12.

23. A: Setting up a proportion is the easiest way to represent this situation. The proportion becomes $\frac{20}{x} = \frac{40}{100}$, where cross-multiplication can be used to solve for x. The answer can also be found by viewing the two fractions as equivalent, knowing that 20 is half of 40, and 50 is half of 100.

Setting up a proportion is an easy way to represent this situation. The proportion is $\frac{20}{x} = \frac{40}{100}$, and cross-multiplication can be used to solve for x. The answer can also be found by writing the question as an equation, such that $40\%(x) = 20$ or $0.4x = 20$. Solving for x gives $x = 50$.

24. A: Flip the second fraction and multiply.

$$\frac{4}{13} \times \frac{169}{27}$$

Simplify the fractions before multiplying to make the numbers simpler to work with.

$$\frac{4}{1} \times \frac{13}{27}$$

246

Multiply across the top and across the bottom.

$$\frac{4 \times 13}{1 \times 27} = \frac{52}{27}$$

The numerator and denominator do not have any factors in common, so this fraction cannot be reduced.

25. A: The relative error can be found by finding the absolute error and making it a percent of the true value. The absolute error is:

$$36 - 35.75 = 0.25$$

This error is then divided by 35.75—the true value—to find 0.7%.

26. B: The y-intercept of an equation is found where the x-value is zero. Plugging zero into the equation for x, the first two terms cancel out, leaving -4:

$$0^2 + 3(0) - 4 = -4$$

27. A: The definition of an even function is that $f(-x) = f(x)$. We can plug in $-x$ to our function to see what we get:

$$f(-2) = \frac{1}{2}(-x)^4 + 2(-x)^2 - 6$$

Since $(-x)^4 = x^4$ and $(-x)^2 = x^2$, we see that $f(-x)$ is equal to the original function, so our function is even.

The definition of an odd function is that $f(-x) = -f(x)$. We can calculate $-f(x)$:

$$-fx = -1\left(\frac{1}{2}\right)x^4 + 2x^2 - 6 = \left(-\frac{1}{2}\right)x^4 - 2x^2 + 6$$

This does not equal $f(-x)$ (which, remember, is the same as our original function), so our function is not odd.

28. C: The equation $x = 3$ is not a function of x because it does not pass the vertical-line test: if any vertical line can intersect the equation's graph at more than one point, the equation is not a function. This test comes from the definition of a function, in which each x-value in the domain must be mapped to no more than one y-value. This equation is a vertical line, so the x-value of 3 is mapped to an infinite number of y-values.

29. B: The table shows values that are increasing exponentially. The differences between the inputs are the same, while the differences in the outputs are changing by a factor of 2. The values in the table can be modeled by the equation:

$$f(x) = 2^x$$

30. B: $\frac{2}{a}$ must be subtracted from both sides, with a result of:

$$\frac{1}{x} = \frac{2}{b} - \frac{2}{a}$$

247

The reciprocal of both sides needs to be taken, but the right-hand side needs to be written as a single fraction in order to do that. Since the two fractions on the right have denominators that are not equal, a common denominator of ab is needed. This leaves:

$$\frac{1}{x} = \frac{2a}{ab} - \frac{2b}{ab} = \frac{2(a-b)}{ab}$$

Taking the reciprocals, which can be done since $b - a$ is not zero, with a result of:

$$x = \frac{ab}{2(a-b)}$$

31. B: The first step is to use the quadratic formula on the first equation ($x^2 - x - 3 = 0$) to solve for x. In this case, a is 1, b is -1, and c is -3, yielding:

$$x = \frac{-b \pm \sqrt{b^2 - 4ac}}{2a}$$

$$x = \frac{1 \pm \sqrt{1 - 4 \times 1(-3)}}{2}$$

$$x = \frac{1}{2} \pm \frac{\sqrt{13}}{2}$$

Therefore, $x - \frac{1}{2}$, which is in our second equation, equals $\pm\frac{\sqrt{13}}{2}$. We are looking for $\left(x - \frac{1}{2}\right)^2$ though, so we square the $\pm\frac{\sqrt{13}}{2}$. Doing so causes the $\pm$ to cancel and we are left with:

$$\left(x - \frac{1}{2}\right)^2 = \left(\frac{\sqrt{13}}{2}\right)^2 = \frac{13}{4}$$

32. B: The origin is $(0, 0)$. The slope is given by:

$$m = \frac{y_2 - y_1}{x_2 - x_1}$$

$$m = \frac{1 - 0}{2 - 0} = \frac{1}{2}$$

The y-intercept will be 0 since it passes through the origin, (0,0). Using slope-intercept form, the equation for this line is:

$$y = \frac{1}{2}x$$

33. C: Let r be the number of red cans and b be the number of blue cans. One equation is:

$$r + b = 10$$

The total price is $16, and given the prices for each can, the second equation is $1r + 2b = 16$. Multiplying the first equation on both sides by -1 results in:

$$-r - b = -10$$

248

Add this equation to the second equation, leaving $b = 6$. So, she bought 6 *blue* cans. From the first equation, this means $r = 4$; thus, she bought 4 *red* cans.

34. D: The first field has an area of 1,000 square feet, so the length of one side is $\sqrt{1,000} = \sqrt{100}\sqrt{10} = 10\sqrt{10}$.

Since there are four sides to a square, the perimeter is $40\sqrt{10}$. The second square has an area of 10 square feet, so the length of one side is $\sqrt{10}$, and the perimeter is $4\sqrt{10}$. Adding these together gives:

$$40\sqrt{10} + 4\sqrt{10} = (40 + 4)\sqrt{10} = 44\sqrt{10}$$

35. C: The $(3x + 1)$ can be factored to get $(2x - 5)(3x + 1)$.

36. D: Because the coefficient of x^2 is negative, this function has a graph that is a parabola that opens downward. Therefore, it will be greater than 0 between its real roots, if it has any. Checking the discriminant, the result is:

$$1^2 - 4(-3)(-8) = 1 - 96 = -95$$

Since the discriminant is negative, this equation has no real solutions. Since this has no real roots, it must be always positive or always negative. Its graph opens downward, so it has at least some negative values. That means it is always negative. Thus, it is greater than zero for no real numbers.

37. A: You can put each answer choice into the expression as an x value and see which value makes it equal zero. Or you can use the quadratic formula, which gives:

$$x = \frac{2 \pm \sqrt{(-2)^2 - 4(1)(-2)}}{2} = \frac{2}{2} \pm \frac{\sqrt{12}}{2} \, 1 \pm \frac{\sqrt{12}}{2}$$

$$1 \pm \frac{\sqrt{4}\sqrt{3}}{2} = 1 \pm \frac{2\sqrt{3}}{2} = 1 \pm \sqrt{3}$$

The only one of these which appears as an answer choice is $1 + \sqrt{3}$.

38. B: The graph of $y = x^2 + 2$ has a vertex at $(0, 2)$ on the y-axis. The circle with a center at $(0, 1)$ also lies on the y-axis. With a radius of 1, the circle touches the parabola at one point: the vertex of the parabola, $(0, 2)$.

39. D: The slope is given by the change in y divided by the change in x. The change in y is $2 - 0 = 2$, and the change in x is:

$$0 - (-4) = 4$$

The slope is $\frac{2}{4} = \frac{1}{2}$.

40. C: Janice will be choosing 4 employees out of a set of 6 applicants, so the number of possibilities will be given by the choice function. The following equation shows the choice function worked out:

$$\binom{6}{4} = \frac{6!}{4!\,(6 - 4)!} = \frac{6!}{4!\,(2)!}$$

$$\frac{6 \cdot 5 \cdot 4 \cdot 3 \cdot 2 \cdot 1}{4 \cdot 3 \cdot 2 \cdot 1 \cdot 2 \cdot 1} = \frac{6 \cdot 5}{2} = 15$$

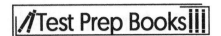

41. C: The triangle in Choice *B* doesn't contain a line of symmetry. The figures in Choices *A* and *D* do contain a line of symmetry, but it is not the line that is shown here. Choice *C* is the only one with a correct line of symmetry shown, such that the figure is mirrored on each side of the line.

42. B: When solving for x, add 3 to both sides to get $4x = 8$. Then, divide both sides by 4 to get $x = 2$.

43. C: The sample space is made up of $8 + 7 + 6 + 5 = 26$ balls. The probability of pulling each individual ball is $\frac{1}{26}$. Since there are 7 yellow balls, the probability of pulling a yellow ball is $\frac{7}{26}$.

44. B: For the first card drawn, the probability of a king being pulled is $\frac{4}{52}$. Since this card isn't replaced, if a king is drawn first, the probability of a king being drawn second is $\frac{3}{51}$. The probability of a king being drawn in both the first and second draw is the product of the two probabilities:

$$\frac{4}{52} \times \frac{3}{51} = \frac{12}{2,652}$$

To reduce this fraction, divide the top and bottom by 12 to get $\frac{1}{221}$.

45. D: If we roll a die twice, there are six possibilities for the first roll and six for the second roll, which gives $6 \times 6 = 36$ total possibilities. Now, how many ways are there to roll exactly one 6? We could get a 6 & 1, or 6 & 2, or 6 & 3, or 6 & 4, or 6 & 5. Or, the 6 could come on the second roll; we could get a 1 & 6, or 2 & 6, or 3 & 6, or 4 & 6, or 5 & 6. Counting these up, we find a total of 10 different ways to roll exactly one 6. That means our event happens in 10 out of 36 possible rolls, so the probability is $\frac{10}{36}$, which reduces to $\frac{5}{18}$.

46. A: If each man gains 10 pounds, every original data point will increase by 10 pounds. Therefore, the man with the original median will still have the median value, but that value will increase by 10. The smallest value and largest value will also increase by 10, so the difference between the two (the range) will remain the same.

47. C: Because the triangles are similar, the lengths of the corresponding sides are proportional. Therefore:

$$\frac{30 + x}{30} = \frac{22}{14} = \frac{y + 15}{y}$$

Using cross multiplication on the first two terms results in the equation:

$$14(30 + x) = 22 \times 30$$

When solved, this gives:

$$x \approx 17.1$$

Using cross multiplication on the last two terms results in the equation:

$$14(y + 15) = 22y$$

When solved, this gives:

$$y \approx 26.3$$

48. B: The technique of completing the square must be used to change the equation below into the standard equation of a circle:

$$4x^2 + 4y^2 - 16x - 24y + 51 = 0$$

First, the constant must be moved to the right-hand side of the equals sign, and each term must be divided by the coefficient of the x^2-term (which is 4). The x- and y-terms must be grouped together to obtain:

$$x^2 - 4x + y^2 - 6y = -\frac{51}{4}$$

Then, the process of completing the square must be completed for each variable. This gives:

$$(x^2 - 4x + 4) + (y^2 - 6y + 9) = -\frac{51}{4} + 4 + 9$$

The equation can be written as:

$$(x - 2)^2 + (y - 3)^2 = \frac{1}{4}$$

Therefore, the center of the circle is $(2, 3)$, and the radius is:

$$\sqrt{\frac{1}{4}} = \frac{1}{2}$$

49. D: When a point is reflected over an axis, the sign of at least one of the coordinates must change. When it's reflected over the x-axis, the sign of the y coordinate must change. The x value remains the same. Therefore, the new point is $(-3, 4)$.

50. D: For manufacturing costs, there is a linear relationship between the cost to the company and the number produced, with a y-intercept given by the base cost of acquiring the means of production and a slope given by the cost to produce one unit. In this case, that base cost is $50,000, while the cost per unit is $40. So,

$$y = 40x + 50,000$$

51. D: We are given an angle (60°), the length of the opposite side (x), and the length of the adjacent side (13 cm). We can use the mnemonic "SOHCAHTOA," where the "TOA" reminds us that tangent equals the opposite side over the adjacent side. In other words, $\tan 60° = \frac{x}{13}$. Since $\tan 60° = \sqrt{3}$, we can calculate:

$$x = 13 \tan 60° = 13 \times \sqrt{3} = 22.52$$

52. D: Let a be the number of apples and b the number of bananas. Then, the total cost is $2a + 3b = 22$, while it also known that $a + b = 10$. Using the knowledge of systems of equations, cancel the b variables by multiplying the second equation by -3. This makes the equation $-3a - 3b = -30$. Adding this to the first equation, the b-values cancel to get $-a = -8$, which simplifies to $a = 8$.

53. A: First, the sample mean must be calculated:

$$\bar{x} = \frac{1}{4}(1 + 3 + 5 + 7) = 4$$

The standard deviation of the data set is $s = \sqrt{\frac{\sum(x - \bar{x})^2}{n - 1}}$, and $n = 4$ represents the number of data points. Therefore,

$$s = \sqrt{\frac{1}{3}[(1-4)^2 + (3-4)^2 + (5-4)^2 + (7-4)^2]} = \sqrt{\frac{1}{3}(9+1+1+9)} = 2.58$$

54. C: The expected value is equal to the total sum of each product of individual score multiplied by its probability. There are 36 possible rolls. The probability of rolling 2 is $\frac{1}{36}$. The probability of rolling a 3 is $\frac{2}{36}$. And so on.

To illustrate this, please see the table below:

Amount Rolled	Probability
2	$\frac{1}{36}$
3	$\frac{2}{36}$
4	$\frac{3}{36}$
5	$\frac{4}{36}$
6	$\frac{5}{36}$
7	$\frac{6}{36}$
8	$\frac{5}{36}$
9	$\frac{4}{36}$
10	$\frac{3}{36}$
11	$\frac{2}{36}$
12	$\frac{1}{36}$

Multiply each possible outcome by its corresponding probability:

$$2 \times \frac{1}{36} = a$$

$$3 \times \frac{2}{36} = b$$

$$4 \times \frac{3}{36} = c$$

And so forth.

Then all of those results are added together:

252

$$a + b + c\ldots = expected\ value = \frac{252}{36}$$

In this case, it equals 7, which makes sense considering it is the value that has the highest probability of being rolled.

Essentially, this is the same as using the expected value formula: $E(X) = \sum x_i p_i$, where x_i represents the value of each outcome and p_i represents the probability of each outcome:

$$E(X) = 2 \times \frac{1}{36} + 3 \times \frac{2}{36} + 4 \times \frac{3}{36} + 5 \times \frac{4}{36} + 6 \times \frac{5}{36} + 7 \times \frac{6}{36} + 8 \times \frac{5}{36} + 9 \times \frac{4}{36} + 10 \times \frac{3}{36} + 11 \times \frac{2}{36} + 12 \times \frac{1}{36} = 7$$

55. 2.73×10^5: The exponent of the ten must be the same before any operations are performed on the numbers. So, $(2.6 \times 10^5) + (1.3 \times 10^4)$ cannot be added until one of the exponents on the ten is changed. The 1.3×10^4 can be changed to 0.13×10^5, then the 2.6 and 0.13 can be added. The answer comes out to be 2.73×10^5.

56. $3(n + 7) \geq 32$: Three times the sum of a number and seven is greater than or equal to 32 can be translated into the equation form shown in Choice *D* by utilizing mathematical operators and numbers.

Practice Test #2

Reading

Questions 1–5 are based on the following passage.

Christopher Columbus is often credited with discovering America. This is a matter of perspective; America was unknown to fifteenth-century Europe, but bear in mind that the places he "discovered" were already filled with people who had been living there for centuries. What's more, Christopher Columbus was not the first European explorer to reach the Americas! Rather, it was Leif Erikson who first came to the New World and contacted the natives nearly 500 years before Christopher Columbus.

Leif Erikson, the son of Erik the Red (a famous Viking outlaw and explorer in his own right), was born in either 970 or 980, depending on which historian you read. In 999, Leif left Greenland and traveled to Norway, where he would serve as a guard to King Olaf Tryggvason. It was there that he became a convert to Christianity. Leif later tried to return home with the intention of taking supplies and spreading Christianity to Greenland, but his ship was blown off course and he arrived in a strange new land: present-day Newfoundland, Canada.

When he finally returned to his adopted homeland of Greenland, Leif consulted with a merchant who had also seen the shores of this previously unknown land. The son of the legendary Viking explorer then gathered a crew of 35 men and set sail. Leif became the first European to set foot in the New World as he explored present-day Baffin Island and Labrador, Canada. His crew called the land Vinland since it was plentiful with grapes. This happened around 1000, nearly 500 years before Columbus famously sailed the ocean blue.

Eventually, in 1003, Leif set sail for home and arrived at Greenland with a ship full of timber. In 1020, 17 years later, the legendary Viking died. Many believe that Leif Erikson should receive more credit for his contributions in exploring the New World.

1. Which of the following best describes how the author generally presents the information?
   a. Chronological order
   b. Comparison-contrast
   c. Cause-effect
   d. Conclusion-premises

2. Which of the following is an opinion, rather than a historical fact, expressed by the author?
   a. Leif Erikson was definitely the son of Erik the Red; however, historians debate the year of his birth.
   b. Leif Erikson's crew called the land Vinland since it was plentiful with grapes.
   c. Leif Erikson deserves more credit for his contributions in exploring the New World.
   d. Leif Erikson explored the Americas nearly 500 years before Christopher Columbus.

3. Which of the following most accurately describes the author's main conclusion?
   a. Leif Erikson is a legendary Viking explorer.
   b. Leif Erikson deserves more credit for exploring America hundreds of years before Columbus.
   c. Spreading Christianity motivated Leif Erikson's expeditions more than any other factor.
   d. Leif Erikson contacted the natives nearly five hundred years before Columbus.

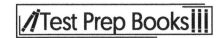

4. Which of the following best describes the author's intent in the passage?
   a. To entertain
   b. To inform
   c. To alert
   d. To suggest

5. Which of the following can be logically inferred from the passage?
   a. The Vikings disliked exploring the New World.
   b. Leif Erikson's banishment from Iceland led to his exploration of present-day Canada.
   c. Leif Erikson never shared his stories of exploration with the King of Norway.
   d. Historians have difficulty definitively pinpointing events in the Vikings' history.

Questions 6–15 are based on the following passage:

"Mademoiselle Eugénie is pretty—I think I remember that to be her name."

"Very pretty, or rather, very beautiful," replied Albert, "but of that style of beauty which I don't appreciate; I am an ungrateful fellow."

"Really," said Monte Cristo, lowering his voice, "you don't appear to me to be very enthusiastic on the subject of this marriage."

"Mademoiselle Danglars is too rich for me," replied Morcerf, "and that frightens me."

"Bah," exclaimed Monte Cristo, "that's a fine reason to give. Are you not rich yourself?"

"My father's income is about 50,000 francs per annum; and he will give me, perhaps, ten or twelve thousand when I marry."

"That, perhaps, might not be considered a large sum, in Paris especially," said the count; "but everything doesn't depend on wealth, and it's a fine thing to have a good name, and to occupy a high station in society. Your name is celebrated, your position magnificent; and then the Comte de Morcerf is a soldier, and it's pleasing to see the integrity of a Bayard united to the poverty of a Duguesclin; disinterestedness is the brightest ray in which a noble sword can shine. As for me, I consider the union with Mademoiselle Danglars a most suitable one; she will enrich you, and you will ennoble her."

Albert shook his head, and looked thoughtful. "There is still something else," said he.

"I confess," observed Monte Cristo, "that I have some difficulty in comprehending your objection to a young lady who is both rich and beautiful."

"Oh," said Morcerf, "this repugnance, if repugnance it may be called, isn't all on my side."

"Whence can it arise, then? For you told me your father desired the marriage."

"It's my mother who dissents; she has a clear and penetrating judgment, and doesn't smile on the proposed union. I cannot account for it, but she seems to entertain some prejudice against the Danglars."

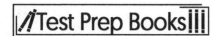
"Ah," said the count, in a somewhat forced tone, "that may be easily explained; the Comtesse de Morcerf, who is aristocracy and refinement itself, doesn't relish the idea of being allied by your marriage with one of ignoble birth; that is natural enough."

Excerpt from *The Count of Monte Cristo* by Alexandre Dumas

6. The meaning of the word *repugnance* is closest to:
   a. Strong resemblance
   b. Strong dislike
   c. Extreme shyness
   d. Extreme dissimilarity

7. What can be inferred about Albert's family?
   a. Their finances are uncertain.
   b. Albert is the only son in his family.
   c. Their name is more respected than the Danglars'.
   d. Albert's mother and father both agree on their decisions.

8. What is Albert's attitude towards his impending marriage?
   a. Pragmatic
   b. Romantic
   c. Indifferent
   d. Apprehensive

9. What is the best description of the Count's relationship with Albert?
   a. He's like a strict parent, criticizing Albert's choices.
   b. He's like a wise uncle, giving practical advice to Albert.
   c. He's like a close friend, supporting all of Albert's opinions.
   d. He's like a suspicious investigator, asking many probing questions.

10. Which sentence is true of Albert's mother?
    a. She belongs to a noble family.
    b. She often makes poor choices.
    c. She is primarily occupied with money.
    d. She is unconcerned about her son's future.

11. Based on this passage, what is probably NOT true about French society in the 1800s?
    a. Children often received money from their parents.
    b. Marriages were sometimes arranged between families.
    c. The richest people in society were also the most respected.
    d. People were often expected to marry within their own social class.

12. Why is the Count puzzled by Albert's attitude toward his marriage?
    a. He seems reluctant to marry Eugénie, despite her wealth and beauty.
    b. He is marrying against his father's wishes, despite usually following his advice.
    c. He appears excited to marry someone he doesn't love, despite being a hopeless romantic.
    d. He expresses reverence towards Eugénie, despite being from a higher social class than her.

256

13. The passage is made up mostly of what kind of text?
    a. Narration
    b. Dialogue
    c. Description
    d. Explanation

14. What does the word *ennoble* mean in the middle of the passage?
    a. To create beauty in another person
    b. To endow someone with wealth
    c. To make someone chaste again
    d. To give someone a noble rank or title

15. From only the information in the passage, why would the Count be said to have a "forced tone" in the last paragraph?
    a. Because he is in love with Mademoiselle Eugénie and is trying to keep it a secret
    b. Because he finally agrees with Albert's point of view but still doesn't understand it
    c. Because he finally understands Albert's point of view but still doesn't agree with it
    d. Because he is only pretending that Albert is his friend to get information out of him

Questions 16–19 are based on the following passage:

Children's literature holds a special place in many people's hearts. The stories that delight young readers can be imaginative and educational, and can help foster a love of reading in children. Stories speak to children in a way adults sometimes do not understand. However, everything is not all joy and happy endings in this genre. Many of the stories, tales, and books that are widely recognized within this category feature darker themes. Some of the stories typically associated with children, including fairy tales and fables, contain more serious issues such as child abandonment, violence, and death. Some of the earliest fairy tales come from the *Brothers Grimm* fairy tale collections. These stories in their original form are surprisingly gruesome. Stories such as *Hansel and Gretel*, *Little Red Riding Hood*, and *Cinderella* all contain elements that many people would consider too dark for children. These early stories often presented these disturbing images and elements in order to serve as a warning for children to induce good behavior.

More recent entries into children's literature, such as *Where the Wild Things Are* and *The Giving Tree*, are less shocking than some of the older tales but still touch on serious issues. When children read about characters in a story dealing with these types of issues, it can help them learn how to process some of the same emotions that occur in their own lives. Whether children are learning a lesson, processing emotions, or just enjoying a good story, reading literature can be an important part of their life's journey.

16. What is the primary topic of this passage?
    a. Children's literature cannot be enjoyed by adults.
    b. Children's literature is universally loved.
    c. Children's literature often contains serious themes.
    d. Children's literature should only have happy endings.

17. What is the meaning of the word "gruesome" in the first paragraph?
    a. Numb
    b. Peculiar
    c. Comfortable
    d. Horrible

18. What does the author mean to suggest by adding the following statement?

These stories in their original form are surprisingly gruesome.

a. The stories were originally written in another language.
b. When the stories were first written, they were grimmer than later adaptations.
c. The original stories have been translated into different formats.
d. Adults, rather than children, were the intended audience for the early stories.

19. What is meant by the figurative language in the following statement?

Stories speak to children in a way adults sometimes do not understand.

a. Adults do not care for children's stories.
b. Children derive meaning from stories that adults do not.
c. Children's stories should always be read aloud to better understand the story.
d. Children's lack of life experiences causes them to sometimes misinterpret stories.

Questions 20–22 are based on the following passage.

Smoking tobacco products is terribly destructive. A single cigarette contains over 4,000 chemicals, including 43 known carcinogens and 400 deadly toxins. Some of the most dangerous ingredients include tar, carbon monoxide, formaldehyde, ammonia, arsenic, and DDT. Smoking can cause numerous types of cancer, including throat, mouth, nasal cavity, esophageal, gastric, pancreatic, renal, bladder, and cervical cancer.

Cigarettes contain a drug called nicotine, one of the most addictive substances known. Addiction is defined as a compulsion to seek the substance despite negative consequences. According to the National Institute on Drug Abuse, nearly 35 million smokers expressed a desire to quit smoking in 2015; however, more than 85% of those who struggle with addiction will not achieve their goal. Almost all smokers regret picking up that first cigarette. You would be wise to learn from their mistake if you have not yet started smoking.

According to the US Department of Health and Human Services, 16 million people in the United States presently suffer from a smoking-related condition, and nearly nine million suffer from a serious smoking-related illness. According to the Centers for Disease Control and Prevention (CDC), tobacco products cause nearly six million deaths per year. This number is projected to rise to over eight million deaths by 2030. Smokers, on average, die ten years earlier than their nonsmoking peers.

In the United States, local, state, and federal governments typically tax tobacco products, which leads to high prices. Nicotine users who struggle with addiction sometimes pay more for a pack of cigarettes than for a few gallons of gas. Additionally, smokers tend to stink. The smell of smoke is all-consuming and creates a pervasive nastiness. Smokers also risk staining their teeth and fingers with yellow residue from the tar.

Smoking is deadly, expensive, and socially unappealing. Clearly, smoking is not worth the risks.

258

20. Which of the following statements most accurately summarizes the passage?
    a. Tobacco is less healthy than many alternatives.
    b. Tobacco is deadly, expensive, and socially unappealing, and smokers would be much better off kicking the addiction.
    c. In the United States, local, state, and federal governments typically tax tobacco products, which leads to high prices.
    d. Tobacco products shorten smokers' lives by ten years and kill more than six million people per year.

21. The author would be most likely to agree with which of the following statements?
    a. Smokers should only quit cold turkey and should avoid all nicotine cessation devices.
    b. Other substances are more addictive than tobacco.
    c. Smokers should quit for whatever reason gets them to stop smoking.
    d. People who want to continue smoking should advocate for a reduction in tobacco product taxes.

22. Which of the following represents an opinion statement on the part of the author?
    a. According to the Centers for Disease Control and Prevention (CDC), tobacco products cause nearly six million deaths per year.
    b. Nicotine users who struggle with addiction sometimes pay more for a pack of cigarettes than for a few gallons of gas.
    c. Smokers also risk staining their teeth and fingers with yellow residue from the tar.
    d. Additionally, smokers tend to stink. The smell of smoke is all-consuming and creates a pervasive nastiness.

23. Jerome K. Jerome's humorous account of a boating holiday, Three Men in a Boat, was published in 1889. Originally intended as a serious travel guide, the work became a prime example of a comic novel. Read the passage below, noting the word in italics. Answer the question that follows.

> I felt rather hurt about this at first; it seemed somehow to be a sort of slight. Why hadn't I got housemaid's knee? Why this invidious reservation? After a while, however, less grasping feelings prevailed. I reflected that I had every other known malady in the pharmacology, and I grew less selfish, and determined to do without housemaid's knee. Gout, in its most malignant stage, it would appear, had seized me without my being aware of it; and *zymosis* I had evidently been suffering with from boyhood. There were no more diseases after *zymosis*, so I concluded there was nothing else the matter with me.

Which definition best fits the word *zymosis*?
    a. Discontent
    b. An infectious disease
    c. Poverty
    d. Bad luck

Questions 24–26 are based on the following passage:

> George Washington emerged out of the American Revolution as an unlikely champion of liberty. On June 14, 1775, the Second Continental Congress created the Continental Army, and John Adams, serving in the Congress, nominated Washington to be its first commander. Washington had fought under the British during the French and Indian War, and his experience and prestige proved instrumental to the American war effort. Washington provided invaluable leadership, training, and strategy during the Revolutionary War. He emerged from the war as the embodiment of liberty and freedom from tyranny.
>
> After vanquishing the heavily favored British forces, Washington could have pronounced himself the autocratic leader of the former colonies without any opposition, but he famously refused and

returned to his Mount Vernon plantation. His restraint proved his commitment to the fledgling state's republicanism. Washington was later unanimously elected as the first American president. But it is Washington's farewell address that cemented his legacy as a visionary worthy of study.

In 1796, President Washington issued his farewell address by public letter. Washington enlisted his good friend, Alexander Hamilton, in drafting his most famous address. The letter expressed Washington's faith in the Constitution and rule of law. He encouraged his fellow Americans to put aside partisan differences and establish a national union. Washington warned Americans against meddling in foreign affairs and entering military alliances. Additionally, he stated his opposition to national political parties, which he considered partisan and counterproductive.

Americans would be wise to remember Washington's farewell, especially during presidential elections, when politics hit a fever pitch. They might want to question the political institutions that were not planned by the Founding Fathers, such as the nomination process and political parties themselves.

24. Which of the following statements is logically based on the information contained in the passage above?
    a. George Washington's background as a wealthy landholder directly led to his faith in equality, liberty, and democracy.
    b. George Washington would have opposed America's involvement in the Second World War.
    c. George Washington would not have been able to write as great a farewell address without the assistance of Alexander Hamilton.
    d. George Washington would probably not approve of modern political parties.

25. Which of the following is the best description of the author's purpose in writing this passage about George Washington?
    a. To inform American voters about a Founding Father's sage advice on a contemporary issue and explain its applicability to modern times
    b. To introduce George Washington to readers as a historical figure worthy of study
    c. To note that George Washington was more than a famous military hero
    d. To convince readers that George Washington is a hero of republicanism and liberty

26. In which of the following materials would the author be the most likely to include this passage?
    a. A history textbook
    b. An obituary
    c. A fictional story
    d. A newspaper editorial

Questions 27–36 are based on the following passage:

We made it. We created it. We brought it forth from the night of the ages. We alone. Our hands. Our mind. Ours alone and only.

We know not what we are saying. Our head is reeling. We look upon the light which we have made. We shall be forgiven for anything we say tonight...

Tonight, after more days and trials than we can count, we finished building a strange thing, from the remains of the Unmentionable Times, a box of glass, devised to give forth the power of the sky of greater strength than we had ever achieved before. And when we put our wires to this box, when we closed the current—the wire glowed! It came to life, it turned red, and a circle of light lay on the stone before us.

We stood, and we held our head in our hands. We could not conceive of that which we had created. We had touched no flint, made no fire. Yet here was light, light that came from nowhere, light from the heart of metal.

We blew out the candle. Darkness swallowed us. There was nothing left around us, nothing save night and a thin thread of flame in it, as a crack in the wall of a prison. We stretched our hands to the wire, and we saw our fingers in the red glow. We could not see our body nor feel it, and in that moment nothing existed save our two hands over a wire glowing in a black abyss.

Then we thought of the meaning of that which lay before us. We can light our tunnel, and the City, and all the Cities of the world with nothing save metal and wires. We can give our brothers a new light, cleaner and brighter than any they have ever known. The power of the sky can be made to do men's bidding. There are no limits to its secrets and its might, and it can be made to grant us anything if we but choose to ask.

Then we knew what we must do. Our discovery is too great for us to waste our time in sweeping the streets. We must not keep our secret to ourselves, nor buried under the ground. We must bring it into the sight of all men. We need all our time, we need the work rooms of the Home of the Scholars, we want the help of our brother Scholars and their wisdom joined to ours. There is so much work ahead for all of us, for all the Scholars of the world.

In a month, the World Council of Scholars is to meet in our City. It is a great Council, to which the wisest of all lands are elected, and it meets once a year in the different Cities of the earth. We shall go to this Council and we shall lay before them, as our gift, this glass box with the power of the sky. We shall confess everything to them. They will see, understand, and forgive. For our gift is greater than our transgression. They will explain it to the Council of Vocations, and we shall be assigned to the Home of the Scholars. This has never been done before, but neither has a gift such as ours ever been offered to men.

We must wait. We must guard our tunnel as we had never guarded it before. For should any men save the Scholars learn of our secret, they would not understand it, nor would they believe us. They would see nothing, save our crime of working alone, and they would destroy us and our light. We care not about our body, but our light is...

Yes, we do care. For the first time do we care about our body. For this wire is as a part of our body, as a vein torn from us, glowing with our blood. Are we proud of this thread of metal, or of our hands which made it, or is there a line to divide these two?

Excerpt from *Anthem* by Ayn Rand

27. What is the overall tone of this passage?
   a. Dreary
   b. Unnerving
   c. Excited
   d. Humorous

28. Why must the invention be kept a secret?
   a. It is illegal to work alone.
   b. The Council of Scholars will try to take credit.
   c. They were supposed to be sweeping streets.
   d. Remains from the Unmentionable Times are off-limits.

29. Which literary device is used in the following sentence from paragraph five?

    "Darkness swallowed us."

    a. Simile
    b. Synecdoche
    c. Flashback
    d. Personification

30. What does the narrator compare their discovery to?
    a. The Sun
    b. A candle
    c. Prison
    d. Blood

31. Why does the narrator expect to be forgiven?
    a. Their invention will save the City money.
    b. The possibilities of the invention outweigh their crime.
    c. They will apologize to the World Council of Scholars.
    d. Their invention is part of their body.

32. What is the meaning of the word *transgression* in paragraph eight?
    a. Obedience
    b. Disruption
    c. Confession
    d. Offense

33. Which quote is an example of personification?
    a. "Our head is reeling."
    b. "Darkness swallowed us."
    c. "We stood, and we held our head in our hands."
    d. "We care not about our body, but our light is..."

34. According to the passage, what will NOT help advance the narrator's discovery?
    a. Using the work rooms of the Home of the Scholars
    b. Gaining wisdom from the brother Scholars
    c. Keeping the discovery a secret from the World Council of Scholars
    d. Stopping the sweeping of the streets

35. How does the narrator feel their status will change as a result of their invention?
    a. They will advance from street sweeper to the Home of the Scholars.
    b. Their status will remain the same after their confession.
    c. They will rise in status from tunnel worker to the Council of Vocations.
    d. They are not sure how their status will change due to the crime they committed.

36. Which transformation has happened by the end of the passage?
    a. The narrator has been forgiven for their transgression.
    b. The gift of electricity has been shared with all the cities of the world.
    c. The discovery has made it easier to sweep streets and light tunnels.
    d. The narrator recognizes the significance of their body.

Questions 37–44 are based on the following passage:

As long ago as 1860 it was the proper thing to be born at home. At present, so I am told, the high gods of medicine have decreed that the first cries of the young shall be uttered upon the anesthetic air of a hospital, preferably a fashionable one. So young Mr. and Mrs. Roger Button were fifty years ahead of style when they decided, one day in the summer of 1860, that their first baby should be born in a hospital. Whether this anachronism had any bearing upon the astonishing history I am about to set down will never be known.

I shall tell you what occurred, and let you judge for yourself.

The Roger Buttons held an enviable position, both social and financial, in ante-bellum Baltimore. They were related to the This Family and the That Family, which, as every Southerner knew, entitled them to membership in that enormous peerage which largely populated the Confederacy. This was their first experience with the charming old custom of having babies—Mr. Button was naturally nervous. He hoped it would be a boy so that he could be sent to Yale College in Connecticut, at which institution Mr. Button himself had been known for four years by the somewhat obvious nickname of "Cuff."

On the September morning consecrated to the enormous event he arose nervously at six o'clock, dressed himself, adjusted an impeccable stock, and hurried forth through the streets of Baltimore to the hospital, to determine whether the darkness of the night had borne in new life upon its bosom.

When he was approximately a hundred yards from the Maryland Private Hospital for Ladies and Gentlemen he saw Doctor Keene, the family physician, descending the front steps, rubbing his hands together with a washing movement—as all doctors are required to do by the unwritten ethics of their profession.

Mr. Roger Button, the president of Roger Button & Co., Wholesale Hardware, began to run toward Doctor Keene with much less dignity than was expected from a Southern gentleman of that picturesque period. "Doctor Keene!" he called. "Oh, Doctor Keene!"

The doctor heard him, faced around, and stood waiting, a curious expression settling on his harsh, medicinal face as Mr. Button drew near.

"What happened?" demanded Mr. Button, as he came up in a gasping rush. "What was it? How is she? A boy? Who is it? What—"

"Talk sense!" said Doctor Keene sharply. He appeared somewhat irritated.

"Is the child born?" begged Mr. Button.

Doctor Keene frowned. "Why, yes, I suppose so—after a fashion." Again he threw a curious glance at Mr. Button.

From *The Curious Case of Benjamin Button* by F. S. Fitzgerald, 1922

37. According to the passage, what major event is about to happen in this story?
   a. Mr. Button is about to go to a funeral.
   b. Mr. Button's wife is about to have a baby.
   c. Mr. Button is getting ready to go to the doctor's office.
   d. Mr. Button is about to go shopping for new clothes.

263

38. What kind of tone does the above passage have?
    a. Nervous and excited
    b. Sad and angry
    c. Shameful and confused
    d. Grateful and joyous

39. What is the meaning of *consecrated* as it is used in the fourth paragraph?

    "On the September morning <u>consecrated</u> to the enormous event he arose nervously at six o'clock, dressed himself, adjusted an impeccable stock, and hurried forth through the streets of Baltimore to the hospital, to determine whether the darkness of the night had borne in new life upon its bosom."

    a. Numbed
    b. Chained
    c. Dedicated
    d. Moved

40. What does the author mean to do by adding the following description?

    "rubbing his hands together with a washing movement—as all doctors are required to do by the unwritten ethics of their profession."

    a. Suggest that Mr. Button is tired of the doctor.
    b. Try to explain the details of the doctor's profession.
    c. Hint to readers that the doctor is an unethical man.
    d. Give readers a visual picture of what the doctor is doing.

41. Which of the following best describes the development of this passage?
    a. It starts in the middle of a narrative in order to transition smoothly to a conclusion.
    b. It is a chronological narrative from beginning to end.
    c. The sequence of events is backwards—we go from future events to past events.
    d. It introduces the setting of the story and its characters.

42. What is the meaning of *anachronism* as it is used in the first paragraph?

    "Whether this anachronism had any bearing upon the astonishing history I am about to set down will never be known."

    a. Comparison
    b. Misplacement
    c. Annoyance
    d. Amelioration

43. The main purpose of the first paragraph is:
    a. To explain the setting of the narrative and give information about the story
    b. To present the thesis so that the audience can determine which points are valid later in the text
    c. To introduce a counterargument so that the author can refute it in the next paragraph
    d. To provide a description of the speaker's city and the building in which he works

44. The end of the passage implies to the audience that:
    a. There is bad weather coming.
    b. The doctor thinks Mr. Button is annoying.
    c. The baby and the mother did not make it through labor.
    d. Something is unusual about the birth of the baby.

Questions 45–50 are based on the following passage:

Knowing that Mrs. Mallard was afflicted with heart trouble, great care was taken to break to her as gently as possible the news of her husband's death.

It was her sister Josephine who told her, in broken sentences; veiled hints that revealed in half concealing. Her husband's friend Richards was there, too, near her. It was he who had been in the newspaper office when intelligence of the railroad disaster was received, with Brently Mallard's name leading the list of "killed." He had only taken the time to assure himself of its truth by a second telegram, and had hastened to forestall any less careful, less tender friend in bearing the sad message.

She did not hear the story as many women have heard the same, with a paralyzed inability to accept its significance. She wept at once, with sudden, wild abandonment, in her sister's arms. When the storm of grief had spent itself she went away to her room alone. She would have no one follow her.

There stood, facing the open window, a comfortable, roomy armchair. Into this she sank, pressed down by a physical exhaustion that haunted her body and seemed to reach into her soul.

She could see in the open square before her house the tops of trees that were all aquiver with the new spring life. The delicious breath of rain was in the air. In the street below a peddler was crying his wares. The notes of a distant song which some one was singing reached her faintly, and countless sparrows were twittering in the eaves.

There were patches of blue sky showing here and there through the clouds that had met and piled one above the other in the west facing her window.

She sat with her head thrown back upon the cushion of the chair, quite motionless, except when a sob came up into her throat and shook her, as a child who has cried itself to sleep continues to sob in its dreams.

She was young, with a fair, calm face, whose lines bespoke repression and even a certain strength. But now there was a dull stare in her eyes, whose gaze was fixed away off yonder on one of those patches of blue sky. It was not a glance of reflection, but rather indicated a suspension of intelligent thought.

There was something coming to her and she was waiting for it, fearfully. What was it? She did not know; it was too subtle and elusive to name. But she felt it, creeping out of the sky, reaching toward her through the sounds, the scents, the color that filled the air.

Now her bosom rose and fell tumultuously. She was beginning to recognize this thing that was approaching to possess her, and she was striving to beat it back with her will—as powerless as her two white slender hands would have been. When she abandoned herself a little whispered word escaped her slightly parted lips. She said it over and over under her breath: "free, free, free!" The

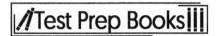

vacant stare and the look of terror that had followed it went from her eyes. They stayed keen and bright. Her pulses beat fast, and the coursing blood warmed and relaxed every inch of her body.

She did not stop to ask if it were or were not a monstrous joy that held her. A clear and exalted perception enabled her to dismiss the suggestion as trivial. She knew that she would weep again when she saw the kind, tender hands folded in death; the face that had never looked save with love upon her, fixed and gray and dead. But she saw beyond that bitter moment a long procession of years to come that would belong to her absolutely. And she opened and spread her arms out to them in welcome.

Excerpt from "The Story of an Hour" by Kate Chopin

45. What point of view is the above passage told in?
   a. First person
   b. Second person
   c. Third person omniscient
   d. Third person limited

46. What kind of irony are we presented with in this story?
   a. The way Mrs. Mallard reacted to her husband's death
   b. The way in which Mr. Mallard died
   c. The way in which the news of her husband's death was presented to Mrs. Mallard
   d. The way in which nature is compared with death in the story

47. What is the meaning of the word *elusive* in paragraph 9?

   "There was something coming to her and she was waiting for it, fearfully. What was it? She did not know; it was too subtle and elusive to name."

   a. Horrible
   b. Indefinable
   c. Quiet
   d. Joyful

48. What is the best summary of the passage above?
   a. Mr. Mallard, a soldier during World War I, is killed by the enemy and leaves his wife widowed.
   b. Mrs. Mallard understands the value of friendship when her friends show up for her after her husband's death.
   c. Mrs. Mallard combats mental illness daily and will perhaps be sent to a mental institution soon.
   d. Mrs. Mallard, a newly widowed woman, finds unexpected relief in her husband's death.

49. What is the tone of this story?
   a. Confused
   b. Joyful
   c. Depressive
   d. All of the above

266

50. What is the meaning of the word *tumultuously* in paragraph 10?

"Now her bosom rose and fell <u>tumultuously</u>."

a. Orderly
b. Unashamedly
c. Violently
d. Calmly

Questions 51-56 are based upon the following passage:

My Good Friends,—When I first imparted to the committee of the projected Institute my particular wish that on one of the evenings of my readings here the main body of my audience should be composed of working men and their families, I was animated by two desires; first, by the wish to have the great pleasure of meeting you face to face at this Christmas time, and accompany you myself through one of my little Christmas books; and second, by the wish to have an opportunity of stating publicly in your presence, and in the presence of the committee, my earnest hope that the Institute will, from the beginning, recognise one great principle—strong in reason and justice—which I believe to be essential to the very life of such an Institution. It is, that the working man shall, from the first unto the last, have a share in the management of an Institution which is designed for his benefit, and which calls itself by his name.

I have no fear here of being misunderstood—of being supposed to mean too much in this. If there ever was a time when any one class could of itself do much for its own good, and for the welfare of society—which I greatly doubt—that time is unquestionably past. It is in the fusion of different classes, without confusion; in the bringing together of employers and employed; in the creating of a better common understanding among those whose interests are identical, who depend upon each other, who are vitally essential to each other, and who never can be in unnatural antagonism without deplorable results, that one of the chief principles of a Mechanics' Institution should consist. In this world a great deal of the bitterness among us arises from an imperfect understanding of one another. Erect in Birmingham a great Educational Institution, properly educational; educational of the feelings as well as of the reason; to which all orders of Birmingham men contribute; in which all orders of Birmingham men meet; wherein all orders of Birmingham men are faithfully represented—and you will erect a Temple of Concord here which will be a model edifice to the whole of England.

Contemplating as I do the existence of the Artisans' Committee, which not long ago considered the establishment of the Institute so sensibly, and supported it so heartily, I earnestly entreat the gentlemen—earnest I know in the good work, and who are now among us,—by all means to avoid the great shortcoming of similar institutions; and in asking the working man for his confidence, to set him the great example and give him theirs in return. You will judge for yourselves if I promise too much for the working man, when I say that he will stand by such an enterprise with the utmost of his patience, his perseverance, sense, and support; that I am sure he will need no charitable aid or condescending patronage; but will readily and cheerfully pay for the advantages which it confers; that he will prepare himself in individual cases where he feels that the adverse circumstances around him have rendered it necessary; in a word, that he will feel his responsibility like an honest man, and will most honestly and manfully discharge it. I now proceed to the pleasant task to which I assure you I have looked forward for a long time.

Excerpt from Charles Dickens' speech in Birmingham in 1853 on behalf of the Birmingham and Midland Institute

51. Which word is most closely synonymous with the word *patronage* as it appears in the following statement:

> "... that I am sure he will need no charitable aid or condescending patronage ..."

a. Auspices
b. Aberration
c. Acerbic
d. Adulation

52. Which term is most closely aligned with the definition of the term *working man* as it is used in the following quotation?

> "You will judge for yourselves if I promise too much for the working man, when I say that he will stand by such an enterprise with the utmost of his patience, his perseverance, sense, and support ..."

a. Athlete
b. Viscount
c. Entrepreneur
d. Bourgeois

53. Which of the following statements most closely correlates with the definition of the term *working man* as it is defined in the previous question?
a. A working man is not someone who works for institutions or corporations but rather someone who is well versed in the workings of the soul.
b. A working man is someone who is probably not involved in social activities because the physical demand for work is too high.
c. A working man is someone who works for wages among the middle class.
d. The working man has historically taken to the field, to the factory, and now to the screen.

54. Based upon the contextual evidence provided in the passage above, what is the meaning of the term *enterprise* in the third paragraph?
a. Company
b. Courage
c. Game
d. Cause

55. The speaker addresses his audience as "My Good Friends." What function does this salutation serve for the speaker?
a. The speaker is an employer addressing his employees, so the salutation is a way for the boss to bridge the gap between himself and his employees.
b. The speaker's salutation is one from an entertainer to his audience and uses the friendly language to connect to his audience before a serious speech.
c. The salutation gives the serious speech that follows a somber tone, as it is used ironically.
d. The speech is one from a politician to the public, so the salutation is used to grab the audience's attention.

56. According to the passage, what is the speaker's second desire for his time in front of the audience?
a. To read a Christmas story
b. To support the idea that the working man should have a say in an institution that is designed for his benefit
c. To have an opportunity to stand in their presence
d. For the life of the institution to be essential to the audience as a whole

Writing

Usage

The following sentences test skills of grammar and usage. Some sentences will contain no error, and the rest will contain only one error.

1. (A) An <u>important issues</u> stemming (B) <u>from this meeting</u> is that (C) <u>we won't</u> have enough time (D) <u>to meet</u> all of the objectives. (E) <u>NO ERROR</u>

2. (A) <u>The rising popularity</u> of the clean-eating movement (B) <u>attributing</u> to the fact that experts say added (C) <u>sugars and chemicals</u> in our food (D) <u>are to blame</u> for the obesity epidemic. (E) <u>No error</u>

3. (A) <u>She's</u> looking (B) <u>for a suitcase</u> that (C) <u>can fit</u> all of her clothes, shoes, (D) <u>accessory,</u> and makeup. (E) <u>No error</u>

4. (A) <u>Shawn started</u> taking (B) <u>guitar</u> lessons (C) <u>while</u> he wanted to become (D) <u>a better</u> musician. (E) <u>No error</u>

5. (A) <u>Considering</u> the (B) <u>recent rains</u> we have had, (C) <u>it's</u> a wonder the plants (D) <u>haven't drowned</u>. (E) <u>No error</u>

6. (A) <u>Since</u> none of the furniture (B) <u>were delivered</u> on time (C)<u>, we</u> have to move in (D) <u>at a later date</u>. (E) <u>No error</u>

7. It (A) <u>is necessary</u> for instructors (B) <u>to offer</u> tutoring to (C) <u>any students</u> who need (D) <u>extra</u> help in the class. (E) <u>No error</u>

8. The (A) <u>fact the</u> train set only (B) <u>includes</u> four cars and (C) <u>one small track</u> was a big (D) <u>disappointment</u> to my son. (E) <u>No error</u>

9. (A) <u>Because</u> many people (B) <u>feel</u> there are too (C) <u>many distractions</u> to get any work (D) <u>done, I</u> actually enjoy working from home. (E) <u>No error</u>

10. There (A) <u>were</u> many questions about (B) <u>why the case went</u> cold, but the detective (C) <u>wasn't</u> willing to (D) <u>discuss the case</u> with reporters. (E) <u>No error</u>

Sentence Correction

Directions for questions 11–21:

Choose the best version of the underlined segment of the sentence. If you feel the original sentence is correct, then choose the first answer choice.

11. Which of the following would be the best replacement for the underlined portion of the sentence reproduced below?

> Since the first discovery of dinosaur bones, <u>scientists has made strides in technological development and methodologies used to investigate</u> these extinct animals.

   a. NO CHANGE
   b. scientists has made strides in technological development, and methodologies, used to investigate
   c. scientists have made strides in technological development and methodologies used to investigate
   d. scientists, have made strides in technological development and methodologies used, to investigate

12. Which of the following would be the best replacement for the underlined portion of the sentence reproduced below?

> However, one has to ask, <u>how if earlier perceptions of dinosaurs</u> continue to influence people's understanding of these creatures?

a. NO CHANGE
b. how perceptions of dinosaurs
c. how, if, earlier perceptions of dinosaurs
d. do earlier perceptions of dinosaurs

13. Which of the following would be the best replacement for the underlined portion of the sentence reproduced below?

> <u>The biggest problem with studying dinosaurs is simply that there are no living dinosaurs to observe.</u>

a. NO CHANGE
b. The biggest problem with studying dinosaurs is simple, that there are no living dinosaurs to observe.
c. The biggest problem with studying dinosaurs is simple, there are no living dinosaurs to observe.
d. The biggest problem with studying dinosaurs, is simply that there are no living dinosaurs to observe.

14. Which of the following would be the best replacement for the underlined portion of the sentence reproduced below?

> To gauge behavioral characteristics, scientists cross-examine these <u>finds with living animals that seem similar in order to gain understanding.</u>

a. NO CHANGE
b. finds with living animals to explore potential similarities.
c. finds with living animals to gain understanding of similarities.
d. finds with living animals that seem similar, in order, to gain understanding.

15. Which of the following would be the best replacement for the underlined portion of the sentence reproduced below?

> Paleontologists know this sail exists and have ideas for the function of <u>the sail however they are uncertain of which idea is the true function.</u>

a. NO CHANGE
b. the sail however, they are uncertain of which idea is the true function.
c. the sail however they are, uncertain, of which idea is the true function.
d. the sail; however, they are uncertain of which idea is the true function.

270

16. Which of the following would be the best replacement for the underlined portion of the sentence reproduced below?

> Some scientists believe <u>the sail serves to regulate the Spinosaurus' body temperature and yet others believe its used to attract mates.</u>

a. NO CHANGE
b. the sail serves to regulate the Spinosaurus' body temperature, yet others believe it's used to attract mates.
c. the sail serves to regulate the Spinosaurus' body temperature and yet others believe it's used to attract mates.
d. the sail serves to regulate the Spinosaurus' body temperature however others believe it's used to attract mates.

17. Which of the following would be the best replacement for the underlined portion of the sentence reproduced below?

> <u>Yet it's quite possible</u> that the sail could hold a completely unique function.

a. NO CHANGE
b. Yet it's quite possible,
c. It's quite possible,
d. Its quite possible

18. Which of the following would be the best replacement for the underlined portion of the sentence reproduced below?

> While it's <u>plausible, even likely that dinosaurs share many</u> traits with modern animals, there is the danger of over-attributing these qualities to a unique, extinct species.

a. NO CHANGE
b. plausible, even likely that, dinosaurs share many
c. plausible, even likely, that dinosaurs share many
d. plausible even likely that dinosaurs share many

19. Which of the following would be the best replacement for the underlined portion of the sentence reproduced below?

> <u>For the longest time this image was the prevailing view on dinosaurs</u>, until evidence indicated that they were more likely warm-blooded.

a. NO CHANGE
b. For the longest time this was the prevailing view on dinosaurs
c. For the longest time, this image, was the prevailing view on dinosaurs
d. This was the prevailing image of dinosaurs

20. Which of the following would be the best replacement for the underlined portion of the sentence reproduced below?

> <u>One of the icon's of romantic and science fiction literature</u> remains Mary Shelley's classic, *Frankenstein, or The Modern Prometheus.*

a. NO CHANGE
b. One of the icons of romantic and science fiction literature
c. One of the icon's of romantic, and science fiction literature,
d. The icon of romantic and science fiction literature

21. Which of the following would be the best replacement for the underlined portion of the sentence reproduced below?

> Besides the novel's engaging <u>writing style the story's central theme</u> remains highly relevant in a world of constant discovery and moral dilemmas.

a. NO CHANGE
b. writing style the central theme of the story
c. writing style, the story's central theme
d. the story's central theme's writing style

Revision in Context

Questions 22-36 are based on the following passage:

> Early in my career, (22) <u>a professor shared this thought with me "Education is the last bastion of civility."</u> While I did not completely understand the scope of those words at the time, I have since come to realize the depth, breadth, truth, and significance of what he said. (23) <u>Education provides</u> society with a vehicle for (24) <u>raising it's children to be</u> civil, decent human beings with something valuable to contribute to the world. It is really what makes us human and what (25) <u>distinguishes</u> us as <u>civelized creatures.</u>
>
> Being "civilized" humans means being "whole" humans. Education must address the minds, bodies, and souls of students. (26) <u>It would be detrimental to society, only meeting the needs of the mind, if our schools were myopic in their focus.</u> As humans, we are multidimensional, multifaceted beings who need more than head knowledge to survive. (27) <u>The human heart and psyche have to be fed in order for the mind to develop properly, and the body must be maintained and exercised to help fuel brain functioning. Education is a basic human right, and it allows us to sustain a democratic society in which participation is fundamental to its success. It should inspire students to seek better solutions to world problems and to dream of a more equitable society.</u> Education should never discriminate on any basis, and it should create individuals who are self-sufficient, patriotic, and tolerant of (28) <u>others' ideas.</u>
>
> (29) <u>All children can learn. Although not all children learn in the same manner.</u> All children learn best, however, when their basic physical needs are met and they feel safe, secure, and loved. Students are much more responsive to a teacher who values them and shows them respect as individual people. Teachers must model at all times the way they expect students to treat them and their peers. If teachers set high expectations for (30) <u>there students</u>, the students will rise to that high level. Teachers must make the well-being of students their primary focus and must not be afraid to let students learn from their own mistakes.

In the modern age of technology, a teacher's focus is no longer the "what" of the content, (31) but more importantly, the 'why.' Students are bombarded with information and have access to any information they need right at their fingertips. Teachers have to work harder than ever before to help students identify salient information (32) so to think critically about the information they encounter. Students have to (33) read between the lines, identify bias, and determine who they can trust in the milieu of ads, data, and texts presented to them.

Schools must work in concert with families in this important mission. While children spend most of their time in school, they are dramatically and indelibly shaped (34) with the influences of their family and culture. Teachers must not only respect this fact, (35) but must strive to include parents in the education of their children and must work to keep parents informed of progress and problems. Communication between the classroom and home is essential for a child's success.

Humans have always aspired to be more, to do more, and to better ourselves and our communities. This is where education lies, right at the heart of humanity's desire to be all that we can be. Education helps us strive for higher goals and better treatment of ourselves and others. I shudder to think what would become of us if education ceased to be the "last bastion of civility." (36) We must be unapologetic about expecting excellence from our students? Our very existence depends upon it.

22. Which is the best version of the underlined portion of this sentence (reproduced below)?

    Early in my career, (22) a professor shared this thought with me "Education is the last bastion of civility."

    a. NO CHANGE
    b. a professor shared this thought with me: "Education is the last bastion of civility."
    c. a professor shared this thought with me: "Education is the last bastion of civility".
    d. a professor shared this thought with me. "Education is the last bastion of civility."

23. Which is the best version of the underlined portion of this sentence (reproduced below)?

    (23) Education provides society with a vehicle for raising it's children to be civil, decent human beings with something valuable to contribute to the world.

    a. NO CHANGE
    b. Education provide
    c. Education will provide
    d. Education providing

24. Which is the best version of the underlined portion of this sentence (reproduced below)?

    Education provides society with a vehicle for (24) raising it's children to be civil, decent human beings with something valuable to contribute to the world.

    a. NO CHANGE
    b. raises its children to be
    c. raising its' children to be
    d. raising its children to be

25. Which of these, if any, is misspelled?

> It is really what makes us human and what distinguishes us as civelized creatures.

a. None of these are misspelled.
b. distinguishes
c. civelized
d. creatures

26. Which is the best version of the underlined portion of this sentence (reproduced below)?

> (26) It would be detrimental to society, only meeting the needs of the mind, if our schools were myopic in their focus.

a. NO CHANGE
b. It would be detrimental to society if our schools were myopic in their focus, only meeting the needs of the mind.
c. Only meeting the needs of our mind, our schools were myopic in their focus, detrimental to society.
d. Myopic is the focus of our schools, being detrimental to society for only meeting the needs of the mind.

27. Which of these sentences, if any, should begin a new paragraph?

> (27) The human heart and psyche have to be fed in order for the mind to develop properly, and the body must be maintained and exercised to help fuel brain functioning. Education is a basic human right, and it allows us to sustain a democratic society in which participation is fundamental to its success. It should inspire students to seek better solutions to world problems and to dream of a more equitable society.

a. There should be no new paragraph.
b. The human heart and psyche have to be fed in order for the mind to develop properly, and the body must be maintained and exercised to help fuel brain functioning.
c. Education is a basic human right, and it allows us to sustain a democratic society in which participation is fundamental to its success.
d. It should inspire students to seek better solutions to world problems and to dream of a more equitable society.

28. Which is the best version of the underlined portion of this sentence (reproduced below)?

> Education should never discriminate on any basis, and it should create individuals who are self-sufficient, patriotic, and tolerant of (28) others' ideas.

a. NO CHANGE
b. other's ideas
c. others ideas
d. others's ideas

29. Which of the following would be the best choice for these sentences (reproduced below)?

> (29) All children can learn. Although not all children learn in the same manner.

a. NO CHANGE
b. All children can learn although not all children learn in the same manner.
c. All children can learn although, not all children learn in the same manner.
d. All children can learn, although not all children learn in the same manner.

274

30. Which of the following would be the best choice for these sentences (reproduced below)?

If teachers set high expectations for (30) there students, the students will rise to that high level.

a. NO CHANGE
b. they're students
c. their students
d. thare students

31. Which of the following would be the best replacement for the underlined portion of the sentence reproduced below?

In the modern age of technology, a teacher's focus is no longer the "what" of the content, (31) but more importantly, the 'why.'

a. NO CHANGE
b. but more importantly, the "why."
c. but more importantly, the 'why'.
d. but more importantly, the "why".

32. Which of the following would be the best replacement for the underlined portion of the sentence reproduced below?

Teachers have to work harder than ever before to help students identify salient information (32) so to think critically about the information they encounter.

a. NO CHANGE
b. and to think critically
c. but to think critically
d. nor to think critically

33. Which of the following would be the best replacement for the underlined portion of the sentence reproduced below?

Students have to (33) read between the lines, identify bias, and determine who they can trust in the milieu of ads, data, and texts presented to them.

a. NO CHANGE
b. read between the lines, identify bias, and determining
c. read between the lines, identifying bias, and determining
d. reads between the lines, identifies bias, and determines

34. Which of the following would be the best replacement for the underlined portion of the sentence reproduced below?

While children spend most of their time in school, they are dramatically and indelibly shaped (34) with the influences of their family and culture.

a. NO CHANGE
b. for the influences
c. to the influences
d. by the influences

275

35. Which of the following would be the best replacement for the underlined portion of the sentence reproduced below?

> Teachers must not only respect this fact, (35) but must strive to include parents in the education of their children and must work to keep parents informed of progress and problems.

    a. NO CHANGE
    b. but to strive
    c. but striving
    d. but strived

36. Which of the following would be the best replacement for the underlined portion of the sentence reproduced below?

> (36) We must be unapologetic about expecting excellence from our students? Our very existence depends upon it.

    a. NO CHANGE
    b. We must be unapologetic about expecting excellence from our students, our very existence depends upon it.
    c. We must be unapologetic about expecting excellence from our students—our very existence depends upon it.
    d. We must be unapologetic about expecting excellence from our students our very existence depends upon it.

Research Skills

37. Firsthand accounts of an event, subject matter, time period, or individual are referred to as what type of sources?
    a. Primary sources
    b. Secondary sources
    c. Direct sources
    d. Indirect sources

38. Which citation style requires a bibliography entry to include the author's last name, the title of the book or article, and its publication date?
    a. MLA
    b. APA
    c. Chicago
    d. All of the above

39. Which citation style requires a bibliography entry to include the author's last name, the title of the book or article, and its publication date?
    a. MLA
    b. APA
    c. Chicago
    d. All of the above

40. A student finds a digital first-hand accounts of an event. What type of source is this?
   a. Primary sources
   b. Secondary sources
   c. Direct sources
   d. Indirect sources

Mathematics

1. 6 is 30% of what number?
   a. 18
   b. 20
   c. 24
   d. 26

2. The value of 6×12 is the same as:
   a. $2 \times 4 \times 4 \times 2$
   b. $7 \times 4 \times 3$
   c. $6 \times 6 \times 3$
   d. $3 \times 3 \times 4 \times 2$

3. After a 20% sale discount, Frank purchased a new refrigerator for $850. How much money did he save off of the original price?
   a. $170
   b. $212.50
   c. $105.75
   d. $200

4. Keith's bakery had 252 customers go through its doors last week. This week, that number increased to 378. By what percentage did his customer volume increase?
   a. 26%
   b. 50%
   c. 35%
   d. 12%

5. A rectangle was formed out of pipe cleaner. Its length was $\frac{1}{2}$ foot and its width was $\frac{11}{2}$ inches. What is its area in square inches?
   a. $\frac{11}{4}$ in^2
   b. $\frac{11}{2}$ in^2
   c. 22 in^2
   d. 33 in^2

6. What is $(2 \times 20) \div (7 + 1) + (6 \times 0.01) + (4 \times 0.001)$?
   a. 5.064
   b. 5.64
   c. 5.0064
   d. 48.064

7. If $6t + 4 = 16$, what is t?
   a. 1
   b. 2
   c. 3
   d. 4

8. On May 1, 2010, a couple purchased a house for $100,000. On September 1, 2016, the couple sold the house for $93,000 so they could purchase a bigger one to start a family. How many months did they own the house?
   a. 76 months
   b. 54 months
   c. 85 months
   d. 93 months

9. Ten students take a test. Five students get a 50. Four students get a 70. If the average score is 55, what was the last student's score?
   a. 20
   b. 40
   c. 50
   d. 60

10. An equilateral triangle has a perimeter of 18 feet. The sides of a square have the same length as the triangle's sides. What is the area of the square?
    a. 6 square feet
    b. 36 square feet
    c. 256 square feet
    d. 1000 square feet

11. Kimberley earns $10 an hour babysitting, and after 10 p.m., she earns $12 an hour. The time she works is rounded to the nearest hour for pay purposes. On her last job, she worked from 5:30 p.m. to 11:00 p.m. In total, how much did Kimberley earn for that job?
    a. $45
    b. $57
    c. $62
    d. $42

12. The perimeter of a 6-sided polygon is 56 cm. The lengths of 3 sides are 9 cm each. The lengths of 2 other sides are 8 cm each. What is the length of the final side?
    a. 11 cm
    b. 12 cm
    c. 13 cm
    d. 10 cm

13. In Jim's school, there are a total of 650 students. There are three girls for every two boys. How many students are girls?
    a. 260
    b. 130
    c. 65
    d. 390

278

14. A piggy bank contains 12 dollars' worth of nickels. A nickel weighs 5 grams, and the empty piggy bank weighs 1,050 grams. What is the total weight of the full piggy bank?
   a.   1,110 grams
   b.   1,200 grams
   c.   2,250 grams
   d.   2,200 grams

15. Mo needs to buy enough material to cover the walls around the stage for a theater performance. If he needs 79 feet of wall covering, what is the minimum number of yards of material he should purchase if the material is sold only by whole yards?
   a.   23 yards
   b.   25 yards
   c.   26 yards
   d.   27 yards

16. Which is closest to 17.8×9.9?
   a.   140
   b.   180
   c.   200
   d.   350

17. There are $4x + 1$ treats in each party favor bag. If a total of $60x + 15$ treats are distributed, how many bags are given out?
   a.   15
   b.   16
   c.   20
   d.   22

18. A rectangle has a length that is 5 feet longer than 3 times its width. If the perimeter is 90 feet, what is the length in feet?
   a.   10
   b.   20
   c.   25
   d.   35

19. Five of six numbers have a sum of 25. The average of all six numbers is 6. What is the sixth number?
   a.   8
   b.   10
   c.   11
   d.   12

20. 4.67 miles is equivalent to how many kilometers, to three significant digits? Use the conversion $1 \text{ mi} = 1.609$ km.
   a.   7.514 km
   b.   7.51 km
   c.   2.90 km
   d.   2.902 km

21. Mom's car drove 72 miles in 90 minutes. How fast did she drive in feet per second?
   a. 0.8 feet per second
   b. 48.9 feet per second
   c. 0.009 feet per second
   d. 70.4 feet per second

22. Last year, the New York City area received approximately $27\frac{3}{4}$ inches of snow. The Denver area received approximately three times as much snow as New York City. How much snow fell in Denver?
   a. 60 inches
   b. $27\frac{1}{4}$ inches
   c. $9\frac{1}{4}$ inches
   d. $83\frac{1}{4}$ inches

23. Which of the following equations best represents the problem below?

The width of a rectangle is 2 centimeters less than the length. If the perimeter of the rectangle is 44 centimeters, then what are the dimensions of the rectangle?
   a. $2l + 2(l - 2) = 44$
   b. $(l + 2) + (l + 2) + l = 48$
   c. $l \times (l - 2) = 44$
   d. $(l + 2) + (l + 2) + l = 44$

24. The table below displays the number of three-year-olds at Kids First Daycare who are potty-trained and those who still wear diapers.

	Potty-trained	Wear diapers	Total
Boys	26	22	48
Girls	34	18	52
	60	40	

If a three-year-old girl is randomly selected from this school, what is the probability that she is potty-trained?
   a. 52%
   b. 34%
   c. 65%
   d. 57%

25. What is the solution to the following system of equations?

$$x^2 - 2x + y = 8$$

$$x - y = -2$$

   a. $(-2, 3)$
   b. There is no solution.
   c. $(-2, 0)\ (1, 3)$
   d. $(-2, 0)\ (3, 5)$

26. Give a numerical expression for the following: "Six less than three times the sum of twice a number and one."
   a. $2x + 1 - 6$
   b. $3x + 1 - 6$
   c. $3(x + 1) - 6$
   d. $3(2x + 1) - 6$

27. $(2x - 4y)^2$ can be expanded to which of the following?
   a. $4x^2 - 16xy + 16y^2$
   b. $4x^2 - 8xy + 16y^2$
   c. $4x^2 - 16xy - 16y^2$
   d. $2x^2 - 8xy + 8y^2$

28. What is the slope of this line?

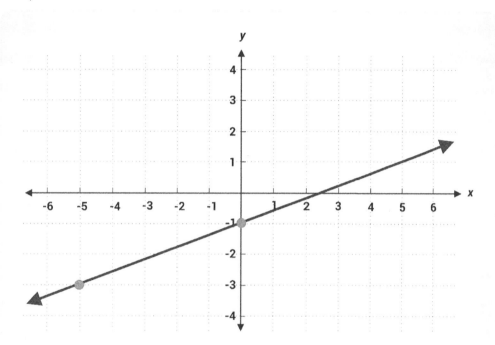

   a. 2
   b. $\frac{5}{2}$
   c. $\frac{1}{2}$
   d. $\frac{2}{5}$

29. If Danny takes 48 minutes to walk 3 miles, how long should it take him to walk 5 miles maintaining the same speed?
   a. 32 min
   b. 64 min
   c. 80 min
   d. 96 min

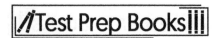
30. Evaluate the expression. Give the result in decimal form.

$$\frac{3}{5} \times \frac{7}{10} \div \frac{1}{2}$$

    a.   0.042
    b.   84%
    c.   0.84
    d.   0.42

31. Solve for x: $\frac{2x}{5} - 1 = 59$
    a.   60
    b.   145
    c.   150
    d.   115

32. A train traveling 50 miles per hour takes a trip lasting 3 hours. If a map has a scale of 1 inch per 10 miles, how many inches apart are the train's starting point and ending point on the map?
    a.   14 inches
    b.   12 inches
    c.   13 inches
    d.   15 inches

33. What is the value of b in this equation?

$$5b - 4 = 2b + 17$$

    a.   13
    b.   24
    c.   7
    d.   21

34. Express the following in decimal form:

$$\frac{3}{5} \times \frac{7}{10} \div \frac{1}{2}$$

    a.   0.042
    b.   84%
    c.   0.84
    d.   0.42

35. Johnny earns $2,334.50 from his job each month. He pays $1,437 for monthly expenses and saves the rest. Johnny is planning a vacation in 3 months that he estimates will cost $1,750 total. How much will Johnny have left over from 3 months of saving once he pays for his vacation?
    a. $948.50
    b. $584.50
    c. $852.50
    d. $942.50

36. What is $4 \times 7 + (25 - 21)^2 \div 2$?
    a. 512
    b. 36
    c. 60.5
    d. 22

37. If the volume of a sphere is 288π cubic meters, what are the radius and surface area of the same sphere?
    a. Radius: 6 meters, surface area: 144π square meters
    b. Radius: 36 meters, surface area: 144π square meters
    c. Radius: 6 meters, surface area: 12π square meters
    d. Radius: 36 meters, surface area: 12π square meters

38. Given the following triangle, what's the length of the missing side? Round the answer to the nearest tenth.

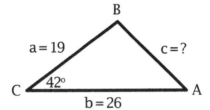

    a. 17.0
    b. 17.4
    c. 18.0
    d. 18.4

39. A six-sided die is rolled. What is the probability that the roll is 1 or 2?
    a. $\frac{1}{6}$
    b. $\frac{1}{4}$
    c. $\frac{1}{3}$
    d. $\frac{1}{2}$

40. Which measure for the center of a small sample set is most affected by outliers?
    a. Mean
    b. Median
    c. Mode
    d. None of the above

41. Before a race of 4 horses, you make a random guess of which horse will get first place and which will get second place. What is the probability that both your guesses will be correct?
    a. $\frac{1}{4}$
    b. $\frac{1}{2}$
    c. $\frac{1}{16}$
    d. $\frac{1}{12}$

42. Which of the following is an equivalent measurement for 1.3 cm?
    a. 0.13 m
    b. 0.013 m
    c. 0.13 mm
    d. 0.013 mm

43. What is $(2 \times 20) \div (7 + 1) + (6 \times 0.01) + (4 \times 0.001)$?
    a. 5.064
    b. 5.64
    c. 5.0064
    d. 48.064

44. Which of the following is equivalent to the value of the digit 3 in the number 792.134?
    a. 3×10
    b. 3×100
    c. $\dfrac{3}{10}$
    d. $\dfrac{3}{100}$

45. Write the following number in standard form:

$$(1 \times 10^4) + (3 \times 10^3) + (7 \times 10^1) + (8 \times 10^0)$$

    a. 137
    b. 13,078
    c. 1,378
    d. 8,731

46. How would the number 847.89632 be written if rounded to the nearest hundredth?
    a. 847.90
    b. 900
    c. 847.89
    d. 847.896

47. What is the sum of $\dfrac{1}{3}$ and $\dfrac{2}{5}$?
    a. $\dfrac{3}{8}$
    b. $\dfrac{11}{15}$
    c. $\dfrac{11}{30}$
    d. $\dfrac{4}{5}$

48. Evaluate the expression: $7^2 - 3 \times (4 + 2) + 15 \div 5$?
    a. 12.2
    b. 40.2
    c. 34
    d. 58.2

49. How would $\frac{4}{5}$ be written as a percent?
   a. 40%
   b. 125%
   c. 90%
   d. 80%

50. A construction company is building a new housing development with the property of each house measuring 30 feet wide. If the length of the street is zoned off at 345 feet, how many houses can be built on the street?
   a. 11 houses
   b. 115 houses
   c. 11.5 houses
   d. 12 houses

51. Kassidy drove for 3 hours at a speed of 60 miles per hour. Using the distance formula, $d = r \times t$ ($distance = rate \times time$), calculate how far Kassidy traveled.
   a. 20 miles
   b. 180 miles
   c. 65 miles
   d. 120 miles

52. If $-3(x + 4) \geq x + 8$, what is the value of x?
   a. $x = 4$
   b. $x \geq 2$
   c. $x \geq -5$
   d. $x \leq -5$

53. A group of 25 coworkers were given a choice of three lunch options: a sandwich, a salad, or a hamburger. If 12 employees chose a sandwich and 5 chose a salad, how many employees chose a hamburger?
   a. 17
   b. 8
   c. 13
   d. 5

54. Cindy makes four trips to the grocery store in March. She spends $42.36, $26.50, $31.71, and $37.23. What is the average amount Cindy spent on groceries per trip in March?
   a. $34.54
   b. $34.00
   c. $35.00
   d. $34.45

55. The hospital has a nurse-to-patient ratio of $1:25$. If a maximum of 325 patients may be admitted at a time, how many nurses are there? Enter your answer in the answer box below.

56. At the beginning of the day, Xavier has 20 apples. At lunch, he meets his sister Emma and gives her half of his apples. After lunch, he stops by his neighbor Jim's house and gives him six of his apples. He then uses $\frac{3}{4}$ of his remaining apples to make an apple pie for dessert at dinner. At the end of the day, how many apples does Xavier have left? Enter your answer in the answer box below.

Essay Prompts #2

Directions: Please read the prompts below and answer in an essay format.

Essay 1

Technology has been invading cars for the last several years, but there are some new high-tech trends that are pretty amazing. It is now standard in many car models to have a rear-view camera, hands-free phone and text, and a touch screen digital display. Music can be streamed from a paired cell phone, and some displays can even be programmed with a personal photo. Sensors beep to indicate there is something in the driver's path when reversing and changing lanes. Rain-sensing windshield wipers and lights are automatic, leaving the driver with little to do but watch the road and enjoy the ride. The next wave of technology will include cars that automatically parallel park, and self-driving cars are on the horizon. These technological advances make it a good time to be a driver, but some features could become distracting or cause drivers to rely too heavily on the car's automation instead of paying close attention to road conditions.

Write an essay to someone who is considering whether to purchase a new car with the latest technological features. Take a stance and argue whether or not he/she should purchase a tech-enhanced car. Use specific examples to support your argument.

Essay 2

Read the two articles below. Then, write a 500-word essay in which you synthesize the two articles with your own opinion of the topic. That is, you must develop a position of the topic then use both sources to draw upon your knowledge of the topic and appeal to your audience. Refer to each source by the author's last name or title.

Passage A

A Defense of Shakespeare

People who argue that William Shakespeare is not responsible for the plays attributed to his name are known as anti-Stratfordians (from the name of Shakespeare's birthplace, Stratford-upon-Avon). The most common anti-Stratfordian claim is that William Shakespeare simply was not educated enough or from a high enough social class to have written plays overflowing with references to such a wide range of subjects like history, the classics, religion, and international culture. William Shakespeare was the son of a glove-maker, he only had a basic grade-school education, and he never set foot outside of England—so how could he have produced plays of such sophistication and imagination? How could he have written in such detail about historical figures and events, or about different cultures and locations around Europe? According to anti-Stratfordians, the depth of knowledge contained in Shakespeare's plays suggests a well-traveled writer from a wealthy background with a university education, not a countryside writer like Shakespeare. But in fact, there is not much substance to such speculation, and most anti-Stratfordian arguments can be refuted with a little background about Shakespeare's time and upbringing.

First of all, those who doubt Shakespeare's authorship often point to his common birth and brief education as stumbling blocks to his writerly genius. Although it is true that Shakespeare did not come from a noble class, his father was a very successful glove-maker and his mother was from a very wealthy land-owning family—so while Shakespeare may have had a country upbringing, he was certainly from a well-off family and would have been educated accordingly. Also, even though

286

he did not attend university, grade school education in Shakespeare's time was actually quite rigorous and exposed students to classic drama through writers like Seneca and Ovid. It is not unreasonable to believe that Shakespeare received a very solid foundation in poetry and literature from his early schooling.

Next, anti-Stratfordians tend to question how Shakespeare could write so extensively about countries and cultures he had never visited before (for instance, several of his most famous works like *Romeo and Juliet* and *The Merchant of Venice* were set in Italy, on the opposite side of Europe). But again, this criticism does not hold up under scrutiny. For one thing, Shakespeare was living in London, a bustling metropolis of international trade and the most populous city in England. In the daily crowds of people, Shakespeare would certainly have been able to meet travelers from other countries and hear firsthand accounts of life in their home country. And, in addition to the influx of information from world travelers, this was also the age of the printing press, a jump in technology that made it possible to print and circulate books much more easily than in the past. This also allowed for a freer flow of information across different countries, allowing people to read about life and ideas from throughout Europe. One needn't travel the continent in order to learn and write about its different cultures.

Passage B

Now there is very good authority for saying, and I think the truth is so, that at least two of the plays published among the works of Shakespeare are not his at all; that at least three others contain very little, if any, of his writing; and that of the remainder, many contain long passages that are non-Shakespearean. But when we have submitted them all the crucible of criticism we have a magnificent residuum of the purest gold. Here is the true Shakespeare; here is the great magician who, by a wave of his wand, could transmute brass into gold, or make dry bones live and move and have immortal being. Who was this great magician—this mighty dramatist who was "not of an age, but for all time"? Who was the writer of *Venus* and *Lucrece* and the *Sonnets* and *Lear* and *Hamlet*? Was it William Shakespeare of Stratford, the Player? So it is generally believed, and that hypothesis I had accepted in unquestioning faith till my love of the works naturally led me to an examination of the life of the supposed author of them. Then I found that as I read my faith melted away "into thin air." It was not, certainly, that I had (nor have I now) any wish to disbelieve. I was, and I am, altogether willing to accept the Player as the immortal poet if only my reason would allow me to do so. Why not? . . . But the question of authorship is, nevertheless, a most fascinating one. If it be true, as the Rev. Leonard Bacon wrote that "The great world does not care sixpence who wrote *Hamlet*," the great world must, at the same time, be a very small world, and many of us must be content to be outside it. Having given, then, the best attention I was able to give to the question, and more time, I fear, than I ought to have devoted to it, I was brought to the conclusion, as many others have been, that the man who is, truly enough, designated by Messrs. Garnett and Gosse as a "Stratford rustic" is not the true Shakespeare. . .

That Shakespeare the "Stratford rustic and London actor" should have acquired this learning, this culture, and this polish; that *he* should have travelled into foreign lands, studied the life and topography of foreign cities, and the manners and customs of all sorts and conditions of men; that *he* should have written some half-dozen dramas . . . besides qualifying himself as a professional actor; that *he* should have done all this and a good deal more between 1587 and 1592 is a supposition so wild that it can only be entertained by those who are prepared to accept it as a miracle. "And miracles do not happen!"

Excerpt from *The Shakespeare Problem Restated* by G. G. Greenwood

The following pages are provided for writing your essays.

Write Your Essay

_____

_____

_____

_____

_____

_____

_____

_____

_____

_____

_____

_____

_____

_____

_____

_____

_____

_____

_____

_____

_____

_____

_____

288

Answer Explanations #2

Reading

1. D: The passage does not proceed in chronological order since it begins by pointing out Christopher Columbus's explorations in America, so Choice *A* does not work. Although the author compares and contrasts Erikson with Columbus, this is not the main way the information is presented; therefore, Choice *B* does not work. Choice *C* is also incorrect because there is no mention of or reference to cause and effect in the passage. However, the passage does offer a conclusion (Leif Erikson deserves more credit) and premises (first European to set foot in the New World and first to contact the natives) to substantiate Erikson's historical importance. Thus, Choice *D* is correct.

2. C: Choice *A* is wrong because it describes facts: Leif Erikson was the son of Erik the Red and historians debate Leif's date of birth. These are not opinions. Choice *B* is wrong; Erikson calling the land Vinland is a verifiable fact, as is Choice *D*, because he did contact the natives almost 500 years before Columbus. Choice *C* is the correct answer because it is the author's opinion that Erikson deserves more credit. Choice *C* is the correct answer because it is the author's opinion that Erikson deserves more credit. Another person could argue that Columbus or another explorer deserves more credit, which makes it an opinion rather than a historical fact.

3. B: Choice *A* is wrong because the author aims to go beyond describing Erikson as merely a legendary Viking. Choice *C* is wrong because the author does not focus on Erikson's motivations, let alone name the spreading of Christianity as his primary objective. Although it's true that Erikson contacted the natives 500 years before Columbus, Choice *D* is wrong because it isn't the author's main conclusion, it is simply a fact used to support the main conclusion. Choice *B* is correct because it accurately identifies the author's statement that Erikson deserves more credit than he has received for being the first European to explore the New World.

4. B: Although the author is certainly trying to tell the readers of Leif Erikson's unheralded accomplishments, the word alert—Choice *C*—carries a sense of urgency or warning that is not found in this passage. Rather, the author would want the reader to be informed about it—Choice *B*.

5. D: Choice *A* is wrong because the author never addresses the Vikings' state of mind or emotions. Choice *B* is wrong because the author does not elaborate on Erikson's exile and whether he would have become an explorer if not for his banishment. Choice *C* is wrong because there is not enough information to support this premise. It is unclear whether Erikson informed the King of Norway of his findings. Although it is true that the king did not send a follow-up expedition, he could have simply chosen not to expend the resources after receiving Erikson's news. It is not possible to logically infer whether Erikson told him. Choice *D* is correct because the uncertainty about Leif Erikson's birth year is an example of how historians have trouble pinning down important details in Viking history.

6. B: This vocabulary question can be answered using context clues. Based on the rest of the conversation, the reader can gather that Albert isn't looking forward to his marriage. As the Count notes that "you don't appear to me to be very enthusiastic on the subject of this marriage," and also remarks on Albert's "objection to a young lady who is both rich and beautiful," readers can guess Albert's feelings. The answer choice that most closely matches "objection" and "not ... very enthusiastic" is *B, strong dislike*.

7. C: This inference question can be answered by eliminating incorrect answers. Choice *A* is tempting, considering that Albert mentions money as a concern in his marriage. However, although he may not be as rich as his fiancée, his father still has a stable income of 50,000 francs a year. Choice *B* isn't mentioned at all in the passage, so it's impossible to make an inference. Finally, *Choice D* is false because Albert's father arranged his marriage, but his mother doesn't approve of it. Evidence for Choice *C* can be found in the Count's comparison of Albert and Eugénie: "she will enrich you, and you will ennoble her." In other words, the Danglars are wealthier, but the Morcerf family has a more noble background

8. D: There are many clues in the passage that indicate Albert's attitude towards his marriage—far from being enthusiastic, he has many reservations. This question requires test takers to understand the vocabulary in the answer choices. *Pragmatic* is closest in meaning to *realistic*, and *indifferent* means *uninterested*. The only word related to feeling worried, uncertain, or unfavorable about the future is *apprehensive*.

9. B: Choice *A* is incorrect because the Count's tone is friendly and conversational. Choice *C* is also incorrect because the Count questions why Albert doesn't want to marry a young, beautiful, and rich girl. While the Count asks many questions, he isn't particularly *probing* or *suspicious*—instead, he's asking to find out more about Albert's situation and then give him advice about marriage.

10. A: Though Albert's mother doesn't appear in the scene, there's more than enough information to answer this question. More than once his family's noble background is mentioned (not to mention that Albert's mother is the Comtesse de Morcerf, a noble title). The other answer choices can be eliminated. She is deeply concerned about her son's future, money isn't her highest priority because otherwise she would favor a marriage with the wealthy Danglars, and Albert describes her "clear and penetrating judgment," meaning she makes good decisions.

11. C: The Danglars family is wealthier, but the Morcerf family has a more aristocratic name, which gives them a higher social standing. Evidence for the other answer choices can be found throughout the passage. Albert mentioned receiving money from his father's fortune after his marriage and implied that his father has arranged this marriage for him. Additionally, the Count speculates that Albert's mother disapproves of this marriage because Eugénie isn't from a noble background like the Morcerf family, implying that she would prefer a match with a girl from aristocratic society.

12. A: This is a reading comprehension question, and the answer can be found in the following lines: "'I confess,' observed Monte Cristo, 'that I have some difficulty in comprehending your objection to a young lady who is both rich and beautiful.'" Choice *B* is the opposite of what the passage states (Albert's father is the one who insists on the marriage), Choice *C* incorrectly represents Albert's eagerness to marry, and Choice *D* describes a more positive attitude than Albert actually feels (*repugnance*).

13. B: The passage is mostly made up of dialogue, or conversation. Narration is when the story is told by the narrator, not the characters. Description is when the narrator describes a specific setting and its images. Explanation is when the author is analyzing or defining something for the reader's benefit.

14. D: The word *ennoble* in the middle of the passage means to give someone a noble rank or title. In the passage, we can infer that Albert is noble but not rich, and Mademoiselle Eugénie is rich but not noble.

15. C: The other choices aren't mentioned anywhere in the passage. Remember, although this passage is part of a larger text, the test taker should only pay attention to what's in the passage itself in order to find the correct answer.

16. C: The primary topic of this passage is the use of serious themes in children's literature. The passage does not state that it is only to be enjoyed by children. The passage does say that children's literature holds a special place in many people's hearts; it does not say that it is universally loved by everyone. Happy endings are mentioned, but only in passing to prove a larger point.

17. D: The word "gruesome" means horrible and grim. In the passage, this word is used to describe stories that contain violence and death. The words numb, peculiar, and comfortable would not be as fitting to describe such stories.

18. B: The statement implies that the original stories were grimmer and darker than more recent adaptations. The passage does not discuss the stories being translated from other languages or formats. While the themes from the original stories were more mature, there is no suggestion that they were intended for adults.

292

19. B: This statement is an example of figurative language called personification, where a thing or an animal has human characteristics. In this example, the stories speak to the children. The passage discusses how children interpret stories, so the correct answer is Choice *B*.

20. B: The author is opposed to tobacco. The author cites disease and deaths associated with smoking, and points to the monetary expense and aesthetic costs. Choice *A* is incorrect because alternatives to smoking are not addressed in the passage. Choice *C* is incorrect because it does not summarize the passage but rather is just a detail. Choice *D* is incorrect because, while these statistics are a premise in the argument, they do not represent a summary of the piece. Choice *B* is the correct answer because it states the three critiques offered against tobacco and expresses the author's conclusion.

21. C: We are looking for something the author would agree with, so it should be anti-smoking or an argument in favor of quitting smoking. Choice *A* is incorrect because the author does not speak against means of cessation. Choice *B* is incorrect because the author does not reference other substances but does speak of how addictive nicotine, a drug in tobacco, is. Choice *D* is incorrect because the author would not encourage reducing taxes to encourage a reduction of smoking costs, thereby helping smokers to continue the habit. Choice *C* is correct because the author is attempting to persuade smokers to quit smoking.

22. D: Here, we are looking for the author's opinion rather than a fact or statistic. Choice *A* is incorrect because quoting statistics from the CDC is stating facts, not opinions. Choice *B* is incorrect because it expresses the fact that cigarettes sometimes cost more than a few gallons of gas. It would be an opinion if the author said that cigarettes were not affordable. Choice *C* is incorrect because yellow stains are a known possible adverse effect of smoking. Choice *D* is correct as an opinion because smell is subjective. Some people might like the smell of smoke rather than considering it "a pervasive nastiness," so this is the expression of an opinion.

23. B: The author implies that zymosis is a disease ("There were no more diseases after zymosis"), so Choice *B* is correct.

24. D: Although Washington was from a wealthy background, the passage does not say that his wealth led to his republican ideals, so Choice *A* is not supported. Choice *B* also does not follow from the passage. Washington's warning against meddling in foreign affairs does not mean that he would oppose wars of every kind, so Choice *B* is wrong. Choice *C* is also unjustified since the author does not indicate that Alexander Hamilton's assistance was absolutely necessary. Choice *D* is correct because the passage states that Washington's farewell address clearly opposes political parties and partisanship. The author then notes that presidential elections often hit a fever pitch of partisanship. Thus, it follows that George Washington would probably not approve of modern political parties and their involvement in presidential elections.

25. A: The author finishes the passage by applying Washington's farewell address to modern politics, so the purpose probably includes this application. The other descriptions also fit the passage to some degree, but they do not describe the author's main purpose, which is revealed in the final paragraph.

26. D: Choice *A* is wrong because the last paragraph is not appropriate for a history textbook. Choice *B* is false because the piece is not a notice or announcement of Washington's death. Choice *C* is false because it is not fiction, but a historical writing. Choice *D* is correct. The passage is most likely to appear in a newspaper editorial because it cites information that is relevant and applicable to the present day, a popular subject in editorials.

27. C: There is a tone of excitement throughout the passage; this tone is conveyed through the narrator's account of the life-changing discovery of electricity. Mentions of tunnels and darkness could evoke a tone of dreariness, but that represents the past. This passage is looking forward to what the future will hold with this new form of light, making Choice *A* incorrect. Choice *B* is incorrect because the narrator does not feel unnerved about the idea of

293

confessing their crime to the Council. This passage does not use humor or lightheartedness, making Choice *D* incorrect.

28. A: Evidence for the correct answer can be found here: "They would see nothing, save our crime of working alone, and they would destroy us and our light." In this society, things must be done as a collective, not individually. The narrator hopes to join the Council of Scholars, and wants their input and work space, which makes Choice *B* incorrect. Street sweeping is the narrator's role, but it's not what makes their discovery a crime. That is why Choice *C* is incorrect. Besides the word *Unmentionable*, nothing indicates that remainders from former times are off-limits, making Choice *D* incorrect.

29. D: The sentence uses personification, whereby darkness is given a human quality—being able to swallow. A simile is a comparison using *like* or *as*, which are not present in this sentence. Synecdoche is a device that uses a part to represent a whole, or vice versa, which is also not present here. A flashback is an interjected scene from earlier in the story, which is not what the author is doing.

30. A: Multiple times the narrator calls their discovery "the power of the sky" which is an allusion to the Sun. For example, in the third paragraph, the narrator reports, "we finished building a strange thing…a box of glass, devised to give forth the power of the sky of greater strength than we had ever achieved before." Candles were a source of light before this discovery, making Choice *B* incorrect. Prison represents the darkness, not the light, making Choice *C* incorrect. The narrator does feel that their invention is a part of their body, the way blood runs through their veins, but does not directly equate it to their overall discovery of electricity. This makes Choice *D* incorrect.

31. B: The narrator is confident their crime will be forgiven by the World Council of Scholars because their "gift is greater than [their] transgression." The passage does not address the money their invention will save the City, making Choice *A* incorrect. It is not the apology alone that will grant the narrator forgiveness, making Choice *C* incorrect. By the end, the narrator does feel a strong connection to their invention, but the wires are only metaphorically part of their body, and the wires are not the reason the narrator believes they'll be forgiven. This makes Choice *D* incorrect.

32. D: *Transgression* most closely means *offense* in paragraph eight. Obedience, or following the rules, is the opposite of transgression, making Choice *A* incorrect. The word *transgression* has a moral or legal connotation that is lacking in the word *disruption*, making Choice *B* incorrect. *Confession*, or admitting to an offense, is what the narrator is going to do as a result of their transgression, making Choice *C* incorrect.

33. B: Personification is a literary device in which human characteristics are attributed to something nonhuman. So, when the narrator says "Darkness swallowed us," they give a human characteristic (swallowing) to something nonhuman (darkness). Choice *A* is incorrect because it is just an expression used to indicate there are a lot of thoughts swirling around in the narrator's head. Choice *C* refers to the human narrator's head and hands; since the narrator is a person, they cannot be personified. Choice *D* is incorrect because it is a thought that trails off, not personification, to indicate that the narrator has changed their opinion on the value of their body.

34. C: The narrator wants to keep their invention a secret until they are able to confess everything to the World Council of Scholars. Paragraph seven lists the resources that are necessary to advance the discovery. Those include work rooms, which makes Choice *A* incorrect. The narrator also wants help and wisdom from the brother Scholars, making Choice *B* incorrect. The narrator feels that they will need to focus all their time on their discovery, which means they will need to stop sweeping the streets, making Choice *D* incorrect.

35. A: Moving from street sweeper to the Home of the Scholars will be an advancement in society because the wisest in all the lands are elected to the World Council of Scholars. Choice *B* is incorrect because the text indicates that being a Scholar is more desirable than being a street sweeper, so their status will not remain the same. The Council of Vocations decides what jobs people will have and would be the group to assign the narrator to the House

of Scholars. This makes Choice *C* incorrect. The narrator is not concerned with the negative consequences of their confession and is confident they will be propelled to Scholar status. This is why Choice *D* is incorrect.

36. D: The last paragraph reveals the shift in how the narrator suddenly cares about their body for the first time after they discover electricity. Choices *A*, *B*, and *C* are all future possibilities, but they have not occurred by the end of the passage.

37. B: The passage begins by giving the reader information about traditional birthing situations. Then, we are told that Mr. and Mrs. Button decide to go against tradition to have their baby in a hospital. The next few paragraphs are dedicated to letting the reader know how Mr. Button dresses and goes to the hospital to welcome his new baby. There is a doctor in this excerpt, as Choice *C* indicates, and clothes are discussed, as choice *D* indicates. However, Mr. Button is not going to the doctor's office, nor is he about to go shopping for new clothes.

38. A: We are told in the fourth paragraph that Mr. Button "arose nervously." We also see him running without caution to the doctor to find out about his wife and baby—this indicates his excitement. We also see him stuttering in a nervous yet excited fashion as he asks the doctor if it's a boy or girl. Though the doctor may seem a bit abrupt at the end, indicating a bit of anger or shame, neither of these choices is the overwhelming tone of the entire passage. Despite the circumstances, joy and gratitude are not the main tone in the passage.

39. C: Mr. Button is dedicated to the task before him. Choice *A*, *numbed*, choice *B*, *chained*, and choice *D*, *moved*, all could grammatically fit in the sentence. However, they do not match the excerpt's use of *consecrated* the way *dedicated* does.

40. D: The author describes a visual image—the doctor rubbing his hands together—first and foremost. The author may be trying to make a comment about the profession; however, the author does not "explain the details of the doctor's profession" as Choice *B* suggests.

41. D: We know we are being introduced to the setting because we are given the year in the very first paragraph, along with the season: "one day in the summer of 1860." This is a classic structure for an introduction of the setting. In the third paragraph we also get a long explanation of Mr. Button, who is related to him, and what his life is like.

42. B: The word *anachronism* most nearly means misplacement (in time). Choice *A*, a *comparison*, shows how two things are alike or different. Choice *C*, *annoyance*, means irritation. Choice *D*, *amelioration*, means improvement.

43. A: The setting of a narrative is the time and place. We see from the first paragraph that the year is 1860. We also can discern that it is summer and Mr. and Mrs. Button are about to have a baby. This tells us both the setting and information about the story.

44. D: The doctor's expression is twice described as "curious," which in this context means strange. He also says that Mr. Button's child is born "after a fashion," which means sort of or in a manner of speaking. All this points to something unusual about the birth.

45. C: The point of view is told in third person omniscient. We know this because the story starts out with us knowing something that the character does not know: that her husband has died. Mrs. Mallard eventually comes to know this, but we as readers know this information before it is broken to her. In third person limited, Choice *D*, we would only see and know what Mrs. Mallard herself knew, and we would find out the news of her husband's death when she found out the news, not before.

46. A: The irony in this story is called situational irony, which means the situation that takes place is different than what the audience anticipated. At the beginning of the story, we see Mrs. Mallard react with a burst of grief to her husband's death. However, once she's alone, she begins to contemplate her future and says the word "free" over

and over. This is quite a different reaction from Mrs. Mallard than what readers expected from the beginning of the story.

47. B: The word *elusive* most closely means indefinable. *Horrible*, Choice *A*, doesn't quite fit with the tone of the word *subtle* that comes before it. Choice *C*, *quiet*, is more closely related to the word *subtle*. Choice *D*, *joyful*, also doesn't quite fit the context here. *Indefinable* is the best option.

48. D: A summary is a brief explanation of the main point of a story. The story mostly focuses on Mrs. Mallard and her reaction to her husband's death, especially in the room when she's alone and contemplating the present and future. Choice *B* is briefly mentioned in the story; however, it is not the main focus of the story.

49. D: The interesting thing about this story is that feelings that are confused, joyful, and depressive all play a unique and almost equal part in this story. There is no one right answer here, because the author seems to display all of these emotions through the character of Mrs. Mallard. She displays feelings of depression in her grief at the beginning; then when she receives feelings of joy, she feels moments of confusion. We as readers cannot help but go through these feelings with the character. Thus, the author creates a tone of depression, joy, and confusion, all in one story.

50. C: The word *tumultuously* most nearly means "violently." Even if you don't know the word *tumultuously*, look at the surrounding context to figure it out. In the next few sentences we see Mrs. Mallard striving to "beat back" the "thing that was approaching to possess her." We see a fearful and almost violent reaction to the emotion that she's having. Thus, her chest would rise and fall tumultuously, or violently.

51. A: The word *patronage* most nearly means auspices, which means protection or support. Choice *B*, *aberration*, means abnormality and does not make sense within the context of the sentence. Choice *C*, *acerbic*, means sour or sharply critical, and it also does not make sense in the sentence. Choice *D*, *adulation*, is a positive word meaning *praise*, and thus does not fit with the word *condescending* in the sentence.

52. D: *Working man* is most closely aligned with Choice *D*, *bourgeois*. In the context of the speech, the word *bourgeois* means working or middle class. Choice *A*, *athlete*, does suggest someone who works hard, but it does not make sense in this context. Choice *B*, *viscount*, is a European title used to describe a specific degree of nobility. Choice *C*, *entrepreneur*, is a person who operates their own business.

53. C: In the context of the speech, the term *working man* most closely correlates with Choice *C*. Choice *A* is not mentioned in the passage and is off-topic. Choice *B* may be true in some cases, but it does not reflect the sentiment described for the term *working man* in the passage. Choice *D* is not a definition, and the topics of the field, factory, and screen are not mentioned in the passage.

54. D: *Enterprise* most closely means cause. Choices *A, B,* and *C* are all related to the term *enterprise*. However, Dickens speaks of a *cause* here, not a *company, courage,* or a *game*. "He will stand by such an enterprise" is a call to stand by a cause to enable the working man to have a certain autonomy over his own economic standing. The very first paragraph ends with the statement that the working man "shall...have a share in the management of an institution which is designed for his benefit."

55. B: Recall from the first paragraph that the speaker is there to "accompany [the audience]...through one of my little Christmas books," making him an author there to entertain the crowd with his own writing. The speech preceding the reading is the passage itself, and, as the tone indicates, it is a serious speech addressing the working man. Although the passage speaks of employers and employees, the speaker himself is not an employer of the audience, so Choice *A* is incorrect. Choice *C* is also incorrect, as the salutation is not used ironically, but sincerely, as the speech addresses the wellbeing of the crowd. Choice *D* is incorrect because the speech is not given by a politician, but by a writer.

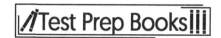

56. B: Choice *A* is incorrect because that is the speaker's first desire, not his second. Choices *C* and *D* are tricky because the language of both of these is mentioned after the word *second*. However, the speaker doesn't get to the second wish until the next sentence. Choices *C* and *D* are merely preliminary remarks before the statement of the main clause, Choice *B*.

Writing

Usage

1. A: Choice *A* is correct because the article (*an*) and the noun (*issues*) do not agree in number. It should be written as "An important issue."

2. B: Choice *B* is correct because it uses an *-ing* verb, "attributing," which does not fit here. The verb phrase most appropriate here is "can be attributed."

3. D: Choice *D* is correct because the phrase "all of" implies that every item in the list should be plural, but "accessory" is singular. It should be "accessories."

4. C: The phrase "while he wanted to" is grammatically awkward; "he wanted to" doesn't imply a time span when Shawn could start taking lessons. Replacing "while" with "because" produces a better sentence.

5. E: There is no error in this sentence.

6. B: The subject "none" sometimes needs a singular verb, such as "was delivered," and sometimes needs a plural verb, such as "were delivered." In this case, "was delivered" would be correct; "were delivered" doesn't fit because "furniture" is not plural. Replacing "furniture" with a plural word would make the sentence correct, for example: "Since none of the boxes were delivered on time ...".

7. E: There is no error in this sentence.

8. A: Choice *A* is missing the word *that*, which is necessary for the sentence to make sense.

9. A: The word "Because" is incorrect here because the sentence is not stating cause and effect. The word "Although" would work much better here because it indicates a contrast.

10. E: There is no error in this sentence.

Sentence Correction

11. C: Choice *C* is correct because it fixes the core issue with this sentence: the singular *has* does not agree with the plural *scientists*. Choices *B* and *D* add unnecessary commas.

12. D: Choice *D* correctly conveys the writer's intention of asking if early perceptions of dinosaurs still influence people. Choice *A* does not make sense the way it is worded. Choice *B* is better, but *how* doesn't coincide with the context. Choice *C* adds unnecessary commas.

13. A: Choice *B* incorrectly replaces simply with simple and adds an unnecessary comma. *Choice C* uses a comma where a semicolon is needed. Choice *D* adds an unnecessary comma.

14. B: Choice *B* is the strongest revision, as adding *to explore* is very effective in both shortening the sentence and maintaining, even enhancing, the writer's point. Choice *A* is not technically incorrect, but it is overcomplicated. Choice *C* is a decent revision, but the sentence could still be more condensed and sharpened. Choice *D* fails to make the sentence more concise and inserts unnecessary commas.

15. D: Choice *D* correctly applies a semicolon to introduce a new line of thought while remaining in a single sentence. The comma after *however* is also appropriately placed. Choice *A* is a run-on sentence. Choice *B* is incorrect because the single comma is not enough to fix the sentence. Choice *C* adds unnecessary commas around *uncertain.*

16. B: Choice *B* changes *its*, which is possessive, to *it's*, which is a contraction of "it is." It also separates the two independent clauses with a comma and streamlines the sentence by eliminating *and*. Choices *C* and *D* are run-on sentences.

17. A: Choices *B* and *C* add unnecessary commas, while Choice *D* uses the possessive *its* instead of the contraction *it's*.

18. C: Choice *C* is correct because the phrase *even likely* is a parenthetical element, which must be set off by commas. Choice *D* does not set off the phrase with commas. Choice *A* omits the second required comma, and Choice *B* misplaces it.

19. D: Choice *D* strengthens the overall sentence structure while condensing the number of words, making the subject of the sentence and the emphasis of the writer much clearer to the reader. Thus, while Choice *A* is technically correct, the language is choppy and over-complicated. Choice *B* is better but lacks the reference to a specific image of dinosaurs. Choice *C* introduces unnecessary commas.

20. B: Choice *B* correctly removes the apostrophe from *icon's* since the *icon* is not possessing anything. Choice *D* is grammatically correct but alters the meaning of the sentence—*Frankenstein* is one of the icons, not the sole icon.

21. C: Choice *C* correctly adds a comma after *style*, successfully joining the introductory phrase and independent clause as a single sentence. Choice *A* is incorrect because the introductory phrase and independent clause remain unsuccessfully combined without the comma. Choices *B* and *D* do nothing to fix this.

Revision in Context

22. B: Here, a colon is used to introduce a quotation. Colons introduce explanations, quotations, or lists. Additionally, the quote ends with the punctuation inside the quotes, unlike Choice *C.*

23. A: This passage is predominantly in the present tense, and the author is describing education as it currently is, so Choice *A* is the correct answer. Choice *B* is incorrect because the subject and verb do not agree; the singular subject "Education" should be paired with the singular verb "provides." Choice *C* is incorrect because the passage is in present tense, and "Education will provide" is future tense. Choice *D* doesn't make sense when placed in the sentence.

24. D: The possessive form of the word "it" is "its." The contraction "it's" denotes "it is." Thus, Choice *A* is incorrect. The word "raises" in Choice *B* makes the sentence grammatically incorrect. Choice *C* adds an apostrophe at the end of "its." While most nouns indicate possession with an apostrophe, adding '*s* to the word "it" indicates a contraction.

25. C: The word *civelized* should be spelled *civilized*. The words *distinguishes* and *creatures* are both spelled correctly.

26. B: Choice *B* is the clearest way to phrase this sentence. It starts by making a statement: schools should not be myopic (which means shortsighted, failing to see the big picture). It then adds detail: schools should not be shortsighted by focusing only on *the mind*. Choice *A*, which inserts the extra detail into the main statement, is grammatically correct but more confusing to read. Choice *C* is also confusing, and it needlessly switches to past tense and changes *the mind* to *our mind*. Choice *D* does not quite make sense.

27. C: The passage's second paragraph can be divided into two paragraphs because it is about two separate topics. The paragraph's first main focus is education addressing the mind, body, and soul. This first section, then, could end with the concluding sentence, "The human heart and psyche ..." The next sentence should start a new paragraph with "Education is a basic human right ..." The rest of this paragraph talks about what education is and some of its characteristics.

28. A: Choice *A* is correct because *others'* is plural and indicates possession. Choice *B* is incorrect because *other's* indicates only one *other* who is in possession of *ideas*, which is incorrect. Choice *C* is incorrect because no possession is indicated. Choice *D* is incorrect because *others's* is not a correct form of the plural possessive word.

29. D: This sentence must have a comma before *although* because it is connecting two independent clauses. Thus, Choices *B* and *C* are incorrect. Choice *A* is incorrect because the second sentence in the underlined section is a fragment.

30. C: Choice *C* is the correct choice because the word *their* indicates possession, and the text is talking about *their students*, or the students of someone. Choice *A*, *there*, describes where something is located. Choice *B*, *they're*, is a contraction and means *they are*. Choice *D* is not a word.

31. B: Choice *B* uses all punctuation correctly in this sentence. In American English, single quotes should only be used if they are quotes within a quote, making Choices *A* and *C* incorrect. Additionally, punctuation should go inside quotation marks (with a few exceptions), making Choice *D* incorrect.

32. B: Choice *B* is correct because the conjunction *and* is used to connect phrases that are to be used jointly, such as teachers working hard to help students "identify salient information" and to "think critically." The conjunctions *so*, *but*, and *nor* are incorrect in the context of this sentence.

33. A: Choice *A* has consistent parallel structure with the verbs *read*, *identify*, and *determine*. Choices *B* and *C* have faulty parallel structure with the words *determining* and *identifying*. Choice *D* has incorrect subject/verb agreement. The sentence should read, "Students have to read ... identify ... and determine."

34. D: The correct choice for this sentence is that "they are ... shaped by the influences." The prepositions *for*, *to*, and *with* do not apply to this phrase. People are *shaped by*, not *shaped for, shaped to,* or *shaped with*.

35. A: To see which answer is correct, it might help to place the subject, *teachers*, near the verb. Choice *A* is correct: "Teachers ... must strive" makes grammatical sense here. Choice *B* is incorrect because "Teachers ... to strive" does not make grammatical sense. Choice *C* is incorrect because "Teachers must not only respect ... but striving" does not use parallel structure. Choice *D* is incorrect because it is in past tense, and this passage is in present tense.

36. C: Choice *C* is correct because it uses an em dash. Em dashes are versatile. They can separate phrases that would otherwise be in parentheses, or they can stand in for a colon. In this case, a colon would be another decent choice for this punctuation mark because the second sentence expands upon the first sentence. Choice *A* is incorrect because the statement is not a question. Choice *B* is incorrect because adding a comma here would create a comma splice. Choice *D* is incorrect because this creates a run-on sentence since the two sentences are independent clauses.

Research Skills

37. A: Firsthand accounts are given by primary sources—individuals who provide personal or expert accounts of an event, subject matter, time period, or individual. They are viewed more as objective accounts than subjective. Secondary sources are accounts given by an individual or group of individuals who were not physically present at the event or who did not have firsthand knowledge of an individual or time period. Secondary sources are sources

that have used research in order to create a written work. *Direct sources* and *indirect sources* are not standard terms.

38. D: Although there are differences between these formatting styles, they all require bibliography entries to include the basic components listed in the question: the author's name, the title of the work, and its publication date.

39. D: Although there are differences between these formatting styles, they all require bibliography entries to include the basic components listed in the question: the author's name, the title of the work, and its publication date.

40. A: Firsthand accounts are given by primary sources—individuals who provide personal or expert accounts of an event, subject matter, time period, or individual. They are viewed more as objective accounts than subjective. Secondary sources are accounts given by an individual or group of individuals who were not physically present at the event or who did not have firsthand knowledge of an individual or time period. Secondary sources are sources that have used research in order to create a written work. *Direct sources* and *indirect sources* are not standard terms.

Mathematics

1. B: 30% is $\frac{3}{10}$. so we can say that $6 = \left(\frac{3}{10}\right)n$, where n is the unknown number. To solve, we can multiply both sides by the reciprocal fraction, $\frac{10}{3}$. We find $n = \frac{10}{3} \times 6 = \frac{60}{3} = 20$.

2. D: By rearranging and grouping the factors in Choice *D*, we can notice that $3 \times 3 \times 4 \times 2 = (3 \times 2) \times (4 \times 3) = 6 \times 12$, which is what we were looking for. Alternatively, each of the answer choices could be prime-factored or multiplied out and compared to the original value. 6×12 has a value of 72 and a prime factorization of $2^3 \times 3^2$. The answer choices respectively have values of 64, 84, 108, and 72 and prime factorizations of 2^6, $2^2 \times 3 \times 7$, $2^2 \times 3^3$, and $2^3 \times 3^2$, so Choice *D* is the correct answer.

3. B: Since $850 is the price after a 20% discount, $850 represents 80% (or 0.8) of the original price. In other words, $850 = 0.8x$ (where x is the original price). Solving this, we find $x = \frac{850}{0.8} = 1,062.5$. Now, to find the savings, calculate the original price minus the sale price: $1,062.50 - $850 = $212.50.

4. B: The first step is to calculate the difference between the larger value and the smaller value.

$$378 - 252 = 126$$

To calculate this difference as a percentage of the original value, and thus calculate the percentage *increase*, 126 is divided by 252, and then this result is multiplied by 100 to find the percentage: 50%, or Choice *B*.

5. D: Recall the formula for area, area = length × width. The answer must be in square inches, so all values must be converted to inches. Half of a foot is equal to 6 inches. Therefore, the area of the rectangle is equal to:

$$6 \text{ in} \times \frac{11}{2} \text{ in} = \frac{66}{2} \text{ in}^2 = 33 \text{ in}^2$$

6. A: Operations within the parentheses must be completed first. Division is completed next, and finally, addition. When adding decimals, digits within each place value are added together. Therefore, the expression is evaluated as:

$$(2 \times 20) \div (7 + 1) + (6 \times 0.01) + (4 \times 0.001)$$

$$40 \div 8 + 0.06 + 0.004$$

300

$$5 + 0.06 + 0.004 = 5.064$$

7. B: First, subtract 4 from each side:

$$6t + 4 = 16$$

$$6t + 4 - 4 = 16 - 4$$

$$6t = 12$$

Now, divide both sides by 6:

$$\frac{6t}{6} = \frac{12}{6}$$

$$t = 2$$

8. A: The question only asks how long they owned the house, so ignore the extra details about prices. There are 6 years between May 1, 2010 and May 1, 2016. There are another 4 months between May 1, 2016 and September 1, 2016. Therefore, they owned the house for a total of 6 years and 4 months. Each year has 12 months, so the total number of months is

$$(6 \times 12) + 4 = 72 + 4 = 76$$

9. A: Let the unknown score be x. The average will be:

$$\frac{5 \times 50 + 4 \times 70 + x}{10} = \frac{530 + x}{10} = 55$$

Multiply both sides by 10 to get $530 + x = 550$, or $x = 20$.

10. B: An equilateral triangle has 3 sides of equal length, so if the total perimeter is 18 feet, each side must be 6 feet long. A square with sides of 6 feet will have an area of $6^2 = 36$ square feet.

11. C: Kimberley worked 4.5 hours at the rate of $10/h and 1 hour at the rate of $12/h. The problem states that her time is rounded to the nearest hour, so the 4.5 hours would round up to 5 hours at the rate of $10/h.

$$(5 \text{ h}) \times \left(\frac{\$10}{\text{h}}\right) + (1 \text{ h}) \times \left(\frac{\$12}{\text{h}}\right) = \$50 + \$12 = \$62$$

12. C: The perimeter is found by calculating the sum of all sides of the polygon:

$$9 + 9 + 9 + 8 + 8 + s = 56$$

Let s be the missing side length.

Therefore, $43 + s = 56$.

The missing side length is 13 cm.

13. D: Three girls for every two boys can be expressed as a ratio: 3 : 2. This can be visualized as splitting the school into five groups: three girl groups and two boy groups. The number of students that are in each group can be found by dividing the total number of students by five:

$$\frac{650 \text{ students}}{5 \text{ groups}} = \frac{130 \text{ students}}{\text{group}}$$

To find the total number of girls, multiply the number of students per group (130) by the number of girl groups in the school (3). This equals 390, Choice *D*.

14. C: A dollar contains 20 nickels. Therefore, if there are 12 dollars' worth of nickels, there are $12 \times 20 = 240$ nickels. Each nickel weighs 5 grams. Therefore, the weight of the nickels is $240 \times 5 = 1,200$ grams. To find the total weight of the filled piggy bank, add the weight of the nickels and the weight of the empty bank:

$$1,200 + 1,050 = 2,250 \text{ grams.}$$

15. D: A yard is 3 feet. The equation to calculate the minimum number of yards is $79 \div 3 = 26\frac{1}{3}$.

If the material is sold only by whole yards, then Mo would need to round up to the next whole yard in order to cover the extra $\frac{1}{3}$ yard. Therefore, the answer is 27 yards. None of the other choices meets the minimum whole yard requirement.

16. B: Instead of multiplying these out, we can estimate the product by using $18 \times 10 = 180$.

17. A: Each bag contributes $4x + 1$ treats. The total number of treats for n bags will be $n(4x + 1)$, or $4nx + n$. We know the total number of treats is $60x + 15$, which means that $60x + 15 = 4nx + n$. Looking at this, we can see that the equation only works when $n = 15$.

18. D: Denote the width as w and the length as l. Then, $l = 3w + 5$. The perimeter is:

$$2l + 2w = 90$$

Substituting the first expression for l into the second equation yields:

$$2(3w + 5) + 2w = 90$$

$$6w + 10 + 2w = 90$$

$$8w = 80$$

$$w = 10$$

Putting this into the first equation, it yields:

$$l = 3(10) + 5 = 35$$

19. C: The average is calculated by adding all six numbers, then dividing by 6. The first five numbers have a sum of 25. This scenario can be expressed by the equation $\frac{25+n}{6} = 6$, where n is the unknown number. After multiplying both sides by 6, we get $25 + n = 36$, which means $n = 11$.

20. B: To convert miles to kilometers, we can multiply the number of miles by the miles-per-kilometer conversion factor:

$$4.67 \text{ mi} \times \frac{(1.609 \text{ km})}{(1 \text{ mi})} = 7.51403 \text{ km}$$

Because the question asks for an answer with three significant digits, 7.51 kilometers is the correct answer.

21. D: This problem can be solved by using unit conversion. The initial units are miles per minute. The final units need to be feet per second. Converting miles to feet uses the equivalence statement 1 mi = 5,280 ft. Converting minutes to seconds uses the equivalence statement 1 min = 60 s. Setting up the ratios to convert the units is shown in the following equation:

$$\frac{72 \text{ mi}}{90 \text{ min}} \times \frac{1 \text{ min}}{60 \text{ s}} \times \frac{5,280 \text{ ft}}{1 \text{ mi}} = 70.4 \frac{\text{ft}}{\text{s}}$$

The initial units cancel out, and the new units are left.

22. D: To find Denver's total snowfall, 3 must be multiplied by $27\frac{3}{4}$. In order to easily do this, the mixed number should be converted into an improper fraction.

$$27\frac{3}{4} = \frac{27 \times 4 + 3}{4} = \frac{111}{4}$$

Therefore, Denver had approximately $\frac{3 \times 111}{4} = \frac{333}{4}$ inches of snow. The improper fraction can be converted back into a mixed number through division.

$$\frac{333}{4} = 83\frac{1}{4} \text{ inches}$$

23. A: The perimeter of a rectangle is $P = 2l + 2w$. We are told $P = 44$, so $2l + 2w = 44$. We are also told that the width is 2 cm less than the length: $w = l - 2$. Substituting this for w in the perimeter equation, we get $2l + 2(l - 2) = 44$, which is Choice A.

Although it's not necessary to answer the test question, we could solve the equation to find the length and width. The equation simplifies to $4l - 4 = 44$, or $l = 12$, and since $w = l - 2$, we find $w = 10$.

24. C: There are 34 girls who are potty-trained out of a total of 52 girls:

$$34 \div 52 \approx 0.65 = 65\%$$

25. D: This system of equations involves one quadratic equation and one linear equation. One way to solve this is through substitution.

303

Solving for y in the second equation yields:

$$y = x + 2$$

Plugging this equation in for the y of the quadratic equation yields:

$$x^2 - 2x + x + 2 = 8$$

Simplify the equation:

$$x^2 - x + 2 = 8$$

Set this equal to zero and factor:

$$x^2 - x - 6 = 0 = (x - 3)(x + 2)$$

Solving these two factors for x gives the zeros:

$$x = 3, -2$$

To find the y-value for the point, plug in each number to either original equation. Solving each one for y yields the points $(3, 5)$ and $(-2, 0)$.

26. D: "Sum" means the result of addition, so "the sum of twice a number and one" can be written as $2x + 1$. Next, "three times the sum of twice a number and one" would be $3(2x + 1)$. Finally, "six less than three times the sum of twice a number and one" would be $3(2x + 1) - 6$.

27. A: To expand a squared binomial, it's necessary to use the first, outer, inner, last (FOIL) method.

$$(2x - 4y)(2x - 4y)$$

$$(2x)(2x) + (2x)(-4y) + (-4y)(2x) + (-4y)(-4y)$$

$$4x^2 - 8xy - 8xy + 16y^2$$

$$4x^2 - 16xy + 16y^2$$

28. D: The slope is given by the change in y divided by the change in x. Specifically, it's:

$$slope = \frac{y_2 - y_1}{x_2 - x_1}$$

The first point is $(-5, -3)$, and the second point is $(0, -1)$. Work from left to right when identifying coordinates. Thus, the point on the left is point 1 $(-5, -3)$ and the point on the right is point 2 $(0, -1)$.

Now we just need to plug those numbers into the equation:

$$slope = \frac{-1 - (-3)}{0 - (-5)}$$

It can be simplified to:

$$slope = \frac{-1+3}{0+5}$$

$$slope = \frac{2}{5}$$

29. C: To solve the problem, we can write a proportion consisting of ratios comparing distance and time. One way to set up the proportion is: $\frac{3}{48} = \frac{5}{x}$. x represents the unknown value of time. To solve this proportion, we can cross-multiply:

$$(3)(x) = (5)(48) \text{ or } 3x = 240$$

To isolate the variable, we divide by 3 on both sides, getting $x = 80$.

30. C: The first step in solving this problem is expressing the result in fraction form. Multiplication and division are typically performed in order from left to right, but they can be performed in any order. For this problem, let's start with the division operation between the last two fractions. When dividing one fraction by another, invert—or flip—the second fraction and then multiply the numerators and denominators.

$$\frac{7}{10} \times \frac{2}{1} = \frac{14}{10}$$

Next, multiply the first fraction by this value:

$$\frac{3}{5} \times \frac{14}{10} = \frac{42}{50}$$

In this instance, to find the decimal form, we can multiply the numerator and denominator by 2 to get 100 in the denominator.

$$\frac{42}{50} \times \frac{2}{2} = \frac{84}{100}$$

In decimal form, this would be expressed as 0.84.

31. C: Set up the initial equation.

$$\frac{2x}{5} - 1 = 59$$

Add 1 to both sides.

$$\frac{2x}{5} - 1 + 1 = 59 + 1$$

$$\frac{2x}{5} = 60$$

Multiply both sides by $\frac{5}{2}$.

$$\frac{\cancel{2}x}{\cancel{5}} \times \frac{\cancel{5}}{\cancel{2}} = 60 \times \frac{5}{2}$$

$$x = 150$$

32. D: First, the train's journey in the real world is:

$$3\,\text{h} \times 50\,\frac{\text{mi}}{\text{h}} = 150\,\text{mi}$$

On the map, 1 inch corresponds to 10 miles, so that is equivalent to:

$$150\,\text{mi} \times \frac{1\,\text{in}}{10\,\text{mi}} = 15\,\text{in}$$

Therefore, the start and end points are 15 inches apart on the map.

33. C: To solve for the value of b, isolate the variable b on one side of the equation.

Start by moving the lower value of –4 to the other side by adding 4 to both sides:

$$5b - 4 = 2b + 17$$

$$5b - 4 + 4 = 2b + 17 + 4$$

$$5b = 2b + 21$$

Then, subtract $2b$ from both sides:

$$5b - 2b = 2b + 21 - 2b$$

$$3b = 21$$

Then, divide both sides by 3 to get the value of b:

$$\frac{3b}{3} = \frac{21}{3}$$

$$b = 7$$

34. C: The first step in solving this problem is expressing the result in fraction form. Multiplication and division are typically performed in order from left to right, but they can be performed in any order. For this problem, let's start with the division operation between the last two fractions. When dividing one fraction by another, invert—or flip—the second fraction and then multiply the numerators and denominators.

$$\frac{7}{10} \times \frac{2}{1} = \frac{14}{10}$$

Next, multiply the first fraction by this value:

$$\frac{3}{5} \times \frac{14}{10} = \frac{42}{50}$$

In this instance, to find the decimal form, we can multiply the numerator and denominator by 2 to get 100 in the denominator.

$$\frac{42}{50} \times \frac{2}{2} = \frac{84}{100}$$

In decimal form, this would be expressed as 0.84.

35. D: First, subtract $1,437 from $2,334.50 to find Johnny's monthly savings; this equals $897.50. Then, multiply this amount by 3 to find out how much he will have (in 3 months) before he pays for his vacation; this equals $2,692.50. Finally, subtract the cost of the vacation ($1,750) from this amount to find how much Johnny will have left: $942.50.

36. B: To solve this correctly, keep in mind the order of operations with the mnemonic PEMDAS (Please Excuse My Dear Aunt Sally). This stands for Parentheses, Exponents, Multiplication & Division, Addition & Subtraction. Taking it step by step, solve inside the parentheses first:

$$4 \times 7 + (4)^2 \div 2$$

Then, apply the exponent:

$$4 \times 7 + 16 \div 2$$

Multiplication and division are both performed next:

$$28 + 8$$

And then finally, addition:

$$28 + 8 = 36$$

37. A: The volume of the sphere is 288π cubic meters. Using the formula for sphere volume, we see that:

$$\frac{4}{3}\pi r^3 = 288\pi$$

We solve this equation for r to obtain a radius of 6 meters. The formula for surface area is $4\pi r^2$, so:

$$SA = 4\pi 6^2 = 144\pi \text{ square meters}$$

38. B: Because this isn't a right triangle, SOHCAHTOA can't be used. However, the law of cosines can be used:

$$c^2 = a^2 + b^2 - 2ab \cos C$$

$$c^2 = 19^2 + 26^2 - 2 \times 19 \times 26 \times \cos 42° \approx 302.773$$

Taking the square root and rounding to the nearest tenth results in $c = 17.4$.

39. C: When a die is rolled, each outcome is equally likely. Since it has six sides, each outcome has a probability of $\frac{1}{6}$. The chance of a 1 or a 2 is therefore:

$$\frac{1}{6} + \frac{1}{6} = \frac{1}{3}$$

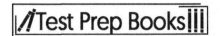

40. A: An outlier is a data value that is either far above or far below the majority of values in a sample set. The mean is the average of all the values in the set. In a small sample set, a very high or very low number could drastically change the average (or mean) of the data points. Outliers will have no more of an effect on the median (the middle value when arranged from lowest to highest) than any other value above or below the median. If the same outlier does not repeat, outliers will have no effect on the mode (value that repeats most often).

41. D: The probability of picking the winner of the race is $\frac{1}{4}$, or $\left(\frac{\text{number of favorable outcomes}}{\text{number of total outcomes}}\right)$. Assuming the winner was picked on the first selection, three horses remain from which to choose the runner-up (these are dependent events). Therefore, the probability of picking the runner-up is $\frac{1}{3}$. To determine the probability that multiple events all happen, multiply the probabilities of the events:

$$\frac{1}{4} \times \frac{1}{3} = \frac{1}{12}$$

42. B: 100 cm is equal to 1 m. 1.3 divided by 100 is 0.013. Therefore, 1.3 cm is equal to 0.013 m. Because 1 cm is equal to 10 mm, 1.3 cm is equal to 13 mm.

43. A: Operations within the parentheses must be completed first. Division is completed next, and finally, addition. When adding decimals, digits within each place value are added together. Therefore, the expression is evaluated as:

$$(2 \times 20) \div (7 + 1) + (6 \times 0.01) + (4 \times 0.001)$$

$$40 \div 8 + 0.06 + 0.004 = 5 + 0.06 + 0.004$$

$$5.064$$

44. D: Digits to the left of the decimal point represent the digit value times increasing multiples of 10 (first 1, then 10, 100, 1,000, and so on). Digits to the right of the decimal point represent the digit value divided by increasing multiples of 10 (first $\frac{1}{10}$, then $\frac{1}{100}$, $\frac{1}{1000}$, and so on). So, the second digit to the right of the decimal point equals the digit value divided by 100.

45. B: The power of 10 by which a digit is multiplied corresponds with the number of zeros following the digit when expressing its value in standard form. Therefore:

$$(1 \times 10^4) + (3 \times 10^3) + (7 \times 10^1) + (8 \times 10^0)$$

$$10,000 + 3,000 + 70 + 8 = 13,078$$

46. A: The hundredths place value is located two digits to the right of the decimal point (the digit 9 in the original number). To decide whether to round up or keep the digit, examine the digit to the right, and if it is 5 or greater, round up. In this case, the digit to the right is 6, so the hundredths place is rounded up. When rounding up, if the digit to be increased is a 9, the digit to its left is increased by one and the digit in the desired place value is made a zero. Therefore, the number is rounded to 847.90.

47. B: To add fractions, we first convert them to have the same denominator. The new denominator should be the least common multiple of the two original denominators (3 and 5), which in this case is 15. Multiply the top and bottom of each fraction by whatever number is required to make the denominator 15:

$$\frac{(1 \times 5)}{(3 \times 5)} = \frac{5}{15}$$

$$\frac{(2 \times 3)}{(5 \times 3)} = \frac{6}{15}$$

Now that the fractions have the same denominator, we add them by adding the numerators and keeping the denominator the same: $\frac{5}{15} + \frac{6}{15} = \frac{11}{15}$.

To determine the numerator of the new fraction, the old numerator is multiplied by the same number by which the old denominator is multiplied to obtain the new denominator.

For the fraction $\frac{1}{3}$, 3 multiplied by 5 will produce 15.

Therefore, the numerator is multiplied by 5 to produce the new numerator:

$$\frac{1 \times 5}{3 \times 5} = \frac{5}{15}$$

For the fraction $\frac{2}{5}$, multiplying both the numerator and denominator by 3 produces $\frac{6}{15}$. When fractions have like denominators, they are added by adding the numerators and keeping the denominator the same:

$$\frac{5}{15} + \frac{6}{15} = \frac{11}{15}$$

48. C: When performing calculations consisting of more than one operation, the order of operations should be followed: parentheses, exponents, multiplication & division, addition & subtraction.

Parentheses:

$$7^2 - 3 \times (4 + 2) + 15 \div 5$$

$$7^2 - 3 \times (6) + 15 \div 5$$

Exponents:

$$49 - 3 \times 6 + 15 \div 5$$

Multiplication & division (from left to right):

$$49 - 18 + 3$$

Addition & subtraction (from left to right):

$$49 - 18 + 3 = 34$$

49. D: To convert a fraction to a percent, we can first convert the fraction to a decimal. To do so, divide the numerator by the denominator: $4 \div 5 = 0.8$. To convert a decimal to a percent, multiply by 100:

$$0.8 \times 100 = 80\%$$

50. A: To determine the number of houses that can fit on the street, we can divide the length of the street by the width of each house's property:

$$345 \div 30 = 11.5$$

However, the construction company is not going to build half a house, so they will need to build either 11 or 12 houses. Since the width of 12 houses (360 feet) would extend past the length of the street, only 11 houses can be built.

51. B: The rate, r (60 miles per hour), and time, t (3 hours), are given. To find the distance, put the values into the distance formula and evaluate:

$$d = r \times t$$

$$d = \left(\frac{60 \text{ mi}}{\text{h}}\right) \times (3 \text{ h})$$

$$d = 180 \text{ mi}$$

52. D: Solve a linear inequality in a similar way to solving a linear equation. First, start by distributing the -3 on the left side of the inequality.

$$-3x - 12 \geq x + 8$$

Then, add 12 to both sides.

$$-3x \geq x + 20$$

Next, subtract x from both sides.

$$-4x \geq 20$$

Finally, divide both sides of the inequality by -4. Don't forget to flip the inequality sign because you are dividing by a negative number.

$$x \leq -5$$

53. B: First, the number of employees who did not choose a hamburger must be found. If 5 employees chose a salad and 12 chose a sandwich, then $5 + 12 = 17$ did not choose a hamburger. This number can be subtracted from the total to find out how many employees chose a hamburger:

$$25 - 17 = 8$$

54. D: The average amount Cindy spent on groceries per trip in March can be calculated by adding all the purchases together and dividing by the total number of purchases.

$$\frac{\$42.36 + \$26.50 + \$31.71 + \$37.23}{4} = \$34.45$$

55. Using the given information of one nurse to 25 patients and 325 total patients, set up an equation to solve for the number of nurses (N):

$$\frac{N}{325} = \frac{1}{25}$$

Multiply both sides by 325 to get N by itself on one side.

$$\frac{N}{1} = \frac{325}{25} = 13 \text{ nurses}$$

310

56. 1: This problem can be solved using basic arithmetic. Xavier starts with 20 apples, then gives his sister half, so 20 is divided by 2.

$$\frac{20}{2} = 10$$

He then gives his neighbor six apples, so 6 is subtracted from 10.

$$10 - 6 = 4$$

Finally, he uses $\frac{3}{4}$ of his remaining apples to make a pie. Since $\frac{3}{4}$ of 4 is 3, he uses 3 apples, so 3 is subtracted from 4.

$$4 - 3 = 1$$

Practice Tests #3, #4, & #5

To keep the size of this book manageable, save paper, and provide a digital test-taking experience, the 3rd, 4th, and 5th practice tests can be found online. Scan the QR code or go to this link to access it:

testprepbooks.com/bonus/praxiscore

The first time you access the test, you will need to register as a "new user" and verify your email address.

If you have any issues, please email support@testprepbooks.com

Index

Dear Praxis Case Test Taker,

Thank you for purchasing this study guide for your Praxis Case exam. We hope that we exceeded your expectations.

Our goal in creating this study guide was to cover all of the topics that you will see on the test. We also strove to make our practice questions as similar as possible to what you will encounter on test day. With that being said, if you found something that you feel was not up to your standards, please send us an email and let us know.

We would also like to let you know about other books in our catalog that may interest you.

Praxis 5001 Elementary Education Multiple Subjects

This can be found on Amazon: amazon.com/dp/1637755651

Praxis Reading Specialist 5302

amazon.com/dp/1637758928

Praxis Math 5165

amazon.com/dp/1637757913

We have study guides in a wide variety of fields. If the one you are looking for isn't listed above, then try searching for it on Amazon or send us an email.

Thanks Again and Happy Testing!
Product Development Team
info@studyguideteam.com

FREE Test Taking Tips Video/DVD Offer

To better serve you, we created videos covering test taking tips that we want to give you for FREE. **These videos cover world-class tips that will help you succeed on your test.**

We just ask that you send us feedback about this product. Please let us know what you thought about it—whether good, bad, or indifferent.

To get your **FREE videos**, you can use the QR code below or email freevideos@studyguideteam.com with "Free Videos" in the subject line and the following information in the body of the email:

     a. The title of your product

     b. Your product rating on a scale of 1-5, with 5 being the highest

     c. Your feedback about the product

If you have any questions or concerns, please don't hesitate to contact us at info@studyguideteam.com.

Thank you!

Made in the USA
Las Vegas, NV
26 December 2024

15360970R00181